AUTHENTIC CLASSROOM MANAGEMENT

Creating a Community of Learners

by **Barbara Larrivee**
California State University, San Bernardino

Allyn and Bacon
Boston London Toronto Sydney Tokyo Singapore

Book Design, Illustrations, and Typography: Constance C. Dickinson and Jan Olsson

Copyright © 1999 by Allyn & Bacon
A Viacom Company
160 Gould Street
Needham Heights, Massachusetts 02494-2130

Internet: www.abacon.com

ISBN 0-205-29739-0

Printed in the United States of America

10 9 8 7 6 5 4 3 2 1   03 02 01 00 99 98

Table of Contents

Preface

Learning Orientation

This approach to addressing classroom management is markedly different in its focus from existing texts. It is predicated on the assumption that the implementation of effective classroom/behavior management strategies requires that teachers engage in self-reflection as the primary vehicle for addressing classroom management issues. This approach integrates best practices for skill enhancement from adult learning theory with the self-reflective process to promote new attitudes and support effective practices.

Teachers are exposed to a variety of approaches that can be effective in certain situations with certain students as well as decision-making criteria to determine when, how, and why specific interventions are likely to be more or less effective.

To facilitate classroom application, implementation activities follow the presentation of each concept. Specific activities include analysis of classroom practices, structured individual and group problem-solving tasks, case studies and role plays. These "tasks" provide a vehicle to enhance and personalize concept understanding, implementation and integration. Two types of learning tasks are provided:

- Learning Practice Task (LPT): Directed learning tasks that provide practice with the concepts and strategies presented to be completed individually, with a learning partner, or in a collaborative learning group.
- Critical Reflection on Practice (CROP): Structured activities to encourage critical reflection on classroom practices and self-reflection on teaching behaviors, interaction patterns and communication styles.

The focus is on providing teachers with opportunities to develop new skills and implement more effective strategies within the context of examining their own values and belief systems. The material presented is structured to provide opportunities for teachers to reflect on their current behavior, develop an awareness of the influence of their own actions on student behavior, and come to personal realizations regarding desired behavior change.

Specifically, this book advocates:

- The self-reflective process for analyzing classroom and behavior problems,
- Continual examination of established patterns, and
- Self-diagnosis and the development of self-efficacy to create personal solutions to problems.

Learning Focus

Development of dynamic and effective classroom management strategies involves the creation of interactive learning formats which facilitate both the understanding of underlying theoretical concepts and the integration of those concepts into classroom practice. The content, format and structure of this book is designed to move teachers beyond a knowledge base of discrete skills to a stage where they integrate and modify skills to fit specific contexts, and eventually, to a point where the skills are internalized enabling teachers to invent new strategies.

The Needs of the Adult Learner

Research findings clearly support the fact that adult learners need to be self-motivated and accept ownership for change to occur. Change only occurs when the person(s) directly responsible for addressing the problem is involved in the design and implementation of the change strategy. Change takes place over time, at a personal rather than system level, and is more likely to happen when it is tailored to the personal needs of those involved (Knowles, 1975, 1992).

Adult learners have the following specific needs:
- To participate in the design of their learning experiences;
- To have their thoughts, feelings and ideas valued;
- To have the opportunity for analysis and self-diagnosis;
- To give and receive feedback;
- To actively engage in learning tasks; and
- To receive information that can be readily applied in their immediate setting.

Current theories add to these notions the belief that learning is enhanced when teachers (as learners) are provided with "mediating structures" or processes that mediate or draw personal connections between existing knowledge and new knowledge. Teachers learn primarily by tapping into their own realm of experiences and reflecting on whether or not their experiences match the new theoretical construct being presented. Mediating structures allow teachers to construct personal meaning to inform their teaching practice.

Every teacher makes the choice to seek growth or resist growth as a learner. If the choice is to stop learning, then students' learning will atrophy as well, and the major satisfaction of teaching will be lost. The position taken in this book is that every teacher seeks perpetual growth—what Maslow referred to as self-actualization.

Guiding Assumptions about Effective Classroom Management

The following assumptions about what constitutes effective classroom management are the guiding tenets for the development of the ideas advocated in this book.

1. Effective classroom management begins with teacher self-awareness, self-control and self-reflection, not with the students.
   - Unless teachers engage in critical reflection and discovery, they stay trapped in unexamined judgments, assumptions and interpretations.
   - Teachers' responses to the various types of behavior students exhibit in the classroom say much about how secure and competent they feel as teachers. If they have confidence in their potential to be effective, successfully solve problems and maintain healthy relationships with students, they employ strategies that humanize rather than dehumanize students.

- Teachers' emotional responses to students' behavior are sometimes based on their own emotional healing that needs to take place.

2. Effective classroom management supports a climate for teaching and learning that validates and accommodates the psychological, emotional, socio-cultural and academic needs of both teachers and students.

   - More students are coming to school neglected, rejected, abused, hungry and ill-prepared to learn and function adequately within the constraints of the classroom setting. Many students have not had the opportunity to learn the prosocial skills needed to work productively with their classmates; social and emotional needs often override academic needs.

   - In daily classroom life, the behavior of individual students will sometimes make teachers uncomfortable, angry, or even furious. These feelings are inevitable and teachers need to balance their own feelings and reactions with their responsibility to serve as role models for their students. The challenge for teachers is to respond appropriately in spite of such feelings—not to deny or invalidate them. Effectively communicating negative emotions is an important teaching function.

3. Effective classroom management is a thoughtful, purposeful and caring way of interacting with students.

   - Teachers must face deeply-rooted personal attitudes concerning human nature, human development, human potential and human learning in their interactions with students.

   - Teachers possess tremendous power to have far-reaching influence on their students. They can be sources of humiliation or inspiration. They can hurt or heal. They can destroy or build.

4. Effective classroom management models democratic values.

   - The classroom is a microcosm of our society and should instill a set of democratic values founded on the principles of tolerance, acceptance, respect and compassion.

   - The teacher's role is to help students internalize these values and learn that freedom is tied to responsibility.

   - In a spirit of equal opportunity for all, teachers have the responsibility to invite, encourage and engage the participation of all their students.

5. Effective classroom management is much more than a compilation of skills and strategies. It's a deliberate philosophical and ethical code of conduct.

   - Without tying management and disciplinary procedures to beliefs about the teaching/learning process and assumptions about, and expectations for students, teachers will have only fragmented techniques—stabs in the dark.

   - If teachers latch onto techniques for handling student behavior without examination of what kinds of responses to students would be congruent with their beliefs, aligned with their designated teaching structures and harmonious with their personal styles, they will have just a bag of tricks.

Learning to manage today's classroom is a challenge of great magnitude. Effective classroom management cannot be prescribed with an intervention formula. The path cannot be preplanned—it must be lived. Meeting the challenge calls for teachers to resist establishing a classroom culture of control in order to create an authentic community of learners.

Demands of Today's Classroom

Classroom management and discipline is a topic of concern to everyone—teachers, parents, administrators, teacher trainers, as well as the community at large as the incidence of violence becomes more prevalent among school-age children. In a Phi Delta Kappa/Gallup poll of the public's attitude, the two concerns most commonly listed as the biggest problems of public schools were fighting/violence/gangs and lack of discipline (Elam, Rose, & Gallup, 1994). For the past decade, NEA's annual surveys consistently report teachers rank classroom management as their number one problem. And, as teachers experience disruptive student behavior with increasing frequency and severity, they report their classrooms increasingly more difficult to manage. Many surveys also report an alarming increase in students' concern for their safety. One-fourth of students in public schools are victims of violent acts (Johnson & Johnson, 1995).

The response to these concerns in many school districts has been reactionary—instituting top-down, unilateral bureaucratic dictums of restrictive zero-tolerance policies to maintain law and order. Schools have built fences, installed weapon detectors, and stationed security forces on school grounds and armed guards at school entrances. Increasingly, schools look and function like prisons.

To many, the term classroom management is synonymous with discipline, or a teacher's ability to control their students' behavior. Hence, the teacher's role is to keep students "in-line" and "on-task," with very little attention paid to the interface with quality instruction or meaningful human relationships. For others, classroom management means instilling self-discipline and a set of values that are the foundation for a democratic society. In accordance with this goal, the teacher's role is to help their students internalize the values of respect, honesty, tolerance and compassion to become responsible citizens.

Given this scenario, teachers often find themselves having to deal with increasingly strict disciplinary procedures for students who disobey school policies. Such policies tend to erode individual teacher efforts to provide a real sense of security, both in terms of physical and emotional security.

Changing Structure of American Society

More and more, schools are battlegrounds for a society in crisis. Below are some relevant and alarming statistics.

- Record high of 6 million children live in poverty, accounting for over 1/4 of all children below the age of 6 in the United States (National Center for Children in Poverty, 1995).

1

- In one day in the life of children there are 5,314 children arrested, 7,945 children reported abused or neglected, and 100,000 children homeless (*State of America's Children Yearbook*, 1994).
- School violence caused death or serious injury of students in 41% of large cities surveyed in 1993 (Arndt, 1994).
- Teens are 2.5 more likely to suffer violence than those over age 20, with most of the violence occurring in or in close proximity to schools (Hodgkinson, 1992).
- Adolescent pregnancy has soared to one of the highest rates among the technologically advanced nations (Hamburg, 1992).
- Over three million assorted crimes (approximately 11% of all crimes) occur each year in public schools which is three times the rate of crime in America's workplace (Sautter, 1995).
- From 1980 to 1990 the number of people in U.S. prisons rose 139% establishing the United States as having the highest percentage of its population in prison of any nation in the world (Hodgkinson, 1992).

An increasing number of students are already severely troubled even before they enter school. The changing family structure and weakened family support system essential for children's normal development put many children at risk for what could be termed "broken cords"—the failure to develop healthy human attachments.

Accommodating Increasing Diversity

Teachers face an ever-present challenge to meet the needs of all students in a diverse society moving toward a global community. In most large American cities, so-called minority students actually have majority representation. All indications are that the current trend will be expanding to an even greater extent in our immediate future.

Those who make the career choice to enter and remain in the teaching profession will need to master skills that go far beyond their ability to teach academic content. Given the scope and intensity of the needs of today's students, it is evident that the teaching function, while necessary and important, is not nearly sufficient to define the inclusive and complex array of skills necessary to render a teacher effective.

Teachers face greater instructional and management challenges as they strive to accommodate increasing diversity of student learning styles and behavior patterns. With growing support for inclusive classrooms, teachers will continue to be called on to enhance their classroom and behavior management skills to effectively address the wider range of educational, psychological and emotional problems students are experiencing.

The onus falls on teachers to create a more responsive educational climate to better serve all students especially those currently at risk of school failure and alienation. For teachers to be successful in today's classroom, they will need to integrate large-group management skills, individual behavior management interventions, counseling techniques, strategies for developing students' social and academic coping skills, and effective communication skills. Educating all learners primarily in mainstream classrooms requires a model of effective classroom management that goes beyond managing instruction and ensuring student compliance.

Current Model for Effective Classroom Management

The model of effective classroom management currently in vogue stems largely from the teaching effectiveness literature which identified teaching skills, strategies and styles associated with high levels of student achievement. This line of research produced, subject to some variability due to subject area, grade level, and student composition, substantial consensus about the kinds of teaching strategies that seem to promote high levels of student achievement and involvement with learning tasks (e.g., Brophy, 1979; Brophy & Evertson, 1974; Brophy & Good, 1986; Gage, 1978; Gersten, Woodward, & Darch, 1986; Medley, 1977; Rosenshine, 1979; Rosenshine & Berliner, 1978; Rosenshine & Stevens, 1984; Slavin, Karweit, & Madden, 1989).

One popular set of instructional methods attempting to capture the results of this research is "direct instruction," calling for teachers to direct instruction, solicit specific student responses, and closely monitor student on-task behavior during independent work (Brophy, 1987; Crocker & Brooker, 1986; Good & Brophy, 1997; Rosenshine & Stevens, 1986).

Not surprising, this instructional approach also produced relatively low levels of student disruption and management difficulties. Subsequent research identified specific strategies and procedures effective teachers used to produce efficiently-functioning classrooms. This line of research resulted in recommendations for teachers based on explicitly teaching students classroom routines and practices for accomplishing learning tasks (e.g., Anderson, Evertson, & Brophy, 1979; Emmer, Evertson, & Anderson, 1980; Evertson, Anderson, Anderson, & Brophy, 1980; Evertson & Emmer, 1982). Within this framework, classroom management is tantamount to effectively "managing instruction."

This research-based approach to classroom management was established during an era in which the predominant instructional model was one of the teacher providing direct instruction and students working independently. Brophy (1988) characterized this approach as the "whole-class instruction/recitation/seatwork" approach. In this instructional orientation, the teacher primarily provides direct instruction, carefully structures student response patterns, closely monitors student feedback and keeps students on-task during seatwork activities, largely completed independently.

Within this instructional framework, the primary intervention model for addressing student behavior is the behavioral paradigm. Student behavior is managed by consequences—rewards when possible, punishment when necessary.

The traditional classroom has evolved since the emergence of this model. The current movement away from teacher-directed classrooms to classrooms in which students are active participants in their learning requires a new model of what effective classroom management should look like. Effectively managing classrooms where students are interactive participants requires a shift away from teacher control/student compliance patterns of interaction. Placing students in such interactive roles in which the predominant work style is no longer independent but cooperative requires students to develop autonomy from the teacher.

Emerging Beliefs about Quality Teaching and Classroom Management

What constitutes effective classroom management needs to be reexamined in light of emerging beliefs about quality teaching. Major curricular changes that provide greater emphasis on curricular integration, teaching for meaning, interactive dialogue, socialization, and collaboration require fundamental changes in the way teachers interact with students and call for different teacher discourse patterns. This shift is characterized by a move from teacher-directed lessons to participatory learning, from predetermined learning outcomes to less-defined learning outcomes, from uniform assessment of performance to varied assessment of mastery of concepts, from sequenced curriculum to integrated curriculum, from teacher solicitation of specific student responses to interactive dialogue, and from the teacher questioning students to reciprocal teaching.

The teacher role is changing from controlling learning to deliberately facilitating learning. The student role is changing from passive recipient of teacher-directed instruction to interactive participant, often functioning in a variety of collaborative modes with peers. This transformation is guided by assumptions about teaching and learning which move us from the belief that students learn from paying attention to the teacher and repetition and rote memory, to the belief that students construct their own meaning and have responsibility for their own learning. These changing classroom demands call for classroom management and interaction styles that better align with emerging metaphors of teacher as social mediator and learning facilitator.

Historically, conceptions of good teaching have evolved from primarily good discipline in the 60s, to efficient and careful monitoring of student work in the 70s, to increasing levels of student on-task engagement in the 80s, to emphasis on how learning occurs and development of lifelong learners in the 90s. The trend represents a gradual redistribution of control and responsibility for learning from teachers to students. Hence, there needs to be a corresponding shift in emphasis in models of classroom management and student/teacher interaction styles to accompany the academic shift from teacher control to development of greater student autonomy (e.g., Bullough, 1994; Larrivee, 1997; Marshall, 1992; McCaslin & Good, 1992; Randolph & Evertson, 1994).

Current approaches to classroom management are antithetical to school reform initiatives and espoused educational goals. A curriculum designed to produce self-motivated, active learners is undermined by classroom management practices that encourage mindless compliance. Preparing students to wait to be told what to do fails to prepare them for the increasingly complex world they will live in. Classroom management should do more than produce obedient followers, it should promote self-management and self-discipline by encouraging self-understanding, self-reflection and critical inquiry—those qualities that are fundamental for a democratic society.

Part I

Creating a Community of Learners

On Becoming a Reflective Practitioner: Developing the Practice of Self-reflection

Classroom management is much more than an accumulation of skills and strategies. Without tying management and disciplinary decisions to personal beliefs about teaching, learning, and development, a teacher will have only the bricks. The real stuff of managing the classroom is the mortar—what holds the bricks in place and provides a foundation. Learning to effectively manage a classroom environment goes beyond taking on fragmented techniques for keeping students on-task and handling student behavior. It requires examination of what kinds of responses to students are congruent with your beliefs and aligned with your personal style.

The classroom is a dynamic, complex, and self-organizing system. Being effective in the classroom setting requires that the teacher remain fluid and able to move in many directions, rather than stuck only being able to move in one direction as situations occur.

On Becoming a Reflective Practitioner

Others have made a distinction between technical reflection and critical reflection (see Sparks-Langer & Colton, 1991; Zehm & Kottler, 1993). Technical reflection is vital to planning and delivery of appropriate learning experiences for students. This is the kind of thinking teachers use to make pedagogical decisions about learning environments, content selection, and teaching methods. On the other hand, critical reflection involves the conscious consideration of the moral and ethical implications and consequences of personal-professional beliefs and practices on students.

The position taken here is that technical reflection is merely analytical thinking, not reflection at all, and critical reflection is an essential element of what is being called *self-reflection* here; it is not synonymous. Self-reflection goes beyond critical reflection by adding to conscious consideration the dimension of critical examination of personal values and beliefs, embodied in the assumptions you make and the expectations you have.

Avoiding the Reflexive Loop

Argyris (1990) pointed out how our beliefs are self-generating, and often untested, based on conclusions inferred from our selected observations. In other words, from all the data available to us, we select data by literally choosing to see some things and ignore others. He coined the term *reflexive loop* to describe the circular process by which we select data, add personal meaning, make assumptions based on our interpretations of the selected data, draw conclusions, adopt beliefs, and ultimately take action. We stay in a reflexive loop where our unexamined beliefs affect what data we select.

Self-reflection involves a deep exploration process which exposes our unexamined beliefs and makes visible our personal reflexive loops. Becoming a reflective practitioner calls teachers to the task of facing deeply-rooted personal attitudes concerning human nature, human potential, and human learning.

Experience is culturally and personally "sculpted." Experience is not pure—everything is contextually bound. We develop mental habits, biases, and presuppositions that tend to close off new ways of perceiving and interpreting our experiences (e.g., Brookfield, 1995; Knowles, 1992; Senge, 1990).

Essential Practices for Becoming a Reflective Practitioner

The process of becoming a reflective practitioner cannot be prescribed. It is a personal awareness discovery process. While it's not possible to prescribe a linear process or define a step-by-step procedure, there are actions and practices that are fundamental to developing as a reflective practitioner. The following three practices are essential.

1. Solitary reflection
2. Ongoing inquiry
3. Perpetual problem-solving

Solitary Reflection

Making time for thoughtful consideration of your actions and critical inquiry into the impact of your own behavior keeps you alert to the consequences of your actions on students.

It's important to engage in systematic self-reflection by making it an integral part of your daily practice. Keeping a reflective journal is one vehicle for ensuring time is set aside for daily reflection.

Ongoing Inquiry

This practice involves unending questioning of the status quo and conventional wisdom by seeking your own truth. Becoming a fearless truth-seeker involves being open to examining the assumptions which underlie your classroom practices. It's a process of identifying and connecting patterns to form personal conceptions for understanding the complexity of what you observe and experience.

To engage in the practice of self-reflection and critical inquiry it is essential to enlist collegial support. Critical reflection is a social process. The support can be in the form of a support group, a "critical friend," or a mentor. The function of the support group or person is not only to empathize with your dilemmas but also to point out incongruencies in practice and fallacies in thinking.

Perpetual Problem-solving

Becoming a perpetual problem-solver involves synthesizing experiences, integrating information and feedback, uncovering underlying reasons, and discovering new meaning. Your *modus operandus* is solving problems not enforcing preset standards of operation. The classroom is a laboratory for purposeful experimentation. A practice or procedure is never permanent. New insights, understandings, and perspectives can bring previous decisions up for reevaluation and consideration. When teachers perpetually seek better solutions, they adjust the power dynamics to turn power *over* into power *with* learners.

Faithfully engaging in these three practices helps teachers recognize their repetitive cycles and reflexive loops which limit their potential for tolerance and acceptance—the vital elements for effectively managing classrooms composed of students from different cultural and social backgrounds who have diverse beliefs and values. Reflective practitioners find a means to catch themselves when they try to unjustly impose their values or dismiss students' perspectives without due consideration.

Critically reflective teachers infuse their practice with a sense of excitement and purpose as they continually forge new ground. While they learn from the past, they thrive in the present. These teachers know that much of what occurs can't be predicted, but they also know that they are not victims of fate. Not to be self-reflective puts teachers in danger of what Freire (1993) calls "magical consciousness," viewing life in the classroom as beyond their control subject to whimsical blessings and curses.

There are many pathways to becoming a self-reflective teacher and each teacher must find his or her own path. Any path a teacher chooses must involve a willingness to be an active participant in a perpetual growth process requiring ongoing critical reflection on classroom practices. The journey involves finding a means of infusing your personal beliefs and values into your professional identity. It results in developing a deliberate code of conduct that embodies who you are and what you stand for. Self-reflection is not only a way of approaching your teaching, it's a way of life. The more you explore, the more you discover. The more you question, the more you access new realms of possibility.

Incremental Fluctuations on the Route to Becoming Self-reflective

The route to becoming self-reflective is plagued by incremental fluctuations of irregular progress, often marked by two steps forward and one step backward. There are necessary and predictable stages in the emotional and cognitive rhythm of becoming a reflective practitioner (Brookfield, 1995; Kasl, Dechant, & Marsick, 1993; Keane, 1987; Larrivee, 1996; Usher & Bryant, 1989). The sense of liberation at discarding a dearly-held assumption is quickly followed by the fear of being in limbo. This state leads to a longing for the abandoned assumption and a desire to revert to the familiar, to keep the chaos at bay. Old ways of thinking no longer make sense but new ones have not yet gelled to take their place and you are left dangling, in the throes of uncertainty. This uncertainty marks transformation and the emergence of new possibilities.

Yet, this inner struggle is a necessary and important stage in the self-reflective process. To break through your familiar cycles, you need to allow yourself to feel confused and anxious, not permanently, but for a time. Fully experiencing this sense of uncertainty is what allows you to come to a personal deeper understanding, leading to a shift in your way of thinking and perceiving. If you can weather the storm, you emerge with a new vision.

Developing Awareness and Self-reflection by Journal Writing

Journal writing is a reflective process that allows you to chart your development and become more aware of your contribution to the experiences you encounter. This process of systematic self-reflection enables you to become more insightful and better attuned to your wants and needs. Journaling can provide the clarification necessary for you to gain, or regain, a sense of meaning and purposefulness in your teaching. Finding personal meaning is the key to preventing burnout.

Journals can be instrumental in helping you unleash your creative powers as well as daily tension. Making regular journal entries helps you remain clear and intensely aware of what is going on in both your inner and outer worlds. Most of all, a journal is a place where you can talk to yourself. The act of maintaining and reviewing a journal over time can serve as a therapeutic tool.

Journal writing develops self-discipline. Attitudes about teaching and interacting with students are the result of attitudes and experiences gained over time. By making journal entries you can look more objectively at your behaviors in the classroom.

Having a record of your thoughts, feelings, concerns, crises, and successes provides a window of the past and a gateway to the future. When maintained over time, it can serve as a database offering both an historical perspective and information about patterns of thought and behavior.

Journals can serve several important purposes for teachers. They can provide a safe haven for:

- Dumping all your daily frustrations
- Storing your most private thoughts and feelings
- Working through internal conflicts and solving problems
- Recording significant events and critical incidents
- Posing questions, naming issues, and raising concerns
- Identifying cause and effect relationships
- Noting strategies that work and those that don't and seeing patterns over time
- Celebrating joys
- Experimenting with new ways of thinking and acting
- Tracing life patterns and themes

A journal can also be a place to set goals for yourself. Committing yourself in writing can be the impetus it takes to move you toward what is really important to you. Keeping a journal can help you map out where you want to be in your teaching 1, 5, 10 years from now.

Journal writing is also an excellent tool for examining personal biases and prejudices that may unwittingly play out in your interactions with students whose backgrounds are significantly different from your own. While you may not be conscious of inappropriate responses to students on the basis of culture, race, gender, or social class, there may indeed be areas where you unknowingly behave in insensitive ways. Making journal entries would allow you to look more objectively at your behaviors toward students from a variety of diverse settings.

The following questions can serve as a guide to beginning the process of making journal writing an integral part of developing the habit of critical reflection.

- What type of schedule would be manageable for you to keep a journal?
- When and where would you make entries?
- Would you do free-form reflection?
- Would you categorize entries?
- Would your entries be crisis or problem-related?
- How would you use your journal to guide inquiry and decision-making?

Critical Reflection on Practice: Daily-reflection

Activity Directions: One way to build reflection into practice is to take some time at the end of the school day and before you go home to reflect on the day. Based on what is important to you and the values you want to uphold in your classroom, write a few personal daily reflection questions. Below are some sample daily reflection questions.

1. Did I speak respectfully to all of my students?
2. Did I use fair and just discipline procedures?
3. Did I remain open to unusual or unexpected student responses?
4. Did I try to teach and reach all of my students?
5. Did I take time to interact with each student?

My personal daily reflection questions:

_____

_____

_____

_____

Developing the Practice of Self-reflection

The challenge of effectively managing today's diverse classroom involves not only self-awareness but self-reflection. By developing self-awareness, teachers become more cognizant of the interdependence between teacher responses to students and student responses to teachers. Through self-reflection, teachers become increasingly aware of how they are interactive participants in classroom encounters, rather than innocent bystanders or victims. By developing the practice of self-reflection teachers learn to:

1. Slow down their thinking and reasoning process to become more aware of how they perceive and react to students, and
2. Bring to the surface some of their unconscious ways of responding to students.

Self-reflection involves developing the ability to look at what's happening, withholding judgment while simultaneously recognizing that the meaning we attribute to it is no more than our interpretation filtered through our cumulative experience. When we are able to acknowledge this, then reality takes on a different meaning. When I can say, "This is my experience, and this is the meaning I attribute to what I am experiencing," I am aware that each person's reality is uniquely defined.

Self-reflection encompasses reflection, deliberation, understanding, and insight turned inward, so we continually discover new dimensions of ourselves. This complex process is not prescriptive in nature, rather it is a process that allows insights to surface which serve to challenge our familiar behavior patterns. It is more a way of knowing than a knowing how.

Developing the practice of self-reflection allows you to recognize that what you see goes through a series of internal, interpretive filters reflecting your belief system. Perception is subjective—it is not pure and it can be distorted. When a student acts out, one teacher sees a cry for help, another a personal attack. It is our interpretation of the student's behavior, or the meaning we attach to the behavior, that determines how we will respond. Through self-reflection we can learn to see beyond the filters of our past and the blinders of our expectations.

Our Screening Process: Examining Our Personal Filtering System

The meaning we attribute to our experiences is influenced by various factors that effectively "screen out" some responses while letting others through. This screening process leads to differing perceptions of circumstances and events, resulting in different interpretations and, subsequently, in different responses. When we critically examine our screens, we can become more aware of how our screens may be "filtering out" potentially more effective responses to classroom situations and students' challenging behavior.

Our actions are governed by multiple screens which can be seen as a series of interpretive filters (see figure). Each level of screen serves to eliminate some potential responses

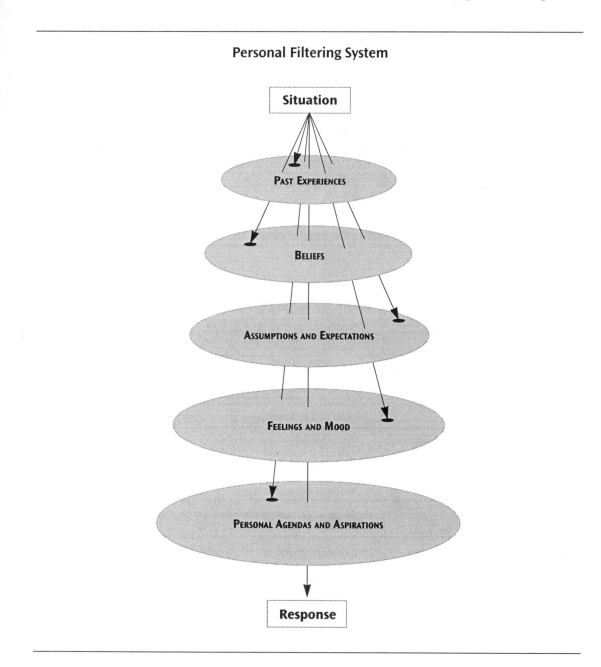

Personal Filtering System

Situation

PAST EXPERIENCES

BELIEFS

ASSUMPTIONS AND EXPECTATIONS

FEELINGS AND MOOD

PERSONAL AGENDAS AND ASPIRATIONS

Response

while allowing others to filter through. Our past experiences, beliefs, assumptions, and expectations, feelings, and mood, and our personal agendas and aspirations can either serve to limit or expand the repertoire of responses available to us in any situation. Beliefs about students' capacity and willingness to learn, assumptions about the behavior of students, especially those from different ethnic and social backgrounds, and expectations formulated on the basis of our value system can potentially be sources for responding inappropriately to students.

Certain responses can be eliminated by being screened through our past experiences. For example, the sight of a snake can conjure up a multitude of differing reactions on a continuum from absolute terror to curiosity to pleasure, based on what our experiences have been. Additional potential responses are ruled out, or in, on the basis of the beliefs we hold. Our beliefs can be affirming or defeating, expansive or limiting, rational or irrational. The assumptions that we make and the expectations that we have can make more responses available, or unavailable, to us. Our feelings, both those directly related to the immediate situation and those resulting from other experiences, can either serve to screen out responses or to avail us to additional responses. And, finally, the agenda we set for ourselves and the aspirations we have act as still another filter. We may become driven by our personal goals and lose sight of what we stand for. For example, we might be so concerned about keeping our job that we go against our own values to keep the classroom quiet because that's what the principal values.

The way we respond is determined by this personal filtering system. This filtering system is a subjective mediating process. At the simplest level, there is an immediate reflexive response with no thought process occurring. A reflexive reaction, like removing your hand from a hot burner, is a reaction without conscious consideration of alternative responses. This type of response is often referred to as a "knee-jerk" response connoting that the response is automatic. Often we operate on "automatic pilot," closed off from entertaining a continuum of responses. When we do this in the complex classroom environment, we run the risk of responding to students in biased and disrespectful ways and can easily escalate, rather than deescalate, student reactions.

Bringing your personal screens into awareness, expands the intermediate thought process between a situation and your resulting reaction. By bringing a greater portion of the mediating process into awareness, you can increase your range of possible responses to the often difficult classroom situations you face daily.

As an example, consider your typical response to being criticized by a student. Suppose your reflexive reaction is to automatically offer a defense to the criticism. Let's say you usually come in with a "but . . .," rather than merely 'taking in' the criticism, or exploring it further. Becoming aware of your own resistance and asking yourself questions like, "Why am I being defensive?" or "What am I defending?" or "Why do I need to be right?" or "Why do I need to have the last word?" would represent challenging your screening process at the assumptions-and-expectations layer. By challenging your usual way of reacting, you thereby allow a greater range of responses to filter through your interpretive screen.

Our cumulative layers of screens can lead to responding to situations in conditioned and rigid ways. To have the greatest freedom of choice and the capacity to respond uniquely to each classroom situation encountered calls for constantly examining your choices to see how your personal screens are influencing your ability to respond in unconditioned ways. As you take time to challenge your screens and consider alternate responses to reoccurring classroom situations, you become open to more possibilities and no possible response is automatically ruled out or in.

Critical Reflection on Practice: Challenging Your Personal Screening Process

Activity Directions: To examine how your filtering screens may result in limiting responses to students, follow the steps below.

1. Think of an area in your teaching where 1 of the 5 filters from the diagram is "clogged" keeping you from a more open response. Is it a bad past experience, a limiting belief, an expectation for how students should act?

   Clogged filter area:

   _____

   _____

   _____

   Describe the specific aspect of the filter area:

   _____

   _____

   _____

2. What types of responses are more likely because of this clogged filter?

   _____

   _____

   _____

3. What other ways of responding are being screened out?

   _____

   _____

   _____

4. List specific classroom actions you can begin to take to curtail your reflexive response.

   _____

   _____

   _____

5. Select one typical response that you want to begin challenging. Write a self-question that will help you.

   _____

   _____

   _____

Question for Self-reflection

What can you do to remind yourself to become more aware of how your filters are screening out potentially more effective responses to students?

Examining Core Beliefs, Assumptions, and Expectations

Examining our core beliefs is a critical aspect of self-reflection. A core belief is a fundamental belief about human nature, development, or learning. Our beliefs are adopted based on conclusions inferred from our observations and interpretations, and they often remain largely untested. Developing the practice of self-reflection involves observing our patterns of behavior and examining our behavior in light of what we truly believe. This process can be envisioned as flowing through several levels, from the level of core beliefs to the level of specific actions. Similar to a model developed by Shapiro and Reiff (1993) to examine the congruence between core beliefs and job performance, this multi-level process has four levels: the philosophical level, the framework level, the interpretive level, and the decision-making level (see figure).

Philosophy of life is the backdrop for all other levels and activities. The philosophical level embodies core beliefs and includes values, religious beliefs, ways of knowing, life meanings, and ethics.

Multi-level Process for Self-reflection

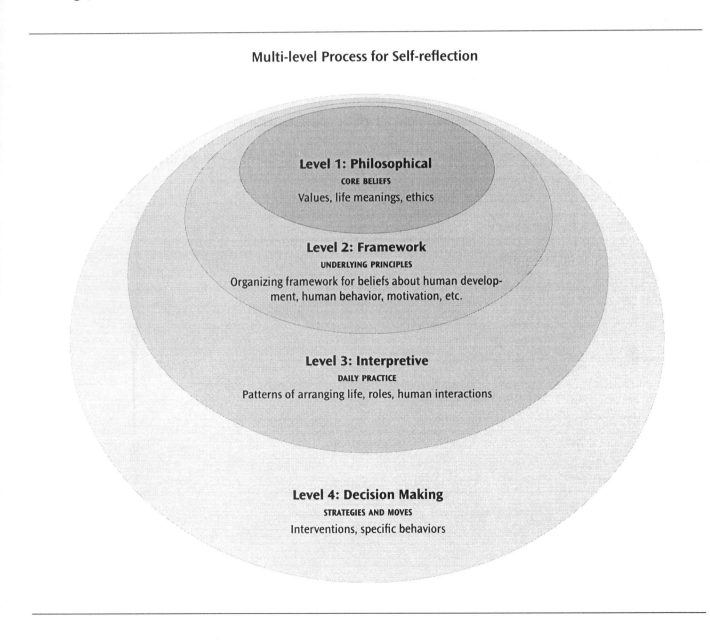

Level 1: Philosophical
CORE BELIEFS
Values, life meanings, ethics

Level 2: Framework
UNDERLYING PRINCIPLES
Organizing framework for beliefs about human development, human behavior, motivation, etc.

Level 3: Interpretive
DAILY PRACTICE
Patterns of arranging life, roles, human interactions

Level 4: Decision Making
STRATEGIES AND MOVES
Interventions, specific behaviors

Level two represents our way of providing an organizational framework for these basic beliefs and includes the theories we espouse, such as theories of human development and human behavior, theories of motivation and learning, theories of organizational development, and chaos theory. It is our framework for attaching meaning to what's happening. These underlying principles serve as the basis for how we organize what we have learned and experienced.

The next level is how we interpret these underlying principles into our general approach to daily practice. This is where we link our beliefs and theories into a way of behaving. Our daily practice is an overriding stance, a pervasive attitude for how we approach life and the situations we encounter. It's a frame of mind.

From our attitude about daily practice evolves our momentary actions. It is our way of making real our ideals and translating them into thoughts, behaviors, and actions. This last level represents the translation into moment-by-moment decision-making.

The four levels of the process for examining a core belief are described below.

Core belief. A fundamental belief about human nature: Each student is doing the best that he or she can at any given moment.

Underlying principle. Principles that organize our experiences and beliefs, or our framework for interpreting our experiences:

- We are all wounded by our unmet needs in childhood and our life experiences.
- Our wounds lead us to act in protective, and sometimes hurtful, ways toward ourselves and others.

Daily practice. Linking of beliefs with actions: If I hold this core belief and understand that behavior is often driven by unmet needs, I will act in a way that reflects the belief and the underlying understanding that:

- Accepts the student's limitations, and
- Refrains from judging the student.

Strategies and moves. If I accept the student's behavior without judgment, then I will respond with compassion. I will:

- Attempt to address the student's unmet need, and
- Choose my behavior knowing that the student is not acting against me.

Aligning Core Beliefs with Classroom Practice

Below is an example of a core belief that is potentially affirming and one that is potentially limiting. For each type of belief, possible underlying principles, daily practice, and specific strategies are described. Some potential questions for self-reflection are also offered.

Affirming Core Belief	**Every student can be successful in my class.**
Underlying Principle	Students have different learning styles and intelligences which need to be addressed.
Daily Practice	Organize lessons to support multiple learning styles.
Specific Strategy	Allow students to select from three alternatives how they will demonstrate that they have learned the major concepts in the science unit on light.
Self-reflective Questions	• Have I given up on any students in my class because I have a limiting belief about their potential to learn?
	• Do all students in my class have daily opportunities to be successful?

Limiting Core Belief	Every student should show respect for the teacher.
Underlying Principle	Adults have the best interests of children in mind.
Daily Practice	Have the following classroom rule: Treat everyone with respect.
Specific Strategy	When a student is disrespectful to me have him/her write 10 times, "I will treat my teacher with respect."
Self-reflective Questions	• Have some of the students in my class experienced adults who do not have their best interest in mind? If so, have they had an opportunity to learn respectful behavior?
	• In what ways might I be modeling disrespect?
	• Am I showing respect for all my students, or just those I think "deserve" it?

Critical Reflection on Practice: Examining Core Beliefs

Activity Directions: To examine whether your actions in the classroom are congruent with what you believe, follow the steps below.

1. Write a belief you hold about education, students, classrooms, schools, learning, or human nature.

   Core Belief: _____

   _____

   _____

2. List the principle(s) that underlie this belief. What are the theories of human development, human behavior, motivation, learning, or organizational development that frame this belief?

   Underlying Principle(s): _____

   _____

   _____

3. List specific ways of approaching classroom practice and the situations you encounter that support this belief.

   Daily Practice: _____

   _____

   _____

4. List specific classroom actions and behaviors that are consistent with this belief.

   Specific Strategies: _____

   _____

   _____

Questions for Self-reflection

What are some of your classroom behaviors and practices that are not in alignment with this core belief? What do you need to do to better align your moment-to-moment choices with this core belief?

Often reflection during, or simultaneously with, our actions is difficult because of the multiple demands we have to juggle in the classroom. For example, focusing our attention on completing a lesson may distract from paying attention to the way in which we interact with students. Hence, self-reflection often requires a perspective of a meta-position, a looking back after the action has taken place.

The self-reflective process raises our level of consciousness and this increased awareness provides an opportunity to spot incongruence or imbalance. Effective classroom management necessitates continual examining and revisiting of our core beliefs and assessing our actions against these beliefs.

Developing the practice of self-reflection keeps us coming back to our core beliefs and evaluating our choices in accordance with these beliefs. Change is an emergent process, requiring that we learn to become increasingly more aware. That consciousness is the source of our capacity to grow and expand, opening up to a greater range of possible choices and responses to classroom situations and individual student behaviors. Becoming a reflective practitioner who engages in critical inquiry and self-reflection is the key to remaining fluid in the dynamic environment of the classroom.

Challenging Your Beliefs

In order to change, you have to challenge the underlying beliefs that drive your present behavior. If you merely try to change a behavior without attacking the belief that drives the behavior, the change is not likely to last long. However, the channel to changing beliefs is not direct; it is through perpetually examining your assumptions, interpretations, and expectations.

Your beliefs about the roles of the teacher and the learner, the nature and purposes of learning, and the teaching and learning environment best suited to these purposes will shape your management decisions. These beliefs disclose your operating principles related to how you view student potential, motivation, development and growth. The following belief statements represent some possible beliefs that teachers may have.

- I believe students learn best in an intellectually challenging yet structured learning environment.
- I believe students misbehave when they feel defeated and become discouraged and are not able to find constructive outlets for their frustrations.
- I believe students will strive in a classroom environment where individual differences are accommodated and where they enjoy each others' company.

Critical Reflection on Practice: I Believe . . . .

Activity Directions: To help you articulate some of your core beliefs about education and examine practices that may not match your beliefs, complete the following:

1. Complete each statement.

   I believe learning is _____

   I believe my classroom _____

   I believe all my students are _____

   I believe my students learn best when I _____

   I believe my students learn best when they _____

2. For each of your core belief statements list some classroom practices and strategies that support the belief.

   _____
   _____
   _____
   _____
   _____
   _____
   _____
   _____
   _____
   _____
   _____
   _____

3. For each of your core belief statements list some classroom practices and strategies that are questionable when aligned with the belief.

   _____
   _____
   _____
   _____
   _____
   _____
   _____
   _____
   _____
   _____
   _____
   _____

4. Select the questionable practice that concerns you the most. Devise some alternative strategies that would be more in line with the belief.

   Alternative strategies: _____
   _____
   _____

Challenging Limiting Expectations

Teacher beliefs are revealed in the expectations they have for students. There is much research to suggest differential teacher responses to students on the basis of their expectations. These expectations can, and often do, serve as self-fulfilling prophecies, when they are acted upon with classroom interaction patterns that are discriminatory (e.g., Rosenthal & Jacobson, 1968). Limiting expectations can be based on gender, race, culture, social status, disability, or academic deficits, to name some. There is also research to suggest the teacher's mediating role in the attitudes that students develop toward their classmates as well (e.g., Larrivee, 1991).

There is a considerable body of research on the differing ways teachers treat and respond to low-achieving students versus high-achieving students. Good and Brophy (1997) list some of the following teacher behaviors that might communicate low expectations for low-achieving students. Teachers tend to:

- Wait less time for low-achieving students than for high-achieving students to answer questions before giving the answer or going to another student;
- Give low-achieving students the correct answer rather than offer clues or rephrase the question;
- Call on low-achieving students less often;
- Ask low-achieving students only easy questions;
- Expect less academic work from low-achieving students;
- Make fewer efforts to improve the performance of low-achieving students;
- Accept and use the ideas of low-achieving students less.

Critical Reflection on Practice: Limiting Expectations

Activity Directions: Answer the following questions thinking of a particular student who is one of your low-achieving students.

1. Describe the student's academic behavior.

   _____

   _____

   _____

2. Now, read over your description. Does it reveal any limiting expectations?

   _____

   _____

   _____

3. Which of the specific behaviors listed above do you find yourself doing with this student?

   _____

   _____

   _____

4. Are there any other behaviors you are engaging in with this student that might be communicating low expectations?

   _____

   _____

   _____

5. What message is the student getting about your expectation for his/her performance?

   _____

   _____

   _____

6. How does your experience relate to the research findings reported here?

   _____

   _____

   _____

7. What lingering questions do you have?

   _____

   _____

   _____

8. What is one thing you want to change when responding to this student?

   _____

   _____

   _____

Teacher Self-efficacy

Teachers' notions of self-efficacy can also play a part in perpetuating their behavior toward certain types of student behavior. Self-efficacy refers to the teacher's perceived ability to be effective, find reasonable solutions to problems, and maintain a belief in their own capacity to effect positive change. When teachers see students' actions as threatening their need for control and as intentional misbehavior, they are often pessimistic about their likelihood of producing positive results or any improvement (Brophy & Evertson, 1981).

Hence, teachers notions of self-efficacy related to their lack of success with students exhibiting such behavior contributes to a sense of powerlessness in being able to affect change. That, in turn, often leads to a continuing pattern of ineffective, even increasingly more hostile, teacher responses.

In contrast, even frequent misconduct does not necessarily impair the teacher/student relationship if it is not disruptive or aggressive, provided the student responds well to the teacher's intervention. Apparently, even if they present behavior problems, students who defer to teachers' authority and respond positively to their interventions are treated with teacher concern and assistance, whereas students who fail to respond appropriately to teacher interventions are treated with rejection and hostility. These findings indicate an interdependence between the teacher's perceived effectiveness, and resulting interaction pattern, and individual student's responses to teacher attempts to curtail inappropriate behavior.

Research findings support the contention that teachers tend to respond with rejection and an orientation toward control and punishment when students are disruptive or threaten the teacher's authority or control (Brophy & Evertson, 1981; Brophy & Good, 1974; Brophy & McCaslin, 1992). Teachers have been found to be especially rejecting and punitive when misbehavior is threatening rather than merely irritating. Students who persistently defy teachers' authority with sullenness or open hostility experience teacher rejection and punishment. Teachers react quite negatively to hostile-aggressive and especially defiant students and to any students who display a surly or insolent attitude. Responses typically depict negative expectations and are characterized by restricted language, often confined to terse demands for behavior change with little emphasis on shaping more desirable behaviors or improving coping skills. Demands are often accompanied by threat or punishment but seldom by rationales or offers of incentives for improved behavior.

Teachers' negative emotional response can trigger a need for control. When student behavior elicits feelings of frustration, irritation, or anger, teachers are more likely to respond with power assertion than to engage in problem-solving negotiations. On the other hand, teachers tend to respond supportively and attempt to help when student problems are purely academic or related to student anxiety or difficulty in coping with the demands of school. Similarly, responses to problems viewed as student-owned, where students are frustrated by people or events that do not include the teacher, are characterized by extensive talk designed to provide support and instruction, with frequent emphasis on longterm goals such as improving students' self-evaluations or teaching them coping techniques.

Critical Reflection on Practice: Self-efficacy

Activity Directions: Follow the steps listed.

1. Think of a particular student with whom your intervention tactics have been mostly ineffective.

2. Describe your emotional response to this student.

_____

_____

3. What specific comment(s) do you find yourself making when you feel threatened?

_____

_____

_____

4. What specific comment(s) do you find yourself making when you fear losing control?

_____

_____

_____

5. What are the physical effects you experience when dealing with this student?

_____

_____

6. What are the mental effects you experience when dealing with this student?

_____

_____

7. How would you classify your usual comments (e.g., demands, threats, put downs)?

_____

_____

8. How does your experience relate to the research findings reported here?

_____

_____

_____

9. What lingering questions do you have?

_____

_____

_____

10. What do you want to pay more attention to when dealing with this student?

_____

_____

_____

Guarding Against Teacher Burnout: Cultivating Teacher Renewal

Teachers are particularly susceptible to burnout because of the high degree of dedication and commitment required, making burnout a definite occupational hazard for those in the teaching profession.

Teacher Burnout Factors

Those in helping professions, such as teaching, often fall prey to burnout as a "consequence of caring," or the emotional response to the chronic strain of dealing with others. Maslach (1982) describes the following eight characteristics of burnout:

- Reluctance to discuss work with others;
- High incidence of daydreaming to escape current plight;
- Attitude of cynicism and negativity toward constituents;
- Loss of excitement and interest in daily activities;
- Emotional exhaustion and feelings of being spent, having nothing more to give;
- Decreased effectiveness in job performance;
- Blaming others for unhappiness;
- Feeling powerless to change the situation.

Friesen, Prokop, and Sarros (1988) offer three main reasons teachers experience burnout: (1) emotional exhaustion, (2) depersonalization, and (3) lack of personal accomplishment. Emotional exhaustion stems from trying to do too much keeping up with a workload that is overwhelming. Depersonalization takes place when teachers develop negative attitudes toward those they work with and become cynical and critical. Burned-out teachers feel a lack of personal accomplishment, becoming disillusioned because they are not satisfying their own needs for challenges, recognition, and appreciation.

Of particular relevance to beginning teachers, Gold (1988) found that those most likely to experience burnout are young and inexperienced. These teachers tend to be ambitious and driven, are likely to be loners who are unable to express feelings, and have a propensity to be depressed. Certain personality characteristics predispose some teachers to greater risk of stress and burnout: being driven, ambitious, competitive, and impatient; needing to be perfect; not feeling in control of emotions (see Mills, Powell, & Pollack, 1992).

Gmelch (1983) coined the term "rustout" to describe a type of professional burnout which afflicts teachers in the form of waning enthusiasm. Rustout is operating when teachers temporarily or permanently cease to be enthusiastic learners. Seeing oneself as a perpetual learner promotes risk-taking, inventing, exploring, and extending—all vital to sustaining excitement about learning. When the desire to keep learning withers, the teacher merely goes-through-the-motions of teaching.

Teachers are also prone to the effects of excessive stress, which if unattended can result in rustout or burnout. Because of the daily unrelenting pressures and demands on teachers from others as well as self, teaching is among the most stressful professions (Blase & Kirby, 1991; Farber & Miller, 1981; Lortie, 1975). Because teachers answer to so many different people, a number of external factors also contribute to burnout. In addition to dealing with students who can be trying and difficult, teachers have irate parents to contend with. The imposing structure of school itself leads to constraints of time and scheduling, as well as the lack of opportunity to collaborate with peers, contributing to a feeling of isolation.

Taking Steps to Inoculate Yourself Against Teacher Burnout

It is not inevitable that such demoralizing feelings will someday infect every teacher's professional life and destroy their idealism. Although feeling demoralized periodically throughout one's career is normal and predictable, teachers can take steps to insulate themselves and keep from surrendering to burnout. As Zehm and Kottler (1993) remind us, burnout doesn't happen all of a sudden, rather it results from an insidious form of self-neglect, a slow deterioration that eventually corrodes the edges of a teacher's compassion.

If teachers recognize the sources of stress and how it affects their perceptions of themselves, their work, their students, and their colleagues, they will be less likely to succumb to potential stressors. Being more aware of the conditions that induce stress, teachers can notice sooner the symptoms of distress and begin to take specific steps to counteract the effects of stress. Teachers will need vehicles to dissipate stress. When feelings of frustration, hopelessness, and isolation cause teachers to feel overwhelmed, it's easy to fall into habits that can exacerbate stress, such as excessive caffeine as a pick up, overeating, skipping meals, or avoiding exercise due to fatigue. Early career teachers will need to prepare themselves for the challenges they will face by equipping themselves with the resources and tools to vigorously counteract the potential destructive effects of burnout.

Believing in what you are doing and deriving personal satisfaction from doing it is one of the best "stress-busters." To guard against the potentially debilitating effects of on-the-job stress, the following strategies are critical.

Ongoing Growth and Development

Become a lifelong learner. Improve your own teaching skills. Teachers who are burned-out feel they no longer make a difference with their students. You can have an impact, and you can improve yourself and your classroom. Feelings about yourself in general, but in particular feelings of competency and control in the classroom, lend a sense of importance and significance to your work.

Be More Authentic

Being genuine and sharing your concerns, fears, and emotions with colleagues as well as students will do much to keep your spirits high. The school culture often promotes the idea that teachers should be able to solve their own problems and should not voice their issues and concerns. This creates a subversive climate in which critical issues are "undiscussable."

Develop a Sense of Belonging to Your School Community

Most teachers are isolated from one another due to the sheer workload involved in teaching. Furthermore, teacher talk often dwells on the undesirable aspects of the job and the shortcomings of colleagues and administrators. Cynicism and pessimism are a common reaction to the stress of teaching. Feeling part of a caring community helps diminish a feeling of solitude while providing a forum for being recognized and appreciated.

Being in a supportive environment promotes satisfaction, enjoyment, and affiliation. When you create a sense of connectedness among your colleagues, you expand your opportunities for authentic discourse. By getting to know each other, you learn each other's strengths as well as limitations. When colleagues respect differences among their peers, they begin to view these differences not as liabilities, rather as assets. Assessing, utilizing, indeed capitalizing on the unique strengths of individual teachers can contribute to the overall resources of the school community to meet the needs of a diverse student population. Because feeling overwhelmed and that there is no-hope-in-sight are major contributors to burnout, it is important for teachers to become resources for each other to counteract such feelings. They can even help each other. For example, a teacher who deals effectively with large-groups and teacher-led lessons can "trade" teaching a science topic for an individual teacher conference with a "problem" student.

Teachers can also create work incentives by reinforcing themselves. One school started a "secret admirer" club where at the beginning of the year all staff members drew a name and became that person's secret admirer (Froyen, 1993). Twice each month they exchanged thoughtful "gifts." The gift might be a solicited note from an appreciative parent, an invitation from a student to share a special box lunch, or a basket of fruit. You can see how tailoring these gifts to the unique preferences and 'soft-spots' of an individual teacher can do much to boost morale. By providing these gifts on different schedules, some teacher is regularly expressing gratitude. The teacher's lounge is buzzing with talk about kind deeds keeping everyone more attuned with the special gifts each person brings to teaching. The elements of mystery, excitement, anticipation, special attention, and personalized affection make this program especially rewarding. The point is, teachers can be proactive and ingenious in inventing ways to create a spirit of mutual support and encouragement.

Have Access to a Support System

It is important to build a support system to provide comfort and compassion as well as understanding, direction, and redirection when necessary. In the normal school structure, teachers have little opportunity to provide emotional support for each other or to share experiences. There is great consolation in knowing your peers have the same struggles and agonize over better solutions to common problems. Recurring problems can erode self-perceptions of ability to find adequate solutions to problems that plague teachers on a day-to-day basis, leading to a preoccupation with negative aspects of self and work.

One vehicle for supplanting negative attitudes and self-appraisals with encouragement is a support group. Support groups can be an uplifting experience, and they can provide a buffer against burnout (Dunham, 1984; Holt, Fine, & Tollefson, 1987; Jenkins & Calhoun, 1991). A support group is an informal group of peers who meet on a regular basis to provide an opportunity for unstructured communication and socialization. The group can be composed of teachers at one school site, within a district, or across districts, such as same-grade teachers or colleagues taking the same class or workshop. It provides a welcome time-out from structured group meetings. Here you can vent emotions and frustrations, give and receive constructive and purposeful criticism, and develop strategies to improve work situations and relations.

A support group is a place where you feel safe and accepted enough to allow yourself to be vulnerable, admit mistakes, and ask for help. Such a group can be rejuvenating and keep you from getting stuck in destructive habits to deal with the stress of teaching. Your peers can help you sift through the maze and acknowledge the good you are doing as well as see how you might be contributing to your own demise. One side effect of support groups is a greater realization and appreciation of the unique abilities and talents of both yourself and your peers.

Enhance Your Communication Skills

Better communication skills can also serve to reduce stress. Having more effective ways to articulate your feelings, frustrations, wants, needs, and desires will help you find the courage to express yourself. Positive and affirming interpersonal relationships are at the heart of feeling good about yourself and what you do. Later chapters in this book address skills for initiating and responding more effectively to both everyday experiences as well as more confrontive encounters.

Critical Reflection on Practice: Dealing with Stress

Activity Directions: Follow the steps below to begin paying more attention to your stress level.

1. Keep a diary of your daily activities for one week.
2. Then go back and reflect on the level of stress you felt on each of those days.
3. Use your entries to make connections between more or less stress and differences in "quality of life" experiences for those days.

Questions for Self-reflection

What did this activity tell you?

What are some cause-and-effect relationships you want to be more aware of?

What seems to serve as a stress buffer for you?

Creating Critical Reflection Support Groups

While adult education advocates emphasize starting with one's personal experiences, they also stress the importance of critical analysis and reformulation of that experience. Brookfield (1995) describes reflection groups as "circles of peers engaged in mutually respectful yet critically rigorous conversation." To serve that purpose, such groups form an emotionally-sustaining peer learning community, providing a safe haven as a buffer against the inevitable low points.

In order to gain insight and a clearer perspective, it may take someone else to mirror back what you are experiencing and perceiving. This process in itself often is enough to open up a new way of seeing things. In fact, your best chance for critical reflection may be through conversations with peers—those with the same struggles and triumphs.

Finding the time and the participants is just the beginning of the process. To ensure a safe climate in which to divulge concerns and personal limitations, the group will have to establish ground rules. While merely being in conversation can foster acceptance and respectful dialogue, it can also silence certain voices and values. Respectful dialogue occurs only when participants bring honorable intentions to the table.

Burbules and Rice (1991) defined several "communicative virtues": tolerance, patience, respect for differences, willingness to listen, inclination to admit being wrong, ability to translate personal concerns to be applicable to others, self-restraint to allow others their turn, and an attitude of open and honest expression. Only when these principles are operational within the group will its members feel safe to be imperfect, vulnerable, and outright wrong.

The group will have to find a way to converse that names, honors, and monitors such virtues. Burbules (1993) warns that the process may initially require an explicit structure to guard against false starts. Because we live in a culture infused with power and status dynamics, we rarely have a chance to participate in group talk that does not mirror societal inequities. Setting expectations and group norms that will guide how teachers talk to each other will require a "mediating structure." The ground rules should ensure that everyone participates with parity, challenging of power tactics, criticism directed at ideas not people, and acceptance of an individual's experiences without judgment.

Learning Stress Management Strategies

Stress management occurs on two levels: prevention and coping. Stress inoculation involves preventative measures that attempt to minimize stress, so that you are "inoculated" against the harmful effects of stress-producing situations. Strategies can be (1) physiological, dealing with the direct effect on the body, such as diet, exercise, or relaxation; (2) cognitive, or increasing your awareness of, and redirecting, your thinking and internal talk; or (3) behavioral, such as time management. A more indepth description of these strategies is provided in Chapter 10.

Some techniques available to help manage stress produce a direct effect on the body. Such techniques help you deal with the physical reactions the body has to stress. We all need some type of physiological coping strategy. Physiological stress coping skills that release the relaxation response include diaphragmatic ("deep") breathing, progressive relaxation techniques, meditation, and visualization techniques. Progressive relaxation produces a deeper and longer-lasting state of relaxation than diaphragmatic breathing (see Cautela & Groden, 1978). It involves alternately making your muscles tense and then relaxed. The idea is to learn the difference between these two states, so that you can better recognize tension in your body and use progressive relaxation techniques to achieve relaxation. Following are two easy to learn deep breathing exercises to release the relaxation response.

Beginning Breathing Exercises

Exercise 1: The Tranquilizing Breath

This simple breathing exercise acts as a natural tranquilizer for the nervous system. While there is only a subtle effect at first, it gains power the more it is practiced. Practice twice a day.

- Sit up comfortably and place the tip of your tongue against the bony ridge near your upper front teeth; you'll keep your tongue in this position throughout the exercise.
- Exhale with a whoosh through your mouth.
- Now close your mouth and breathe in quietly through your nose to the count of four.
- Hold your breath easily to the count of seven. Then exhale through your mouth with a whoosh to the count of eight.
- You have completed one breath. Repeat the cycle three more times for a total of four breaths.

Do not do more than four breaths at one time for the first month of practice. Over time you can work up to eight breaths.

Exercise 2: The Mindfulness Breath

The following exercise will help you learn to relax to handle stress better. Practice this exercise daily.

- Assume a comfortable posture lying on your back or sitting. Close your eyes if it feels more comfortable.
- Bring your attention to your stomach, feeling it rise or expand gently on the inbreath and fall or recede on the outbreath.

- Keep the focus on your breathing, staying with each inbreath and outbreath for its full duration, as if you were riding the waves of your own breathing.
- Every time you notice that your mind has wandered off the breath, notice what it was that took you away, then bring your attention back to your stomach and the feeling of the breath coming in and out.
- Practice this exercise for 15 minutes at a convenient time every day, for one week, to experience how it feels to incorporate a disciplined breathing practice into your daily routine.

Managing Stress at the Mental Level

When faced with a problem, you basically have two choices—change the situation or change your reaction to the situation. Often you can't change the situation, but you can change how you emotionally respond, by using tension-releasing strategies to help you experience some relief and cope more effectively. You can learn to reframe, reposition, and restructure classroom situations and work circumstances by monitoring your self-talk and altering limiting self-appraisals of events and situations.

Beliefs and attitudes materialize in the form of internalized self-talk. You continually talk to yourself throughout the day and throughout the hours you're in school, and you talk to yourself as you're interacting with students. Often with a student who poses a problem, your internal talk is about how impossible the student is. Try stepping back and listening in on your internal talk for a few seconds, and you will notice the kind of running commentary you have about the student.

Your mind is typically engaged in anxiety-producing thoughts which trigger the fight-or-flight response keeping your body in a state of arousal. Your body's other response is the relaxation response, a state of lowered arousal which diminishes many adverse symptoms brought on by stress. It is your perspective on things, your mental appraisal of external events, that determines your emotional tone and, hence, your level of stress. The secret to effectively regulating stress is to learn to cultivate the ability to monitor and regulate harmful thought patterns (Ellis, 1974; Ellis & Bernard, 1984; Ellis & Harper, 1975; Harvey, 1988). Control in this sense means that you are aware of and can exercise choices that direct you away from patterns that create anxiety and stress toward patterns that lead to satisfaction and coping.

Many methods and techniques are available to handle stress at the mental or cognitive level. Meditation is a popular strategy, but any strategy that creates an internal stillness that stops the endless flow of noise and interference constantly parading through your mind can precipitate the relaxation response. The idea is to create an observation point from which you can begin to notice your thoughts and then let go of your old dialogues.

It is important to have a way to access the body's relaxation response. You need to find ways to catch yourself in the act of constructing your familiar stories, so you can make the shift from thought to awareness of what is immediately happening. In its normal state, your mind is preoccupied with an inner dialogue, which is an endless stream of thinking, providing commentary on your experiences. Our mind is a realm of metaphors, myths, and movies. The repetitive stories you tell yourself about how things should be serve to perpetuate automatic ways of interpreting your experiences. These stories serve the function of putting your immediate experiences into your past experience framework, continuously replaying the past.

Your self-created storylines can wreak havoc in the classroom by creating a mental picture of how things ought to be—stories such as "It's impossible to teach this class the way they behave"; or "These kids just don't want to learn"; or "I should be able to control all the students in my class." These stories provide the backdrop for the expectations you have for your classroom and can set you up for disillusionment, loss of a sense of vision, and, ultimately, burnout.

The vast majority of self-talk is learned. It is learned from families, friends, and society. If self-talk is learned, then you can learn to use different self-talk. Your old patterns of responding create a groove in your mind, making it difficult to take a different route. The path of critical inquiry involves examining the filters through which you see and interpret the world and disputing, altering, and acting against your familiar internal verbalizations. It is possible to accomplish considerable change in your way of behaving through learning to rechannel your thoughts. If you fail to break out of your destructive thinking patterns, you stay trapped behaving automatically.

The goal is not to be worry-free, rather to keep the harmful effects of cumulative stress at bay. A certain level of discomfort is healthy and leads to taking necessary action. Also, stress is a subjective response to potentially stressful events. Different individuals function more or less effectively with differing amounts of stress. Some teachers seem to be able to manage great amounts of stress, while others become overwhelmed with modest amounts.

Critical Reflection on Practice: Inoculating Yourself Against Stress

Activity Directions: Answer questions 1 to 4 by yourself. Then conduct a brainstorming session with several peers for question 5.

1. Write a general statement about your ability to handle stress.

   _____
   _____
   _____

2. What school or classroom events or situations do you find most stressful?

   _____
   _____
   _____

3. Considering your personal qualities and your own idiosyncrasies, what aspects of the job of teaching are likely to be stress-producing for you?

   _____
   _____
   _____

4. Of the potential sources of personal and job-related stress discussed, which are you most susceptible to?

   _____
   _____
   _____

5. What can you do to make yourself less vulnerable to, or to inoculate yourself against, the sources of stress that are potentially most debilitating to you?

   _____
   _____
   _____

Guarding Against Setting Unattainable Expectations

In addition to the anxiety created by the often unreasonable demands of today's classroom, a teacher's own dissatisfaction with self adds to the feelings of helplessness. Sometimes teachers need help in discriminating between the actual demands of teaching and their own self-imposed demands. Idealism, dedication, and commitment can result in unreasonable and virtually unattainable expectations. Your own limiting assumptions about a problem, or student perceived as a problem, can drive behavior in unproductive directions.

The pressure to conform to a picture of the perfect teacher lies at the root of much self-induced stress. Your own thoughts and feelings undermine more effective behavior. Such limiting beliefs are expressed in self-verbalizations. As a stress inoculation strategy, you can learn to replace negative thought patterns with affirming ones. Two especially destructive ways of thinking about problems and issues are (1) all-or-none and (2) catastrophic thinking.

All-or-none Thinking

Ms. Morris doesn't like me, so none of the teachers here like me.
My principal let me down. I'll never trust him again.

Catastrophic Thinking

I messed up again, I can't do anything right.
Why even try, it won't do any good—she's a hopeless case.

Combating Commonly-held Teaching Myths

Some beliefs can be especially devastating for teachers to try to measure up to. When teachers set unattainable standards for themselves, they are headed for disillusionment at the very least.

The following I-should statements represent some commonly-held teaching myths.

I should:

- Like and care for all students equally.
- Have no preferences or prejudices.
- Be consistent in my actions with students.
- Remain calm and collected at all times.
- Hide my true feelings and place students' feelings above mine.
- Be able to readily solve all problems.
- Cope with all situations without anxiety, stress, or conflict.
- Run my classroom so that there is no confusion, uncertainty, or chaos.

Critical Reflection on Practice: Combating Teaching Myths

Activity Directions: For each of the eight teaching myths, write a corresponding belief that is more realistic and accepting of being human.

Limiting Belief   **Accepting Belief**

I should like and care for all students equally.   _____

                                                       _____

I should have no preferences or prejudices.   _____

                                                       _____

I should be consistent in my actions with students.   _____

                                                       _____

I should remain calm and collected at all times.   _____

                                                       _____

I should hide my true feelings and place students'
feelings above mine.   _____

                                                       _____

I should be able to readily solve all problems.   _____

                                                       _____

I should cope with all situations without anxiety,
stress or conflict.   _____

                                                       _____

I should run my classroom so that there is no
confusion, uncertainty or chaos.   _____

                                                       _____

Teacher Burnout and Renewal Cycles

Curwin and Mendler (1988) described a phenomenon they labeled the discipline-burnout cycle. When teachers respond ineffectively to student misbehavior, typically using either denial or attacking tactics, their response leads to continuation or worsening of the student's behavior, causing tension and frustration. Faced with not knowing what to do, the teacher either holds in the tension or yields to explosive outbursts. If the tension accumulates with no relief in sight, the teacher responds with either withdrawal or aggression.

When the cycle becomes repetitive, burnout sets in. "Burnout victims" suffer from both physical and mental side effects. Signs of imbalance due to burnout can take the form of preoccupation with negative thoughts, lack of motivation to go to work, fatigue, irritability, muscular tension, high blood pressure, or ulcers.

On the other hand, when the teacher's interventions result in appropriate student responses, it leads to the teacher's enhanced sense of self-efficacy. Believing that they are capable of finding reasonable solutions to the day-to-day problems they face helps keep teachers actively engaged and enthusiastic about their work. As teachers learn to use more effective interventions for both teacher-owned and student-owned problems, they become more confident of their own resources for solving problems. They stay in a renewal cycle.

One of the best buffers against undue stress and potential teacher burnout is to learn intervention strategies that get you the student responses you desire.

The following diagrams provide a graphic display of teacher burnout and renewal cycles.

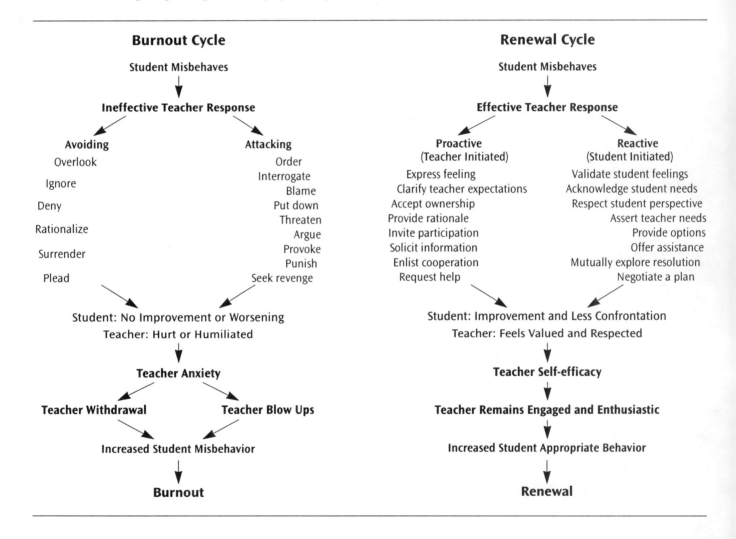

Chapter 2

Classroom Management: A Multidimensional Perspective

Effective classroom management is inextricably tied to the quality of educational experiences in which students engage as well as the teacher's skill in organizing the class structure to facilitate efficient teaching and learning. In order to provide the necessary foundation for effective classroom management, several conditions should be in effect. The following three conditions are integral to effective classroom management.

1. A stimulating and supportive setting for learning to occur.
2. Reasonable expectations established with consideration given to student characteristics.
3. Opportunities provided for all students to experience success.

The teacher's ability to effectively orchestrate the learning environment to enhance the competence of all students is also clearly related to student behavior. In a setting in which students typically fail, students will be less motivated to follow the established rules and expectations. If students' sense of self-efficacy is not supported in positive ways, then again misbehavior is likely to occur. That is, when students feel helpless and powerless they are less likely to comply with expected classroom norms.

The Balancing Act: The Many Faces of Classroom Management

Developing a personal system of classroom management involves considering instructional issues, management issues, discipline strategies, as well as interpersonal relationships. Effectively managing the classroom setting requires a multidimensional approach. Several authors have delineated the multiple phases of classroom management from different perspectives—as faces, stages, and aspects.

Charles (1996) refers to the three faces of discipline. He labels these faces of classroom discipline: preventive, supportive, and corrective.

1. Preventive disciplinary steps are those taken to prevent misbehavior from occurring.
2. Supportive disciplinary measures are strategies that assist students in self-control by helping them get back on task.
3. Corrective disciplinary steps are called for when students misbehave and need to be corrected.

Grossman (1995) discusses the three stages of management.

1. At stage one, management is directed at organizing classroom routines and procedures to avoid behavior problems.
2. Stage two includes those general strategies for solving behavior problems.

3. Stage three techniques involve those primarily geared toward strengthening personal relationships.

Kounin (1970) talks about the three aspects of a teacher's role: instructor, manager, and person.

1. The role as instructor calls for teachers to provide appropriate instructional activities.
2. The role as manager stresses effective group management techniques.
3. The role as person is concerned with positive human interactions.

12 General Principles of Effective Classroom Management

The following behavior management principles provide the foundation for maintaining an effective classroom. They represent key management concepts which are embellished to varying degrees in many of the models of discipline to be presented in subsequent sections. These recurring themes form the basis for establishing a healthy and productive teaching and learning environment.

1. Demonstrate caring.
2. Take charge—be in control of yourself.
3. Communicate regularly and clearly with students.
4. Establish enforceable rules and enforce them.
5. Hold high expectations for students.
6. Persistently confront unproductive behavior.
7. Invoke consequences in a calm manner.
8. Comment only on students' behavior, not personal traits.
9. Model desirable behavior.
10. Teach students to make appropriate choices.
11. Organize teaching activities to avoid boredom and wasted time.
12. Provide ample opportunities for students to experience success and receive recognition.

Setting Reasonable and Ethical Expectations

Behavior management should not be thought of as a set of procedures to make students conform to a rigid, inflexible value system or to squelch creativity or to force compliance. Any behavior management strategies utilized in the classroom should be for the purpose of facilitating the learning environment and bringing about meaningful learning, not merely to squelch noncompliant behavior. Before attempting to modify individual student's classroom behavior, teachers need to assess how they have structured their classroom environment to support learning.

The following questions will help teachers reflect on their personal "classroom ecology."

Ask Yourself

- Do your classroom rules and procedures really benefit students, or are they primarily for your own comfort level and convenience?
- What type of behavior is annoying to you but essentially harmless to the learner and his/her peers?
- Is the student's behavior irritating to you because it offends your personal values or sensitivities?

- What classroom freedom can be permitted without infringing on the rights of other students?
- Under what conditions do you have a right to impose your personal standards on your students?
- When do your students have a right to behave as they wish?
- Should silence be maintained while children are working, or should reasonable communication among students be permitted?
- Do you react intensely to a particular student's behavioral characteristics?
- Does the student's behavior violate your rights? Those of others?
- Does the student's behavior interfere with his/her academic learning? That of peers?

Learning Practice Task: Instructor, Manager, and Person

Activity Directions: Think of a class you really enjoyed and where you were motivated to learn.

1. List five characteristics of this teacher and/or class.

_____

_____

_____

_____

_____

2. Then join with three other colleagues and share them.

3. On a sheet of paper create three columns labeled: Instructor, Manager, and Person.

4. Take the 20 characteristics listed by the four members of your group and place each under one of the three columns.
   - Place items which are primarily functional in nature such as grouping structure and class format under the heading "Manager."
   - Place items which are primarily related to the teacher's effectiveness in teaching the content and personally involving you under the heading "Teacher."
   - Place items which are primarily related to the teacher's personal characteristics or traits under the heading "Person."

5. Discuss what the results suggest.

6. Write three observations your group made.

_____

_____

_____

_____

_____

_____

Learning Practice Task: Applying Key Concepts for Effective Classroom Management

Activity Directions: Write a statement about what each of the 12 principles means to you and why the principle is important.

1. Demonstrate caring. _____

_____

_____

2. Take charge—be in control of yourself. _____

_____

_____

3. Communicate regularly and clearly with students. _____

_____

_____

4. Establish enforceable rules and enforce them. _____

_____

_____

5. Hold high expectations for students. _____

_____

_____

6. Persistently confront unproductive behavior. _____

_____

_____

7. Invoke consequences in a calm manner. _____

_____

_____

8. Comment only on students' behavior; not personal traits. _____

_____

_____

9. Model desirable behavior. _____

_____

_____

10. Teach students to make appropriate choices. _____

_____

_____

11. Organize teaching activities to avoid boredom and wasted time. _____

_____

_____

12. Provide ample opportunities for students to experience success and receive recognition. _____

_____

_____

Critical Reflection on Practice: Analyzing Your Use of Effective Management Principles

Activity Directions: Follow the steps below.

1. List the three (3) principles you most consistently follow.

_____

_____

_____

2. List the three (3) principles you least consistently follow.

_____

_____

_____

3. Select and list one principle you most want to be more evident in your classroom.

_____

_____

_____

4. Decide on one specific behavior you could engage in to enhance adherence to the selected principle.

_____

_____

_____

Setting the Stage: Preventive Planning

Successful teachers actually avoid many potential behavior problems by using effective teaching techniques, appropriately challenging students, promoting group accountability and cohesiveness, preventing potentially disruptive situations from occurring, establishing reasonable procedures and rules, modeling desirable behavior, satisfying students' basic needs, and maintaining good relationships with students.

For many students who behave inappropriately in spite of their teachers' best efforts at preventive planning, eliminating situational or contextual barriers, teaching students coping skills, or reasoning with them will often be all that is needed.

Preventive Planning by Effectively Managing Teacher-led Activities

Many authors talk about preventive planning as the foundation for effective classroom management (e.g., Charles, 1996; Curwin & Messler, 1988; Grossman, 1995; Kounin, 1970; Jones, 1987; Redl, 1966). Preventive planning is what the teacher does strategically in planning that actually prevents management and discipline problems from occurring.

Several authors take the position that mastery of group management techniques will enable teachers to be free from concern about classroom management problems. They emphasize the teacher's role in contributing to smooth activity flow, primarily by keeping students on-task and effectively managing teacher-led activities (e.g., Kounin, 1970; Redl & Wattenberg, 1959; Jones, 1987). Clear-cut directions, instructional clarity, careful sequencing of activities, and adequately preparing students for doing follow-up activities will do much for keeping the classroom running smoothly.

Kounin's Techniques for Group Management

Kounin, like Gordon, believes many classroom problems are clearly teacher-owned. He described several factors related to whole class instruction, interactive group activities, and smooth activity flow that characterize effective classrooms. When the lesson flow keeps students' attention without frequent interruptions, distractions, or diversions there is less opportunity for off-task behavior and less competition for student attention from what is external to the lesson. On the other hand, by issuing vague and indefinite directions, presenting information out of sequence, backtracking, inserting extraneous information, moving from one topic to another without warning, making assignments without first checking for understanding, and giving assignments that do not align with the content development activities, teachers leave students floundering, leading to a greater tendency for students to go off-task.

According to Kounin, the following factors prevent misbehavior: withitness, overlapping, smoothness, momentum, and maintaining group focus by ensuring attention to the task with high response rates and general accountability. By using specific teacher techniques that maintain constant alertness to the sights and sounds of the classroom, teachers can attend to multiple events at the same time, manage lesson flow and transitions, keep all students alert, and insulate lessons from distractions from student intrusions or external interruptions.

Kounin's categories for maintaining group focus are especially helpful for teachers for preventing student off-task behavior. Below are examples of these techniques.

Technique	Description	Example
Group alerting	Engages attention of whole class while individuals are responding	Using designation such as thumbs up for agreement
Encouraging accountability	Lets students know everyone's participation is expected	Pairing with a partner and explaining a concept to each other
High participation formats	Involves students other than those directly responding to teacher question	Writing a question about the concept being studied to be put in a pool for later whole-class discussion

When teachers provide lesson continuity by thinking more about the whole than the lesson pieces and react promptly to problems, they will often be able to use simple, unobtrusive measures (e.g., eye contact, quiet correction) that don't interfere with ongoing activities or distract students from the task.

Jones' Techniques for Group Management

Jones, like Kounin, focuses on prevention by calling on teachers to look at their ability to manage groups, lessons, and the overall classroom environment. His main emphasis is on managing group behavior to reduce disruptions and increase cooperative behavior. Jones identifies three clusters of skills that help to prevent misbehavior when it occurs: (1) using body language to set and enforce limits; (2) using formal and informal incentives; and (3) providing efficient help for students. According to Jones, teachers should know exactly what they want done and have routines in place for getting things done that are simple and effective. In addition, teachers should use incentives to get students to be at the right place at the right time with the right materials doing the right thing.

Having a good structure, including rules, routines, standards of appropriate behavior, and positive student/teacher relations, avoids many problems. When students misbehave despite good structure, he advises limit-setting that clearly communicates that the teacher is in charge at all times and means business, expecting and teaching students to assume responsibility and using an incentive system of gaining and losing positive consequences (favored over punishment).

Redl's and Wattenberg's Techniques for Group Management

Like Kounin and Jones, Redl and Wattenberg stress surface management techniques for general managing of groups, but they add a "mental hygiene" component. They adapted their work with students with emotional problems for use in regular classrooms. Their focus is on managing students without resorting to negative consequences and accommodating the classroom environment to students' emotional needs. Like others concerned with students' unmet needs, they stress taking the conscious and unconscious motivation of students into consideration. They recommend techniques for managing surface behavior of students and preventing dangerous or disruptive behavior in nonpunitive ways.

Redl and Wattenberg advocate that the teacher must understand group processes in addition to individual differences, noting that the group is distinctly different from the individual. How teachers behave as well as how they handle the misbehavior of one student, affects the way their students behave. Furthermore, group behavior in the classroom is influenced by how students perceive the teacher. In translating their psychodynamic concepts into classroom practice, they provide insight into both the psychological and social forces that affect student behavior, both individually and within a group. They suggest that teachers need to identify the various roles the student may play, such as leader, clown, fall guy, or instigator, to provide the student with a sense of belonging to the group.

According to Redl and Wattenberg, teachers maintain group control by (1) addressing the problem before it becomes serious; (2) helping students to regain control; (3) teaching students the underlying causes of misbehavior and helping them to foresee probable consequences; and (4) rewarding good behavior and punishing negative behavior.

Some Teacher-owned Group Management Problems

Teachers often condition students to misbehave by their actions and policies. Cangelosi (1997) notes the following ways teachers condition students.

- When a teacher demonstrates that he/she is aware of off-task behavior but does not make an effective effort to lead students to redirect off-task with on-task behavior, students surmise that the teacher is not serious about expecting them to be on-task.
- When a teacher tells students how to behave without taking any action to lead them to follow what is said, students are conditioned not to bother to listen.
- When the teacher repeats demands for students to be on-task over and over without compliance until finally the teacher gets angry and upset, it conditions students not to listen until the teacher becomes upset.

If the teacher is confronted with off-task behavior and is not, at the moment, in the position to apply a strategy that has a reasonable chance of working, then the teacher should delay a response until the teacher can implement a suitable strategy.

Some types of teacher commands or directives can actually lower the rate of student compliance, such as chain commands or vague commands delivered as questions. Several authors suggest ways for teachers to give directives to students that are more likely to get students to comply (Barkley, 1987; Morgan & Jenson, 1988; Forehand & McMahon, 1981).

- Be specific and direct by phrasing requests and directives in descriptive terms, so students know exactly what is expected, using language that can be clearly understood.
- Get the student's attention and pause until eye contact is established.
- Give only one directive at a time.
- Avoid chain commands such as "Take out your math books, turn to page 56, do the odd-numbered problems, check your answers, and then report to me."
- Pause for sufficient time following the directive (minimum of 5 seconds) for the student to respond. During this period don't reissue the directive or a new one, or argue, prompt, or try to coerce the student.
- For noncompliance within the allotted time, repeat directive only once.
- When giving directives to individual students, it is preferable to be within close proximity to the student and to speak to the student quietly.

In setting the stage for their classroom, teachers should consider the following classroom structure variables.

Ask Yourself

- Are there long periods of non-functional time?
- Are there many unexpected changes in schedules, procedures, and routines?
- Are the assigned tasks made relevant to students?
- Are the classroom activities stimulating and thought-provoking?
- Is each student given ample opportunity to experience success?
- Are there too many failures?
- Is there too much emphasis on competition?
- Is there more criticism than encouragement?
- Are students encouraged to strive for improvement, not perfection?

Summary

While being able to manage group functions is certainly a necessary set of skills, it's only a partial answer to a total management system. There is much more to managing today's classroom than getting the classroom to function like a well-oiled machine with everything regulated for students. This approach has the drawback of the potential for teachers to lose sight of other essential elements of the student/teacher relationship.

Teachers need to create a balance between overdirecting students and leaving them too much on their own without providing a structure. Emphasizing group management techniques tends to tip the scale in favor of overdirecting.

Highlighting the instructional efficiency aspect as the major route to effective classroom management, creates a tendency to move from a functional dimension directly to applying consequences for misbehavior and rule infractions. This sequence virtually eliminates the middle ground—what to do between relatively minor infractions and the teacher taking charge. In addition to group management structures, teachers also need to develop structures for helping students take responsibility before the teacher reverts to applying consequences.

A teacher's capacity for self-reflection and self-analysis is a key element in the ongoing challenge to balance the three interfacing roles of instructor, manager, and person. The teacher must balance regulating student behavior, to maintain an environment conducive to teaching and learning, with potentially stifling student creativity, decision-making power, and problem-solving autonomy. The ability to balance the teacher's inner comfort with setting and upholding reasonable expectations for students is another critical dimension.

Learning Practice Task: Classroom Grouping Practices

Activity Directions: Working in pairs, discuss each of the following questions.

1. Why do you group your students?
2. What student characteristics would be important to consider in composing a small group?
3. Do the same groups work together most of the time?
4. Are there opportunities for students to move out of their groups?
5. Under what circumstances would you allow students to choose a group for membership?
6. Do you provide each group with similar academic experiences?
7. Do you spend more time with one group than others?
8. Do you direct your comments to one group more than others?
9. Do you tend to stand and teach on the side of the room where one group sits?
10. Do you actually work more often with one group than others?

What did you discover about your attitudes and practices toward grouping and cooperative learning?

Question for Self-reflection

Did this activity lead you to question any of your grouping policies? If so, what grouping policies or interaction patterns are you bringing into question?

Deciding to Intervene

The question of when a teacher should intervene is an important classroom management decision. Determining when to intervene involves three considerations. First, whether an intervention is warranted; second, at what point to intervene; and third, whether it would be most effective or efficient to intervene immediately or delay an intervention. Determining if and when to intervene involves consideration of the following:

- Whether the teacher owns the problem.

  Teacher-owned problems are problems that interfere with their needs, such as the need to maintain an orderly environment or the need to have students be respectful, both to the teacher and to classmates.

- At what point intervention is warranted.

  When teachers fail to set limits or intervene when first necessary, they can develop counter-aggressive feelings toward students when their behavior has escalated.

- Whether immediate or delayed intervention would be most effective.

  Sometimes immediate intervention can be counterproductive when the student is in a disturbed state or the teacher is at a critical point in a lesson activity.

Determining When to Intervene

Several authors offer guidelines for making the best choice. Gordon (1989) suggests that teachers learn to determine who owns the problem; Redl (1966) suggests specific situations where intervention is necessary; Grossman (1995) suggests that teachers consider the classroom context in determining whether intervention should be immediate or delayed.

Prior to determining when to intervene, the teacher first has to determine whether a problem is teacher-owned. The teacher owns a problem when it either actually or potentially interferes with the teacher's legitimate needs. Unacceptable student behaviors that have a tangible negative effect on teachers cannot be ignored and call for teachers to assume an active posture and deal with the behavior.

When teachers identify a student behavior as unacceptable, they have several options available to them. In attempting to modify unacceptable behavior, teachers have three variables to work with: the student, the environment, and their own behavior. They can:

- Confront the student and attempt to modify his/her behavior.
- Modify the learning context, by altering the task, their expectation, or the learning situation.
- Modify their own reaction to the behavior.

The following example illustrates these choices.

Ms. Peters is repeatedly interrupted by Brian who seems to be unable to go ahead with an assignment without constant checking and reinforcement. This is unacceptable to Ms. Peters, so she owns the problem. What can she do?

1. She can confront Brian, sending some message that will cause him to stop interrupting. [Modify the student.]

2. She can provide the student with an alternative way for checking other than directly with the teacher. [Modify the environment.]

3. She can say to herself, "He's just a dependent student and he'll out-grow it soon," or "He obviously needs more reassurance than the others." [Modify the self.]

These are not clear-cut distinctions and often more than one or all three variables might be involved in the most effective solution to a classroom problem. In this example, the teacher might pair some nonverbal cue to the student with designating a willing classmate to answer the student's frequent questions.

When teachers make a conscious choice to try to modify student behavior which they consider unacceptable, they usually send a confrontative message. However, the messages they send often have negative effects on students and fail to bring about the desired results. According to Gordon, most teachers have simply never considered the potential impact of their messages on students. Typically, the messages teachers send when confronting students fall into three general categories:

1. Power play, or telling students what to do.
2. Put-down, or personal assault.
3. Guilt trip, or trying to shame students.

More effective confrontive strategies are presented in later sections.

Situations Warranting Immediate Interventions

Redl also offers criteria for determining when to intervene. Teachers are often not sure whether they should interfere or not when faced with a particular student behavior. When teachers fail to set limits or interfere until they are overcome with negative feelings toward a student, they are likely to use an intervention which is too severe. Redl suggests nine situations in which immediate intervention is warranted (Fagen & Hill, 1977). In these situations, student behavior needs to be regulated immediately. These situations require an on-the-spot reaction which will contain the problem behavior, without regard to underlying causes or motives. Such techniques are referred to as "surface management" techniques and will be discussed in the next section. The nine situations are listed below, along with an example of each.

Situations Warranting Immediate Intervention	Example
1. Reality dangers	Fighting
2. Psychological protection	Calling another student a derogatory name
3. Protection against too much excitement	A game getting out of hand
4. Protection of property	Destroying desktop
5. Protection of an on-going program	Disruption of a group activity
6. Protection against negative contagion	Tapping on desk with pencil
7. Highlighting a value area or school policy	Smoking in school bathroom
8. Avoiding conflict with the outside world	Following rules on a field trip
9. Protecting a teacher's inner comfort	Noise exceeding teacher's level of tolerance

Several of these suggestions are described more specifically below.

Reality dangers

Adults are usually more reality-oriented than students and have had more practice predicting the consequence of certain acts. If students are playing some crazy game, fighting or playing with matches and it appears as if they might injure themselves, then the teacher moves in and stops the behavior.

Psychological protection

Just as the teacher protects a student from being physically hurt, he/she should protect the student from psychological injury. If a group is ganging up on a student or using derogatory racial nicknames, then the teacher should intervene. The teacher does not support or condone this behavior and the values it reflects.

Protection against too much excitement

Sometimes a teacher intervenes in order to avoid the development of too much excitement, anxiety, or guilt. For example, if a game is getting out of hand and continues another 10 minutes, the student may lose control, mess up, and feel very unhappy about his/her behavior later. Once again, the teacher should intervene to stop this cycle from developing.

Protection of an on-going program

Once a class is motivated in a particular task and the students have an investment in its outcome, it is not fair to have it ruined by one student who is having some difficulty. In this case, the teacher would intervene and ask the student to leave or to move next to him/her in order to insure that the enjoyment, satisfaction, and learning of the group is not impaired.

Protection against negative contagion

When a teacher is aware that tension is mounting in the classroom and a student with high social power begins tapping the desk with a pencil, the teacher might ask the student to stop in order to prevent this behavior from spreading to the other students and disrupting the entire lesson.

Protecting a teacher's inner comfort

It is important for a teacher to recognize his/her personal idiosyncrasies and realize when he/she might be overreacting to a student's behavior. On the other hand, it's better to try to stop the behavior than do nothing and inwardly reject the student. Protecting a teacher's inner comfort points out the need for teachers to create a balance between personal idiosyncrasies and reasonable expectations for students. This is a critical decision point in determining whether intervention is appropriate.

When to Delay Intervention

Grossman (1995) has identified some specific situations which warrant either immediate or delayed intervention. Some situations require immediate intervention, such as when the behavior is dangerous, destructive, or contagious. It is also important to step in right away when the behavior could get worse or the behavior is self-perpetuating. Behavior problems that are likely to intensify if not corrected should be "nipped in the bud." For example, an argument between two students that appears about to lead to a real fight needs to be stopped immediately. Likewise, misbehavior that is intrinsically rewarding, such as cutting ahead in line, needs to be stopped before students receive any reinforcement for their actions.

Sometimes it is preferable to delay intervention rather than respond immediately to student misbehavior. Grossman provides the following examples of situations in which immediate intervention can be counterproductive.

When the teacher does not have all the facts

For example, when you overhear someone say something nasty to another student, while you might get angry, it could be that the other student provoked the response. In this case, it may be better not to correct the first student, since you may have an incomplete understanding of the situation. Here you would want to wait to deal with it until you know all the circumstances.

When the timing is wrong

In the following situations, it may not be the right time to intervene. It may be preferable to postpone dealing with it until a more convenient time, when the immediate circumstances will not allow you to deal with the problem effectively.

Insufficient time. If a student misbehaves at dismissal time, you may have to wait if you want to discuss the behavior at length. A simple statement such as, "We'll have to discuss what you just did tomorrow morning," will suffice to let the student know that you are planning to handle it.

Disruptive effects of intervening. If you are at a point in a lesson when it would be too disruptive to stop to handle a behavior problem, you might want to briefly signal your disapproval to the student and deal with it in a more constructive manner at a less disruptive time.

When students are too sensitive to be exposed publicly. If dealing with students' behavior publicly might embarrass them, wait until you can talk to them in private.

When students are too upset to deal with their behavior rationally. When students are extremely angry, it will be more effective to discuss their behavior with them after they have calmed down. Students are not likely to be receptive to teacher intervention when they are in a highly emotionally-charged state.

Learning Practice Task: Identifying and Prioritizing Problem Behaviors

Activity Directions: Think of yourself as the teacher in each situation described below. You are to make three determinations for each situation. First, whether or not there is a problem; second, who "owns" the problem (i.e., the teacher "owning the problem" means that the teacher would intervene to deal with the problem); and third, whether the particular problem would be of high or low priority for you to take action on. If you determine there is no problem in the situation, there is no need to fill in the other two columns. Code your responses as follows: Problem (Y), No Problem (N); Teacher Owns (T), Other Owns (O); High Priority (H), Low Priority (L).

	Problem Yes/No Y/N	Who Owns Teacher/Other T/O	Intervention Priority High/Low H/L
1. Several of your students are whispering loudly while you are giving instructions.	_____	_____	_____
2. Dennis tells you that he is having trouble with his friend and is too upset to do his work.	_____	_____	_____
3. Marvin glares at a classmate and threatens to punch him if he doesn't shut up.	_____	_____	_____
4. Harmony enters your room, drags herself to her seat, and puts her head down on her desk.	_____	_____	_____
5. A student has just handed in her homework late for the second time this week.	_____	_____	_____
6. Jessica has come up to you for the fourth time this morning complaining that her classmates are teasing her.	_____	_____	_____
7. You notice that the private reading area has been left in a mess (e.g., books left out, scrap paper lying around).	_____	_____	_____
8. Tanya keeps using obscene language in class, both to you and her classmates.	_____	_____	_____
9. A student is roaming around the room checking up on friends instead of doing the assignment.	_____	_____	_____
10. Juan has come in crying from recess for the third time this week.	_____	_____	_____

Learning Practice Task: Immediate or Delayed Intervention Exercise

Activity Directions: Match each of the following situations or consequences with the most appropriate time to intervene. Use "I" for Immediate and "D" for Delayed.

_____   If student's behavior is likely to spiral

_____   If student may be embarrassed

_____   When lesson interruption may lead to group confusion

_____   If behavior may cause psychological damage to another student

_____   If there is potential for blaming innocent student(s)

_____   When student is too upset to be rational

_____   When teacher's inner comfort is violated

_____   If student's behavior can cause harm

_____   When student uses derogatory racial nickname

_____   When student's behavior disrupts class activity

Managing Surface Behavior

Many behavior problems can be controlled or circumvented by the use of instructional methods that take into consideration group dynamics, socialization needs, characteristics of the particular group, as well as individual learner characteristics. Effective instructional strategies provide structure to the learning environment that prevents problems from occurring. When problems do occur, teachers need to clarify behavior expectations and assist students in acting in acceptable ways to prevent more serious problems from developing.

There are many times throughout the school day when disruptive behavior requires teacher intervention. Teachers need to have a variety of interventions "at their fingertips" in order to deal effectively with the inevitable, everyday minor disruptions, distractions, rule infractions, and off-task behaviors. Teachers need a repertoire, or a set of "surface management" techniques. Surface management techniques should serve several purposes. They should:

1. Maintain the ongoing instructional program;
2. Deter any minor student problem from becoming a major one;
3. End disruptive behavior on-the-spot;
4. Reduce student's stress;
5. Maintain a positive student/teacher relationship; and
6. Occur before the teacher begins to harbor negative feelings.

These techniques have also been referred to as hurdle help because they are designed to help students over rough spots, not as substitutes for well-planned instructional activities or as a total management plan. The goal is to provide situational assistance to help students cope with the instructional situation and stay on-task or get back to the task. The term also connotes that these behaviors are normal and to be expected. Teachers need to have a systematic plan to deal with the many disruptive behaviors that routinely occur in the classroom, such as whispering, calling out, laughing, off-task behaviors, passing notes, doing other work, walking around, talking back, arguing, teasing, and name-calling.

Surface management techniques are designed to deal with mild behavior difficulties that occur on a regular basis, but that have the potential to inhibit the smooth functioning of the classroom. Such overt student behavior needs to be addressed immediately, without regard (at the time) to underlying causes or motives. These techniques are meant to be shortterm, surface-level strategies. The idea with surface management techniques is to effectively stop behaviors early before they escalate and to intervene in such a way that the teacher doesn't actually have to interrupt the lesson flow.

Techniques for managing the surface behavior of students

The following techniques are designed to be used by teachers to maintain the surface behavior of students in the classroom. They are meant to be used in conjunction with a well-planned program based on the teacher's knowledge of each individual student's needs (Fagen & Hill, 1977).

Planned ignoring. Much student behavior carries its own limited power and will soon exhaust itself if it is not fueled, especially if the behavior is done primarily to annoy the teacher. If it is not likely to spread to others, it is sometimes possible for the teacher to ignore the behavior and thus extinguish it.

Signal interference. Teachers use a variety of signals to communicate expected behavior to students. These nonverbal techniques include such things as eye contact, hand gestures, tapping or snapping fingers, coughing or clearing one's throat, facial frowns, and body postures. These techniques are usually most effective at the beginning stages of misbehavior.

Proximity control. Teachers know how effective it can be to merely stand near a student who is having difficulty. The teacher's presence serves as a source of comfort and protection and helps the student control his/her impulses.

Interest boosting. If a student's interest in his/her work is declining, and the student is showing signs of boredom or restlessness, it may be helpful for the teacher to show an interest in the student. The teacher may engage the student in a conversation about a topic which is of interest to him/her. Stimulating the student's interest may motivate him/her to continue working and/or help the student view the teacher as a person who takes a personal interest.

Tension decontamination through humor. A funny comment is often able to defuse a tense situation. It makes everyone feel more comfortable.

Hurdle help. Some students who experience difficulty with classroom assignments may seek help from the teacher or peers when appropriate. Other students skip over the difficulty and go on to work they can do. But some students stop working and don't know what to do next. They need to be able to overcome the obstacle that has them stopped. The teacher can be helpful in getting the student back on task by doing (or solving) the problem with the student, thus removing the hurdle and allowing the student to continue.

Restructuring the classroom program. How much can a teacher deviate from a scheduled program and still feel that teaching responsibilities are being met? Some teachers feel compelled to follow their class schedule rigidly. They feel students should learn discipline and self-control. Other teachers feel it is necessary to be flexible and sensitive to students' needs and concerns. Some middle ground seems most sensible. Discipline and structure are valuable, but not when they fly in the face of a general class need. Moderate restructuring based on affective as well as academic goals can be a very effective technique. Restructuring is appropriate when it is necessary to drain off high tension or emotion in the classroom. The technique is, as its name implies, simply a change of plan, format, task, or location based on a perceived need to drain off tension or high emotion in the total class.

Direct appeal to values. A teacher can often appeal to a student's values when intervening in a problem situation. The teacher might:

1. Appeal to the relationship of the teacher with the student, for example,

   "You seem angry with me. Have I been unfair with you?"

2. Appeal to reality consequences, for example,

   "I know you're angry, but if you break that aquarium, the fish will all die, and you'll have to replace it with your own money."

3. Appeal to a student's need for peer approval, for example,

   "Your classmates will get pretty angry if you continue to interrupt them and correct them."

4. Appeal to the student's sense of the teacher's power of authority, for example,

   Tell the student that as a teacher you cannot allow a behavior to continue, but that you still care about the student.

5. Appeal to the student's self-respect, for example,

   "I know you'll be upset with yourself if you tear up that paper you worked on all period."

Removing seductive objects. It is difficult for the teacher to compete with certain objects. Sometimes removing seductive objects leads to power struggles. Take a strong interest in the object and politely ask to see it or handle it. Once in your hand, you have the option of returning it with a request for it to disappear for the remainder of the period or to keep it with a promise to return it at the end of the period. This technique is most effective if you have a relationship with the student.

Antiseptic bounce. When a student's behavior has reached a point where the teacher questions whether or not the student will respond to verbal controls, it is best to ask the student to leave the room for a few minutes—perhaps to get a drink or deliver a message. In antiseptic bouncing, there is no intent to punish the student, but simply to protect and help the student and/or the group to get over their feelings of anger, disappointment, or uncontrollable laughter. Unfortunately, many schools do not have a place the classroom teacher can send a student that the student will not think of as punishment.

Examples of Surface Management Techniques

Planned ignoring
Several students enter the classroom acting very rowdy. I ignore their behavior at first. As soon as they settle down at their desks, I smile at them.

Signal interference
Matt has a very low self-esteem. Often he will belittle his own efforts. When he starts this behavior, I lower my glasses on my nose and gaze over them. He grins and usually stops his self-berating behavior.

Proximity control
During math class, Dennis frequently tries to distract others during independent work time. Today, when he begins poking the girl in front of him, I walk over and stand near her desk. He begins to work quietly.

Interest boosting
Sammy daydreams a lot and is often quiet but off-task. I've started talking to him for about five minutes each morning. He is now more interested in most class activities.

Tension decontamination through humor

We had made kites and were flying them outside when one student's string broke and his kite sailed away. There was shocked silence, and I could see a face ready to cry. I quickly said, "Well, Ricky wins the High Flyer Award—he gets to choose the story this afternoon." Suddenly faces brightened and there were no tears.

Restructuring the classroom

During recess I overhear several students making unkind comments to a homeless person. During Social Studies class that day, we discuss the homeless situation in America. I have the students do research projects on the problem.

Direct appeal to value areas

One day Glen refused to come to his small group when they were called together. I said, "Glen, the group will be pretty upset with you if you don't join us." He came, joined in, and cooperated actively.

Hurdle help

Robin was having difficulty researching a social studies question. She was becoming frustrated and did not know what to do. I suggested a procedure for her to use and a place to look for the answer.

Antiseptic bouncing

I have a student who often gets over-excited and becomes very loud. I sometimes find an excuse to send him out of the room to do an errand. When the student returns he is usually calmer.

Removing seductive objects

Anytime students bring objects from home to school, they have a basket (with their name) to put the object in until a designated time to share it with others.

Learning Practice Task: Managing Surface Behavior Exercise

Activity Directions, Part 1: Identify which of the following surface management techniques the examples below represent. In the space provided, write-in one of the 10 techniques.

a. Planned ignoring
b. Signal interference
c. Proximity control
d. Interest boosting
e. Tension decontamination through humor
f. Restructuring the classroom program
g. Direct appeal to values
h. Removing seductive objects
i. Antiseptic bounce
j. Hurdle help

1. Change in plan, format, task or location based on perceived need _____
2. Eye contact, snapping fingers, body posture _____
3. Seating student who often needs help close to teacher's desk _____
4. Have student leave room for a few minutes to defuse situation _____
5. Engage students in class discussion on an emotional incident that just occurred _____
6. Appraise student of reality consequences _____
7. Stand next to student who is having trouble _____
8. Show genuine interest in student's assignment _____
9. Gently touch student on shoulder _____
10. Engage student in conversation on a topic of interest to the student _____

Activity Directions, Part 2: For each of the following situations identify the appropriate surface management technique(s).

Situation or Characteristic	Technique(s)
1. Does not embarrass student	_____
2. Used when student is frustrated by class assignment	_____
3. Used when behavior is likely to exhaust itself	_____
4. Most effective for students with whom you have developed a relationship	_____
5. Does not identify student within the group	_____
6. Used when student shows signs of boredom, restlessness	_____
7. Used when behavior is not likely to spread	_____
8. Could be used to drain off tension	_____
9. Can use without interrupting classroom program	_____
10. Most effective at beginning stages of misbehavior	_____
11. Used not to punish but to protect student or help student get over the immediate situation	_____

Alternatives for Managing in the Multicultural Classroom

Teachers have three major alternatives available to them. Teachers can allow student behavior, intervene to try to change student behavior, or adapt the teaching/learning environment to accommodate students. That is, teachers can choose to:

1. Allow behavior
2. Intervene
3. Accommodate

Allow Behavior

Here the teacher makes a conscious choice to allow the behavior. This category includes permitting, tolerating, and accepting student behavior.

Permitting

This is behavior that is generally accepted for all members of the class. It includes specifying routine procedures, like being able to get a drink, sharpen pencils, or get materials without teacher permission. Another example of permitting is having a specified policy in place, such as allowing students to go to the book corner after they complete their assignments.

Tolerating

Tolerating problem behavior means accepting it temporarily. When teachers tolerate students' behavior problems, they may choose to allow students to misbehave, give up too soon, withdraw from the group, or pout or cry because they know that the students can't help themselves for the moment, so they tolerate the behavior temporarily. It might also be appropriate to tolerate misbehavior due to extenuating circumstances or the "heat of the moment" if students are unlikely to repeat the behavior. Long and Newman (1961) describe the following three conditions where toleration is warranted.

Learner's leeway

Whenever a student is learning a new concept, experimenting with ideas, or trying to win status in the group, the teacher expects that the student will make mistakes. Teachers often actually tell their students that they are not going to be upset when they err in trying to master new academic and social skills.

Behavior that reflects a developmental stage

Some behavior is age-typical and will change as the student becomes more mature. Any attempts on the part of teachers to alter or inhibit this behavior will likely result in such negligible changes that it is usually not worth the inevitable fight.

For example:

- Students in the early grades are impulse-ridden and motor-oriented. Kindergarten teachers generally accept the fact that very little can be done about it except tolerate it. Such tolerance should not be confused with sanctioning it or permitting wild behavior.
- Students in the late third or early fourth grade, caught between group pressure and allegiance to the teacher, are notorious for tattling, e.g., "Johnny pulled a leaf off your flower when you were in the hall."
- Other illustrations of age-typical behavior are the unscrubbed appearance of the preadolescent boy, the primping of sixth-grade girls, the secrets of preadolescent girls, and the sex language and behavior of adolescent boys.
- All adolescents sometimes feel the need to show their increasing autonomy and individuality to prove they can win with an adult, and this often leads to verbal confrontations. In their struggle to develop their own identities, they often reject adult characteristics. Such rejection may take the form of teasing or badmouthing, as in "Did you try to get your hair to look like that?" or "Did your mother pick out that dress for you?"

It's important to keep behaviors like these in developmental context and not participate in these confrontations, because it is likely to make matters worse. A better response might be to poke fun at yourself to lessen the tension.

Behavior which is symptomatic of an illness, disability, or undeveloped skill

Behaviors that students engage in because they are incapable of doing otherwise will need to be tolerated. This is not to say that the teacher will not have to control some student behavior to prevent students from doing things that will harm themselves or others. Tolerance as well as control, when managing techniques don't work to stop harmful behavior, may both be necessary while the teacher tries to deal with the causes, not just the symptoms.

Accepting

When teachers accept the fact that students are who they are and have individual needs, teachers accommodate their demands, expectations, routines, and disciplinary techniques to the unalterable aspects of their students. This also includes adjusting their behavioral expectations to their students' culturally-determined behavior patterns, as long as their behavior is not negatively effecting their learning or interfering with the rights of others.

Teachers also need to accept certain aspects of a student's personality, such as moodiness or temperament, again providing the particular behavior does not have a negative impact on the learning environment.

Accepting and Tolerating Compared

On the surface, accepting and tolerating look similar. In both cases teachers allow their students to behave in ways that sometimes differ from how the majority of students are expected to act. The difference is that teachers permanently accept the unchangeable aspects of their students' personalities or their cultural behavior patterns but tolerate only temporarily their alterable, yet presently problematic, behavior. For example, a teacher would choose to accept different discourse styles based on cultural background as a general code of conduct, but only temporarily tolerate the moodiness of a student who lost a ring during lunch.

Intervene

When student behavior impinges on the rights of others, disrupts learning or threatens the safety of the student or others, the teacher needs to intervene. Here the situation requires that the teacher use an intervention to attempt to alter the situation. This category includes controlling, changing and modifying behavior.

Changing

Techniques for changing behavior try to modify the attitudes, values, motives, beliefs, expectations or the self-concepts of students so that they won't have to behave in the same inappropriate way in given situations. Helping students develop coping skills and social skills are examples. Changing techniques require time, so the teacher may also pair these strategies with other shortterm interventions. Changing techniques include teaching, modeling and supporting students in learning alternative behaviors.

Modifying

When the teacher attempts to modify a student's behavior, the teacher uses means other than coercion. The teacher manages students' behavior without resorting to consequences or using authoritarian power. Meeting the psychological needs of a student is also included here, or responding to the communicative intent of the inappropriate behavior, rather than the symptom.

Examples of this approach are diverting a student's attention, making a joke out of something a student might be taking too seriously, or speaking calmly to a student when the student is upset. Such techniques do not involve the use of consequences or direct control. Because changing students' behavior takes a considerable time commitment, teachers usually have to manage their students' behavior as well. Modifying refers to techniques that modify a situation enough to make it less likely that students will continue to exhibit inappropriate behavior. Modifying techniques aren't designed to change students, but to help students control their behavior. They may also be thought of as place holders, or strategies that do damage control or contain the situation. Strategies such as antiseptic bouncing, hurdle help, direct appeal to values, signal interference, and proximity control may also be used to modify behavior.

Controlling

Controlling management techniques involve using consequences and are concerned only with stopping inappropriate behavior. Teachers using consequences to manage students' behavior are using their power or authority. They reward students for behaving the way they want them to behave and punish them for behaving in inappropriate ways.

Intervening Techniques Compared

Controlling and modifying techniques handle misbehavior for the moment while changing techniques try to modify students' attitudes, motives, and self-concepts so they will not misbehave in the future. Convincing students likely to misbehave that they have to behave or they will be punished is an example of controlling students. Motivating students to want to behave appropriately even when they won't be punished is changing them. Ignoring the attention-seeking behavior of students who play the clown is modifying, while teaching them how to obtain attention in more acceptable ways is changing.

Accommodate

Here the teacher takes primary responsibility for making adjustments to accommodate students. The onus for change is primarily directed toward the instructional context. This may include adjusting expectations and procedures as well as instructional format to accommodate individual differences in learning rate and style. Accommodations could be at the class-level or the individual student-level. This category includes preventing, supporting, and adapting.

Adapting

Both contextual and individual adaptations are included here. Some examples of adapting include defusing tension using humor, interest boosting, and restructuring the classroom program. At the individual student level, the teacher might adapt the length of a seatwork assignment without a break to the shorter attention span of a student or the length of an individual reading assignment.

Supporting

Supporting techniques provide encouragement and emotional support for students. Here the intent is to provide personal support to help a student exercise self-control. It also includes a restorative aspect intended to restore positive relations.

Preventing

Preventing is proactive and involves developing classroom procedures which will avoid problems anticipated beforehand based on previous experience. Included here are planning for providing students with help when they are uncertain about assignments and planning lesson flow and activities to accommodate different lengths of time needed for task completion.

In deciding on an intervention, the teacher needs to weigh a range of contextual variables by considering the following questions.

Ask Yourself
- When a student misbehaves, am I thinking about how the student can be helped to learn better—or just how the disruptive behavior can be eliminated?
- Is the intervention accompanied by a plan for the student to learn a new way of behaving?
- Does the intervention strategy for changing a student's behavior also include an external component to make it easier for the student to learn a more appropriate behavior?
- Is the intervention designed to initiate change to come from within the student?
- Is the student emotionally ready for the intervention?
- What types of student misbehavior can I control to a significant degree by restructuring expectations and/or classroom procedures?
- Do students have other ways of obtaining acceptance and recognition besides behaving appropriately?

- Is the intervention goal merely to gain the student's compliance for the moment?
- After an intervention, is the student typically angry? passive aggressive?
- After an intervention, is the student typically back to work, or not participating?
- Is the student/teacher relationship after an intervention enhanced, maintained, or eroded?
- Does the intervention help the student learn anything about his/her behavior?

Critical Reflection on Practice: Assessing Your Intervention Pattern

Activity Directions: Write several statements to describe each of the following aspects of your intervention pattern.

Behaviors which I choose to permit in my classroom:

_____
_____
_____

Behaviors which I consciously accept:

_____
_____
_____

Behaviors/situations which I decide to tolerate:

_____
_____
_____

I intervene with student behavior when:

_____
_____
_____

Working with a partner compare and contrast your patterns, then list some key similarities and differences.

Similarities   **Differences**

_____   _____
_____   _____
_____   _____

Complete: This exercise led me to ask myself the following question(s) about my intervention pattern.

_____
_____
_____

Student/Teacher Classroom Interaction Patterns: Are They Equitable?

Many teachers think that they treat all of their students the same. They think that they do not exhibit any favoritism. However, research has shown that the quality of student/teacher interactions sometimes contradicts the idea that all students are treated the same.

Research indicates that teachers tend to have more interactions relating to classroom behavior with low-achieving students and fewer interactions regarding learning activities. Consider the following questions and ask yourself if you engage in any of these behaviors.

Ask Yourself

- Do you ask some students to analyze, synthesize, and evaluate answers to your questions while you ask others non-stimulating fact-type questions?
- Do you give students time to think about a question before expecting an answer, or do you ask the question and then move quickly to another student because you think that the first student will not be able to answer correctly?
- Do you give some students more encouragement or assistance after you have called on them?
- Do you merely give some students the answer to the question?
- Do you give briefer and less informational replies to questions to some students?
- Do you probe for deeper meaning behind only certain students' responses?
- Do you fail to tell some students their answer is incorrect?
- Do you actually praise some students for answers that really aren't correct?
- Do you avoid eye contact with some students?
- Do you differentiate between work and worth in your praise to students?
- Do you accept student answers to open-ended questions without judgment, or do you question the novel or nontraditional responses?
- Do you interact with the same students most of the time?
- Do you expect, tolerate, or demand different behavior from male students than you do from female students? If so, are these different standards justified?

Promoting Acceptance of Students from All Cultural and Social Backgrounds in Your Classroom

In order to ensure equity, you will need to be proactive in your planning of classroom practices and teaching/learning structures.

Ask Yourself

- During group work, do you ensure that students from different cultural and social backgrounds have the same responsibilities and duties as other students?
- What do you do to ensure that students from different backgrounds will participate in group work?
- What strategies do you use to raise the academic image of students from different cultures in the eyes of all students?
- What strategies do you use to bridge the gap between a student's culture and school?
- What strategies do you use that incorporate the cultural background and community of students?
- What resources (individual/group) from the community have you brought to class?

- Do your bulletin boards and overall classroom appearance reflect the culture(s) of your students' backgrounds?
- What methods do you use to enhance the self-esteem of students from different cultures?
- Have you tried to accommodate the family structure of students from different social and cultural backgrounds?
- Have you considered the family discipline style of students from different cultural backgrounds in your management plan?
- Do you differentiate between behavior that is culturally-based and behavior that is not? Do you respond accordingly?
- Are the behavior problems you identify more often attributed to one group?
- Have you considered the values of your students and their cultural backgrounds in setting standards? Are your behavioral standards in conflict with theirs?

Critical Reflection on Practice: Assessing Your Interaction Pattern

Activity Directions: Follow the steps below.

1. Record the names of students called on for an entire day.
2. Then, calculate the percentage of your students you called on. _____
3. What do the data tell you? Do you see a pattern?

   _____

   _____

   _____

4. On another day, record all the names of students you interact with for inappropriate behavior.
5. Then calculate the percentage. _____
6. Compare these two lists. What does the comparison reveal?

   _____

   _____

   _____

Exploring Student Status within Groups in the Classroom

Individual students have "status" within groups in the classroom. This status can be related to gender, ethnicity, race, color, social class, knowledge, perceived ability, peer group membership, personality characteristics, or physical attributes. Such status can be a function of role status such as leader, clown, or bully. Status can also be inadvertently, covertly, or overtly, "assigned" to certain students on the basis of gender, social status, or cultural background. Or, that status might be a function of group members' attitudes about others' potential to contribute meaningfully to the learning task on the basis of their assessment of perceived ability or achievement level.

Carefully observing how students interact during assigned group learning tasks can furnish teachers with valuable information. Systematic observation provides a way to assess interaction patterns that could reveal biases that serve to impede some students' opportunities to learn. Such data can help teachers assess whether they need to intervene with a structure that offers greater potential for fair and just treatment of all members of the class, regardless of status or ability. This may involve teaching communication skills, developing problem-solving strategies, or creating awareness of inequities.

By proactively identifying students who are relegated to "low-status" teachers have the opportunity to restructure group norms to improve the status of these students. Low-status students could be ridiculed, ostracized, criticized, or ignored by other students. In the multicultural classroom, it is essential that teachers have a way to monitor interaction patterns and intervene when necessary to ensure unbiased treatment and opportunity to learn.

Assessing Interaction Patterns: The Moon Problem Exercise

The following structured experience developed by Hall (1971) is being used here as an attempt to simulate experiences your students may experience in group learning tasks. The purpose of the exercise is to disclose how role perceptions are always operating in any group setting.

Guidelines for the moon problem exercise

- It is not necessary to complete the exercise. The purpose of this activity is to provide a simulation for observing behavior during a problem-solving task.
- The participants should interact as naturally as possible.
- The observer should keep the focus of the feedback on the interaction and give objective, nonjudgmental feedback.

Learning Practice Task: The Moon Problem Exercise

Activity Directions: You will be working in groups of five to seven for this activity.

1. Select one member to serve as an observer of the process. The observer will record information on the interaction pattern among the group members. After the structured activity, the observer will give specific feedback using the following questions to guide their observations and subsequent feedback to the group.
   - Who initiates the ideas?
   - Who complies with the ideas?
   - Who verbalizes the most in the activity?
   - Who controls the situation in the activity?
   - Who is "silenced" by other group members?
   - What do the physical movements tell you about the interaction?
   - What does other nonverbal behavior tell you about the interaction?

2. Once the groups and the observers have been established, engage in the activity for approximately 15 minutes.

3. Have the observers give feedback based on the specific behaviors they observed.

Note. While the focus of the activity was the process, not getting the right answers, the participants will most likely be curious about the "right" answers, hence the NASA solution is included.

The Moon Problem Exercise

You are a member of a spaceship crew originally scheduled to rendezvous with a mother ship on the lighted surface of the moon. Due to mechanical difficulties, however, your ship was forced to land at a spot some 200 miles from the rendezvous point. During reentry and landing, much of the equipment aboard was damaged and, since survival depends on reaching the mother ship, the most critical items available must be chosen for the 200 mile trek.

Below are listed 15 items left intact and undamaged after landing. Your task is to rank order them in terms of their importance for your crew in allowing them to reach the rendezvous point. Place number 1 by the most important item, the number 2 by the second most important, and so on through number 15, the least important.

Undamaged Equipment	Ranking Importance
Box of matches	_____
Food concentrate	_____
Fifty feet of nylon rope	_____
Parachute silk	_____
Portable heating unit	_____
Two .45 caliber pistols	_____
One case dehydrated Pet milk	_____
Two 100 pound tanks of oxygen	_____
Stellar map (of the moon's constellations)	_____
Life raft	_____
Magnetic compass	_____
Five gallons of water	_____
Signal flares	_____
First-aid kit including needles	_____
Solar-powered FM receiver/transmitter	_____

There are no right or wrong answers to this exercise.

NASA Solution to The Moon Problem Exercise

This is the order in which these items have been ranked by NASA. Remember, there are no right or wrong answers. What is important is why you decided to rank the items the way you did.

1. Two 100 pound tanks of oxygen. — *Fills respiration requirement.*
2. Five gallons of water. — *Replenishes loss by sweating, etc.*
3. Stellar map (of the moon's constellations). — *One of principal means of finding directions.*
4. Food concentrate. — *Supply daily food required.*
5. Solar-powered FM receiver/transmitter. — *Distress signal transmitter, possible communication.*

6. Fifty feet of nylon rope.	*Useful in tying injured together, help in climbing.*
7. First-aid kit including needles.	*Oral pills or injection medicine valuable.*
8. Parachute silk.	*Shelter against sun's rays.*
9. Life raft.	*CO_2 bottles for self-propulsion across chasms, etc.*
10. Signal flares.	*Distress call when line of sight possible.*
11. Two .45 caliber pistols.	*Self-propulsion devices could be made from them.*
12. One case dehydrated Pet milk.	*Food, mixed with water for drinking.*
13. Portable heating unit.	*Useful only if party landed on dark side.*
14. Magnetic compass.	*Probably no magnetized poles; thus useless.*
15. Box of matches.	*Little or no use on the moon.*

Using structured exercises with students

This is an excellent activity to engage students in to watch their interaction patterns. For this and similar activities, varying group composition will allow teachers to observe interaction patterns among many different combinations of gender, ethnicity, and ability during the group process. Systematic observation in such settings can provide teachers with valuable insight.

This exercise or similar activities can be used by teachers to assess how students in their classroom, especially those from different backgrounds, engage in group problem-solving tasks. Teachers can also use similar activities to gauge the social interaction between students from different cultural and social backgrounds and other students in group academic tasks. Activities like these can also help teachers identify individual student's status within the group. Once "low-status" students are identified, the teacher can make concerted attempts to provide structures which will help enhance the status of these students. Some potential interventions and general strategies teachers can use include the following:

- Teach problem-solving strategies to limit decision-making by power, status, aggression, and so forth;
- Give low-status students specific responsibilities;
- Assign roles to low-status students that will necessitate interacting with all students in the group;
- Provide task directions which call for all students to make contributions; and
- Engage low-status students in learning activities in which they can exhibit or demonstrate their strengths or expertise.

Integrating Theories of Human Development into Classroom Practice

The foundation for what has been called the humanistic education movement which began in the 60s is the acceptance of basic human needs and the drive to satisfy those needs, coupled with the development of the person as a whole or complete person. This movement was an offshoot of the larger human potential movement, spearheaded by such pioneering psychologists as Abraham Maslow (1968) and Fritz Perls (1976). Maslow has been called the father of humanistic psychology; Perls is the founder of Gestalt therapy. Gestalt psychology is predicated on the notion that the whole person is greater than the sum of its parts.

Pertinent to this discussion is the notion that a student is greater than the sum of his or her behavior. Given the confines of the classroom setting, inappropriate behavior has to be managed, but at the same time the teacher needs to look beyond the student's action and consider the student's development as a whole. This is not to imply that creating an understanding of the depth of a student's need deprivation and resulting emotional turmoil means that the teacher should excuse inappropriate behavior. Quite the contrary, the position advocated here is that the teacher help the student gain competence by giving the student alternatives and helping the student learn new tools to engage in more productive behaviors.

In the past, most students arrived at school relatively well-adjusted psychologically, having benefited from early nurturing and healthy family connections. In today's classroom, more and more students begin their school careers maladjusted. Many models of psychological development are based on the importance of getting basic human needs met. What the models all have in common is that the environment should be need-fulfilling for developing and sustaining healthy psychological well-being. The following chart compares and contrasts the viewpoints of six authors who propose theories of psychological development useful to educators.

Theories of Basic Need Fulfillment and Lack of Fulfillment

Maslow	Glasser	Brendtro, Brokenleg & Van Bockern	Dreikurs	Erikson	Wood
Hierarchy of Needs	Basic Human Needs	Essential Developmental Needs	Mistaken Goals	Psychosocial Developmental Needs	Developmental Anxieties (When Needs are Unmet)
Survival	Survival				
Safety or security				Trust (lack of security)	(Anxiety of abandonment/lack of security)
Belonging and affection	Belonging and love	Belonging	Recognition/attention	Identity (lack of belonging)	(Anxiety of identity/lack of acceptance and belonging)
Esteem, recognition, and achievement		Mastery/competence	(Inadequacy/lack of mastery)	Industry (lack of self-esteem)	(Anxiety of inadequacy/lack of self-esteem)
Self-actualization					
	Power/control	Interdependence/autonomy	Power/control	Autonomy (self-doubt)	(Anxiety of conflict/lack of power and autonomy)
	Freedom/choice		(Revenge—for lack of freedom)		
	Enjoyment/fun/satisfaction				
		Generosity			
				Initiative (guilt)	(Anxiety of guilt/lack of self-worth)

Note: Parentheses ( ) are used to indicate unmet need or response to unmet need.

As can be seen in the chart, belonging is a need common to five of the six models. When a student feels "I'm worthy—there's a place for me" and "I'm needed and I can contribute," the student is well on his/her way to school adjustment. In the school setting, the teacher is the primary provider for students' needs and the school is the context for building a sense of belonging. If this doesn't happen, students suffer alienation and seek other avenues for need-fulfillment. The need for students to develop a sense of competence, particularly related to school expectations, was also a common element in five of the models. Successful school experiences and academic accomplishments lead a student to feel "I am capable" and to want to participate in what school has to offer.

Also common to five of the models, is the need for power, control, and autonomy, typically defined as personal power to influence one's environment. Feeling a sense of empowerment leads to the belief that "What I do makes a difference." (This is similar to what is commonly referred to as an internal versus an external locus of control.)

Maslow (1968) proposed a hierarchy of five levels of needs that motivate human behavior. In his model, the lowest level of need must be satisfied in order to seek out the next level. If students' are deprived of food, shelter, and safety needs, they will be stifled in their drive to seek the fulfillment of higher needs. Glasser (1986) posited five fundamental needs, the fulfillment of which he considers critical to students' psychological welfare. He puts the omen on teachers and schools to create learning opportunities that meet these needs. Both Glasser and Maslow concur on the need for survival and belonging. Glasser's theories are discussed in greater detail in Chapter 5.

Building on native American child-rearing practices, Brendtro, Brokenleg, and Van Bockern (1990) propose four essential needs of developing children. Their model is based on the symbol of the Indian medicine wheel or Circle of Courage. They believe all children, regardless of culture, will become healthy adults if their needs for belonging, mastery, independence, and generosity are met. Characteristics of their model are described below.

- Children need to belong to the tribe by having many 'mothers.' Over time, children become a part of a larger community with a clear identity and sense of trust regarding their cultural roots and feelings of belonging.
- Children develop mastery by observing and listening to their elders and participating in tribal games, stories, and work. This process of learning reflects the importance of mastering a skill, based on the value of cooperative achievement, personal persistence, creativity, and problem solving.
- Children are encouraged to hunt by themselves, to be accountable for their actions, and to take risks by adventuring into the unknown. These expectations develop autonomy, responsibility, assertiveness, and self-discipline.
- Children are taught the importance of giving and sharing their resources instead of accumulating them for personal wealth. Personal acts of generosity are a significant way of building the importance of helping others.

They advocate that the way to reclaim troubled youth is by promoting the fulfillment of these four needs.

These first three authors describe needs that, when fulfilled, lead to healthy personality adjustment and development of skills to successfully navigate life. Implicit in these models is the idea that students whose needs for attention, approval, and acceptance have not been met by primary caretakers will bring a greater range of problematic behaviors to the classroom.

The next three authors specifically address what happens when these needs are not met in childrearing and the longterm psychological consequences of need deprivation.

Dreikurs was one of the first to address this issue for teachers. Like Glasser, Dreikurs believed that students will behave in ways that they think will get their needs met (Dreikurs, Grunwald, & Pepper, 1982). His position was that students misbehave because they think that's what will get them what they want (i.e., attention, power, revenge, to be left alone). Dreikurs' theories are also presented in more detail in Chapter 5.

Both Erikson and Wood, like Maslow, propose a hierarchical relationship, noting that if children fail to advance successfully from one stage to the next they will be inhibited in their capacity to develop a well-balanced personality, with diminished capacity to respond productively to life experiences. Erikson's first five developmental stages are presented in the chart below.

Erikson's Stages of Psychosocial Development

Psychosocial Stage	Psychosocial Development	Need Fulfillment
Trust versus mistrust (Approximate age: Birth to 18 months)	Develops varying degrees of trust and mistrust depending on the degree of support and nurturing provided by primary caretaker; quality of initial care will have a profound effect on the degree to which the maturing child expresses trust.	Need to trust that the basic needs of nourishment, caring and safety will be met.
Autonomy versus self-doubt (Approximate age: 18 months to 3 years)	Begins to express a strong sense of self; attempts to gain a degree of independence and competence; intensely investigates environment.	Need to explore the environment for the sake of curiosity; should be encouraged to express themselves verbally.
Initiative versus guilt (Approximate age: 3 to 6 years)	Begins to explore sexual identity; begins to identify with male and female role models.	Need to establish a sense of self and own identity; should reinforce their identity at this point.
Industry versus inferiority (Approximate age: 6 to 12 years)	Forms social alliances reflecting growing interest in other people and in things beyond the family; actively explores; tests themselves; works hard to achieve goals.	Need to develop confidence in ability to do things successfully, such as schoolwork.
Identify versus role confusion (Approximate age: 12 to 18 years)	Uses logic to solve hypothetical problems; makes decisions based on objective evidence; develops capacity for empathy; develops need to improve things; acquires personal responsibility for growth.	Need to develop an identity not based on the desires of others, but based on one's own interests and desires; should be given real, self-directed experiences.

Erikson stressed the importance of the quality of early childrearing to the child's later psychological adjustment, noting that if the child is not supported in developing trust and a sense of self during infancy and the toddler years, the effects of mistrust and self-doubt will haunt the child throughout his or her adult life.

Wood (1986) proposed that unmet emotional needs at early stages result in persistent anxieties. Her theory is that all children experience five developmental anxieties throughout childhood. If an anxiety is not resolved at the appropriate age, it carries onto the next developmental level, creating more intense unmet emotional needs. Wood, like Maslow, emphasized that unresolved developmental anxieties will eventually become a primary motivation for students, interfering with all future relationships. The following chart shows the types of anxiety and the associated unmet needs and the resulting behavior.

Wood's Stages of Intrapsychic Anxiety

Stage	Anxiety Development	Unmet Need (Unresolved (Anxiety)	Resulting Behavior
Anxiety of abandonment (Birth to 2 years)	If young child bonds with significant adult, receiving care and nurturing, feelings of abandonment will be resolved and a growing sense of trust will develop.	Love, safety	Develop superficial relationships, hoard objects, have overriding desire to be accepted by others.
Anxiety of inadequacy (3 to 6 years)	Feelings of inadequacy and self-doubt are normal for children as they come to understand the expectations of the important adults in their lives. If the child experiences success rather than failure and the ability to meet adult standards, feelings of inadequacy are resolved.	Self-worth	Learn to deny or justify mistakes by blaming others, lying, projecting feelings on others.
Anxiety of guilt (6 to 9 years)	If children have not resolved anxiety of inadequacy and come to think they are unworthy, they will put themselves down for not meeting their own standards.	Self-esteem, empowerment	Actually seek out punishment; become scapegoats and willing victims of exploitation; engage in self-abusive behavior.
Anxiety of conflict (9 to 12 years)	This anxiety emerges when the need for budding independence conflicts with the will of authorities. If this is resolved, self-confidence to solve conflicts, independence and a sense of freedom emerge. Also, one becomes personally accountable for one's decisions and behaviors.	Self-confidence, independence	Fights with authority figures; may come to believe there is status and power in being bad.
Anxiety of identity (12 to 18 years)	Adolescents struggle with such questions as "Who am I?" and "Can I handle this?" These questions reflect the dynamic interplay between feelings of independence and feelings of dependency. The struggle is intensified by the adolescent's maturing body to create additional concerns about sexuality, attractiveness, and group acceptance.	Acceptance, belonging	Develop false identity and seek recognition and status in inappropriate ways; reject adult values and put down adults; have no direction.

Consequences of Failure to Develop Secure Attachments

Students who fail to develop healthy, secure attachments to significant adults are typically products of inconsistent, detached, neglected, or abused caregiving at significant developmental stages. Children whose primary caretakers oscillated between giving adequate to effusive attention and being indifferent to totally inaccessible, become insecure. The uncertainty and unpredictability they experience lead to obsessive attachments which may play out in the form of anxious obedience or over-reliance on external comfort (Bowlby, 1982; Herman, 1992). Because children who fail to develop healthy attachments anticipate abandonment, they try to do whatever they can to prevent it. They can become clinging vines, hovering about and constantly requiring attention.

Students who suffer from detached caregiving fail to have their needs for touch, love, affection, and genuine interest met. When caregivers are rejecting, and/or detached, with no affirmation or support forthcoming, children come to feel worthless. Hostility and rejection of adults may become their protection against the possibility of rejection. They may crave closeness, but the fear of the pain they may endure if they fail becomes unbearable, something to avoid at all cost (Morrow, 1987). In more extreme cases, they may operate by the motto: "I'll reject you before you reject me." They come to find solace in being the rejecter instead of the rejected. The inner turmoil created by avoiding while desperately seeking connection causes anger to ferment and frequently the teacher is the object of their sting of rejection (Gootman, 1997).

With abusive parents, they may be kind and loving and then, in a rage, beat their children then hug them and beg forgiveness. Neglected children suffer the pain of knowing no one cares. Disinterest in and hostility to others is their protective shield to guard themselves against the overwhelming effect of apathy and rejection.

Children who have experienced such emotional deprivation may be less socially competent, fight more, bully others, and engage in other behaviors that cause teachers concern. Students who have such unresolved anxieties and unmet needs often behave in ways that drive teachers away, and yet these are the very students teachers have the greatest potential to influence by providing an alternative adult role model. Understanding the dynamics of insecure attachment and how it manifests can help teachers to go beyond simply trying to control or to retaliate for a student's inappropriate and abusive behavior. By finding ways to provide secure attachment, without feeling overwhelmed themselves, teachers can do much to bolster the development of feelings of worthiness.

Troubled students who have experienced such early, intense, and prolonged abuse, neglect, and rejection no longer are motivated by personal trust or the spirit of human kindness. These students come to the classroom with the intent to avoid interpersonal closeness. Teachers who reach out to these students can be the victims of "psychological biting of any hand that tries to feed them" (Long & Morse, 1996). Their well-honed negative attitudes and rejecting behaviors are difficult for teachers to accept and deal with productively. Students who are seriously troubled typically do not readily respond to teacher attempts to be supportive and nurturing. They seem to have developed psychological antibodies against the warmth of healthy relationships. They have been conditioned to consider close relationships as toxic rather than enriching. For these students, closeness holds the despair of a new cycle of rejection and abandonment, not the hope of affection, trust, and bonding. It feels much safer to try to manipulate others than to take charge of their lives.

Going Beyond Reacting to Responding to Students' Misbehavior

These models of psychological needs and development provide a more holistic framework for conceiving students' misbehavior. The same underlying problem (unmet need, unresolved anxiety, mistaken goal) can be expressed in a multitude of ways. The corollary of this statement is also true: different behaviors that are problematic in the classroom setting can be motivated by the same underlying cause. The message these authors have for teachers is that, in the long run, it is far more beneficial to students to try to identify the unmet needs they have and then to attempt to address those needs within the confines of the classroom setting. The unmet need might be safety, belonging, competency, attention, identity, power, status, recognition, satisfaction, or control.

It is this author's belief that nearly all inappropriate classroom behavior stems from unmet needs, undeveloped skills, or expectations incompatible with individual student's personality, preferences, learning style, or cultural background. When the problems that students experience and act out are positioned within this framework, the teacher is empowered as the critical force, because it is the teacher who controls whether the classroom climate is need-satisfying, whether students are taught skills they lack, and whether the range of individual differences are accommodated.

Some students may need to learn how to make friends or to respond to frustrating life events, not only to function more effectively in the classroom but to be successful in life. As Kohn (1996) points out, what matters is the reasons and feelings driving the behavior. Viewing student behavior from this perspective will require a very different orientation than discipline programs that merely control or attempt to change behavior temporarily.

All behavior is purposeful and, according to the beliefs of many, this author included, most behavior is an attempt, albeit misguided, to satisfy a need. Most misbehavior teachers confront is sending out a signal. When teachers learn to read these signals, they go beyond reacting to students' misbehavior to responding beneath the surface behavior. They are willing to adjust their methods, routines, and expectations and assess the teaching/learning environment they create against potential student unmet needs. They examine classroom policies and practices to determine factors that may be contributing, even exacerbating, student anxiety or frustration. Rather than blaming the student, teachers first consider factors within their power to change, such as instructional format, grouping, testing practices, curriculum content, peer relationships, or student/teacher relationship.

The message for teachers is to channel basic drives, which are expressed disruptively, into socially-acceptable expressions. The goal then becomes discovering the student's motive and attempting to rechannel the unacceptable behavior by offering the student acceptable options, as the following example illustrates.

Misbehavior	Unmet need	Alternative Teacher Response
Frequent arguing with teacher	Independence, status	Allow student to be teacher for a specified time
		Allow student to critique teacher or a lesson

The current conditions in many classrooms warrant a need for deeper understanding of the socio-emotional problems many students experience. Teachers need to uncover the reason or function of a particular misbehavior, then formulate a strategy likely to have an impact on the motive that is driving the behavior.

Long and Morse (1996) suggest that teachers might respond by "regulated permission" or providing an outlet for the student, for example, allowing the student to express anger by flattening clay or banging erasers. Similarly, they cite the example of the teacher asking a student why she always calls out answers, and the student replying "cause those dummies think I don't know anything." Such a retort should give the teacher a pretty clear indication that attempting to devise ways for this student to have increased competence status among her peers would be a more meaningful intervention than attempting to squelch her calling-out behavior.

The Challenge to Reposition Student Behavior

Thoughts like the following serve to limit your range of responses to classroom problems:
- "If it wasn't for him, my class would run fine;" or
- "If I didn't have these kinds of kids to contend with, maybe I could actually teach!"

The term "repositioning" connotes the idea of changing your perception by "moving out of" your old position and creating a new position from which to view a situation. It's your personal framing that shapes how you attribute meaning to your experiences. Seeing new ways of interpreting a situation enables you to move beyond a limited perspective. By challenging yourself to think in a different way, you can assign new meaning to the classroom situations you confront.

Some helpful ways of repositioning for the classroom setting include:

- Repositioning conflict as opportunity,
- Repositioning confrontation as energy,
- Repositioning aggression as a cry for help,
- Repositioning defiance as a request for communication, and
- Repositioning attention-seeking as a plea for recognition.

Repositioning calls for a change in your perception of misbehavior, by making the shift in thinking from:

"This kid is a problem." to *"This kid poses a problem for me to solve."*

So rather than try to teach the kid a lesson for misbehaving with cease and desist tactics, you really do teach the kid a lesson by using the problem situation as an opportunity to teach a skill that the student lacks. By using a problem-solving approach instead of just trying to stop the behavior, you work with rather than against the student by seizing "teachable moments" to teach students how to get what they want in more appropriate ways.

Learning Practice Task: Examining Your Own Issues

Activity Directions: Different beliefs are based on who we are, how we were raised, how we define our role, and what we believe is good for students. Working with at least three others, discuss your answers to the following questions.

Should students be allowed to wear hats in class? _____

Should students be allowed to talk quietly while doing individual work? _____

Should students be allowed to call out answers to questions? _____

Instead of advocating for your position or trying to get consensus, listen for the differences of opinions. Try to identify factors that underlie these differences.

What factors did your group identify?

_____

_____

_____

How do you think examining your personal history and your own issues relating to your expectations and discipline can be helpful to setting reasonable disciplinary procedures?

_____

_____

_____

_____

What Pushes Your Buttons

Teachers, like everyone else, are sensitive to, or self-conscious about, some aspect of their background, status, or image. However, in their position as role model to developing students they are often "put to the test" to examine their reasons for the way they respond. Physical attributes, appearance, lack of content knowledge, computer illiteracy, and need for acceptance are a few of the areas that may be a source of insecurity or concern.

Students are astute observers of teachers' reactions, and teachers often reveal much about themselves in how they react when their students find the right button to push.

Learning Practice Task: What Pushes Your Buttons?

Activity Directions: Working with a partner, take turns sharing the following.

Think about an area that represents a source of insecurity to you.

Briefly describe what it is.

_____

_____

_____

What is your typical reaction when this button is pushed?

_____

_____

_____

How might that effect students?

_____

_____

_____

What message do they get?

_____

_____

_____

Who's to Blame and Who Can Fix

Much of the psychological literature addresses only the negative behavioral aspects of students who are conveniently labeled *at-risk* (i.e., violence, aggression, crime, pathology) and how these behaviors can be ameliorated and these students remediated (Goldstein, 1991). Such a fixation with controlling deviance translates into a curriculum of control, crisis intervention, and obedience training as the major vehicles for addressing the management of deviant behavior.

When we target what is wrong, focusing on a philosophy of "lacking," we are likely to overlook students' strengths and resources. Rarely is the focus on the facilitation and expansion of the strengths the "at-risk" student may bring to a situation, such as resiliency, risk-taking, a spirit of adventure, fortitude, coping, and survival skills. Much of the terminology used to describe such students is pejorative and demeaning. We label students as disruptive, disobedient, defiant, disordered, disturbed, deviant, disabled, deprived, and disadvantaged. We also label parents and families as dysfunctional, when that label may more aptly describe schools, bureaucratic organizations, and society in general.

Traditional ways of thinking about students who experience problems in school embrace either a deficit mentality, viewing students as deficient and rendering them disabled, or take a compensatory position in which the target of the intervention encompasses not only the deficit functioning of students but the deficient nature of their environment, rendering students disadvantaged. Both orientations require bringing students up to snuff with little regard for the social context within which learning occurs or the quality of instruction delivered. While the latter orientation still focuses interventions at the child level, it does advocate teaching coping skills, appropriate social skills, and learning strategies.

The prevailing focus is on identifying and delineating the source of disability or deficit, with little regard to the classroom context in which a student is considered deficient. We need to refocus our emphasis to pay greater attention to dimensions of the teaching/learning process rather than learner characteristics which may inhibit learning, such as class organization, task structures, and performance expectations. The contextual makeup of the classroom environment which has been referred to as the "classroom ecology" needs to be examined to assess aspects of instructional programming, curriculum content, social organization, and classroom demands that may cause student alienation and student/teacher conflict.

Attributes for Behavior

Most belief systems for attributing cause for student behavior include biological, environmental, and psychological factors.

Biological. Physiological or biochemical factors such as:
• Brain damage, neurological impairment.
• Learning disability, abnormal development.
• Disease, drug addiction.
• Hunger, malnutrition.

Environmental. Contextual factors based on experience. This category covers a lot of ground, including:
• Debilitating effects of poverty.
• Learned consequences of behavior based on what child is rewarded and punished for.
• Social and cultural norms.
• Community, family, school, and peer group influence.
• Cultural misperceptions.
• Situational stressors (such as parental unemployment, serious illness or death).
• Social cognitive skill deficits such as:
   —Lack of opportunity to learn (due to lack of examples provided by others in child's environment).
   —Lack of appropriate experiences from which to learn (due to lack of exposure).
   —Not knowing what is expected (due to lack of understanding of social expectations).

—Inability to read social cues and signals (that certain behavior is expected or pro-hibited).

—Not foreseeing possible results.

—Lack of appropriate role models.

Psychological. Factors related to personality and emotional development. Development is primarily governed by need-fulfillment. The host of needs human beings have include the need for:

- Survival, safety, security;
- Belonging, love, affection;
- Recognition, achievement, status;
- Power, control, freedom;
- Identity, competence, mastery;
- Curiosity, challenge, stimulation;
- Enjoyment, adventure, satisfaction.

Development can be normal, delayed, or abnormal; needs can be met or unmet at age-appropriate developmental levels. When needs are met, healthy or normal development occurs; when needs are not met unhealthy or pathological behavior results. Early emotional deprivation in the form of abuse, abandonment, neglect, or rejection has devastating, longterm impact potentially causing the child to suffer from feelings of insecurity, anxiety, helplessness, hopelessness, low self-esteem, anger, and rage.

Teacher and Student Attributions

While no one category is entirely discounted, most teachers give more credence to some explanations than others. Teachers make certain assumptions about why students behave the way they do. Teachers have both conscious, expressed attributions and unconscious attributions that affect their interactions and relationships with students. They may assume a student is restricted in the capacity to make good choices, or they may assume a student chooses inappropriate behavior. Here they also make the assumption that other choices are readily accessible to the student.

Learning Practice Task: Looking at Your Attributes for Student Behavior

Activity Directions: Working with a peer, review the factors in each of the three categories of attributes for student behavior.

1. Each individually list the five top reasons why you believe students behave the way they do.

_____

_____

_____

_____

_____

2. Compare your list with your peer. How are your lists similar?

_____

_____

_____

How are your lists different?

_____

_____

_____

3. Discuss the differences in your lists.

   What can you attribute your differences to?

_____

_____

_____

Teachers' general notions about the causes of human behavior significantly influence how they attempt to intervene and their attitudes about changing student behavior. Teacher attributions about blame and control are critical because they frame their beliefs about their personal potential to impact students, and that affects the teachers' own sense of power and control. In attempting to influence students, teachers can fail to go far enough or go too far. They can err in either direction; and each is a judgment call. Teachers can give up too soon, if the student is not immediately responsive to their overtures, or they can go too far and fail to require student accountability or responsibility at some point. They can try too hard, give too much.

Teacher attributions for blame and control will be a key factor in how teachers answer questions like:

- How do I help?
- Who do I help?
- Who can be helped?
- How far do I go?
- What is the extent of my responsibility to students?

Teachers must face deeply-rooted personal attitudes concerning human nature and causation of behavior to answer these questions for themselves.

Both teachers and students hold attributions about their responsibility for situations and solutions. Teachers range in attributions from taking on total responsibility (it's all up to me) to relinquishing all responsibility (you can't teach these kids anything). Generally speaking, such attributions are age-related, with the pattern being the younger the student the more responsible the teacher feels for providing the solution. Younger children are usually deemed helpless primarily due to environmental and biological factors. As they grow older, especially as they reach adolescence, teachers tend to assign personal blame for their mistakes and assume students have the power to change their behavior. A choice to behave inappropriately is seen as willful. Hence, the teacher's perception of student misbehavior moves from helplessness to defiance as the child gets older.

Students have their own list of attributions—bad luck, unfair treatment, peer pressure, life sucks, I'm learning disabled, I can't read, I have a bad temper, I was abused, I was too drunk. Both teachers and students have their own role perceptions and interpretations of motives and intentions.

Learning Practice Task: Looking at the Helper Role

Activity Directions: Working with a partner, take turns sharing the following:

1. As a child, who did you go to with your problems?
2. As an adolescent, who did you go to with your problems?
3. What did the person do that was helpful?
4. Did you move from relying on your parent(s) to your peer group as you got older?
5. Generally, did you see your teachers as a source of help or part of the problem?
6. Think of the last time you had a crisis to deal with in your life.

How did you handle it?

_____

_____

_____

What seemed to help you get through it?

_____

_____

_____

What were you able to do to move through the crisis?

_____

_____

_____

What label would you give the coping skill(s) you used?

_____

_____

_____

Questions for Self-reflection

Do you try to teach your students such coping skills?

What does this say about how you might work with students who experience difficulty and may act inappropriately?

Learning Practice Task: When Your Help was Rejected

Activity Directions: Think of a time when you tried to help a student, and the student refused your attempts to help. Working with a partner, take turns sharing the following:

1. How did you feel?
2. What were some of your frustrations?
3. How has it affected your willingness to try to help another student?

Role Models for Discipline

The literature on parenting provides some insights on communicating caring to children. In light of the similarity of the teacher/student relationship, it seems reasonable that the ways that promote closeness between parent and child might also promote closeness and trust between teacher and student. The practices advocated by the authoritative parenting model have been shown to increase feelings of closeness and trust between child and parent and have particular relevance in that they are grounded in the belief that children warrant respect (McNabb, 1990). A major tenet of this approach to parenting is treating children firmly, but with dignity and respect (Glenn, 1982; Glenn & Nelson, 1989). Parents espousing this model believe that the rights of parents and children are reciprocal and that children are capable (Cole & Cole, 1989).

The attitudes and behaviors that emanate from this approach to parenting include:

- Explaining rules and decisions and the reasoning behind them to the child.
- Listening to the child's point of view, even if they don't accept it.
- Setting high standards for behavior.
- Encouraging the child to be individualistic.
- Making demands that are within what is developmentally appropriate for the child.
- Separating the child's personal worth from his or her behavior.
- Using discipline as an opportunity to teach the child, so that the child can internalize the learning and become independent.

The type of discipline received as a child, both at home and at school, leaves a lasting imprint. These earlier models can provide a useful guide for managing problems of varying severity in the classroom setting. They can also serve to limit the range of potential responses to situations.

Learning Practice Task: Examining Your Past Experiences

Activity Directions: Working with a partner, take turns sharing the following:

1. How were you disciplined as a child?

2. Did your mother and father discipline in different ways? How were they different? Did you learn to use this difference to your advantage? How?

3. In general, what was your parents' demeanor during discipline situations? Angry? Calm? Disappointed? Patient? Conciliatory?

4. Did you feel good about some of the ways you were disciplined?

5. Think of a situation where an adult in your life handled a discipline situation badly. From your perspective, what was wrong with the way that person handled the situation? Why do you think you remember this incident?

6. Think of a situation where an adult in your life handled a discipline situation effectively. Why was it memorable?

7. Can you recall a time when you were disciplined and you felt you really learned a lesson? What was the lesson you learned? How has this lesson served you in your life?

Questions for Self-reflection

Would the strategies that were effective for you be equally appropriate or effective for the various types of students you may teach?

What aspect of your approach might you need to challenge to better align with today's classroom?

What aspect of your approach might you need to challenge to better align with your core beliefs?

Teachers' reactions to problem behaviors are influenced by the adult models they experienced. Many of our ways of disciplining stem from our own experiences as children. The way we respond to particular types of behavior in the classroom, likewise, says much about how we were brought up and what our early school experiences were like. In addition, our current school norms and expectations provide further enculturation. There is some evidence that teachers' childhood disciplinary experiences in their family of origin affect their disciplinary styles. Teachers who use more punitive consequences experienced more punishment as children, experienced more harsh physical punishment as children and as teenagers, were less likely to have been told the reasons behind their parents' rules, and were more likely to have been prohibited from questioning parental authority (Hyman, 1990; Kaplan, 1992).

Learning Practice Task: Role Models for Discipline

Activity Directions: Working with a partner, take turns sharing the following:

Parental Discipline

1. What aspects of parental discipline are you carrying over to your classroom?

2. Have you made a conscious choice to use these disciplinary procedures, or is it merely habit?

3. Conversely, what aspects of parental discipline are you deliberately choosing not to use in your classroom? Why?

School Discipline

1. What aspects of school discipline are you carrying over to your classroom?

2. Have you made a conscious choice to use these disciplinary procedures, or is it merely habit?

3. Conversely, what aspects of school discipline are you deliberately choosing not to use in your classroom? Why?

Chapter 3

Building Democratic Learning Communities

Moving away from the traditional management role of providing rewards and punishments, delivering praise and judging student behavior calls for a fundamental shift in the way teachers and students relate to each other. Changing the metaphor of teacher from manager to facilitator significantly transforms student/teacher interaction patterns. Below the climate dimensions of the teacher role in the traditional authoritarian hierarchy is contrasted with the role in a democratic community.

Authoritarian Hierarchy		Democratic Community	
Manages	Dominates	Facilitates	Guides
Demands respect	Evaluates product	Commands respect	Encourages effort
Orders	Punishes	Invites	Acknowledges human error
Controls	Tells	Supports	Suggests
Imposes beliefs	Decides	Offers ideas	Discusses

Developing a safe environment calls for attending to students' emotional and personal needs concurrently with their academic and social needs. In such a teaching and learning climate, emphasis is placed on the quality of human interactions, both between teacher and student and student to student. Creating a classroom environment that breeds mutual tolerance and respect is the foundation for a caring learning community. Creating a classroom climate that honors participation, equity, and inclusiveness is the foundation for a democratic community.

Support for Community-building in Schools

Several arenas converged to give impetus to the concept of creating the school as a community of learners. Those include:

- The effective schools research,
- The concept of emotional intelligence (EQ) popularized by Goleman (1995),
- The demise of the traditional family support structure,
- Increase in violence and alienation among youth, and
- A growing literature base on the importance of caring.

All these avenues converge in support of the necessity to give equal attention to the emotional, social, and psychological development of students. This belief shapes the focus of this book.

The literature on school community clusters several sets of attributes in the term *community*. Specifically, three aspects of community have been discussed: (1) community as applied to an external social setting, (2) an identifiable constituent group, and (3) a coherent quality of the school itself (Merz & Furman, 1997).

The position supported in this text is that the aspect that the teacher has the greatest potential to achieve by virtue of his/her own actions is that of "school as community," actually "classroom as community." The level of networking with the community to achieve a sense of community requires a schoolwide effort, indeed a communitywide effort, clearly beyond the individual efforts of a teacher. Hence, the focus here is on developing the classroom as community and the characteristics that need to be in place so that students develop a sense of belonging as a member of that community. This author takes the position that until the teacher defines community for him/herself, *community* is only convenient rhetoric. At the heart of community is the principle that the people are more important than any information to be learned or techniques to be used.

Research Findings on the School as Community

Impetus for the community movement, as it might be called given its recent insurgence of popularity, grew out of several bodies of research, the major one being the effective schools research of the 70s and 80s. This line of research identified characteristics of schools that were considered effective primarily on the basis of achievement at the school-level. From this literature base, a composite of desirable outcomes emerged to shape the concept of school as community (e.g., Purkey & Smith, 1983; Rowan, 1990), typically including mutually-shared values, a common agenda highlighting academic standards, and emotional connections. This latter variable cluster was clearly related to the quality of interpersonal relationships and came to be labeled an *ethic of caring* (Grant, 1988; Sizer, 1984; Lightfoot, 1984; Halliger & Murphy, 1986). The concept of shared values and shared responsibility has come to be framed as a *democratic community*.

In order to try to capture the key concepts that have emerged from the research and literature on school as community, the following chart summarizes the attempts to decipher specific variables that contribute to the concept of community.

Identified Factors Defining Community

McMillan & Chavis (1986)	Sergiovanni (1994)	Meier (1995)	Boyer (1995)	Bryk & Driscoll (1988)	Battistich et al. (1995)
Sense of Community	Democratic Community	Democratic Community	Community for Learning	Community Index	Democratic Community
Influence	Democratic	Democratic/ respect	Self-discipline/ respect		Autonomy
Emotional connection/ membership	Caring	Trust/collabo- ration	Caring	Caring	Belonging
	Shared values/ common purpose	Shared values	Shared purpose	Shared values	
		High standards for intellectual develop- ment	Curriculum coherence	Common agenda	Competence
Fulfillment of needs					

Utilizing the concept of sense of community, McMillan and Chavis (1986) and Sergiovanni (1994) synthesized existing research; each described several components of sense of community. Based on empirical research (correlational studies reanalyzing existing data), Battistich, Solomon, Kim, Watson, and Schaps (1995), and Bryk and Driscoll (1988) each identified three clusters. Boyer (1995) and Meier (1995) "operationalized" the research literature to develop school-based models built on the concept of the school as a caring, democratic community.

As can be seen in the chart, four factors were common to several of these composite definitions for community. Two factors are at the student-level: (1) a positive, caring, and connected relationship with others and (2) the ability to influence their environment by both having an influence on and accepting group norms and values (achieved principally through being able to exercise choices, autonomy, and self-discipline). The consistency of the presence of these factors gives further momentum to the critical elements of bonding relationships (identified by all six of the data sources) and a democratic-like community that is based on mutual participation, responsibility, and acceptance of group norms (identified by five of the six data sources).

As shown in the chart, the other two factors are at the school-level: (1) mutually-derived purpose, values, and curriculum agenda and (2) high academic standards. Each of these factors were identified by four of the six sources.

The research findings indicate that community variables are usually related to affective outcomes, assessed by attitudinal responses of teachers and students, but not necessarily to achievement outcomes. Only Bryk and Driscoll (1988) specifically identified academic achievement performance as a documented outcome; they found students achieved higher math scores when community variables were present. However, those who advocate for a caring community see caring as a goal in itself, not a means to an end.

Additionally, the general finding of the effective schools research was that a cluster of variables was more related to outcomes than a single aspect. This finding has evolved into using the term democratic community to connote a merging of the ideas of shared values, belonging, autonomy, and competence.

The School as Caring Community

The literature on the school as a caring community calls for equal status for caring and nurturing with other educational agendas (e.g., Sergiovanni, 1992; Noddings, 1992; Beck, 1994; Boyer, 1995). This literature is primarily philosophy-based and espouses that teaching students to care is a primary goal, not just a means for accomplishing other academic goals. They espouse Dewey's (1963/1938) notion that school is "about life" not preparation for life.

Some authors advocate that the school be designed to function as surrogate family. The underlying assumption is that students today have fragmented home lives and require greater nurturance in the school setting. Because of the disconnectedness of the lives of many children outside of school and the lack of stable family relationships, many educators are advocating that the schools create a community within the school itself (see Noddings, 1992; Sergiovanni, 1992, 1994). Recognizing the paucity of social, psychological, and emotional support systems available for many of our youth, they advocate that schools provide some of that missing support.

In addressing the concept of school as a caring community, authors emphasize the importance of emotional connecting for schools to be successful with today's student population. They describe relationships within the school community as personal, committed, and familial. They also stress the importance of forging shared values and providing a sense of security and identity to both teachers and students (e.g., McLaughlin, 1991, 1993). Underlying the concept of school as a caring community is a commitment to shared values and relationships that foster interdependence. Others urge that school staffs redefine colleagueship in order to evolve into a professional community (Johnson, 1990; Sergiovanni, 1994). A professional community strives toward an ideal that includes exemplary practices in an atmosphere of friendship and caring.

With the traditional family structure and access to extended family weaning, some educators are calling for schools to support families in meeting these needs by taking a more active role in nurturing students. They advocate that schools must become more nurturing places to better serve the emotional as well as the academic needs of students (Goodlad, 1990; Lieberman & Miller, 1984; Martin, 1992; McLaughlin & Talbert, 1990; Sergiovanni, 1994).

When one defines community as an organization committed to shared values and relationships that foster interdependence, such relationships, based on mutual commitments, render much traditional management and control tactics moot. Utilizing family as the metaphor for management, the terms *classroom management* and *discipline* don't begin to capture the teacher/student relationship. A relationship of family with shared responsibilities, calls for the teacher to guide students, to facilitate their development and to connect, confer, and collaborate with students. As Bullough (1994) aptly states: when the focus is on building caring relationships, teachers participate with students "in their journey to make the world their own."

This line of research coalesces with those educators who take a more psychological framework for defining the goals of schooling by suggesting that the school should provide for the basic needs all human beings have. Moreover, they suggest that the school should try to compensate for the devastating and debilitating effects of abuse, neglect, rejection, abandonment, and other psychological deprivation caused by lack of appropriate bonding at the early stages of development.

As Goleman (1995) pointed out, success in life is only partially attributed to intellectual capacity. Emotional intelligence is just as important. Being able to persist in the face of disappointment, handle frustration, control the desire for immediate gratification, and empathize and get along with others are also critical factors in one's success.

What Research Says about Student Resiliency

Another branch of related literature is that of students who are resilient. When students are resilient they develop a set of attributes that provide them with the strength and fortitude to confront the overwhelming obstacles they face in their life. Resilient students have the ability to rebound or recover from adversities that might have caused serious debilitating effects.

The literature on resilient children, those who thrive in spite of potentially devastating experiences, shows that what frequently makes the difference is one caring adult who gets involved in their lives—often that person is a teacher. This literature would support that a sense of connectedness that comes from establishing the school as a caring community, even if direct links to academic performance can't be drawn, is important in itself because teachers have the proven potential to be the primary impetus and support for turning a child's life around.

Studying Asian-American children living in adverse home conditions who were resilient and became successful adults, Werner and Smith (1992) found that these children most frequently mentioned a teacher as the person who really made a difference for them. Moskovitz (1983) studying Nazi concentration camp survivors found that they attributed their resilience to their connection with warm, caring, and encouraging teachers. Another study identified a teacher as the primary source in helping children from a disadvantaged, urban neighborhood to overcome adversity and become successful adults (Pederson, Faucher, & Eaton, 1978).

Even when children grow up in the worst circumstances, some are able to thrive. What makes children resilient in the face of tremendous odds is often the dedicated commitment of a teacher. Teachers are consistently credited as a significant protective factor in ameliorating the response to high risk factors and stressful life circumstances (Boyer, 1983; Cicchetti, 1989; Garmezy, 1984; Hawkins, Catalano, & Miller, 1992; Lynch & Cicchetti, 1992; Masten & Garmezy, 1985; O'Donnell, Hawkins, Catalano, Abbott, & Day, 1995; Werner, 1990; Zimrin, 1986). Caring teachers can be a child's salvation against all odds (Gootman, 1997).

How Teachers Create a Sense of Community

While the need for teachers to assume a role in meeting the social and emotional needs of children is clear, the form that role may take is less clear. After all, teachers are not parents, social workers, therapists, or counselors (Deiro, 1996). Clearly, there are alternative paths to creating a classroom culture for emotional support and comfort.

Outstanding teachers who have significant impact on the lives of children and youth and are able to develop healthy bonds with students do so without necessarily becoming intimate, affectionate, or indulgent (e.g., Deiro, 1996; Gootman, 1997; Ladson-Billings, 1995). Teachers with very different personalities and with very different teaching styles can find ways to nurture their students. Research findings dispel three common myths relating to being a caring teacher. The first is that caring is gender-specific, based on the assumption than women are more effective nurturers than men. This has not been found to be the case, especially in Deiro's (1996) study. The second myth is that developing caring connections requires that the teacher touch students and show overt affection. Teachers need not be sweet, affectionate, or gentle; they can also be stern and professionally detached yet still be nurturing. The third misconception is that nurturing is synonymous with permissiveness. Caring is often associated with leniency and indulgence, even weakness. Those studying teachers who are able to make a difference in students' lives by making healthy connections often describe teachers as strict disciplinarians.

What emerges as the critical variable is treating students with dignity and respect. And, there are diverse ways teachers can do this. Depicting caring and respect means listening to students, engaging in dialogue with students, showing interest in them, soliciting their opinions, valuing their ideas, and demonstrating a belief that they are capable. What is critical is that students perceive the teacher as caring; and that perception is created by a communication style that is respectful. (The next chapter provides some specific strategies for effective communication that is respectful.)

Recently, Deiro (1996) studied teachers who were able to build close and trusting connections to students. The teachers she studied were selected on the basis of having both excellent reputations among peers, students, and staff as teachers who develop caring connections with students and, simultaneously, having expert reputations for their ability to teach and expertise for their subject area. This set of criteria was used to ensure that the selected teachers nurture students in ways that do not compromise their primary teaching responsibility. The strategies listed below were derived from this qualitative study.

Create one-to-one time with students. These teachers remained accessible to students before and after school, between classes, during extracurricular activities, or during class periods by using a delivery style that maximizes individual or small-group contact.

Use appropriate self-disclosure. These nurturing teachers disclose personal information about themselves that is pertinent to the needs of the students, while exercising discretion about what information to share.

Have high expectations of students while simultaneously conveying a belief in their capacities. These teachers establish and maintain high academic standards for their students while communicating a belief in their students' capacity to meet these expectations.

Network with parents, family members, friends, and neighbors of students. By creating intergenerational networks, they establish a common ground with common histories on which to build healthy connections.

Build a sense of community among students within the classroom. They encourage students to take risks in the classroom, make honest disclosures, and share personal information with classmates.

Use rituals and traditions within the classrooms. By developing rituals and traditions in which everyone participates, they help to build a sense of community by fostering a feeling of comfort and belonging.

While these strategies are not the only role-appropriate ways for developing bonds with students, they represent a variety of ways secondary teachers bond successfully with their students without compromising their primary responsibility for the cognitive development of students.

Developing Rituals and Traditions for Community-building

Rituals and traditions provide a familiar routine and create a common experience for students and serve to enhance teachers' connections with students. They may be incorporated into learning activities or used as noncurricular activities. Rituals are activities that are done the same way each time, such as having the last ten minutes of every class period on Friday reserved for open discussion or beginning a social studies class with a current event introduced by a student. Traditions are customs, practices, or special events that are routinely acknowledged and honored, although they need not be honored the same way each time. In fact, by design they may be celebrated differently each time. Below are some examples of rituals teachers have.

As a daily ritual, one teacher at the beginning of her classes reads or has a student read a "one-minute message" from an inspirational reader. They read different messages about life, hope, and all kinds of human experiences providing food for thought.

A junior-high teacher has her students periodically stand and yell at the end of class what she calls the "PMA" (positive mental attitude) cheer. When she asks them how their positive mental attitude is today, they answer: "Happy, healthy, feel fantastic, boy are we enthusiastic!"

To let students know it's OK to talk about their feelings and what's important to them and to encourage them to talk about what's happening in their lives, one teacher saves time at the beginning or at the end of the week for talking about topics unrelated to the class focus, such as movies or current events in the news.

Such small rituals in which everyone participates help teachers develop close connections with students. One ritual teachers may want to institute is a ritual that ends each day or class period on a positive note.

By finding opportunities to follow rituals and traditions and create special events and celebrations, teachers develop cultural norms that support community. When teachers help students learn the value of supporting one another in their trials and tribulations, they convey the notion that everyone has something worthwhile to say and reinforce the values of dignity and respect.

Teachers should create rituals that align with their teaching goals and subject area, while highlighting values they want their students to develop. A tradition already in place at the school can be adapted to fit a particular teacher interest or goal. Below are some examples.

Developing the Habit of Questioning

Asking questions that encourage students to think beyond their own self-interest, consider the implications of their ideas and actions on others, and apply standards of fairness and justice.

- *How would this action help, hurt, or affect others?*
- *Would this action help make the world a better place?*
- *How would you feel if you were on the other side?*
- *Is this just a matter of personal choice, or is it a question of right or wrong?*

Creating the Ritual of "Calling the Circle"

This is a ritual that calls students together for the purpose of creating a safe "container" for students to voluntarily express both negative and positive emotional experiences. They may express anger and frustration as well as joy and appreciation. Students are taught to honor the circle as a special time and space by doing a simple ritual to mark the beginning and end of the circle time. That simple ritual might be holding hands, taking several deep breaths, or reading a selection from a book or a poem.

The use of an object such as a "talking stick" or rock can also be incorporated during this time, so that everyone who wishes can speak and be heard without interruption. The object is taken by the person who wishes to speak. The person holding the object speaks without interruption and then returns the object to the center when he/she has finished speaking.

The teacher may also want to create a saying that students can recite before the circle begins. The following is an example.

> *"We're here to listen to what each other has to say with thoughtfulness and to be a compassionate witness for everyone in our community."*

Morning Announcements

Some examples of morning announcement rituals include:

- *Acknowledging students who have demonstrated respect, thoughtfulness, authenticity, or emotional integrity*
- *Reciting a cheer or pledge that the class has created*
- *Telling a story or reading a poem, newspaper, or magazine article that delivers an important message*
- *Having a moment of silent reflection, unstructured or directed, to reflect on something in particular*

- *Daily quote containing thought-provoking or inspiring message*
- *Thanking anyone for a kind deed*
- *Having a good news/bad news format*
- *Having a selected student deliver quote or thought-of-the-day*

Practicing Listening Skills

Listening games such as "telephone" where one student whispers something to another student, that student whispers the message to the next student, and so on. After the message has traveled from ear to ear, the last person says the message aloud. Usually what the last person heard bears little resemblance to the original message. This can provide an opportunity to discuss the listening process with students and show how messages can easily get distorted, highlighting the importance of listening and clarifying skills.

Schoolwide Opportunities for Rituals, Ceremonies, and Traditions

There are also many schoolwide opportunities for promoting community values with rituals, ceremonies, and traditions.

- *Awards ceremonies*
- *Appreciation days for support staff, teachers, and others*
- *Awareness days or weeks*
- *Value of the week or month*
- *Service days*

Creating Community Spirit

Kirschenbaum (1995) offers some ideas for teachers to teach their students values that are also useful for building a community spirit. Some of these suggestions are listed below.

Appreciation time: *Daily or weekly ritual time for sharing appreciations. This is a time for students to appreciate one another, the teacher to appreciate students, and for students to appreciate the teacher for things the teacher has done or said. Initially, teachers can provide a "sentence stem" to help students develop the habit and keep focused, such as:*

- *"I appreciate . . . ."*
- *"I feel really good when . . . ."*
- *"The most helpful thing someone did for me this week was . . . ."*

Opinion time. *Set aside a particular time each week for the ritual of students speaking out on current topics. The teacher can make a greater ceremony by setting up a lectern. During this time any student may come up to the lectern and deliver an opinion or editorial on any topic they choose, or it can be confined to a particular topic area. This ritual inculcates the values of independent thought and respect for others' views.*

Open forum. *Create a forum:*
- *Where students listen to each other's dilemma and provide feedback*
- *Where students listen to each other without feedback*
- *Where students discuss events in their lives*
- *Where students talk about a set question like:*
  - *What's your favorite hobby?*
  - *What do you do when you're feeling down?*

Song. *At lower grade levels, teachers can have the tradition of the class singing a song at the beginning or end or at a regular time during the school day. These songs can have a particular theme to highlight a value area, such as friendship, helping others, family, or making the world better. This ritual can contribute to caring and cohesiveness of the class.*

Applause. *Student applause or other nonverbal expressions of appreciation for designated things, such as when a student volunteers to do something less than desirable, performs a service to the class, or accomplishes a difficult task. By creating this type of ritual, students know that when they extend themselves their classmates will be appreciative.*

Some Definitions of Community

In all types of communities members are bonded together for a common purpose, for the "communal good" of the group, as well as to meet their individual needs for belonging and acceptance. When people come together in a spirit of community, they embrace a collective concern for humankind.

The principles of natural sustainable communities are the very same principles that sustain human communities (Capra, 1983). These basic principles of ecology are the principles of interdependence, partnership, and diversity. The principle of interdependence is our appreciation that we need each other. The principle of partnership is working together toward mutually-valued goals. The principle of diversity is embracing diversity as a resource rather than a liability and appreciating differences.

Scott Peck (1987) defined community as a group of people who have learned to communicate honestly with each other, whose relationships go deeper than their masks of composure, and who have developed a commitment to rejoice together, to delight in each other, and to make others' conditions their own. The underlying principles here are those of open and honest communication, mutual vulnerability, significant commitment to each other, and collective responsibility for sustaining the community. These are at the heart of community-building.

Fundamentals of a Caring, Democratic Community: Respect, Authenticity, Thoughtfulness, and Emotional Integrity (RATE)

Establishing the foundation for a caring, democratic community begins with the way the teacher interacts with students and filters through to student-to-student interactions. The teacher serves as role model by living by the principles he/she espouses.

In a caring, democratic community, as the acronym suggests, everyone "rates."

Creating such a community has two levels and involves teachers being both proactive and reactive. These levels are:

1. Teachers demonstrate the value they place in the quality of relationships with students, by showing their commitment—of time, resources, and emotional energy.
2. Teachers monitor how students treat each other. They intervene, redirect, and challenge students when they violate community norms. (This requires that the teacher use assertion and confrontive skills discussed in detail in a later section.)

Concern for the welfare of the members of the community, open communication, and honest interactions define a caring community. In a caring community, members are thoughtful and respectful and are not afraid to be real, wrong, or vulnerable. Community members engage in direct and nonmanipulative dialogue that is accepting of each others' perspective. Students come to know each other and learn to value what each has to offer. In the next section, the four fundamentals of authenticity, thoughtfulness, emotional integrity, and respect are described.

Authenticity

Being authentic means being real. Teachers who are authentic do not act out assumed roles or roles others expect them to play. They know who they are and are clear about what they stand for. They have let down their masks and disguises. To use the colloquial expression, authentic teachers "walk their talk."

They use appropriate self-disclosure. Self-disclosure that is appropriate considers the context, the type of relationship, and the desired outcome of the communication. It's a judgment call, involving the ability to assess the depth of the disclosure that is desirable or warranted in a particular situation.

They validate their right to the feelings they experience, respond honestly to students, and share what's really going on with them without trying to sugarcoat it. Authentic teachers communicate to their students that it's OK for them to make mistakes and create a climate where their students feel safe enough to also be real, or authentic.

In the classroom where authenticity is valued, both the teacher and the students share and express what they care about. Authentic teachers exude self-acceptance and self-confidence and inspire these qualities in their students.

Being open and accepting of students and encouraging students to express a variety of feelings and opinions helps develop a sense of connectedness and emotional intelligence.

The specific communication skills for teachers to develop that align with authenticity are the connecting skills of validating, self-disclosing, and accepting personal ownership and responsibility.

Thoughtfulness

The word *thoughtfulness* was purposefully chosen instead of the word *caring* to connote the concept that mutual consideration is what is called for in the large-group structure of the classroom. We can't demand or dictate caring. Caring requires a special connection. While teachers can exhibit caring in their relationships with students, it might be more appropriate to expect that students show tolerance and acceptance for their classmates, rather than expect a caring relationship with everyone. In the classroom setting, it may be more reasonable to strive for tolerance of individual differences, not necessarily caring the way it is normally defined, while reserving caring for those we choose to have more connected relationships with, such as family members and close friends.

In the thoughtful community, members know others in the community accept them as they are. Students cooperate by working together for a common purpose and collaborate toward mutual goals. Students can rely on one another to be considerate of their needs, wants, desires, and fears.

The thoughtful teacher considers the emotional well-being of students in every interaction he or she has with students. The skills that contribute to thoughtfulness on the part of the teacher are primarily listening skills, such as reflecting, paraphrasing, and clarifying.

Emotional Integrity

Having emotional integrity means communicating with emotional honesty. Emotional integrity is imbedded in honest communication and mutual vulnerability. Teachers who have emotional integrity are aware of what is happening in the present moment and act on that awareness. They have the ability to be fully present and to share thoughts and feeling as they experience them. They also validate students' right to express their feelings. They deal with emotions as they emerge. This keeps "lingering resentment" from settling in to erode the relationship. They don't dismiss challenges from students and aren't afraid to be wrong.

Emotional integrity also means being proactive and confronting students' behavior by respectfully challenging them and calling students to accountability. The following examples of teacher talk exemplify emotional integrity.

Directly discuss with the student your perception of the state of the relationship at any moment: *"I'm sensing an edge in your voice in your last comment. I'm wondering if you had a negative reaction to what I just said. I'd like to get some feedback before we go on."*

Challenging student: *"Wait a minute, I'm really uncomfortable with the tone of this conversation, and I don't want to start this way."*

Calling student to accountability: *"When you call me names, I get upset and want to attack you too, and I don't want to do that. I'd like you to speak respectfully to me."*

Being proactive and confronting students' behavior: *"I'm disappointed in this class. Just yesterday we talked about the importance of respecting one another and how, if you have any problems with something someone does, you should talk it over with them, and if you can't work it out, you should come to me. So when there was a fight on the playground at recess, I was very upset because I think you can handle conflicts without trying to hurt each other."*

Although teachers may be aware of and sympathetic to students' feelings, they may not communicate that to students. Learning to explicitly validate students' feelings can help build bridges to students whose behavior teachers find difficult and can be the starting point for changing ways of responding to students.

Some teachers find it easier to share their positive feelings with students but not their sadness, hurt, or frustration. Others have no difficulty communicating such feelings, but seldom communicate their positive emotions and reactions to students. Teachers tend to have a predisposition either to openly express more negative, or more positive emotions with their students. It is important for teachers to consider if they are predisposed to expressing either type of emotion more exclusively, and to work to try to create more balance in their expression of emotions.

The behavior of students will sometimes cause teachers to be uncomfortable or angry. These feeling are natural and teachers are entitled to have these feelings without also experiencing guilt or shame. Teachers are also entitled to express their feelings as long as they do so in a way that doesn't harm students. The teacher serves as a role model for students when he/she appropriately displays negative emotions.

Constantly stuffing your feelings or trying to act as if nothing bothers you can be as much a problem as expressing your feelings in inappropriate ways. The balance comes with "emotional integrity." Not acknowledging and expressing your true feelings is emotional dishonesty. The idea is to express your feelings in a way that both reflects emotional honesty on your part and is helpful to your students. The goal is to express your feelings appropriately by modeling constructive outlets for your emotions while providing students with feedback regarding their behavior.

Trying to deny or suppress your feelings typically leads to lingering resentment. When resentment is left to fester, it can eventually lead to rejection of the student—a far worse option than dealing with your anger when it happens.

Teachers are human and they have strong feelings about what is important to them. The way they interact with students tells students what they value. When a teacher expresses anger and disappointment about a cheating incident, he or she is showing students the value he or she places on honesty and integrity. When a teacher expresses a deep concern after some students are picking on another student, he or she is communicating the importance he or she attributes to the value of kindness and respect. On the other hand, when a teacher also calls a student an unkind name or uses sarcasm, students see the incongruence in what they expect from them and what they expect from themselves.

As Long (1996) tells us, no teacher enters the classroom with a "symptom-free" personal history, nor a perfect psychological fit to work equally successfully with all students with whom they happen to be assigned. Each teacher's psychological makeup is better suited for dealing with some students, and necessarily not others. The teacher's journey begins by "digging through one's developmental past and uncovering those powerful and buried life events that have affected the teacher's attitudes and behaviors toward select students."

Questions for Self-reflection

Self-reflection is an essential tool for the democratic classroom. Below are some questions to pose that foster emotional integrity.

- What am I feeling?
- Am I feeling hurt? What is my hurt about?
- What is keeping me from expressing my feeling?
- Is it fear of rejection? Is it fear of disapproval?
- Is there something I need to say to a student? the class?
- What message is my behavior communicating to the student?
- What need might the student be trying to get met?

The specific communication skills for teachers to develop that align with emotional integrity are confronting skills, involving stating concerns, asserting and challenging.

Promoting Emotional Integrity with Students

The teacher not only demonstrates emotional integrity, but also encourages students to express a variety of feelings and opinions. Learning to deal with their feelings and to look within for the motives of their actions helps students develop their emotional intelligence. It also creates a sense of connectedness to others. Teachers can also help students go beyond words like angry and mad to get to the feelings that lie below the surface, or to a deeper feeling. This level of feeling communicates the students' vulnerability. Getting to the emotion that lies behind what they are feeling and then expressing it honestly is integral to a classroom community that values emotional integrity. The following examples illustrate deeper level feelings.

Surface Feeling	Deeper, Vulnerable Level
I'm mad because you won't let me play.	I feel left out when I'm not allowed to join the game.
I get angry when you ignore me.	It makes me sad when I think no one likes me.

When the classroom community values emotional integrity, group members feel secure that their challenges will be acknowledged and considered. They also come to value having access to feedback from class members and see it as an opportunity to learn about themselves from the eyes of others.

Respect

Respect is a less tangible concept. The key concept that underlies respect is acceptance. Teachers demonstrate acceptance by listening respectfully and honoring multiple voices. Oldfather (1993) coined the term "honored voice" to connote giving students a voice in the classroom and valuing what they have to say.

Respect is communicated through carrying on respectful dialogue with students, by not talking at students, rather talking with students. By listening to students' perception of life, caring about what they have to say and thoughtfully responding to their ideas, teachers help honor their voices.

Respect is earned. You can gain it and you can lose it based on your deeds. Teachers communicate respect when they show regard for students' capacity to manage their own lives successfully. Dignity is the quality of being worthy of respect, a personal attribute of self-worth. Treating students with dignity means honoring their individual worth.

In respectful classrooms, differences are acknowledged and appreciated and everyone strives to listen to each other in search of common understandings. Students value what each other has to offer and express what is important to them without the fear of judgment.

Teachers who respect their students also create trust, by being both trustworthy and trusting at the same time. They are willing to try to understand students' point of view and opinions. They are not afraid to discuss controversial issues—they speak the unspeakable, discuss the undiscussable.

Teachers who value respect know the rights of students and teachers are reciprocal. It's a two-way street—everyone's equal. The teacher is not above recrimination.

When students know that they can share concerns and difficulties with a teacher who will not stand in judgment but who will attempt to understand from the students' perspective, it helps them understand more about their own experiences and their reactions to them.

When children have not been shown respect, they have trouble internalizing this value in ways that allow them to express it appropriately. In some neighborhoods, youngsters have seen or heard of so many killed in random violence, they come to feel disposable and expendable, and without a future worth planning for. Young teens often confuse respect with fear and self-gratification and seek to intimidate others as a way of surviving. To respect others, one must have been shown respect. When you are treated with disrespect, over time you grow to feel worthless.

It is from the experience of being shown consideration and care that children learn to feel valued. Feeling valued is at the heart of self-respect. Rather than blame the student for being disrespectful, teachers can show him/her how it feels to be respected.

The teacher's communication skills that contribute to being respectful are primarily the skills of acknowledging, encouraging, appreciating, and inviting.

Establishing and Sustaining a Sense of Community

Establishing and sustaining a sense of community has to be "operationalized" and played out in daily interactions and moment-to-moment decisions. First and foremost, promoting a spirit of community requires that the teacher make the quality of relationships equally as important as the teaching/learning process. Transforming the culture of the classroom from a climate of competitiveness to a climate of cooperation can create the necessary buffer to help insulate students from the often hostile world they live in.

Putting community-building in operational terms includes:

- Responding with acknowledgment and acceptance rather than defensiveness, judgment, or denial;
- Creating a vehicle for open and ongoing dialogue with students;
- Getting to know students and their backgrounds by taking an interest in students' life stories;
- Infusing the classroom with community-building experiences imbedded in methods, structures, and content learning;
- Creating classroom norms that balance the growth of the individual and the well-being of the community.

Communities that honors the four fundamentals of relationships do not emerge from a step-by-step formula. It is not enough for teachers to try to show authenticity and respect; they also need to be perceived by students as authentic and respectful. No matter how hard a teacher tries to connect with students, if students do not interpret what teachers do as authentic and respectful, bonds between teachers and students will not develop.

When teachers are committed to creating such communities, they:

- Act authentically by speaking the truth with care and thoughtfulness;
- Pay attention to what's being said without interpretation, judgment, or trying to rescue;
- Listen beneath the surface, remaining open to discovering something about themselves in the stories of their students.

Acting in a spirit of community changes not only the community but each person as well. When the climate of the classroom is transformed from "me against you" to "us against the world," the classroom becomes a safe haven. When teachers enlist cooperation, create allies in their students and use the language of respect, they promote mutual acceptance, dignity and emotional literacy.

Learning Practice Task: Making Connections

Research has shown that teachers who are able to build close and trusting connections to students do the following: Create one-to-one time with students, create networks with parents, family members, friends, and neighbors of students, build a sense of community among students within the classroom, and develop rituals and traditions within the classroom.

Activity Directions: Working with a peer, list some ways you could develop these aspects.

1. Create one-to-one time with students.

_____

_____

_____

_____

_____

2. Create networks with parents, family members, friends, and neighbors of students.

_____

_____

_____

_____

_____

3. Build a sense of community among students within the classroom.

_____

_____

_____

_____

_____

4. Develop rituals and traditions within the classroom.

_____

_____

_____

_____

_____

Learning Practice Task: Demonstrating Caring

Activity Directions: Working in groups of three or four:

List all the ways you might ascertain from students whether they perceive you as caring.

_____

_____

_____

Some important characteristics of a caring community are: (1) respectful listening, (2) honoring multiple voices, (3) self-disclosure and sharing what's important, (4) maintaining personal safety, and (5) building trust.

For each characteristic, list some ideas about how you could promote these principles.

1. Engage in respectful listening?

_____

_____

_____

2. Honor multiple voices?

_____

_____

_____

3. Support students in disclosing and sharing what's important to them?

_____

_____

_____

4. Maintain personal safety?

_____

_____

_____

5. Build trust?

_____

_____

_____

Questions for Self-reflection

What makes you feel safe?

What would you need to communicate to students so that they feel safe to be vulnerable?

How can you create that kind of safety in your class?

Chapter 4

Keeping Communication Channels Open

Styles of Talk

To transform the traditional classroom into a learning community, students need to feel secure, not only in terms of physical safety but psychological security as well. Students need to feel free to express themselves, feel valued as group members, and accepted as individuals. By the dialogue they create with students, teachers play a critical role in modeling freedom of expression and acceptance. Creating a classroom environment that embraces a spirit of acceptance necessitates that the teacher's style of talk manifests the language of acceptance, encouragement and respect.

Fostering student self-evaluation will require that teachers restructure their discourse patterns and pay particular attention to the language they use when giving feedback to students. Most responses to others in general, but especially to students, are judgmental. Certainly teachers must at times exercise control and serve in an evaluative and judgmental role, but there are many instances in which teachers can allow students to make their own judgments about the appropriateness of their behavior and the quality of their work. The process of evaluating and judging students inhibits acceptance.

The Potential Perils of Praise as a Management Tool

Promoting a democratic classroom involves supporting students in self-evaluation and self-reflection so that they will learn self-management and self-control. With this end in mind, the traditional wisdom of teacher praise can be challenged on the grounds that praise conditions students to seek outside evaluation for accomplishments rather than develop responsibility for their own behavior (Larrivee, 1997).

Although praise can have positive effects on student behavior, there is substantial evidence that the use of praise can also have undesirable effects. Effective use of praise is not related to quantity or the frequency of praise but rather the qualitative use of praise, considering when and how to use praise.

As students get older they become less extrinsically motivated and more intrinsically motivated. Hence, in order for praise to remain effective, it needs to be matched to students' developmental levels. This calls for teachers to move away from strictly evaluative praise and move toward encouraging personal satisfaction, self-reflection, and analysis by calling on students to assess their performance by their own standards, feelings, and sense of accomplishment. This shift is illustrated in the following examples of age-appropriate teacher responses.

Primary (Evaluative)	Upper Elementary (Personal Satisfaction)	Secondary (Self-reflection)
That's a wonderful drawing.	I bet you're proud of your drawing.	Your drawing has a a unique perspective.
You did a great job on the test.	You must be very pleased about getting nearly every answer correct.	Your reading comprehension score was lower than your vocabulary score. Is that what you expected?

In discussing the conditions for delivering effective praise, Brophy (1981) noted that depending on a student's prior experience with feedback and the way it is delivered, praise may serve as a reinforcer, a punisher, or as a powerless antecedent that has no effect on either the alteration of inappropriate behavior or the continuation of desired behavior. He made the distinction between feedback relative to the accuracy of a student's answer and praise in general, concluding that providing feedback about whether student answers are correct, not indiscriminate praise, relates positively to student learning. While it is often recommended that low-achieving students be praised for putting forth minimal effort, Brophy also questioned the practice of profusely praising low-achieving students for trivial accomplishments.

If students get used to being praised all the time, they come to interpret the absence of praise as a negative statement. Although praise can generate disappointment for those students who don't receive it, it can make others frightened at the prospect of not being able to live up to expectations. "Will I be able to keep this up?" "What if I mess up? Then what will my teacher think of me?" It's important to be realistic in giving praise. If everything is *super*, *great*, or *right on*, these words lose their meaning as superlatives. Too much of the same pat phrase leads to satiation, and the praise dissolves into meaninglessness. Praise should be gauged to fit the accomplishment. The amount and degree of praise should be commensurate with the extent of effort rendered.

If you praise students just to try to make them feel better, they'll see right through it. Such false praise can cause students to lose faith and become discouraged, thinking "Gee, am I really that bad that he has to praise me for this!" Nonetheless, honest, sincere, realistic praise that is not manipulative and that stays focused on both the issue at hand and the student can be helpful (Gootman, 1997).

Dreikurs clearly distinguishes between praise and encouragement and makes a strong case against the use of praise, favoring instead the language of encouragement (Dreikurs, Grunwald, & Pepper, 1982). Praise positively evaluates students' performance, on the other hand, encouragement conveys teacher respect and belief in students' capabilities. Through encouragement teachers give purpose to learning and facilitate the development of a positive self-image. When teachers construe ability as an acquirable skill, deemphasizing competitive social comparison while emphasizing self-comparison of progress and personal accomplishments, they help students build a sense of self-efficacy that promotes academic achievement (Bandura, 1993).

Praise conditions students to seek outside evaluation for their accomplishments rather than develop responsibility for their own behavior. Encouragement recognizes efforts, not necessarily achievements, and stimulates motivation from within allowing students to become aware of their own strengths. While praise conditions students to measure their worth by their ability to please others, encouragement teaches students to evaluate their own progress and make their own decisions, which is in line with Dreikurs emphasis on the democratic classroom.

Ginott (1972) is similarly concerned about the drawbacks of using praise, especially when it is judgmental. He distinguished between evaluative (judgmental) praise and appreciative (nonjudgmental) praise. As with negative comments, praise can have detrimental effects on forming a positive self-image. Using praise to tell students they are good because they know the right answer, or equating "knowing the right answer" with "being good," is dangerous. Teachers should refrain from making character judgments when commenting on correct answers.

Gordon (1974) also makes several assertions about praise. Teachers almost universally resist the notion that praise could serve as a roadblock or nonfacilitative response when responding to messages that indicate a student is experiencing a problem. He notes that praise can often "fall on deaf ears" when the student is experiencing a problem. In these times, even positive evaluation in the form of praise can bring about defensiveness.

Brophy on Praise

Teacher praise can include both general praise and praise specific to academic performance, as well as attempts to provide positive encouragement, control behavior, or model appropriate behavior. Brophy (1981) in his review of the research on teacher praise concluded that indiscriminate praise or mere frequency of praise is not positively related to student learning. However, providing feedback as to the correctness of student responses, with moderate levels of praise issued for quality responses, is positively related to student learning. He cautioned that when students are praised every time they sit up straight, wait in line, listen, or engage in routine behaviors, they may experience rewards as silly or irrelevant.

In order for praise to be effective, it should be:

- Spontaneous rather than planned;
- Sincere rather than insincere or rote;
- Credible rather than given effusively for trivial accomplishments;
- Specific rather than general, specifying the particular behavior being praised; and
- Contingent on performance which warrants recognition, rather than random.

Additional characteristics of effective praise include:

- Praise should reward effort as well as success.
- Praise should be given because students deserve it, not because they seek it.
- Praise should be accompanied by congruent nonverbal actions (e.g., voice, gestures, body language). If students get conflicting messages they can respond negatively.
- Praise given to low-achieving students for trivial accomplishments can actually worsen, rather than improve students' functioning. Students may doubt their own ability or lose confidence, if they perceive that their performance does not warrant praise, leading students to have thoughts such as:

"She must really think I'm hopeless if she praises me for that!"

"What's the matter with him? How could he think that was good?"

Gordon on Praise

Teachers have been trained to reinforce good behavior, as determined by the teacher, by systematically dispensing rewards, and among these are praise, positive evaluation, or kind words of support.

Gordon (1974) makes the following points about praise.

- When a student is experiencing a problem, it is often accompanied by personal dissatisfaction. Praise when the student is in this state either goes "unheard," makes the student feel that the teacher doesn't really understand, or provokes an even stronger defense of the student's low evaluation of him/herself. If the positive evaluation does not fit with the student's self-image, it may invoke anger as the student may perceive it as an attempt at manipulation.

- When praise is consciously employed as a technique for influencing students to choose some behavior deemed desirable by the teacher, there is a good chance that students will perceive such praise as insincere, intended primarily to meet the teacher's needs.

- In the classroom setting, praise given to one student, or a few, often will be translated by the other students as negative evaluation of them. Similarly, a student who has become accustomed to receiving frequent evaluative praise may feel negatively evaluated when he/she does not get praised. Students grow to depend on praise—even demand it.

- For some students, public praise can be embarrassing.

- When the student is not experiencing a problem, praise which is a spontaneous and genuine verbal response to a student's performance can be effective.

Ginott on Praise

Ginott warns of the "perils of praise." His concern with praise relates to the potential negative effects on the development of a positive self-image. He makes the following points about praise.

- Teachers use praise to manipulate students' feelings about themselves. Praise such as "You are such a good girl" creates a dependence on others for approval and self-validation. A preferable response would be "I can see you've really been working hard."

- Teachers should comment on specific acts and refrain from attributing qualities of a student's work to the student's personality. By merely describing the circumstances, students can then draw their own conclusions and make their own judgments about their behavior and/or work. For example, when commenting on written work the teacher can give personal reactions (e.g., "I'm really excited about this idea.") or pose questions which will extend the student's thinking (e.g., "How has this awareness affected you?").

- When teachers use praise to tell students they are good because they know the right answer, students logically conclude that they are bad when they do not know the answer. This equating of knowledge with goodness is dangerous. Teachers should use comments for correct answers which carry no evaluation of the student's personality, such as "fine," "exactly," "that's correct," or "you're right."

- When teachers praise students for behavior they want to encourage, the message students get is that poor behavior is what the teacher expected. Students often live up to such perceived negative expectations.

- Teachers should express their appreciation without using evaluative language. Rather than saying, "You behaved so well at the assembly," a comment such as "I'm delighted we could all enjoy the assembly" is preferable. Evaluative praise puts teachers in a position of judgment, signifying a higher status level.

- Evaluative praise is often an attempt by the teacher to ensure desired behavior. When students feel that the praise is not sincere, but delivered to manipulate them into behaving in a certain way, they can harbor resentment.

Would you appreciate this comment from a student?

"You can teach a fine lesson, when you want to."

You would probably consider it disrespectful. In the same vein, you shouldn't say to students what you yourself would find condescending.

Rather than evaluative praise, teachers should:

- Provide honest recognitions without value judgments,
- Describe their own feelings,
- Comment on student efforts.

In summary, nonevaluative praise communicates appreciation and acceptance while allowing students to make their own evaluations about their behavior and work.

Dreikurs on Praise

Dreikurs makes a clear distinction between praise and encouragement. He takes the position that continuous encouragement is a crucial element in the prevention of problem behavior. Through encouragement teachers give purpose to learning and facilitate the development of a positive self-image.

Praise consists of words that positively evaluate students' performance.

- Praise promotes the idea that a product is worthless unless it receives praise.
- Praise conditions students to seek outside evaluation for their accomplishments.
- Praise perpetuates the attitude, "What am I going to get out of this?"

Encouragement consists of words or actions that convey teacher respect and belief in students' capabilities.

Praise versus Encouragement

With Praise Students Learn:	With Encouragement Students Learn:
1. To measure worth by ability to conform.	1. To be self-confident and responsible for their own behavior.
2. To measure worth by ability to please others.	2. To evaluate their own progress and make their own decisions.
3. To fear disapproval.	3. To accept their imperfections.
4. To set unrealistic standards for themselves.	4. To accept efforts of self and others.
5. To fear failure.	5. To want to persevere with tasks.
6. To be competitive.	6. To use talents and efforts for the good of all.
7. To get ahead at the expense of others.	7. To appreciate the successes of others as well as their own.

Learning Practice Task: Considering Teacher Praise

Activity Directions: Based on the material presented on teacher praise, answer the following questions.

1. What are the common themes that emerge regarding the potential dangers of teacher praise?

_____

_____

_____

2. What is your own position on the use of teacher praise?

_____

_____

_____

3. Complete the following: This exercise has caused me to reconsider my thinking about teacher praise in the following way:

_____

_____

_____

Alternatives to Praise: Encouraging Personal Satisfaction, Self-reflection, and Self-evaluation

Transforming the classroom into a democratic community requires that the teacher support student self-evaluation, self-management, and self-control by finding ways to give students decision-making power. Styles of talk that support such learning communities make two very important distinctions:

1. Teacher talk to students distinguishes between the *deed* and the *doer*.
2. Teacher talk to students distinguishes between a student's *work* and a student's *worth*.

When these two distinctions are made clear, the teacher communicates the fundamental principle of valuing. The type of teacher talk that aligns with this principle is nonevaluative and nonjudgmental. It is the language of respect.

Distinguishing Between the Deed and the Doer

Most of our responses to others, especially students, are judgmental. We judge a behavior to be positive or negative and respond accordingly in judgmental language—"that's good" or "that's bad." Often we judge a behavior as good or appropriate based on our own comfort zone. We project our own intolerance for certain behaviors and consequently make a value judgment about the behavior of others. More simply stated, because we don't like a particular behavior, we don't want others to act that way. We decide that they shouldn't act that way, and we reject their behavior. Sometimes we may go even further to reject the person as well.

One alternative to using evaluative language when responding to students is to provide a simple description of the student's behavior, ensuring that the words chosen are not value-laden. When responding to inappropriate behavior, nonjudgmental descriptions of the student's behavior communicate that while you may disapprove of the behavior you don't reject the student. The following examples compare nonjudgmental descriptions of student behavior with judgmental statements about the student.

Nonjudgmental Description	Judgmental Statement about Student
This is the third time this week you've been late.	You're being irresponsible.
Your work hasn't been turned in for the past two days.	You're just lazy.
Tyrone, you're not contributing to your group.	You're being inconsiderate.

Clearly, nonjudgmental descriptions of a student's behavior are far more likely than judgmental statements about the student to solicit a dialogue in which the student takes responsibility for his/her behavior.

Descriptive Not Personality Praise

Although the use of praise is usually heralded as a desirable way to build up students' self-concept, praising students who are troubled often has a negative effect. According to Long and Morse (1996), when working with students with low self-esteem and a history of failure, praise can have effects opposite of those intended. These students may feel comments such as "you're great" and "you're the best" are not an accurate assessment. Instead of making the student feel better, they introduce additional stress and often lead to feelings of guilt. Such students may draw any of the following conclusions.

- My teacher is a jerk and is lying to me.
- I guess I had a lucky day. I happened to hit the bulls-eye today, but it will never happen again.
- I'm not worthy of such wonderful praise, and I find it hard to take.
- I'll have to show you I don't deserve such praise.

They recommend that teachers differentiate between descriptive and personality praise, advocating for the latter. Descriptive praise deals only with the students' efforts and behavior without attaching any evaluation. The important impact is the positive message the student self-imposes after assessing the teacher's comment. Teachers telling students they are terrific is not as helpful as when students tell themselves they are competent and worthy. Such positive appraisals promote self-esteem and investment in learning.

Descriptive praise: "Jerome, I noticed you worked at your desk for 15 minutes, and when you needed some help you raised your hand and waited until I could get to you."

Self-appraisal: "I showed a lot of self-control today, and I'm learning to follow the rules, good for me!"

Nonjudgmental responses facilitate the development of responsible behavior by granting students the responsibility for their behavior. Transforming from evaluative to nonevaluative responses will require a restructuring of classroom discourse. While for some, self-reflection in the form of self-questioning will be all that it will take to curtail judgmental responses, for those whose judgmental behavior is more entrenched, it will take a more concerted effort.

Because evaluative responses are so ingrained, making the change to giving nonevaluative feedback to students will take a sustained effort to monitor responses to students. Learning to respond in nonjudgmental ways involves changing behavior that is well-ingrained. As a beginning step to learning to replace judgmental responses with non-judgmental responses, teachers may need to devise ways to actively practice new speaking patterns, involving specific self-prompting or cueing strategies for overtly monitoring the way they talk to students.

Personal Rather Than Evaluative Feedback

Evaluative feedback is characterized by judgment (I am the judge, you are the judged) and typically takes the form of "you are ...," "you are a ...," or "your ... is ...." On the other hand, personal feedback makes a personal connection, communicating that you are aware of what's going on with the student and that you want to be supportive. It's feedback from the heart rather than the head. Here are some ways to respond that are personal, supportive, and nonjudgmental.

Response Option	Examples
Share personal position	"I sometimes have the same fears."
	"I'd be angry too."
	"I remember how I felt when that happened to me."
Describe your own feeling about the student's behavior	"I was moved by how you were able to comfort Jake."
	"I appreciate the way you expressed your feelings."
Provide acknowledgment of student's emotional state	"It must be hard to accept that."
	"I know this is a difficult time for you."
Pose questions that help student consider others' perspective	"Have you considered other possible reasons for what he did?"
	"How do you think he is feeling now?"

Monitoring your verbal acceptance of behavior may also be helpful in situations in which you and a particular student are having problems. You could enlist a colleague or another student to record your verbal responses to the particular student. If you find your responses are typically judgmental (negative), you may want to try making acceptant responses and note the student's response.

Your students could also benefit from using acceptant responses with their peers. Students of all ages can be made aware of the difference between judgment and acceptance.

Distinguish Between a Student's Work and a Student's Worth

Teachers promote self-evaluation when they provide encouragement rather than praise, respond with acceptance not judgment, and offer constructive interpretations rather than evaluative feedback or destructive criticism. By encouraging students to set their own standards and deal with their feelings, they learn to look within for the motives of their actions.

When you want to help students solve problems or deal with difficult situations, your job is to build trust in their own capacity to deal effectively with their life situations. What you want to do is facilitate development of their own problem resolution, not provide a solution. Interacting with students in nonjudgmental ways allows new alternatives to surface and helps students become aware that they don't have to accept other's judgments of their actions.

Encouragement

Encouragement consists of words or actions that convey teacher respect and belief in students' capabilities. The following are some characteristics of encouragement.

- Encouragement is available to all, not just to those who achieve at the highest levels.
- Encouragement decreases competition for limited rewards.

- Unlike praise which diminishes in effectiveness as students mature, encouragement is equally effective at any age.
- Encouragement tells students that how they feel about themselves and their own efforts is what is important.
- Encouragement gives students the support they need to continue their efforts.
- Encouragement stimulates motivation from within.
- Encouragement allows students to become aware of their own strengths.
- Encouragement increases risk-taking behaviors and the possibility of students constructing new knowledge because the focus is on effort and not on a certain outcome.
- Encouragement increases the likelihood that students will develop an internal value structure.
- Encouragement supports cooperation and working to make everyone a winner.

By using encouragement, teachers communicate the following messages to students:
- They are accepted as they are.
- Their effort is recognized.
- Their improvement is noticed.
- Trust in their ability to manage themselves constructively.
- The process is as valuable as the end result.

Encouragement is grounded in the core belief that each student can be successful. When teachers use encouragement, they help students feel and believe that they are capable of taking charge of their own lives. Encouragement focuses on what students are doing, rather than on what they are not doing. Giving encouragement recognizes individual differences in the learning style, rate, and effort it takes to achieve desired results. A fundamental premise for using encouragement over praise is the separation of a student's *work* and *worth*. It communicates that the teacher supports progress and values process rather than end products. It helps students feel accepted for who they are, not for what they can do.

The purpose of encouragement is to provide a description of the students' accomplishment that will enable the student to understand what qualities made the accomplishment possible and worthwhile. It merely describes, leaving students to draw their own conclusions and take control of their own behavior. Encouragement does not evaluate or attempt to control students, rather it leaves an opening for student self-evaluation. When teachers use encouragement they give students the courage to contribute and participate fully by sending the message that everyone's contribution is important.

The Language of Encouragement
The following remarks exemplify encouragement.

- *I noticed you got right to work and got the whole assignment done.*
- *You used very descriptive words in your paragraph.*
- *I know you can do it.*
- *I see you've figured it out.*
- *What did you learn from that mistake?*
- *You have really spent a long time working on your project.*
- *It looks like you put a lot of work into that paper.*
- *You must be proud of the job you did on this.*
- *I see you thought of a new way to put those together.*

Learning Practice Task: Practicing Nonevaluative Praise

Activity Directions: For each of the five alternatives to praise listed below, write two examples.

1. Description of what you see.

_____
_____
_____

2. Personal reaction without value judgment.

_____
_____
_____

3. Description of your own feeling evoked by the student(s).

_____
_____
_____

4. Honest acknowledgment for the student's situation or effort.

_____
_____
_____

5. Question which expands the student's thinking.

_____
_____
_____

Question for Self-reflection

What will you need to do to begin using less praise and more nonjudgmental responses to students?

Responding to Students with Acceptance

In addition to using descriptive, personal, and encouraging feedback, nonjudgmental responses can also communicate acceptance. By using validating, acknowledging, or appreciating responses, teachers not only refrain from evaluating and judging students, they communicate acceptance and respect for students. When teachers respond with acceptance, it keeps the responsibility with the student, yet maintains the teacher's involvement. Such responses help students solve their own problems.

With all of these types of responses, the student is granted the responsibility for his/her behavior. Although we have been socialized to respond to others in judgmental ways, acceptant responses are preferable to judgmental responses, whether they be judgmental-positive or judgmental-negative, because they recognize that each individual is ultimately responsible for him/herself.

Validating Acceptant Responses

When teachers respond with validating responses to students, they recognize and respond to the feelings that underlie students' behavior by conveying understanding and acceptance of their feelings. In doing so, the teacher neither encourages nor discourages the feelings. Often teacher messages tell students to stop feeling, as if they can turn their feelings off on notice. Feelings are what they are; they need to be acknowledged. They should not be evaluated in terms of right or wrong, good or bad.

Validating feelings means accepting without evaluation, but it doesn't mean the teacher has to condone students' behavior as a result of the feeling. Validating communicates acceptance, while not necessarily agreement. Validating feelings is an important way to connect with students and can help students work through their feelings and move on. Students can have intense feelings, and often they don't know what to do with them (and sometimes teachers don't either). Validating these feelings can make a difference to the student and serves to strengthen relationships between the student and the teacher.

It is important to attend to feelings first, because the student who is upset is not likely to be receptive of any information, directives, or corrections. When teachers validate feelings they show concern and give words to feelings by describing what they see.

"I can see you're very involved in your discussion, but you need to put your materials away now."

Validating feelings doesn't mean that students are exempt from classroom responsibilities, but it does tell them the teacher understands and accepts their frustrations, anger, or hurt.

"Oh, clean up time came too soon. I know it's hard to stop playing."

It acknowledges students' right to have such feelings and lets them know the teacher cares about what they are feeling.

"You look really upset. Do you need to take a break?"

Sometimes the validation may be merely saying you're sorry for the student's feelings without retracting your position about the action you expect from the student.

"I'm sorry about what happened in science class, but you need to calm down and start your work."

Validating feelings helps the teacher to stay in tune with students' feelings. It also helps the teacher refrain from blaming, criticizing, or attacking. When you merely acknowledge your students' feelings, it keeps you from becoming defensive and taking on responsibility for those feelings. When you validate feelings, you are honoring your students' feelings rather than evaluating or denying those feelings. When you become accustomed to hearing an issue with concern for the student, you don't hear it as a criticism and have a need to defend, take responsibility for, or counterattack.

Learning Practice Task: Invalidating Responses

Activity Directions: Working in groups of three, share your responses to the following:

1. Think of a situation where you were disappointed, frustrated, even angry by the way someone responded to you when you were distressed. Briefly describe what happened.
2. Categorize the person's response (e.g., judging, correcting, fixing, denying feelings).
3. What response did you want to hear?
4. How did the response effect how you felt about yourself?
5. How did the response effect how you felt about that person?

Questions for Self-reflection

What type of responses don't you find consoling?

How often do you respond to students in ways that you find supportive or consoling?

When do you want someone to notice your efforts, initiative, or ingenuity?

When do you want someone to validate your feeling?

When do you want someone to show appreciation for who you are?

Appreciating Acceptant Responses

Letting students know that you appreciate them helps students feel important. Taking notice of what students do and what's important to them communicates that they are valued members of your class. Simple statements expressed with interest and enthusiasm communicates to students that the teacher values what they do. Students interpret such acknowledgment to mean they have importance and status. Teacher comments such as the following communicate that the teacher notices what a student does.

"I appreciate the way you worked with Angelo today."

"I know you've worked hard today."

Expressing appreciation is important in several ways. It:
• Communicates interest and enthusiasm,
• Shows recognition,
• Makes students feel valued, and
• Creates a sense of importance.

All these lead to building positive relationships. It's hard to find time to appreciate each student, but students respond to even the slightest signs of attention. Teachers can show appreciation by seizing "appreciation opportunities" to build small rituals into the day that provide moments to connect with students. Some simple ways teachers can show appreciation are:
• Greeting each student every morning or as they enter class;
• Using students' names;
• Making eye contact, nodding, smiling;
• Stopping what you are doing when a student comes to you;
• Shaking hands; and
• Showing obvious pleasure for something a student does.

When teachers make an effort to show appreciation, students get the message: "You don't have to do everything perfect to be accepted. The little things count too—your presence counts."

Learning Practice Task: When No One Notices

Activity Directions: Remember a time you were in a situation where no one noticed you. Working with a partner, share your responses to the questions below.

1. Describe what it felt like not to be appreciated, to be left out.
2. What did you decide to do?
3. Was it helpful or not helpful in dealing with your feelings?

Acknowledging Acceptant Responses

When teachers acknowledge, they accept and show respect for students' point of view or position. They encourage students to express their opinions and show that they value what students have to say. The teacher acknowledges that each student has a right to his or her perspective and thoughtfully responds to student ideas without judgment, as in:

"That's an interesting position. We hadn't been thinking along those lines."

"Suki, I never would have thought of that one!"

Acceptant versus Judgmental Responses

Teacher responses to students' behavior can be categorized as either acceptant or judgmental. Judgmental responses can be either judgmental-positive or judgmental-negative.

- Acceptant responses: recognizing that each individual is ultimately responsible for him/herself and responding with acceptance by a response which is validating, acknowledging or appreciating.
- Judgmental-positive: judging the behavior to be desirable, good or right and responding with an attempt to reinforce it.
- Judgmental-negative: judging the behavior to be undesirable, bad or wrong and responding with an attempt to change it.

Note the difference between acceptant and judgmental responses in the next example:

Leslie slams into your room, throws down his books, and tells you how unfair Mr. James is for reprimanding him.

- **Judgmental (positive):** *"That's OK. When you have problems with him, you can just come in here."* (Leslie is likely to repeat the behavior, since he was rewarded by the teacher solving the problem for him.)
- **Judgmental (negative):** *"Well, if you acted with him the way you are acting right now, I don't blame him."* (Leslie's feelings are ignored, and the relationship between him and the teacher is not enhanced. The problem remains.)
- **Acceptant:** *"I can see you're very upset because Mr. James yelled at you (validating). I'd like to talk with you about it later. Right now we have to get started with math."* (Leslie's feelings are recognized and the teacher communicates concern while still letting him know what's expected.)

Learning Practice Task: Practicing Acceptant Responses

Activity Directions: Working in groups of three, take turns practicing making accepting responses to the following situations. Use each other to get feedback on whether your responses are accepting or judgmental.

1. An upper-elementary age student refuses to work with another student, saying that "He keeps picking on me."

2. A junior-high student hands you a bedraggled-looking homework assignment, sheepishly explaining that she dropped it in a puddle on the way to school.

3. A high-school student tells you he's thinking of dropping out of school.

Critical Reflection on Practice: Analyzing Your Responses to Students

Activity Directions: In your classroom, use a tape recorder or have an observer (peer, aide, student, parent, volunteer) record every personal response you make to students during one lesson or class period. Then transfer the data to the worksheet provided, and classify each response as judgmental-positive, judgmental-negative, or acceptant.

Questions for Self-analysis

1. In which category did most of your responses fall?

2. Combining the first two categories, did you make more judgmental or more acceptant responses?

3. Which type of response is easiest for you? What does that tell you?

4. Select one response you are especially pleased with. What was the probable effect of that response on the student? (You might ask the student for verification.)

5. Select the response you are least satisfied with. What was the probable effect of that response on the student? (Again, you might ask the student for feedback.) Write a better response.

6. Complete the following sentence:

   From my analysis of this data, I see _____

   _____

   _____

   _____

   _____

Suggested Follow-up

As with any activity in which you collect data concerning your classroom behavior, significant changes will occur only with a longterm commitment. Continuous analyses over time, with comparisons drawn and trends noted, are essential if you are serious about changing any aspect of your behavior. Therefore, it is recommended that you repeat this activity several times to monitor your progress.

Worksheet for Analyzing Judgmental and Acceptant Responses to Students

Response	Category Type		
	Judgmental-negative	Judgmental-positive	Acceptant

Another Nonevaluative Response: Asking Students to Make Value Judgments

The idea of acceptance versus judgment is closely aligned with Glasser's (1986) notion of control theory which posits that while we may try to control others' behavior, in actuality, we can only control our own behavior. When we evaluate students' behavior, even with a positive evaluation, we are assuming responsibility for them and attempting to exercise control over them. If you say "That's excellent!" you are implicitly reserving the right to also say "That's awful!" In either case, it is most likely an attempt to control the student by judging the student by some set of standards external to the student.

Glasser (1993) offers another alternative to judgmental responses to students, advocating that teachers call on students to make value judgments about their own behavior. Comments such as "Is that helping the group?" or "What might you do that would be more helpful?" call on students to take responsibility for their behavior and recognize its effect on self as well as others. Glasser challenges teachers to teach students that freedom is tied to responsibility by attempting to motivate students from within, help students establish inner controls, and learn to regulate their own behavior.

Constructive Comments versus Destructive Comments

Constructive comments offer specific assistance while supporting students' efforts and building self-confidence. They communicate acceptance and allow students to draw their own conclusions and make their own judgments about their work. Destructive comments point out errors and are interpreted by students as evidence of their incompetence.

While teachers may fear that correcting students' mistakes diminishes their self-esteem, the sense of not being competent is far more damaging. Self-esteem is enhanced when students experience the confidence of correcting their own mistakes by hard work.

Constructive criticism lets students know they have made a mistake while helping them to embrace feedback as an opportunity to learn and improve. The following comment illustrates constructive criticism.

> *"I see why you might have thought that, but it's not the correct answer. There's one piece of information you overlooked."*

Purposeful critique is constructive feedback that is descriptive, sensitive, and offers a next step for the student to move toward self-correction and, ultimately, the sense of satisfaction of having gotten it right. Purposeful critique is feedback that specifically shows students the way, allowing them to construct what to do next, rather than feel helpless.

> Example: *"That's not the answer. Let's see how you came to that conclusion."*

By interacting with students in a nonjudgmental fashion, teachers encourage student self-evaluation and support student development of self-management skills. Below are some additional examples.

Give personal reactions without value judgments:

> *"I like how you tell a story to make your point."*

> *"I enjoyed the humor in your presentation."*

Describe your own emotional reaction evoked by the student:

> *"I was moved by how you were able to capture what Jake felt like."*

> *"I appreciate the way you expressed your feelings."*

Pose questions which expand the students' thinking:

> *"Have you considered other possible interpretations of what the author meant?"*

> *"Can you relate those two ideas?"*

Such constructive comments support students' efforts and build self-confidence while allowing students to evaluate their own work. Giving constructive criticism and purposeful critique enables students to develop confidence by knowing they can do something about their errors and seeing their own improvement.

Constructive versus Destructive Written Comments on Student Papers

Teachers can spend hours responding in writing to the written work of students. Many teachers fall victim to the "red-pencil syndrome" where they merely mark everything that's wrong with the student's work. Most of the comments that teachers put on student papers serve to destroy rather than enhance the student's self-concept. Many teacher-made comments and corrections, however subtle, contribute to a hostile environment for students.

Students pay little or no attention to the responses so laboriously made by their teachers. But why should they? Most people try to ignore or downgrade anything that tells them they are less than worthy. No one enjoys having their weak points and mistakes paraded before them, and especially not students.

When commenting on written work, teachers can avoid judgmental responses by sharing personal reactions (e.g., "I'm really excited about this idea") or posing questions which extend the student's thinking (e.g., "How has this awareness affected you?"). They can also make specific comments acknowledging progress (e.g., "You've become much clearer in organizing your points") or state a need for greater clarity (e.g., "I'm not sure what you mean here, can you make this clearer?").

Many of the comments that teachers write on student work or deliver personally can be classified into one of ten categories (Curwin & Fuhrmann, 1975). Five are generally destructive in that they point out errors that students interpret as evidence of their inadequacies. The other five are constructive in that they support the student's efforts and offer specific assistance. While destructive comments discourage students from trying, constructive ones help them build their skills and self-confidence.

––––––––––––

Destructive Comments

1. Simple corrections.

   Mistakes are indicated by a mark, usually an X or a check in red. At a glance, a student can measure his/her inadequacy.

2. Vague references to needed improvement with no specifications of what is needed.

   Often a question mark or a vague reference like *unclear*, *poor*, or *vague* is written in a margin. The student is given no assistance in understanding the reference or how to improve.

3. Comments that indicate the teacher's disagreement but do not provide factual data.

   The student is told that he/she is wrong but not why, or told that his/her opinion is unacceptable. Comments like *"No, Your thinking is fuzzy,"* and *"That's not what the book said,"* especially in matters of opinions, are examples.

4. Sarcastic put-downs.

   "Sure!," "Oh, really?," "Come on, now!," "You don't say!," and similar statements serve only to belittle students and tell them their ideas are unacceptable.

5. Prescriptive corrections of spelling, punctuation, grammar, and other skills.

Students, especially those who are unsure of their skills to begin with, are taught only that they have failed. (These do not include judicious and meaningful suggestions and help in these skill areas.) Examples include: *awkward, poor sentence, rewrite, these aren't sentences, fix.*

Constructive Comments

1. **Personal reactions in which a dialogue between student and teacher is initiated.** Examples:

   This idea excites me.

   Your account of your anger here brought back vivid memories of a similar situation in my life;

   I'm not sure I understand you here, let's talk about it.

2. **Specific suggestions for improvement in which the emphasis is not on what is wrong, but on what can be done to improve.** Examples:

   This argument will be stronger if you use specific examples;

   How did this event follow from the one preceding it? Show the relationship clearly.

3. **Questions designed to extend the student's thinking, especially on the meaning of events and information to him/her.** Examples:

   How has this value affected your life?

   How difficult is it for you to uphold this opinion?

   How has this discovery been important to you?

4. **Corrections of grammar, spelling, punctuation, and other skills that are used sparingly for the purpose of clarifying thought.**

   No more than two or three such corrections on any one paper can probably be assimilated. Unlike the prescriptive corrections indicated previously, which are used simply to show students their mistakes, the focus here is on improving the meaning through better writing, not on pointing out errors. Examples:

   These are fragments, try joining them together to make one complete sentence.

   I can't tell whether you mean … or … . Can you clarify which by rewriting this sentence?

5. **Specific supportive comments that indicate progress and recognize achievement.**

   General supportive comments like *good* and *well done,* though not destructive, are not as constructive as more specific comments that provide definitive and meaningful feedback. Examples:

   You've become much clearer in organizing your presentation.

   This is an excellent use of metaphor!

   _____

Learning Practice Task: Using Constructive Comments

Activity Directions: For each of the five categories of constructive comments, write one of your own comments. Remember the idea is to provide purposefully constructive comments that show students the way to move toward self-correction.

Personal reactions.

_____

_____

_____

Specific suggestions for improvement.

_____

_____

_____

Questions designed to extend the student's thinking.

_____

_____

_____

Corrections of grammar, spelling, punctuation, and other skills for the purpose of clarifying thought.

_____

_____

_____

Specific supportive comments that indicate progress and recognize achievement.

_____

_____

_____

Worksheet for Analyzing Written Comments on Student Papers

Comment	Destructive	Constructive

Critical Reflection on Practice: Evaluating Your Written Comments on Student Papers

Activity Directions: Using the ten categories of destructive and constructive comments, analyze the comments you wrote on at least twenty student papers from a recent set of papers. You can use your latest batch of papers or you can ask students to return old papers and choose some at random. Copy each comment you made onto the worksheet provided. Then classify each one as either destructive or constructive. You can also categorize them by type, using the numbers of the ten types in the list, if you wish. Questions for consideration:

1. Add up the number of destructive comments and the number of constructive comments. What do these numbers say to you about the comments you put on these papers?

2. Which kind of comment, destructive or constructive, is easier for you to make? What does that mean to you?

3. Pick out three comments that you classified as destructive. What do you imagine the students' reactions to these might have been? Rewrite each as a constructive comment.

4. What implications does this activity have for you?

Suggested Follow-up

On the next set of papers that you collect, make only constructive comments. When you return the papers to your students, you might choose to tell them that you have attempted to use only constructive responses. Point out the kind of comments you have made and explain the rationale for doing so. Observe student reactions to the comments.

Inviting versus Inhibiting Communication

Often our communication is all about our personal needs (one-way) and is delivered as a statement of blame (I feel this way . . . and it's your fault). Instead, you want to "invite" your students to participate in a two-way communication, rather than defend against an attack. Inviting communication is reciprocal, with both teacher and student participating in the communication.

When the communication process is no longer reciprocal, that is, one party has taken over the communication, that's an indication that the communication has moved from inviting to inhibiting. Inhibiting communication:
- Invalidates others' feelings, thoughts, wants, and needs;
- Tells others what they should want, feel, think, or do; and
- Advocates for your own position without acknowledging others' positions.

When you inhibit, you shut down two-way communication. You:
- Use the language of disrespect,
- Invoke defenses, and
- Create an adversary.

When you invite, you keep the communication channels open or two-way. You:
- Use the language of respect,
- Enlist cooperation, and
- Create an ally.

Barriers to Communication

Gordon (1974) identified 12 roadblocks to communication. He called them "the dirty dozen" because they all represent messages that inhibit the communication process. When teachers make a conscious choice to confront students with their unacceptable behavior, their confrontation messages typically not only fail to bring about the desired results, they also have a negative effect on students. The best teachers can hope for with such messages is submissive compliance, frequently accompanied by a negative attitudinal response. These roadblocks contain only information about the student, never about the teacher. Hence, students are not likely to be motivated to take the teacher's needs and feelings into consideration. On the contrary, students are usually motivated to fight back or develop other strategies to defeat teachers' attempts to impose their solutions.

The Language of Unacceptance: Roadblocks to Communication

Gordon describes categories of messages that serve to block further communication. Such messages inhibit and sometimes completely stop the two-way process of communication necessary for helping students solve the problems that interfere with their learning. For each category the teacher's behavior and language pattern, the message it sends to students, and students' typical reactions are described.

Gordon's Roadblocks to Communication

Roadblocks 1–5, ordering, threatening, preaching, advising and lecturing in one way or another all communicate unacceptance by offering a solution to the student's problem.

Roadblock	Teacher Behavior	Language Pattern	Message to Student	Typical Reaction
1. Ordering, Commanding, Directing	Telling the student to do something, giving him/her an order or a command.	"You must …." "You will …."	Your feelings or needs are not important.	Fear, resentment, active resistance, testing
2. Warning, Threatening	Telling the student what consequences will occur if he/she does something.	"If you don't, then …." "You'd better, or …."	I have no respect for your needs or wants.	Fear, submission, hostility, testing of threatened consequences
3. Moralizing, Preaching	Telling the student what he/she should or ought to do.	"You ought to …." "You shouldn't …." "It is your responsibility …."	Your judgment cannot be trusted.	Guilt feelings; resistance; defending position even more strongly
4. Advising, Giving Solutions or Suggestions	Telling the student how to solve a problem, giving him/her advice or suggestions, providing answers or solutions.	"Why don't you …." "What I would do is …." "I suggest you …."	You're not capable of solving you own problems.	Dependency on others; feeling misunderstood
5. Lecturing, Teaching, Giving Logical Arguments	Trying to influence the student with facts, counter-arguments, logic, information, or personal opinions.	"Yes, but …." "The facts are …." "You must learn to …."	You're inferior, ignorant.	Feelings of inadequacy, defensiveness, resentment; rejection of argument

Roadblocks 6–8, blaming, labeling and diagnosing all communicate judgment, evaluation, or put-downs.

Roadblock	Teacher Behavior	Language Pattern	Message to Student	Typical Reaction
6. Judging, Criticizing, Blaming	Making a negative judgment or evaluation of the student.	"You're wrong about …." "You're being immature." "You're not thinking clearly."	You're no good.	Accepts judgment as true and feels incompetent, or retaliates with counter-criticism

Roadblock	Teacher Behavior	Language Pattern	Message to Student	Typical Reaction
7. Name-calling, Stereotyping, Labeling	Making the student feel foolish, categorizing, or trying to shame.	"You're just a procrastinator." "You're acting like a baby."	You're unworthy.	Verbal retaliation; making excuses
8. Analyzing, Diagnosing, Interpreting	Telling the student what his/her motives are or analyzing why he/she is doing or saying something.	"You don't really mean that." "You're just trying to get out of doing it." "You feel that way because …."	I have you figured out.	Feel threatened, frustrated, exposed, embarrassed, falsely accused

Roadblocks 9 and 10, praising and reassuring, represent attempts by the teacher to make a student feel better by making a problem go away or denying that a real problem exists.

Roadblock	Teacher Behavior	Language Pattern	Message to Student	Typical Reaction
9. Praising, Agreeing, Giving Positive Evaluations	Offering a positive evaluation or judgment, agreeing	"You're pretty smart. I'm sure you'll figure it out" "Well, I think …."	You don't really have a problem. Your problem is not important.	Dependency, embarrassment; feeling patronized or manipulated to behave in desired way
10. Reassuring, Sympathizing, Consoling	Trying to make the student feel better by talking the student out of his/her feelings, trying to make the feelings go away, or denying the strength of the feelings	"You'll feel better tomorrow." "All students feel …."	Stop feeling the way you do.	Feeling misunderstood; reacting with hostility

Roadblock 11, questioning, is probably the most frequently used. Teachers most often use questions when they feel they need more facts because they intend to solve the student's problem by coming up with the best solution, rather than help the student to solve the problem him/herself.

Roadblock	Teacher Behavior	Language Pattern	Message to Student	Typical Reaction
11. Probing, Questioning, Interrogating	Trying to find reasons, motives, causes; searching for more information to help student solve the problem	"Why did you wait so long?" "What made you do that?"	I don't trust you.	Defensiveness; feeling interrogated; reacting with avoidance, non-answers, half-truths or lies

Roadblock 12, diverting, consists of messages teachers use to avoid having to deal with the student at all by trying to change the subject or divert the student.

Roadblock	Teacher Behavior	Language Pattern	Message to Student	Typical Reaction
12. Withdrawing, Diverting, Being Sarcastic, Humoring	Trying to get the student away from the problem; withdrawing or pushing the problem aside; distracting or kidding	"Let's talk about more pleasant things." "Come on, let's …." "Just forget about it."	I'm really not interested. I'd rather not deal with this.	Hurt, put down, put off, dismissed

Learning Practice Task: Personal Reaction to Roadblocks

Activity Directions: Think of a time when you shared a problem situation with another person who responded with roadblocks.

• How did you react?

_____

_____

_____

Spend a few minutes discussing your situation and your response with a peer.

• Were your reactions similar?

_____

_____

• Were your feelings similar?

_____

_____

Remember, if roadblocks have these effects on you, they will have the same effects on your students.

Inhibiting Communication: The Language of Disrespect

Sending you-messages, moralizing with *should*s, and using trigger words such as *always* and *never* communicate a lack of respect for students. The following section points out some communication-inhibiting traps to avoid and inauthentic talk patterns that foster distrust.

Inhibiting Communication: Using You-language

Meaningful communication often breaks down when teachers continually tell students what's wrong with them and what they shouldn't be doing. By pointing an accusatory finger, they put students on the defensive. Such messages are usually expressed in you-language and often frame problems in the past, i.e., you'll never . . ., you always . . ., can't you ever . . . .

You-language is harmful in several ways because it:

• Denies students responsibility for themselves,
• Fails to show understanding or empathy for students,
• Implies blame, and
• Ignores the teacher's own feelings (which the teacher may or may not be aware of).

Making "should" statements has a similar effect. Saying to students "You should do this" or "You should have done this" makes you their voice of conscience. The typical response to such moralization or implied or expressed criticism is for the student to attempt to prove that what he or she did was right, as in the statement "I wasn't being disrespectful, I was just telling it like it is." Often the student takes it one step further by trying to justify the behavior under the circumstances. Having to defend oneself is often accompanied by a counterattack in retaliation for a character assault, either implicitly or explicitly making the teacher just as bad, or even worse, as in the following example. "I can talk however I want to you. You never say anything nice to me, or anyone else for that matter!" The battle lines are drawn as each tries to be right and make the other wrong.

These kinds of messages serve to block further productive communication and typically move the interaction to confrontation, a battle of attack and counterattack, creating an adversarial climate rather than a spirit of cooperation. Such messages inhibit, and sometimes completely stop, the two-way process of communication that is essential for building and maintaining relationships.

Inhibiting Communication	You-language
Demanding	You will ....
Threatening	You better or ....
Moralizing	You should learn to ....
Name calling	You are rude.
Blaming	You made me ....
Judging	You are being immature.
Interrogating	Why did you ...?
Humiliating	You should have ....
Degrading	If you had any feelings you would ....
Invalidating	You'd feel better if ....
Manipulating	Don't you think you should ...?
Globalizing	Why can't you ever ...?

The first seven ways of inhibiting communication above were described previously as part of Gordon's "dirty dozen." Descriptions of the remaining five types of inhibiting communications follow.

- Humiliating is trying to instill guilt or shame with comments like, "You ought to know better."
- Degrading comments are indirectly derogatory, as in "That wasn't too bright" implying that only someone who is stupid would do that!
- Invalidating is dismissing feelings, ideas or opinions, as in the comment "You shouldn't feel that way."
- Manipulating comments indirectly try to get others to do what you think they should do, as in "It's none of my business, but I wouldn't do that."
- Globalizing frames behavior in global terms by using words like *always, never*, or *ever*, such as "You're never doing what you are supposed to be doing."

Habits of Language to Break

Communicating in inauthentic language is demeaning and disrespectful to students. While these language differences may seem subtle to teachers, students know exactly what the teacher means. Older students think the teacher is "talking down" to them. Inauthentic language also gives students an opening to mock teachers, as in the following example:

"Don't you think we've had enough of that!" leaves the teacher wide open for a retort from the student like *"No, I don't"* or *"Who's had enough?"*

Third Party Talk: We, Let's, It, Some People

Using *we* and *let's* is inauthentic communication because it implies that the teacher will participate too, and that's usually not true.

Let's see if we can all sit up straight.
Let's cut it out.
We are supposed to . . . .
Some people in here . . . .

Providing Ultimatums Disguised As Choices

Telling students that they have a choice is a popular recommendation. However, when the real message is "Do what I say, or I will punish you" it is an inauthentic choice. The following example is an ultimatum.

> *"You can put that away or go to the principal's office,"* [really says, do one of the two things I tell you].

Telling Students What They Need

Need statements should be about what the teacher needs, not what he/she wants students to do. Rather than say "You need to put that away now" the teacher should say directly what the teacher needs or wants, as in "I need you to stop talking until I finish giving the directions" or "I want you to put that away."

Psuedodirections: Directions Disguised as Questions

When giving directions, teachers give "psuedodirections," often in the form of questions that aren't really questions at all—they're directives. Rather than direct language, they use indirect language, hinting instead of issuing clear directives. Teachers give psuedodirections because they do not want to sound harsh or autocratic. They want to appear to be nice by making their directives more pleasing and friendly. They think they are being tactful by not using direct language, but such psuedodirections not only fail to give students clear direction, they make teachers appear weak and phony, fostering distrust. Speaking to students directly, unambiguously, and honestly builds trust. Following are examples of psuedodirections.

Appearing to give students choices

Asking if the student is able to or if the student would like to, as if there is a choice.

- *Would you like to answer the next question?* [means answer the question]
- *Bud, could you do the next problem?* [means do the problem]
- *Can you write your name in the upper right corner?* [means write your name]

Disguised solicitation of students' opinion

The real intent is to tell students what they should be doing, not soliciting an opinion.

- *Don't you think it would be better if you . . . ?*
- *Isn't it time to . . . ?*
- *Don't you think you should clean out your desk?*

Hedging with Tag-on Questions

When you hedge saying what you want or need by adding tag-on questions you give the impression that you need to seek approval for your requests.

- *It's time to put that away, don't you think?*
- *You've had enough time to work on that, haven't you?*

Sarcastic Questions

Rather than make a direct request of a student, the teacher sarcastically asks a rhetorical question.

- *Could we now get back to work?*
- *Don't you think that's enough?*
- *Are you done yet?*

Other Communication-inhibiting Traps to Avoid

Teachers often think they have to prove to students that they are right. Doing that serves to inhibit communication and is likely to start a fault-finding cycle with the student.

- Trying to prove you're right (I'm not being unfair. You ....)
- Having to have the last word (But you ...; I did it because ....)
- Extracting a confession: attempting to get the student to admit wrong-doing (Here's why you are wrong ...; Do you realize ...?; Why did you ...?)
- Giving logical arguments for why the student is wrong (Can't you see that ...?)

Inviting Communication: The Language of Respect

The goal of any relationship is the mutual meeting of needs and desires. Expressing dissatisfaction can be done in a way that is either facilitative and respectful or in a way that is obstructive and disrespectful, making it more difficult to maintain an amicable relationship. Using I-language and making impact-statements are two approaches that are facilitative and respectful.

Using I-language to Invite Communication

The term I-language represents a broader concept than the term I-message which connotes a particular format. I-language serves the primary function of allowing students to maintain self-respect and responsibility for their own behavior. With I-language, teachers speak from their own perspective and clarify for students why they're concerned while respecting students' capacity to make appropriate adjustments on their own. Using I-language instead of you-language helps maintain a positive relationship by promoting consideration by others of the impact of their actions and fosters a willingness to change. Such nonblameful messages don't require justification because they don't imply a negative evaluation. When there is no accusation of wrongful behavior, there is no need to become defensive, self-worth is not at stake.

Contrary to what is typically presented, the main purpose of using I-language is to avoid attributing blame, by keeping the focus on why the behavior is a problem; expressing feelings is secondary. Teachers don't have strong feelings about everything that happens in the classroom. Frequently, in the classroom setting, clarifying the impact is more essential than expressing the feeling. The goal is to effect a change in disposition, allowing students the opportunity to correct their own behavior.

When teachers use I-language, they encourage students to choose to change the behavior that is causing a problem. They provide students with data for stopping and thinking about the ramifications of their actions, while leaving the decision in their hands.

I-language has a very different affect on students than you-language. As an example, suppose you are frustrated because one of your students is constantly interrupting you while another student is responding to a question. The behavior (interrupting) is causing you a problem—you are feeling frustrated. If your message to the student is "Jack, you're being rude" you are in effect transferring your frustration into a label of the student's character. By labeling the student's behavior, you avoid communicating your own feeling of frustration. If you send a message that accurately portrays what is going on with you, it will inevitably be in I-language, as in:

"Jack, I get frustrated when you keep interrupting, because I can't hear either of you when you're both talking."

While using I-language communicates what the teacher is experiencing, you-language is a negative judgment about the student. From Jack's perspective, he hears an evaluation of how bad he is in the first case and a statement about the teacher in the second case. When you use I-language, you take responsibility for your own reaction and you leave the responsibility for the student's behavior with the student.

I-language has the following advantages.

I-language:

- Doesn't require justification from the student,
- Is nonthreatening,
- Provides a concrete reason for the teacher's concern,
- Doesn't imply a negative judgment of the student,
- Supports students' consideration of the impact of their behavior,
- Fosters acceptance of responsibility for change,
- Promotes a willingness to change the behavior,
- Maintains a positive relationship, and
- Models appropriate expression of negative (or positive) emotions.

Making students aware of the impact of their actions, without trying to make them feel guilty or ashamed, tends to put them in a cooperative frame of mind. Stating the impact of the actions of students is valuable for two reasons. First, it helps the teacher see more clearly why he/she was bothered (or pleased) by what the student did. Pointing out why the behavior is a problem can sometimes help the teacher recognize when feelings are stemming from enforcing an expectation that may not be interfering with a productive learning climate. And secondly, telling students about the impact of their actions can help clarify for them the results of their actions.

Constructing an I-Message

I-messages convey only the teacher's reaction and concern. Using I-messages transfers the focus from students to teacher by refocusing attention on the needs and feelings of the teacher. I-massages communicate far more than you-messages. They let students know how the teacher feels, why he or she feels that way, and what they can do. I-messages communicate the teacher's feelings to students about how their behavior affects the teacher's ability to teach and maintain a productive learning environment. When teachers send I-messages they share personal feelings by stating facts about their feelings in the situation without blaming the student for those feelings.

In contrast to expressing irritation using I-language, aggressively expressing irritation using you-language tries to make the student responsible for causing the teacher's feelings. In the following example, the first statement is a you-message, and the second statement is an I-message.

"You really make me mad when you always butt in! Why do you have to do that?"

"When I'm constantly interrupted, I lose my train of thought and then I start to get irritated. I'd like you to wait until I've finished speaking."

Typically, an I-message has three parts. First, students need to know exactly what's causing the problem.

- Part 1 is a nonblameful description of the behavior, situation or event. For example:

  "When materials are left everywhere, ..." [represents a condition or situation, whereas]

  "When you interrupt, ..." [represents a specific student behavior of concern].

- Part 2 is the feeling or emotional state associated with the behavior or situation. This component states the feelings generated as a result of the problem. For example:

  "When your feet are in the aisle [description], *I'm afraid someone might fall"* [feeling].

- Part 3 is the tangible or concrete effect of the behavior, or the condition it brings about. This component addresses the tangible effect on the teacher by describing why the teacher has a problem. For example:

  "When materials are left everywhere [description], *I get annoyed* [feeling] *because I have to spend my time picking them up"* [effect].

Using I-language also provides an opportunity to help students develop empathy for others. While students may not agree with your policies and classroom practices, they can't argue with your feelings. Likewise, you shouldn't argue with theirs. A statement like the following leaves little opportunity for students to take issue.

"I'm disappointed about the way you behaved when I was out of the room."

It is important to make sure that your claimed effect is credible in the eyes of your students. Actually stating why the behavior is a problem causes teachers to consider whether student behaviors actually have a tangible effect. If there is no tangible effect, it will be hard to convince students they should change their behavior.

The usual format of an I-message is:

"When ... [description of behavior], I feel ... [feeling state] because ..." [concrete effect or problem the behavior creates].

"When ... I feel ... because ...," or *"I feel ... when ... because ...."*

Learning to Use I-language

The following two questions can help guide teachers in effectively utilizing I-language:

1. Will students identify with my concern?
2. Will students be invited to make the right choice on their own?

It is not necessary to always use the specific components, you can begin to practice I-language by just beginning your communication with the word *I*, as in:

"I'm very tired because I only got three hours sleep last night. I just can't take all this noise right now."

"I don't want you to ... because ...."

"I'd like you to ...."

"I have a problem with ...."

Sometimes you may just want to make a statement about what you are worried or concerned about, as in

"I'm concerned that everyone won't get to say what they want to say."

"I'm worried for you when I hear you talk like that, because I'm afraid that ...."

When commenting about something that has already happened it may only be necessary to say:

"I was disappointed that you missed class yesterday."

It might also be helpful to think to yourself, "This is a problem for me because I have to . . . ." If you can complete the sentence to yourself, then you can communicate exactly why the behavior is causing a problem.

I-language is particularly effective for helping teachers express difficult negative feelings, as in:

"I don't like stuff being thrown at me."

"I don't want to be treated that way."

"I'm really angry because . . . ."

"I'm becoming more and more aggravated by your tone of voice."

Sometimes for the classroom setting, it is also helpful to add what you'd like the student to do, what you want to happen, or what would improve the situation, by adding a fourth component. This last component could be in addition to or in place of either the feeling or the effect, as in:

"When . . . I feel . . . because . . . and I'd like . . . ."

"When you're out of your seat, it distracts the students around you. I want you to stay in your seat until this activity is over."

The "I want" part of the I-message should be used purposefully. While excluding it gives the student maximum opportunity to offer his/her own ideas for dealing with the situation, including it gives the student specific information as to what you want to see happen.

I-messages don't always have to express a concern or negative feeling. They can be used to make a positive assertion, as in:

"I felt really proud when you were selected as student-of-the-month."

I-language may at first seem artificial, but much of the awkwardness is due to unfamiliarity. As you practice and adapt the language to your own style, I-language will begin to sound more and more natural. While the I-statement format is initially presented as a formula, after you become comfortable using I-language, you can interchange the three components or omit parts so that your message matches your own natural style of speaking. For example, the "I feel" part of the statement can be omitted. While saying *I feel* does clarify precisely what you're feelings are and may reduce misunderstandings, describing your feelings may be inappropriate in some situations or you may not think stating your feelings is necessary.

Some teachers may not be comfortable expressing their feelings in the classroom or may think that a statement of feelings is inappropriate in certain situations or with particular students. The primary reason for using I-language in the classroom is to avoid blame-attributing language by focusing on the impact of the behavior, not the students' shortcomings. Often clarifying the impact is more important to communicate than the teacher's feeling.

Summary

The critical elements of I-language are that it: (1) speaks from the teacher's perspective, (2) clarifies why the behavior is a problem, (3) gives students data about their behavior, (4) communicates respect for students' ability to make their own choices, and (5) is non-blameful. Delivering an I-message is usually just the first move. You want the I-message to begin a dialogue which leads to students solving their own problems.

Once teachers are well-versed in delivering I-messages, they can teach their students to use them. With students, it's important to stress that sharing their feelings helps others understand why they might be acting the way they are. Students can be coached to make statements like the following.

"When you interrupt me, I get confused and forget what I was saying," [rather than] *"Hey man, I'm talking."*

"I feel sad when you won't let me in the game because I have no one to play with," [rather than] *"You jerks, who wants to play with you anyway!"*

Cautions

It is important to note that while I-messages have many advantages over you-messages, there are some potential drawbacks to consider. I-messages can:

- Involve the risk of self-disclosure,
- Reveal your own vulnerability,
- Elicit inappropriate levels of intimacy or self-disclosure, or
- Go "unheard" by some students.

Even the best I-statement won't be effective unless it is delivered appropriately, that is, unless there is congruence between your nonverbal and verbal message. If your words are perfect but your tone of voice, facial expression, and posture all are communicating a you-message, the student is likely to hear a blaming message and respond defensively. And even if both your words and stance are sending an I-message, the student may still become defensive. Sometimes students can be so uncooperative or unreachable that even an I-message will not facilitate communication. However, I-messages certainly have a far greater potential than you-messages for keeping the communication channels open.

When you send an I-message you are exposing yourself as you really are and revealing your own vulnerability for being hurt or upset. Occasionally, I-messages can elicit inappropriate levels of intimacy or self-disclosure.

Potential Pitfalls to Avoid When Learning to Use I-language

When you let others know exactly what's causing the problem with a nonblameful description of the situation and address the concrete effect on you, it communicates why the behavior is causing a problem for you. It is a factual account without "editorial commentary." When evaluation creeps in, you get messages that may sound nonblameful but are actually blameful. They are in an I-language format, but are actually you-messages in disguise, as the following examples illustrate.

"When I find I can't trust certain troublemakers in here . . . ."

"When you act like a bully . . . ."

Often when you attempt to communicate your true feelings, you actually express not your feelings but attitudes, interpretations, or opinions. For example, if you say "I feel you did that on purpose," you have expressed only your interpretation. If you say "I feel like leaving," you have expressed what the behavior leads you to want to do, not a feeling. In this case, the feeling behind this statement is most likely hurt or anger.

Or, you may disguise a feeling behind a message that's a statement of opinion such as saying "I feel you're wrong." This phrase doesn't express any feeling; it is merely your position. Another example of a disguised you-message is: "When you . . ., I feel you are being inconsiderate." "I feel" is substituted for "I think" transforming the message from a true feeling message to a blaming, judgmental, "You're inconsiderate," message.

Avoid using the words *you*, *that* or *like* after *I feel*.

――――――――――――

"*I feel that* ...." Once you use *that*, the message is an opinion and is usually a judgment not a feeling.

"*I feel you should know better than to do that* ...." The real message is, "You're inconsiderate."

"*I feel that you were acting childish* ...." The real message is, "You're immature."

"*I feel like you don't care* ...." The real message is, "You're uncaring."

――――――――――――

The following sequence of practice activities asks you to recognize examples and non-examples of I-messages, convert you-messages to I-messages, put parts together, and finally to construct I-messages without prompts.

Learning Practice Task: Recognizing I-messages

Activity Directions: Classify each of the statements below as either a you-message or an I-message. Remember, if the message blames or orders, regardless of the words, it is a you-message.

Teacher Response	You-message	I-message
1. Quit fooling around.	_____	_____
2. It's impolite to speak out of turn.	_____	_____
3. When you're late for class, I get frustrated because it's distracting.	_____	_____
4. Are you enjoying making me angry?	_____	_____
5. The hair on my arms stands on end when you shout like that.	_____	_____
6. Stop that yelling. You're driving me crazy.	_____	_____
7. I'm very tired and just can't take extra noise right now.	_____	_____
8. Mind your own business.	_____	_____
9. I really get annoyed when people get pushed around in this room.	_____	_____
10. I'm becoming more and more aggravated by your tone of voice.	_____	_____

Learning Practice Task: Rewriting You-messages

Activity Directions: For the two situations below, rewrite the you-message as an I-message.

Situation: Eddie knocks his books off the desk.
You-message: "Eddie, you pick up those books right now! I don't want to see that again."
I-message: _____

_____

Situation: Sally and Sue are talking while Thea is giving a presentation.
You-message: "Pay attention. You're being rude."
I-message: _____

_____

Learning Practice Task: Constructing I-messages

Activity Directions: 1. List three student behaviors that cause a problem for you. 2. Describe the effect on you and your feeling. 3. Join these separate components and write the three I-messages the way you would actually deliver them. Use the examples provided as a guide.

Behavior: Nonjudgmental description of the problem.	Effect: Concrete effect of the behavior on me.	Feeling: My feeling about the behavior.
Example		
John interrupts another student.	*I can't hear what either student is saying.*	*frustration*
1. _____	_____	_____
2. _____	_____	_____
3. _____	_____	_____

Example

John, I get frustrated when you interrupt Sue, because then I can't hear what either of you is saying.

1. _____

_____

2. _____

_____

3. _____

_____

Learning Practice Task: Writing I-messages

Activity Directions: Write an I-message for the three frequent classroom problems listed below.

1. Student is late.

_____

_____

_____

2. Student is talking while you are giving directions.

_____

_____

_____

3. Student puts down another student.

_____

_____

_____

Questions for Self-reflection

For what type of classroom situations do you think I-messages are most appropriate?
For what type of classroom situations do you think I-messages are least appropriate?

Using Impact-statements to Invite Communication

When you think stating your feelings is inappropriate, undesirable, or unnecessary an "impact-statement" can be used rather than an I-statement. An impact-statement is similar to an I-statement, without the statement of feeling component. Both impact-statements and I-statements have three components. In an impact-statement there is a non-blameful description of the behavior and a statement of its tangible effect, as in an I-statement, but instead of stating your resulting feelings, you specify the person affected by the behavior. In the classroom setting, the person affected could be the teacher directly or the learning activity, the student engaging in the behavior, or other students.

Impact-statements are less personal and appeal to the student's sense of responsibility, rather than feelings for the teacher. The idea of an impact-statement is to state the actual consequence and what direct effect it has on the classroom situation or learning environment. The impact on the teacher could be in terms of ability to maintain the lesson flow, manage the total classroom environment, or sense of responsibility for students (e.g., their learning, security, or safety).

Delivering an Impact-statement

An impact-statement includes three components:

- A nonblameful description of the behavior,
- The direct impact of the behavior, and

• The person(s) affected or the situation created as a result of the behavior or resulting situation.

Impact-statements could describe the impact on (1) the teacher directly, (2) the teacher's sense of responsibility, (3) the lesson or learning activity, (4) the student(s) engaging in the behavior, or (5) other students. The following example illustrates an impact-statement:

"When you ask me a question when I'm with another group [behavior]*, I have to stop what I'm doing* [impact] *and the students in the group have to wait for me"* [person(s) affected].

The focus is on the immediate impact of the behavior rather than on the feelings the teacher has, as in an I-statement. Also, as is the case with I-statements, the direct impact as well as the resulting consequence should be believable to your students. Often in delivering the impact-statement, you would combine the impact and the effect or just state the person(s) affected (part 3) and omit the impact (part 2) because it is unnecessary or implicit.

"When you ask me a question when I'm with another group, the students in the group have to wait for me."

The following example illustrate various effects of the same behavior.

"When you call out the answer . . . ."

Effect on other students: *Other students don't have a chance to think of their own answers.*

Effect on teacher: *I'm not able to call on another person and give everyone a chance to answer.*

Effect on student's own learning: *You don't have a chance to learn from other students who may have different ideas.*

Learning Practice Task: Developing Your Skill at Delivering I- and Impact-statements

Activity Directions: The following activities can help you develop your skill at delivering I-statements and impact-statements.

Activity 1: Think of a time when you have sent the following you-messages:

"You really make me mad!"

"You are so self-centered!"

Practice writing alternative messages in I- and impact-language.

_____

_____

_____

Activity 2: Write three you-messages you could send: One to a student, one to a peer, and one to an administrator in your school. Transform each of these statements into I- or impact-language and rehearse them with a peer.

_____

_____

_____

Activity 3: Practice making I-statements and impact-statements in a safe setting. Try them out on people you feel comfortable with on relatively minor issues. Solicit feedback on others' reactions.

Activity 4: Take a few minutes twice per day during the coming week and reflect on the language you use with students. List any you-messages you can remember and write them as either an I- or impact-statement.

The Two Rules for Inviting Communication

Inviting communication creates a climate of honesty, acceptance, and safety. When you invite communication, you:

- Tell your side without judgment or blame. This means you communicate only your own feelings, needs, wants, and intentions. As soon as you judge or attribute blame to the other person(s), you have crossed the line.
- Respect the rights and needs of the other person(s). This means you communicate without projecting or invalidating others' feelings, thoughts, needs, or intentions.

While you might like to think you control students, you don't. What you do control is how you interact with, and respond to, students. You are in control of:

- What you send out (initiate) and
- How you respond to what you get and/or get back.

You can't control what a student may send your way or how a student will respond to what you do or say. But you can do "damage control" or turn around the tone of the interaction from adversarial to cooperative. As in the martial arts, you use your opponents' attack as an opportunity to move fluidly without becoming rigid. You take in the attack and redirect the energy for cooperative problem-solving, using the energy to move through the conflict to a mutually-agreeable resolution.

Learning Practice Task: Inviting Communication

Activity Directions: Pair up with other person and role play the situation described. Take turns being sender and receiver. After you have both had a turn, then discuss the three questions.

Situation to role play: You are feeling hurt because Ms. Jackson, the teacher in the room next to you, complained to you about too much noise in your class. You didn't say anything at the time, but it's still bothering you, so you decide to discuss it with her.

Task 1: As the sender, try to send messages that invite communication and keep it two-way by:

1. Telling only your side without judgment or blame (you communicate only your own feelings, needs, wants, and intentions).
2. Respecting the rights and needs of the other person (you communicate without projecting or invalidating the other person's feelings, thoughts, needs, or intentions).

Task 2: As the receiver/listener, listen and whenever you hear a "communication violation" put up your right hand as a stop sign and then describe the violation. For example:

You're invalidating my feeling.

You're trying to tell me what I should want.

You're advocating for your position and not acknowledging mine.

[Hint. When the receiver feels the communication process is no longer reciprocal, that probably means that the communication has moved from inviting to inhibiting.]

Task 3: The sender then restarts (as often as needed) until he/she ends up with a clear communication that honors the two "rules" of inviting communication.

Questions for Discussion

What communication-inhibiting behaviors did you use?

What inviting behaviors did you use?

What was especially hard for you?

Learning to Listen

The basis for many communication problems lies in the inability of individuals to listen effectively. Listening is perhaps the most overlooked form of communication. Genuine listening requires much practice to become an effective listener. Listening skills are used both proactively and reactively. When the teacher owns the problem, the teacher uses listening skills as part of the problem-solving process, to transition to a mutually-acceptable solution. When teachers place themselves in a helping role in response to a student-owned problem, they are in more of a reactive mode.

Listening is probably the most essential element of any supportive relationship. Listening is at the core of acknowledging and comforting students. When a teacher listens to a student with quiet attention and silent affection, the teacher supports the student in discovering what to do about the problem he/she is experiencing. By listening to students, the teacher serves as the mirror of reflection, so the picture become clearer. By facilitating self-reflection, the teacher helps to unmuddy the waters enabling students to tap their own resources for coping with their problems.

Developing the Art of Listening

Developing the art of listening means learning to really listen, rather than rehearsing in your mind the next thing you are going to say as you wait for the other person to finish talking. Often you get caught up in a "your turn/my turn" response format in which each person is only waiting for the other to stop talking so he or she can have his or her own turn to talk. This is the kind of nonlistening characterized by fragmented conversation in which neither person really listens to or cares what the other person has said.

Probably the most exasperating nonlistening is when the person appears to be listening but responds with a comment completely unrelated to what you said. That's when you want to scream, "You didn't hear a word I said!" Nonlistening can be extremely frustrating because the person is hearing the words but not listening to the message, often preoccupied with his or her own thoughts. These ways of interacting masquerade as listening but are poor substitutions for the real thing.

For many, it's difficult to just listen. The tendency is to want to jump in with your own solutions to the student's problem. Hence, the first tool to develop in learning to listen is to catch yourself before you move in with a solution, by controlling the impulse to talk and just remaining silent. While silence communicates some degree of caring by just being there, it doesn't necessarily communicate acceptance. So the second tool in developing the art of listening is to demonstrate acceptance. You show acceptance by letting the person know you are really present by providing nonverbal and verbal support.

Being silent and demonstrating that you are truly present communicate caring and acceptance, but they don't necessarily communicate that you are willing to take the time to help the student delve into and explore issues and concerns. So you need to move to the next tool in developing the art of listening which is to explicitly provide an invitation to talk. This involves a more proactive role on the part of the listener to ask open-ended, nonevaluative questions that invite the student to talk more. With the final tool, active listening, you become an active participant with the student, by reflecting, paraphrasing, and clarifying what you are hearing.

Styles of Listening

The following diagram shows the characteristics and the interaction of the two components of listening style: listening and responding. You can either listen or not listen (depicted in the vertical axis). Likewise, you can either respond or not respond (depicted in the horizontal axis). The interaction of these two components produces four styles of listening:

- Active nonlistening (quadrant 1)
- Passive nonlistening (quadrant 2)
- Passive listening (quadrant 3)
- Active listening (quadrant 4)

Active and passive nonlistening represent ineffective styles of listening, while passive and active listening represent more effective styles. In quadrant 1, the individual is only waiting for the speaker to stop so he/she can have his/her own turn to talk. The quadrant 2 passive nonlistener can be extremely frustrating since he or she fails to capture what's really going on with the speaker. The quadrant 3 passive listener communicates acceptance and empathy thereby encouraging the speaker to continue. In quadrant 4, the active listener goes one step further by trying to "hear" the underlying emotions as well as the words.

Styles of Listening

		Ineffective Listening Styles	
No	**Active Nonlistening** • Talking *to* not *with* • Showing no acknowledgment for what person has said • Your turn/my turn response mode • Response is superficial, unrelated to what was said	**Passive Nonlistening** • Hearing but not listening • Preoccupied with own thoughts • Unaware of emotions being expressed	
	Q1	Q2	
Listening	Q4	Q3	
		Effective Listening Styles	
Yes	**Active Listening** • Reflecting • Exploring • Paraphrasing • Perception Checking • Clarifying	**Passive Listening** • In accepting silence • Showing nonverbal support • Expressing encouragement • Providing invitation to talk	
	Yes	No	
		Responding	

Nine Ways to Listen

Developing the art of listening can be thought of as progressing through four levels. At each level, the listener becomes a more active participant in the process. Moving through the levels involves the nine listening skills described below.

Level 1: Passive Listening

In passive listening, the listener just listens without any interaction with the speaker.

1. **Silence.** Merely listening is an effective tool because it invites the person experiencing a problem to talk about what is bothering him or her. Remaining a silent listener allows the person to release feelings and emotions.

   While silence does communicate some degree of acceptance by just being there, it does not communicate empathy or warmth. The student doesn't know if the teacher is really paying attention and/or understanding what's going on with the student. Students may even think that the teacher is evaluating them while being silent.

Level 2: Acknowledgment

These types of responses indicate that the teacher is really listening.

2. **Nonverbal Support.** Nonverbal messages help communicate that you are really paying attention. Cues such as nodding, smiling, or leaning forward indicate to the person that you are tuned-in.

3. **Encouragers.** Minimal verbal responses can offer encouragement to the student to continue and serve to reassure the student that you are still attentive and interested in the student's problem.

Expressions such as "Uh-huh," "Oh," "I see," or "Really" let the student know that it is okay for him or her to continue. While these types of responses do communicate some empathy, they do not indicate acceptance or understanding of the situation.

Level 3: Invitation to Talk

This skill is primarily used at the beginning to let students know you want to help and are willing to take time.

4. **Opening.** This skill involves a more active role on the part of the teacher to ask open-ended, nonevaluative questions that serve as a "door-opener" to get the student to talk more. Some examples are:

   "Do you want to tell me about it?"

   "That's interesting, want to tell me more?"

   "Would you like to tell me what happened?"

   Openings are genuine invitations to students to share their feelings or concerns. They open the door but do not necessarily keep the door open because, while they do demonstrate caring, they do not demonstrate understanding.

Level 4: Active Listening

Levels one to three have limitations in that they do not provide much interaction nor do they let the student know that he or she is being understood.

Active listening is when you try to understand the feelings being expressed or what the real message means (i.e., hearing the emotions as well as the words) and then putting your understanding into your own words and sending it back to the person for consideration and/or verification. Active listening involves interaction with the student and it provides feedback (proof) to the student that the teacher understands. The process of active listening involves several specific skills.

5. **Reflecting.** When you reflect, you verbalize the feelings and attitudes that you perceive lie behind the message. The purpose of reflecting is to let the student know you are aware of the emotions involved as well as the words. Because spoken words often don't clearly articulate how one is feeling, responding in terms of the student's perspective, not your own, by feeding back the feelings perceived can help bring a troublesome emotion to the surface. In many cases, going beyond the spoken word to the often unspoken emotions can actually help the student identify his or her feelings and assume ownership for those feelings. The following are examples of reflective statements:

   "Cindy really irritates you when she acts like that."

   "You seem disappointed with your assignment."

   "I can see you're angry with me right now."

Sometimes reflective statements may be rejected by the student. It's important to realize you won't always be exactly on the mark. You don't have to be right every time. One of the advantages of reflection is that it conveys that you are trying to understand the feelings, and when you are off target the relationship is not hindered. The student will generally feel comfortable restating his or her feelings and you'll have another chance.

6. **Exploring.** This technique calls for questioning in an open-ended way to extend the student's thinking and expand the student's range of consideration. It can be used when the student is only telling feelings not facts or when there are missing links in the story. The following are examples.

> *"Can you tell me more about ... ?"*
>
> *"What's causing you the most trouble?"*
>
> *"I'm wondering if the plan you chose is really what you want. It seems to me that you are experiencing some doubt. Are you?"*

The following example illustrates a teacher response to help the student explore other options:

> **Student:** *"There's nothing else I can do."*
>
> **Teacher:** *"Are you sure you've considered all your options?"*

7. **Paraphrasing.** Paraphrasing calls for translating or feeding back to the student the essence of his or her message but in a simpler, more precise way. In paraphrasing, you listen for the basic message, summarize what you heard in your own words, and restate it in fewer but similar words. The following example illustrates paraphrasing:

> **Student:** *"Sometimes I think I'd just like to quit school. Then I wouldn't have to put up with all this crap from everyone, but then I start to feel like that would just be copping out."*
>
> **Teacher:** *"So you think you'd be ashamed of yourself if you gave up now."*

In paraphrasing, you make sure that you are clear about what the student said. You demonstrate understanding without adding ideas, clarifying, or trying to interpret. Paraphrasing not only demonstrates understanding of what was said, it communicates that you care enough about what the student said to get it right. While the simple step of restating what you thought you heard and playing it back to the student might seem unnecessary, it often helps the student take a more objective look at what he or she is saying. Sometimes you may want to follow up your paraphrase with an additional question if you think you need to clarify a certain point.

8. **Perception Checking.** The purpose of perception checking is to make sure you are interpreting what the student said, the way it was intended. In perception checking, you verify any confusion you might be having in understanding the message. To do this, you pose a question, usually providing more than one possible interpretation, and ask for feedback. The goal of perception checking is to verify the accuracy of your interpretation, not to be right. In the following example, the teacher checks to see if the student thinks the material is too difficult versus another issue, like too much work.

> **Student:** *"I'll never be able to learn all this. I don't even know what to do."*
>
> **Teacher:** *"Is it that the material seems too hard for you, or is it that it's too much work?"*

Perception checking reflects an attitude of respect and concern for the student, saying in effect, "I need your help to make sure I'm correctly interpreting what you're saying." The following is another example.

> *"I'm not sure I understand. Was it that she left, that really made you mad?"*

9. **Clarifying.** Sometimes there is a need to sort out something you are confused about. Clarifying involves restating what the student has said to clear up any confusion. Often it involves stating your own confusion and asking for help to clarify your understanding. The following are examples of clarifying:

> *"I'm not sure how you feel. Earlier you said .... Now you seem to be saying .... I'm confused."*

> *"Can we stop here? I really don't understand what you mean. Can you tell me more?"*

> *"Let me see now, in other words you ...."*

Sample Teacher/Student Dialogue Using Active Listening

Student: *I don't want to stay in school today. Can I go home?*
Teacher: *You do sound unhappy, Manny.* [reflecting]

Student: *I just hate those fifth graders. They think they're really hot stuff.*
Teacher: *Hmm.* [encouraging]

Student: *Leroy Brown is the worst one. He thinks he's a big shot, just because he has a new baseball glove.*
Teacher: *I see.* [encouraging]

Student: *They always make fun of me because I have to play with my dad's old glove.*
Teacher: *You get upset when they make fun of you.* [reflecting]

Student: *Yeah. Dad said he would get me a new glove but I have to pay for half of it. And I only have two dollars.*
Teacher: *It's pretty discouraging when you can't see how you're going to get the glove.* [reflecting]

Student: *Yeah, it sure is! I've been trying to save my allowance but it's hard to do. I'll bet Leroy Brown didn't have to buy half of his glove.*
Teacher: *You think it's not fair for you to have to spend your money on a glove when the other kids don't.* [paraphrasing]

Student: *Well, I guess it's a fair way to do it. But I just can't save money, that's all.*
Teacher: *Oh. You think it's an OK idea, if you could only do it.* [paraphrasing]

Student: *Yeah, that's right. How can I save $10 more when my allowance is only $2 a week?*
Teacher: *Wow! You would have to save all your allowance for five whole weeks.* [paraphrasing] *That's pretty frustrating, huh!* [reflecting]

Student: *Yeah—what I need is money quicker. Maybe my dad would give me my allowance early.*
Teacher: *Do you think that could be the answer?* [exploring]

Student: *Yeah—no. Then I'd have no allowance for anything else for a long time!*
Teacher: *Hmm.* [encouraging]

Student: *Yeah! I'll bet my mom would let me help her pull weeds from the garden. And I could clean up Mr. Smith's yard. He's already asked me about that!*
Teacher: *Wow! Sounds like you're pretty excited about all these new ideas you've come up with.* [reflecting]

Student: *Yeah. Gosh, thanks. You've really helped me out.*

Teacher: *I'm glad I was here to help, Manny. I want to see that new glove when you get it, OK?* [appreciating]

Student: *Sure! Thanks. See you later.*

Learning Practice Task: Recognizing Active Listening Responses

Activity Directions: For each of the following student statements, several teacher responses are given. For each one, decide which response is closest to an active listening response, that is, a response that invites further discussion or best reflects the idea or feeling being communicated.

1. "Sometimes I think I'd like to drop out of school, but then I start to feel like a quitter."
   a. "Maybe it would be helpful to take a break. You can always come back, you know."
   b. "You're afraid that you might fail if you stay in school now, is that it?"
   c. "I can really relate to what you're saying. I feel like that myself sometimes."
   d. "So you'd feel ashamed of yourself if you quit now, even though you'd like to?"

2. "I hate David! I hate him. I hate him. I hate him."
   a. "You must never hate people, Monica."
   b. "David really makes you mad when he bothers you."
   c. "What did he do?"
   d. "Oh, you really don't feel that way, do you?"

3. "I don't get it. Why do we have to learn this stuff anyway?"
   a. "You'll need it to get into college."
   b. "Just keep at it. It'll make sense after a while."
   c. "Something isn't making sense to you?"
   d. "Would you like to come in for extra help after school?"

4. "I don't want to sit near Juan anymore."
   a. "Sorry, but seats have been assigned."
   b. "If he's bothering you, just ignore him."
   c. "You ought to be able to handle this on your own."
   d. "Would you like to tell me what happened?"

5. "Mr. Jones, can a person die from chicken pox?"
   a. "No."
   b. "Don't be silly."
   c. "Do you have chicken pox?"
   d. "Sounds like you're a little worried about somebody."

6. "Ms. Adams, look at my math paper! I got an 'A'."
   a. "Hey, you must be pretty proud of yourself today!"
   b. "That's very nice, Angie."
   c. "See what happens when you really try."
   d. "Well, don't let it go to your head!"

Learning Practice Task: Categorizing Active Listening Responses

Activity Directions: For each of the following student statements, decide which response is an active listening response. Then decide which type of active listening response it is. For each response which is not an active listening response, indicate which type of roadblock is being used. Follow the example provided.

**Type of Roadblock or
Active Listening Response**

"This school sucks!"

   a. "Don't use that language."   *Ordering*

   b. "Come on, things aren't so bad."   *Diverting*

   c. "That attitude will get you nowhere."   *Judging*

   d. "School's getting you down these days?"   *Active listening-reflecting*

"Ms. Smith, I don't think I'll ever learn to read."

   a. "Of course you will, Jamie. You just need to try harder." _____

   b. "Well, it really doesn't matter, honey. Everyone will like you anyway." _____

   c. "Why do you think that?" _____

   d. "You sound pretty discouraged about this." _____

"My daughter is very upset. She says she doesn't understand anything."

   a. "She needs to pay closer attention in class." _____

   b. "Please go on. I'd like to hear more about this." _____

   c. "She's very anxious but she'll do just fine." _____

   d. "Most students find my explanations quite clear." _____

Learning Practice Task: Writing Active Listening Responses

Activity Directions: During this activity you will work with a partner to analyze your active listening responses. Follow the steps listed below.

Step 1: Working independently, write an active listening response for each of the following statements.

Peer: "My fifth period class is driving me up a wall."

_____

_____

_____

Friend: "I'm so fat! Nobody can stand me!"

_____

_____

_____

Student: "I tried to explain to Mr. Adams why my assignment was late, but he wouldn't listen to me."

_____

_____

_____

Parent: "I've tried to get Johnny to do his homework but he won't, and I just don't know what to do about it."

_____

_____

_____

Step 2: Exchange task sheets with your partner. For each of the active listening responses, determine the following:
   a. Are there any roadblocks?
   b. Are there any you-messages (either direct or disguised)?
   c. For responses that are active listening responses, what type of active listening response is it (e.g., clarifying, reflecting)?

Step 3: Exchange task sheets and rewrite your responses based on your partner's feedback.

_____

_____

_____

_____

_____

_____

_____

_____

Paraphrasing is an especially helpful strategy when conferencing with parents. It demonstrates an understanding of what was said. In paraphrasing the teacher does not add any new ideas or try to impose the teacher's own frame of reference. Such restatement helps the parent to feel understood and encouraged to continue the dialogue.

Learning Practice Task: Recognizing Paraphrasing Responses in Conferencing with Parents

Activity Directions: For each situation below decide which response is the most complete and accurate paraphrasing of the parent's message.

1. "Cindy is very upset and needs more help or she won't be able to pass. She says she doesn't understand anything."
   a. "Cindy needs to pay closer attention in class."
   b. "She's very anxious but actually she'll do just fine. She only needs to review more before tests."
   c. "Most students find my explanations to be quite clear. Perhaps she isn't listening."
   d. "You're concerned because Cindy can't keep up, and you think she needs more help."

2. "I don't know what to do about my son. His whining is driving me crazy."
   a. "Even though whining is natural, it's getting to you?"
   b. "Sometimes you really get fed up with his complaining?"
   c. "You're getting angry at him?"
   d. "Even the best parents get irritated sometimes."

3. "Every day there seems to be a new crisis with Mike. He's constantly on the go and I just can't seem to settle him down."
   a. "You're really having difficulty keeping up with Mark."
   b. "Oh, he'll outgrow it sooner or later."
   c. "You need to set limits for Mark."
   d. "Perhaps he needs more physical activity."

4. "I've heard kids calling the special class kids 'retarded.' I don't want Billy made fun of. I definitely don't want him to be in a special class."
   a. "You really don't believe that do you?"
   b. "But we have a good program here."
   c. "You're worried about the other students' reactions to Billy."
   d. "What would make the other kids say that?"

Your perception check response should have three parts:

1. A description of the comment, behavior or situation,
2. Offering of alternative interpretations, and
3. A request for feedback.

Example

Special Education Teacher: *"The committee has recommended that we put Mary into the regular class. She will be given one hour a day special assistance."*

Parent: *"I don't want Mary in a regular class for any part of the school day. I don't want her to suffer setbacks."*

Perception check: *"When you say you don't want Mary to suffer setbacks are you worried about how she will react to the new situation or are you more concerned about the other students' reactions? Could you clarify what you're worried about?"*

Learning Practice Task: Perception Check Exercise

Activity Directions: Write a perception check response for the situations below.

Teacher: "I'm going crazy with Donny. He doesn't seem to want to do anything right."
Perception check:

_____

_____

_____

_____

Parent: "My child is floundering in your class."
Perception check:

_____

_____

_____

_____

Student: "I'm not putting up with that crap from him."
Perception check:

_____

_____

_____

_____

Questions for Self-reflection

What effect does offering more than one interpretation have?

In what school/classroom situations might perception checking be a useful strategy?

Communication Skills for Inviting Communication and Problem Solving

Inviting student participation in problem-solving involves moving through three stages. First, the teacher uses listening skills to engage students and check for understanding. Stage 2 involves both self-disclosing and demonstrating acknowledgement of the student's perspective. The final stage incorporates inviting cooperation, focusing on the issues, and directly confronting problem areas.

Three Stage Model of Communication Skills

Stage 1: Listening	Level 1: Engaging	Level 2: Checking	
	Opening	Paraphrasing	
	Exploring	Clarifying	
	Reflecting	Perception Checking	

Stage 2: Connecting	Level 1: Accepting/Self	Level 2: Accepting/Others	
	Being Authentic	Acknowledging	
	Accepting Ownership	Encouraging	
	Verifying Assumptions	Validating	
		Appreciating	

Stage 3: Resolving	Level 1: Inviting	Level 2: Focusing	Level 3: Confronting
	Inviting Cooperation	Inquiring	Challenging
	Requesting	Summarizing	Asserting
	Enlisting	Sharing Information	Restoring
	Soliciting	Suggesting	Stating Concern

Below each of the 25 communication skills in this model are described with examples. Some of these skills are presented in greater detail in earlier sections.

Stage 1: Listening. Level 1: Engaging

Skill	Description	Example
Opening	Opening the door by inviting the person to talk (sometimes referred to as door openers).	Do you want to talk about it? Do you want to tell me what happened?
Exploring	Questioning in open-ended way to try to extend the person's thinking about the issues. To help the person to consider alternative perceptions.	Have you thought about . . . ? How is this related to . . . ?
Reflecting	Responding to the emotions expressed or implied.	You sound disappointed. You want me to know that you are very frustrated with this situation.

Stage 1: Listening. Level 2: Checking

Skill	Description	Example
Paraphrasing	Repeating what the person has said in your own words.	I think I got the message. You said you are feeling anxious about this class and you think I'm moving through the material too quickly. His behavior is causing you to doubt your effectiveness as a teacher.
Clarifying	Requesting restatement to ensure understanding. Used when one point in the story doesn't seem to follow from the one before or when facts and feeling don't seem to match.	I'm confused about this. I'll try to state what I think you have said. First, ... Let me see if I got what you said. You said . . . .
Perception Checking	Offering more than one interpretation and asking for help or clarification. Acknowledging the possibility of an interpretation other than the one you are making.	I'm having a hard time getting clear about what you're saying. When you said . . . did you mean . . . or . . . ? I'm not sure what you mean when you said . . . . To me it means . . . . Is that what you meant?

Stage 2: Connecting. Level 1: Accepting Self

These three skills are all proactive and represent a person's ability to be reflective and recognize that one's own way of seeing things is influenced by who they are and the beliefs they hold.

Skill	Description	Example
Being Authentic	Being "up front," honest and self-disclosing.	I'm so angry about this I can't talk to you right now. This is a difficult time for me.
Accepting Ownership	Owning your own interpretations and not projecting intentions. Not expecting others to do or think the way you do.	I'm concerned about the way I've been acting toward you. Using that tone of voice really aggravates me.
Verifying Assumptions	Rather than projecting intentions or attributing motives without verifying, explicitly stating your assumptions.	Taylor, I assume that means . . . . When you do that, I think you don't care.

Stage 2: Connecting. Level 2: Accepting Others

Acknowledging, encouraging, validating and appreciating all communicate respect for, and acceptance of, the other person(s). Also, these skills all are nonjudgmental and communicate understanding and caring. In acknowledging, the acceptance is of rights, needs and viewpoints; in appreciating, it is actions and interests; in validating, it is feelings and mood; and in encouraging, it is efforts and individual valuing.

These skills attempt to join the needs and wants of both parties and represent an effort on the part of the person initiating the communication to connect to the other person. These skills are sometimes referred to as blending skills, in that they represent joining the other person's world and seeing things from that person's perspective.

Skill	Description	Example
Acknowledging	Accepting and showing respect for others' point of view, position or opinion. Accepting without judgment others' rights and needs.	I can appreciate why you think that. That's an interesting perspective.
Encouraging	Valuing effort, accepting individual worth and respecting others' competence.	OK, you know what to do. I see you found your own way to do that.
Validating	Communicates acceptance of feelings. Can go further to communicate concern and understanding. Acknowledges others' right to have and experience whatever emotion they are experiencing.	I can see you are angry now. I understand that you feel . . . when I . . . .
Appreciating	Appreciates actions and interests. Recognizes what others do.	I appreciate your willingness to work this out. I'm pleased to see you are enjoying yourself.

Stage 3: Resolving. Level 1: Inviting

Inviting skills attempt to ensure mutual participation.

Skill	Description	Example
Inviting Cooperation	Communicates that you need or desire the other person's help and cooperation.	I'd like you with me on this, Frieda. I need your help on this.
Requesting	Communicates that you need or desire the other person's input or advice.	I see it this way . . ., how do you see it? I would like your input about how we might resolve this.
Enlisting	Asking what the other person wants, needs or feels. Includes what the person may want from you.	Are you feeling alright? What would you like to see happen? How can I help?
Soliciting	Asking what the person would like to do. Asking what the person wants you to do.	Would you like to leave the room? What do you think I should do about this?

Stage 3: Resolving. Level 2: Focusing

Focusing skills involve trying to help move the issue toward resolution.

Skill	Description	Example
Inquiring	Involves asking questions to move the issue toward problem solving. Inquiry rather than advocacy—remaining open, not advocating for your own needs and position. Focuses on specific information. Asking open-ended questions. Asking questions for reflection.	I'm wondering . . . . What do you think would happen if . . . ?
Summarizing	Pulling together ideas, themes. Reviewing the ground covered. Summarizing where you are.	Here's what we have so far . . . . Did I miss anything? Let's take a look at all the issues we've discussed so far. So, you're proposing that . . . .
Sharing Information	Sharing ideas and information. Includes statements about personal experience.	I think I know a strategy that may be helpful here. My experience is . . . .
Suggesting	Making suggestions.	What do you think about using . . . ? I have an idea that might work. How about . . . ?

Stage 3: Resolving. Level 3: Confronting

Confronting skills take a proactive stance for addressing issues and concerns.

Skill	Description	Example
Challenging	Confronting others when they attempt to get their own needs met without considering others' needs. Challenging others to reflect on, or consider their own actions and weigh their appropriateness.	That sounded like an accusation to me. How would you feel if it were you?
Asserting	Expressing your rights and needs.	I don't like that idea because . . . . I'd like . . . .
Restoring	Acting as the gatekeeper, monitoring the communication process, and intervening to keep it on track.	We're getting off track. We haven't heard from everyone. Is there anyone else who wants to add something?
Stating Concern	Expressing a concern, either about the process or about a particular idea or potential solution.	I'm concerned that we don't have enough information. I'm worried that if we do that . . . .

Below are some examples of combining these communication skills to deliver messages to students that keep the communication channels open.

Inviting Communication Sequences	Language of Respect
Encouraging/Appreciating	"I know this is a struggle. I'm glad you're sticking with it."
Being Authentic/Inviting	"I'm frustrated. I don't like the way I am acting toward you. I'd like to change, but I need your help."
Acknowledging/Enlisting	"You're angry because you think I wasn't considering your needs. What can I do that would make you feel like your needs were taken into account?"
Validating/Soliciting	"I can see you're upset. Do you want some time to yourself right now?"

Questioning

This is a particularly difficult skill for teachers to master because so much of their questioning is typically of a fact-finding nature where the major purpose is to get specific data or answers they are looking for. When questioning is used as part of an inviting communication, it is not a fault-finding mission. When questions are for the purpose of finding out who's wrong and doling out a fitting punishment, the teacher is acting as both jury and judge, rendering his/her decision of authority.

Questioning as part of inviting communication assumes both or all parties are active participants and have input in the problem-solving process for the purpose of arriving at a mutually-agreeable resolution. Here the goal of questioning is to explore and clarify.

In the communication model proposed here, questioning is at both Stage 1 and 3. In the initial stage, the idea is to open-up a potentially limiting perspective of the problem or possible solutions (exploring), to clear-up confusion or get more information if there seems to be missing pieces in the story or accounting of an incident (clarifying), or clarify meaning or potential misperceptions (perception checking). In Stage 3, questioning is used to invite participation at Level 1, to get more information at Level 2 and to challenge attempts to get personal needs met at the expense of others at Level 3.

Using Listening and Connecting Skills to Transition to Problem-solving

Teachers who invite communication see issues from students' point of view and can communication understanding of what their students' are experiencing. Though they may not always agree with the actions students take to deal with their feelings, they do accept that students have a right to their feelings. However, they clearly differentiate between the right to have strong feelings and the right to act aggressively. Teachers show appreciation for how and why students feel and think the way they do, and still assert their position that students don't have the right to harm others, disrupt the class, or destroy property. They use listening and connecting skills to transition to problem-solving. They do this by speaking respectfully and showing faith in the students' ability to find a solution.

This problem-solving process moves through three phases:
- Phase 1: Accept/validate/respect.
- Phase 2: Connect with the student.
- Phase 3: Transition to problem-solving.

The following examples illustrate transition to problem-solving.

"I can see you're furious about what he said about your mother. I don't blame you for being angry. I'd be angry, too. But I'm responsible for everyone's safety here, so you'll have to find another way to deal with your anger."

In this example, after validating the student's feeling and acknowledging the student's right to feel angry, the teacher expresses appreciation for the feeling, but then moves to asserting her need for a reasonable solution.

"I know you feel bad about knocking over Thinh's project and that it really wasn't your fault, but for Thinh, all his hard work was wasted. What do you think you should do now?"

In this example, the teacher moves from validating the student's feeling to connecting, and then to resolution.

Learning Practice Task: Using Inviting Communication for Problem-solving

Activity Directions: Pair up with another person. Follow the sequence of steps listed.

1. Review all of the skills in the communication chart.
2. Select one of the following common classroom problems to work with:
   • Student is usually late for class.
   • Student is abusive to other students.
   • Student does very little classwork.
3. Write an initial response for each of the categories below by selecting those types of responses from the 25 skills presented that seem appropriate for the situation.

1. Showing respect.

   _____

   _____

   _____

2. Connecting personally.

   _____

   _____

   _____

3. Confronting the issues.

   _____

   _____

   _____

4. Asserting the teacher's needs.

   _____

   _____

   _____

5. Problem-solving negotiation.

   _____

   _____

   _____

6. Resolution.

   _____

   _____

   _____

Part II

Ways of Managing

Chapter 5

Managing for Collaborative Decision-making

Several authors who have translated principles of human behavior into strategies for classroom teachers offer alternative models to compliance models for creating an optimal atmosphere for teaching and learning. The work of William Glasser, Rudolph Dreikurs, and Haim Ginott has been selected for inclusion here. These three authors encompass the range of orientations to addressing classroom and behavior management that align with the principles of building a caring, democratic community. The principles they espouse are most consonant with those emerging from the school-as-community literature.

Their theories provide the cornerstone for establishing the communication, interaction and intervention strategies necessary for creating classrooms that embrace the principles of respect, authenticity, thoughtfulness, and emotional integrity (RATE) described in Chapter 3.

While a number of other authors of approaches and programs recommend strategies which are also consistent with the basic tenets of caring communities, the work of these three theorists provides the foundation which comprises the underlying theories of these other approaches as well (e.g., Curwin & Mendler, 1988; Freiberg, 1996; Queen, Blackwelder, & Mallen, 1997; Rogers, 1969; Rogers & Freiberg, 1994). They offer "mixes" of approaches, strategies, and techniques that represent different renditions of similar themes.

The work of William Glasser, from the 1960s through the 1990s, emphasizes the importance of satisfying students' basic needs as a necessary condition to establishing a learning community. These basic human needs include the need to belong, the need to have power and freedom, as well as the need to experience personal satisfaction. Understanding the motivation that drives students' behavior, based on the work of Rudolph Dreikurs and colleagues (1968, 1972, 1982), offers another perspective. Dreikurs reminds us that we all need to have avenues for receiving recognition. If the classroom environment fails to offer students opportunities to get recognition, students will find ways (often inappropriate) to get the recognition they thrive on. Enhancing student self-esteem through continuous encouragement and validating and accepting both teachers' and students' feelings is the means for developing a positive socio-emotional climate advocated by Haim Ginott (1972).

Dreikurs, Glasser, and Ginott all focus on meeting the psychological needs of students by calling on teachers to:

- Show genuine concern for students.
- Support student emotional growth and development.
- Respect the rights and needs of students.

- Deal honestly and openly with students.
- Recognize both their own and their students' feelings.

From the work of these authors several themes relative to classroom interactions emerge. These consistent themes call for minimizing blame by clearly differentiating between rejection of the student's behavior and rejection of the student, allowing and encouraging student choices, and providing continuous encouragement while, at the same time, calling on students to take responsibility for their own behavior.

Glasser's Managing Without Coercion: Satisfying Student Needs

William Glasser's early work in reality therapy represented a shift from psychoanalysis to assessing present reality. According to Glasser, individuals need to fulfill two basic needs—for belonging and to have a sense of worth to self and others. Students need to accept the reality of classroom demands. The primary vehicle for implementing reality therapy is the individual student conference.

Glasser's New Views

Glasser's newer views are geared primarily toward secondary schools.
- Schools need to be restructured to provide more satisfying experiences for students.
- Schools need to find ways to reduce both teacher and student frustrations.
- Less than 50% of students are willing to make an effort to learn.
- Only a discipline program that produces classroom satisfaction can work.
- Four fundamental needs play powerful roles in student behavior: the need to belong, the need for power, the need for freedom, and the need for fun.
- In our present organization of schools, cooperative learning offers the greatest promise for providing for these four needs.
- Although much of what teachers do is an attempt to control others' behavior, in reality we can only control our own behavior (i.e., control theory). Hence, students will control their own behavior so that what they choose to do is the most need-satisfying thing they can do.
- Integrating leadership style theory with his other notions, Glasser defines what he calls "the quality school" where:
  —Students' needs are satisfied.
  —Teachers don't try to coerce students.
  —Teachers "lead" not "boss" students.
  —Teachers build the link between classroom tasks and student's perception of quality.

Comparison of Glasser's Earlier and Current Work

In his earlier work, Glasser maintained that schools offered students the best, and sometimes their only, chance to interface with adults who genuinely cared about them. Thus schools afforded students an opportunity for belonging, success, and positive self-identity. To avail themselves of this opportunity, students were continually called on to make value judgments about their behavior, make appropriate choices, and accept the consequences of their good and bad choices.

In Glasser's more recent work, he places greater onus on the schools to meet student needs, rather than molding students, to deal more effectively with the conditions they encounter in school.

Key Principles for Teachers: Glasser's Reality Therapy

Glasser developed reality therapy as an alternative to conventional psychotherapy. In his book, *Reality Therapy: A New Approach to Psychiatry* (1965), he called for a shift in focus from uncovering conditions in one's past that contribute to inappropriate behavior (psychoanalysis) to assessing the present reality of the current situation. The underlying premise of reality therapy is that an individual must face reality and assume responsibility for his or her own actions. Reality therapy attempts to guide the individual toward competent functioning in the real world by assisting him or her to effectively deal with his or her environment to fulfill personal needs. The following principles are integral to Glasser's beliefs:

Individuals need to fulfill two essential psychological needs:

1. To love and be loved, and
2. To feel worthwhile to self and others.

The primary objective of reality therapy is to teach the ill/irresponsible person responsible behavior. Thus, therapy and the teaching/learning process are the same.

Reality therapy is the process of teaching an irresponsible person to face existing reality, to function responsibly, and as a result fulfill one's personal needs for love and self-worth.

Responsibility is the ability to meet one's own needs in a manner that does not deprive others of their ability to fulfill their personal needs.

Classroom Application

Applied to the classroom, Glasser (1969) maintained that a student's background and/or socioeconomic status does not exempt a student from his/her responsibility to behave appropriately. The present reality of the classroom is what matters. Teachers should not excuse irresponsible behavior. Rather, they should guide a realistic assessment of not "why" but "what" behavior the student engaged in and its impact. Glasser's basic tenet is that students are capable of controlling their behavior. They choose to act the way they do.

The reality therapy teaching/learning process requires:

1. Involvement with a person perceived by the student as caring about him or her.
2. A teacher who is able to accept the student while rejecting the irresponsible behavior.
3. For the student, learning responsible means of fulfilling personal needs.

Reality therapy applied to the classroom is viewed as a cooperative interchange in which both the teacher and the student commit to the process. The process calls for teachers to engage in direct instructions, discussions, conferences, planning sessions, and group meetings. In essence, in reality therapy, the teacher provides emotional support while maintaining focus on deriving a resolution to the problem at hand (i.e., calling for responsible behavior on the part of the student). In order to guide the student toward more responsible behavior, the recommended vehicle is the reality therapy interview or individual conference. The following guidelines are offered for teachers during the student conference.

Student Conference Guidelines

1. Demonstrate caring.
2. Provide emotional support and security.
3. Use active or empathic listening.
4. Do not probe by asking why questions.
5. Ask what, who, how questions.
6. Focus on present behavior, not past behavior.
7. Curtail excessive "venting."
8. Refrain from judging the student's behavior.
9. Call on students to make value judgments about their behavior; offer suitable alternatives when necessary.
10. Help students "make a plan" to increase responsible behavior.

A New Beginning: Ten Steps to a Fresh Start with a Problem Student

When nothing you do seems to work and you're at your wits end, it's time for a fresh start. Glasser (1974) offers the following sequential steps for dealing with your "behind-in-his-work, disruptive, doesn't-listen, never-on-time, always-picking-fights Tom (or Susan)."

The process begins with an attitude adjustment on your part. Let's face it—you've tried everything you know and still the student is driving you crazy. Steps 1 to 3 provide a systematic way for you to change your own attitude and resolve to start fresh. The intermediary steps suggest nonpunitive, nonblameful responses to the student when he/she breaks a rule. The strategy is to keep the tone "cool and crisp," until the student makes some effort to comply, and to continue to try to "inject some warmth and recognition into the student's day." Steps 4 and 5 call for you to be warm and supportive and minimize teacher-talk. In step 6 you call for conference time and engage in structured dialogue. The remaining steps are a graduated series of "benching techniques" to be used when the student's behavior is so serious he/she has to be removed. The process is slow and you'll need to commit at least a month, since progress is not likely before then.

Ten Steps to a Fresh Start with a Problem Student

Step 1: Commit to Changing Your Approach

If what you're doing hasn't worked by now—it probably won't. Itemize all the things you're doing now when Tommy misbehaves. For the next four weeks try to refrain from doing anything on your list.

Step 2: Make Your Motto: *Every Day's a New Day*

When Tommy misbehaves, try to act and react as if it is the first time he's ever behaved inappropriately. Avoid comments like: "I've had enough of that!" When he does something right, give him verbal or even physical recognition. Example:

> *"I appreciate your staying in your seat this morning."*

Step 3: Make an Effort to Make Tomorrow a Better Day

Find something (no matter how small) that you can do to help Tommy have a better day tomorrow—and every day for at least four weeks. It could be just a simple warm gesture—20 seconds of unexpected recognition. The next time you need to send a message to the office, you might ask Tommy to delivery it. The objective here is to try to break the pattern of recognition only for misbehavior.

Step 4: Quiet Correction

This step involves confronting the student with short, simple directives. The following are examples:

> *"Tom, put the ruler down and get back to work."*
>
> *"Tom, take a seat until you've finished your work."*

When the student does not comply, the strategy is to calmly pose short questions to focus the student on his/her present behavior and to help him/her think rationally about the behavior he/she is engaging in. Remember to establish the mind set that this is the first time the student has misbehaved.

When a straightforward directive doesn't work, then use the "broken record" technique in which you repeatedly ask "What did you do?" until you get an answer. You relentlessly press the student to admit his/her behavior. As an example, let's say this time Tommy cuts in line and starts a fight in the process. You say, "Tommy, stop fighting and go to your place in line." He continues. The ensuing dialogue might go something like this.

> **Teacher:** *What did you do, Tom?*
> **Tom:** *What?*
>
> **Teacher:** *What did you do, Tom?*
> **Tom:** *Nothing.*
>
> **Teacher:** *Please, Tom, I just asked you what you did. Tell me.*
> **Tom:** *Well, this is my place in line, and they won't let me in.*
>
> **Teacher:** *What did you do, Tom?*
> **Tom:** *It's my place, so I pushed my way in.*

Then, with no further discussion, you take him by the hand and walk him to his correct place and stay with him, maybe still holding his hand.

> **Teacher:** *Can you walk quietly now?*
> **Tom:** *What are you going to do?*
>
> **Teacher:** *I just asked you if you can walk quietly now; we'd all like lunch.*
> **Tom:** *OK, I'll try.*

When this step doesn't work you continue with the next step. With this procedure you are attempting to establish that, while Tom needs to take responsibility for doing something wrong, if he accepts your correction, it's over—no blaming, yelling, or threatening.

Step 5: Insist on a Plan

In this step you press for a plan from the student. You will need to be very insistent and continually focus on following the rules. Your agenda is to tell the student he/she broke the rule; of course the student's agenda will be to evade this issue in every possibly way. The following prototype questions are recommended.

> *What did you do?*
>
> *Just tell me what you did.*
>
> *Please tell me what you did.*
>
> *Where are you supposed to be now?*
>
> *What are you supposed to be doing now?*
>
> *Do you think you can* [appropriate behavior] *now?*

What's the rule?

Was it against the rules?

Are you willing to [appropriate behavior]?

Can you make a plan?

Step 6: Conference Time

Up to this point, you kept your talking at a minimum. If the behavior persists, a conference is in order. You tell the student you want to talk over the problem. The message you want to try to communicate to the student is:

Yes, we have a problem; I want to help; I think you are capable of coming up with a solution.

During the conference you should make clear that you appreciate the student's wants/needs; however you cannot allow the student to hurt or take advantage of others. Appeal to the student's sense of fairness. The following phrases are illustrative of the suggested language:

I know you want to . . . .

I can't allow you to . . . .

Can you think of a way to . . . .

It is sometimes helpful to put the plan in writing to reinforce the commitment.

Step 7: Off to the Castle

This is isolation within the classroom. It differs from the traditional "time out" in that the designated area is not meant to be unpleasant. The teacher should create a private space within the classroom, making it a comfortable retreat so that any student wouldn't mind spending time there. In fact, it should be available to any student who might on occasion want a private place.

When the student's behavior is so serious he/she has to be removed, the student is sent "off to the castle" with a simple directive—"Go sit in the castle." The teacher should pay no obvious attention to the student and should not worry about how long the student stays there. Later the teacher asks the student if he/she is ready to return and insists on some plan of action, regardless of how simple.

Step 8: Off to the Office

When steps 1 to 7 haven't worked, the student has to be removed from class. This step requires the principal's support in two ways. First, in providing a nonpunitive environment or "rest-spot" and, second, in using consistent dialogue and insisting that the student make a plan for getting back into class. To enact this phase, the teacher should simply say: "Go down to the office and take a rest."

It is imperative that the student come to realize that he/she has only two choices: To be in class and behave appropriately, or to be out of class and sit.

Step 9: A Tolerance Day

If the student is totally out of control and can't be contained in the office rest area, then the student is sent home. The student is then put on a "tolerance day" in which he/she comes to school in the morning and stays until step 9 is reached.

Step 10: Removal from School with Hope for Reentry

If the student can't be contained in school, then he will have to stay at home and/or be served by some other agency. When the student seems ready, he/she can reenter at the lowest possible step. However, step 10 should be necessary only in very rare instances.

Critical Reflection on Practice: Analyzing Your Current Behavior Pattern

Activity Directions: Think of a student you are having trouble with now or have had trouble with in the past. During this activity you will be working with a partner to analyze your current behavior pattern in dealing with your problem student. Follow the steps listed below.

1. List the student's most frequent inappropriate behaviors.

_____

_____

_____

_____

2. List what you currently do when this student misbehaves.

_____

_____

_____

_____

3. Compare your behaviors with those of your partner and list similarities and differences.

Similarities   **Differences**

_____   _____

_____   _____

_____   _____

_____   _____

_____   _____

4. Switch cases and complete the following sentence: "I think the message your behavior would be giving the student is . . . ."

_____

_____

_____

_____

Critical Reflection on Practice: Planning an Attitude Adjustment

Activity Directions: Using your own problem-student case, work with your partner to develop a self-prompting strategy to systematically change your attitude and start every day with a "clean slate."

Strategy 1: **Start fresh every day.** Develop a self-regulation strategy to prompt yourself to "erase the slate" and begin anew each day with your student.

_____

_____

_____

_____

Strategy 2: **Plan for a better day tomorrow, and the next day . . . .** Find something you can do to help your student have a better day tomorrow. List things you could do for the student and to the student to make his/her day a little brighter. It doesn't have to be much—a simple gesture can go a long way. Try to list at least 10 things.

_____

_____

_____

_____

_____

_____

_____

_____

_____

_____

_____

_____

Glasser on Classroom Rules

For Glasser, classroom rules are essential. He considers rules to be especially critical for students who have not been successful in school. Permissiveness for such students is often counterproductive and fosters lack of respect for teachers and others. Rules should be jointly formulated by teachers and students, reasonable, related to efficient learning, and always enforced. Classroom rules should support a learning environment that facilitates individual and group achievement. Rules should be constantly reevaluated for utility and purpose and should lead to class and individual success.

Rules should be adapted to the age and ability of the students as well as other realities of the classroom situation. Below are some examples of appropriate rules at various grade levels.

Examples of Appropriate Classroom Rules

Primary level	1. Help others.
	2. Take turns.
	3. Walk in the classroom.
	4. Raise your hand to talk.
Upper-elementary level	1. Do your best work.
	2. Be kind to others.
	3. Follow directions.
	4. One person may talk at a time.
Secondary level	1. Be on time.
	2. Come to class with the materials you need.
	3. Be considerate of others.
	4. Return materials you use.

Characteristics of effective classroom rules

Effective rules should be:

- **Jointly established.** Students should take part with the teacher in establishing class rules. Rules should address both personal behavior and work habits.
- **Reasonable.** Rules should focus on important behavior and be reasonable both in terms of duration of time and performance capabilities.
- **Clearly defined.** Rules should be clear and understandable. It should be clear to both the student and the teacher when the rule has been broken.
- **Observable.** Rules should address behaviors that can be observed. Words which are value-laden should be avoided (e.g., good, nice, polite).
- **Positive.** Rules should be phrased in positive rather than negative terms. They should state what students should do and emphasize positive actions.
- **Succinct.** Rules should be brief and specific. Rules that are short and to the point are easily remembered.
- **Few in number.** There should be only enough rules to address areas of main concern. From three to six rules are adequate depending on the situation. Rules should govern general behaviors; specific instructions for special occasions can be given when the occasion arises.
- **Enforceable.** If the teacher cannot enforce a rule consistently, he/she cannot expect students to follow it. Teachers should ensure that the established rules can be adhered to.
- **Enforced.** Rules must be enforced. Students should know the consequences of breaking a rule in advance.
- **Constantly evaluated.** Rules are established to support individual and class success. Rules should be constantly reevaluated to ensure their continued utility.

Learning Practice Task: Evaluating Your Classroom Rules

Activity Directions: Follow the steps below to evaluate your classroom rules.

Step 1: List your class rules below.

Step 2: Applying the 10 characteristics of effective classroom rules to your rules, list any of the criteria you have violated.

Step 3: For each rule, check the categories which are met.

Classroom Rules	Clear	Observ-able	Succinct	Positive	Reason-able	Enforce-able
1.						
2.						
3.						
4.						
5.						
6.						

Effective Rule Criteria

Classroom Meetings

For Glasser, the classroom meeting is essential for maintaining an effective system of discipline. Classroom meetings provide a forum to continually review rules, responsibilities, and problems and to explore and clarify student responsibility. It is a way of involving students and keeping the communication channels open. Glasser (1969) suggests that the class be viewed as a problem-solving group, with the teacher serving as the group leader. A description of the essential elements of the classroom meeting is provided below.

Description

The classroom meeting is a regularly scheduled time when the whole class engages in openminded, nonjudgmental discussion of personal, social, or academic problems in an effort to find collective solutions.

Purpose

1. To foster caring and supportive relationships which help students satisfy their needs to belong, have power, feel in control, and experience satisfaction or enjoyment.
2. To identify and discuss problems.
3. To seek mutually agreed-upon solutions.

Kinds of meetings

1. Problem-solving meetings.
   - Attempt to solve problems that arise among people living and working together in a school setting.
   - Opportunity to consider matters of discipline.
   - Usually initiated by the teacher but could be initiated by anyone.
   - Group-oriented.

- Discussion is directed toward arriving at a solution.
- Solution should not include punishment or fault-finding.
- Focus should be on the situation, rather than the individual(s).
- Discussion can be facilitated through storytelling, role-playing, and pictures depicting specific situations or incidents.

2. Open meetings. These open-ended meetings could take a variety of forms such as:
   - An opportunity for an individual to express frustrations or feelings resulting from another member(s).
   - Focus on intellectually important subjects.
   - Can address any topic of concern to students (e.g., homeless people, war).
   - Could address any current topic or experience of a class member.

3. Educational decision-making meetings.
   - Need not be "a problem."
   - Address issues such as curriculum, instructional activities, tasks, assignments.
   - Could address how well students understand concepts in the curriculum.
   - Planning events, trips.
   - Discussion of classroom procedures, such as subject or activity order, furniture arrangement, rewards, and so forth.

Setting and time allotment

Meetings should be conducted with the teacher and all students seated in a tight circle. This seating arrangement fosters interaction, student involvement, and a sense of equal status. At the early grades (K-2) 10 to 20 minutes should be allotted, increasing to 30–45 minutes at the upper grades.

Glasser's Newer Views

Glasser's more recent position has evolved from focusing on helping students deal with the conditions they encounter in schools ("reality") to calling for a restructuring of schools to provide more satisfying experiences for students. He now says if schools are to enjoy good discipline, they must reduce both teacher and student frustrations by creating a more need-satisfying environment.

Glasser's (1986) recent views are geared primarily toward secondary schools. He takes the position shared by many that major restructuring is needed because in our current system less than one-half of the students are willing to make an effort to learn and thus cannot be taught. In fact he goes as far as stating, "I believe that we have gone as far as we can go with the traditional structure of our secondary schools." (p. 6) In *Control Theory in the Classroom* (1986), Glasser emphasizes the school's role in meeting student basic needs as a prime factor in discipline and work effort. He contends that only a discipline program that is concerned with classroom satisfaction can work. He calls for schools to be restructured to fulfill four fundamental needs that play powerful roles in student behavior. Those needs are:

1. **The need to belong,** to feel accepted, to be a member of the group or class.
2. **The need for power,** not so much power over others as power to control part of one's own life and power to do things competently.
3. **The need for freedom,** to feel at least partly in control of self, self-reliant, without constant direction from others.
4. **The need for fun,** for enjoyment, for pleasure, for satisfaction.

Glasser and others advocate cooperative learning as an instructional strategy that is most likely to provide for these four needs in our present organization of schools. Cooperative learning provides a structure that allows students to meet their need for belonging and acceptance, since all members of the group participate and have a role. Talking and working with others fulfills the need for fun and enjoyment. Shared leadership offers some freedom in making decisions and serves students' need to have some control. Most important, cooperative learning gives students power—power to influence others, power to do something well, and power to be recognized. Glasser sees the power need as central for secondary-level students.

In cooperative learning, small groups of students work together to complete instructional activities. Students work collaboratively and share responsibility for task completion. Of course not all working together in a group setting constitutes cooperative learning. Johnson and his colleagues in their book, *Circles of Learning: Cooperation in the Classroom* (1984, p. 8), identified the following four elements as necessary for cooperative learning to be effective.

1. **Positive interdependence.** This distinction is critical. Students must be dependent on each other in the completion of the assigned activities. This dependency is generally accomplished by assigning students to different roles within the group. However, the overall task cannot be completed without the contributions of each member.

2. **Face-to-face interaction.** Students must be able to interact with one another and exchange information easily.

3. **Individual accountability.** Each member is held individually accountable for accomplishing the intended learnings. Students are assigned to groups to provide a mix of abilities, so that students comprising each group have different ability and achievement levels. This allows students to learn from each other while providing mutual assistance and support.

4. **Use of interpersonal and small-group skills.** Students must use effective social skills for collaborative learning to be successful, but often such skills are lacking. Therefore, students must be taught how to use such skills as leadership, effective communication, and conflict management. In their groups they are given time and procedures for analyzing the overall effectiveness of their group work.

Control Theory

According to Glasser (1986), the need for control is one of the basic needs we all have. Whenever people feel that they do not have control, they will do whatever they think is necessary to regain control. Attempting to control another's behavior ultimately only leads to conflict as that person attempts to meet his or her own need for control.

Control theory posits that most of what we do is not a reaction or response to events around us. We are not controlled by external forces outside of our control, rather we control ourselves by forces that lie within. How we feel is not controlled by others or events. It is our nature to try to satisfy, as best we can, basic needs for survival, acceptance, freedom, power, and satisfaction. We control our own behavior by choosing to do things that satisfy these basic needs. All any of us do, think, or feel is always our best attempt at the time to satisfy the drive to meet one of these needs. And often, our attempt is an ineffective response.

The notion of control viewed from this perspective is an inner action rather than a response to events, people, or situations. It is not about controlling others' behavior, it is about self-control.

In contrast, in the behavioral model of reinforcement theory, behavior is controlled by external stimuli, or reactions to behavior. Adhering to this theory leads to trying to manipulate the behavior of others by dispensing rewards and delivering punishments. If on the other hand, you believe control to be an inner action governed by an internal thought process and mediated by inner speech, or self-talk, the way to exercise control is to monitor and regulate what you think and what you tell yourself. Clearly, this is a very different way of perceiving control. So if, as the teacher, I think and say to myself, "I'll show him who's boss," then I will impose a negative consequence. But, if I think and say to myself, "I'll remain calm," then I will respond by helping the student exercise self-control.

Calling for students to make value judgments

When students behave inappropriately, teachers should ask questions to help them make value judgments about their behavior. Glasser (1977) suggests the following procedure when a student is misbehaving:

Teacher: *"What are you doing?"* [Asked in nonthreatening tone of voice.]
Student: [Will usually give an honest answer if not threatened.]

Teacher: *"Is that helping you or the class?"*
Student: *"No."*

Teacher: *"What could you do that would help?"*
Student: [Names better behavior; if can think of none, teacher suggests appropriate alternatives and lets student choose.]

Of course, the student won't always respond in an acceptable way. When that happens, Glasser offers the following protocol teacher responses:

Student: [Behaving irresponsibly.]
Teacher: *What are you doing? Is it against the rules? What should you be doing?*

Student: [Responds negatively, unacceptably.]
Teacher: *I would like to talk with you privately at* [specifies time].

During private conference between teacher and student.

Teacher: *What were you doing? Was it against the rules? What should you have been doing?*
Student: [Agrees to proper course of behavior.]

Later the student repeats the misbehavior and the teacher calls for another private conference.

Teacher: *We have to work this out. What kind of plan can you make so you can follow the rules?*
Student: *I'll stop doing it.*
Teacher: *No, we need a plan that says exactly what you will do. Let's make a simple plan you can follow. I'll help you.*

Clarifying ownership of the problem

Glasser suggests that teachers make it perfectly clear that the student's disruption is her or his own problem, not the teacher's, and that the teacher knows exactly what to do. The teacher should say something like the following to the disruptive student:

It looks like you have a problem. How could I help you solve it? If you'll just calm down, as soon as I have the time, I'll talk it over with you and I think we can work something out. As long as you're doing what you're doing now, we can't work anything out.

Sometimes a joking remark (at the teacher's expense, not the student's) can help relieve the tension. The teacher might try saying in a mock serious tone:

Wow, you're upset. I must be doing something really terrible. Calm down, and as soon as I can, we'll get together and maybe you can help me work things out.

Glasser maintains that, if the student will not calm down after this reasonable request, there is no good way to deal with him or her in class. The teacher should not get into an argument or even a long discussion with an angry student. Above all, the teacher should never threaten the student.

In order to solve problems that arise, teachers need the cooperation of the student. If the student refuses to cooperate, he or she must be asked to leave the room. The teacher should say something like:

Since you won't calm down, I have to ask you to leave. I hope we can get together later and work this out, but if you are not willing to settle down, it's better that you leave now.

The disruptive student is often looking for someone to blame in order to sustain his/her grievance. But it's hard to stay angry at a teacher who is saying, in words, attitude, and behavior:

I want to help you work this out. I am not looking to punish you for what you have just done. If there is a problem, let's solve it.

The only reasonable solutions to discipline problems are systematic and long term, and thus must be developed while the student is in control. So the first strategy should be to get the student to calm down. Then you need to find a few minutes to talk to him/her; either in class, between classes, before or after school, or any time you can spare a few minutes. When you have the time, you should say something similar to the following:

What were you doing when the problem started? Was this against the rules? Can we work it out so that it doesn't happen again? If this situation comes up in the future, let's work out what you could do and what I could do so we don't have this problem again.

The Quality School

Glasser's more recent book, *The Quality School: Managing Students Without Coercion* (1990), again emphasizes the importance of meeting students' basic needs within the learning environment. He reiterates that although much of what we do is an attempt to control others, in reality we can only control our own behavior (i.e., control theory). It is human nature to try to satisfy as best we can our basic needs for survival, belonging, freedom, power, and enjoyment.

Translating control theory to the classroom setting means that students will control their own behavior, so that what they choose to do is the most need-satisfying thing they can do at a given time. And, more often than not, something other than the learning task is more need-satisfying at the time.

Glasser also integrates organizational theory and leadership style theory with his other notions to define what he calls "the quality school." Thus in the quality school the following conditions prevail:

1. Students' basic needs are satisfied.
2. Teachers recognize that they can only control their own behavior and do not try to coerce students.
3. Teachers "lead" rather than "boss" their students.

4. Teachers manage their class so that students can easily see the connection between what they are asked to do and what they believe is quality work.

His ideas about quality work are based on the work of Dr. W. Edwards Deming who tried after World War II to promote the power of participatory management for workers in order to achieve quality products. Applying Deming's notions to education, Glasser notes that students are both the workers and the products of schooling. The theory is that once students see that they themselves are gaining in quality they will make an effort to continue. So the role of the teacher becomes one of building the link between what students believe to be quality and what they are expected to accomplish.

Glasser draws an interesting parallel:

> *Just as the American auto industry in the 1970s concentrated on building low-quality, high-profit cars, schools have concentrated on getting more students to meet the low-quality standards required for graduation. Thus we produce students who, like workers, merely "lean on their shovels."*

A comparison of managers who "lead" and those who "boss" is provided below.

Comparison of boss-management and lead-management

The lead-manager:

- Confers with students when deciding about the work to be done, the time needed to do it, and the quality standard.
- Models the job and seeks student input about better ways to achieve quality.
- Invites students to evaluate their own work for quality.
- Provides the tools and setting that promote self-confidence and congeniality among students.

In contrast, the boss-manager:

- Does not consult students about what work needs to be done.
- Tells students what to do without asking them how it might be done better.
- Sets quality standards and evaluates work without involving them in the process.
- Relies on coercion to get students to do what they are told, creating an adversarial climate.

Quality teaching leads to quality learning

Glasser (1993) in his latest book advises teachers to support quality teaching, quality learning, and quality student work by striving to:

- Make the classroom warm and supportive. Let students know you and like you by sharing who you are and what you stand for. Show you're always willing to help. Clarify what you will expect from them as well as what you will do for them.
- Ask students to do only useful work, consisting of skills, not just information, that students and teachers view as valuable.
- Ask students to do quality work, the best work they can do.
- Discuss quality work often so students know what you mean by quality work.
- Then ask students to evaluate their own work and improve it.
- Help students to see that doing quality work makes them feel good. When they experience this feeling of pride and accomplishment they will want more.
- Help students to see that quality work is never destructive to oneself, others, or the environment.

Learning Practice Task: Case Study of Stan-the-man

Activity Directions: Working with a partner, develop some strategies that would be consistent with Glasser's views on discipline for the problem situation below.

Stan has arrived for class in his usual nasty mood. He goes to sharpen his pencil and while in route he can't resist giving Joe a "friendly" shove. Joe responds with a complaint to the teacher. The teacher asks Stan to return to his seat at which point Stan retorts with "I'll go when I'm damned good and ready!"

How would Glasser deal with Stan?

_____

_____

_____

_____

Critical Reflection on Practice: Is Your Classroom Need-satisfying?

Activity Directions: Take a few minutes to think about the procedures and strategies which are part of your classroom organization which address Glasser's view of students' four basic needs. Then share your list with a peer and complete Part 2 together.

Part 1: Complete independently.

Student Needs	Ways I Address this Need in My Class Structure
1. Need to belong and be accepted.	1. _____
2. Need to have some power and to influence others and be recognized.	2. _____
3. Need to have freedom and to be in control of self.	3. _____
4. Need for enjoyment and satisfaction from learning.	4. _____

Part 2: Work with a peer.

Are you satisfied that you are sufficiently meeting your students' needs?

List other things you might do to make your classroom a more need-satisfying environment.

_____

_____

_____

_____

_____

List the one thing you are willing to commit to that will make classwork more satisfying for students.

_____

Dreikurs' Democratic Discipline: Identifying Students' Mistaken Goals

Rudolf Dreikurs, long associated with psychiatrist Alfred Adler, immigrated to the United States to eventually become director of the Alfred Adler Institute. Throughout his long career, he continued to focus on family-child counseling, but became well-known in the area of classroom behavior through his books *Psychology in the Classroom* (1968), *Discipline Without Tears* (1972) and *Maintaining Sanity in the Classroom* (1982).

Dreikurs' approach to discipline is based on understanding the motivations behind student behavior. He believed that students react to negative feelings by developing defense mechanisms to protect their self-esteem and called on teachers to identify students' goals and use that information to help students recognize the purpose of their inappropriate behavior. All students want recognition, and most misbehavior occurs when they attempt to get it. When unable to get the recognition they want, they turn to misbehavior to gain the recognition they are seeking.

Dreikurs' approach to classroom discipline is based on three key ideas:

1. Students are social beings and as such their actions reflect their attempts to be important and gain acceptance.

2. Students are capable of controlling their behavior and choose either to behave or to misbehave.

Combining these two points, Dreikurs contends that:

3. Students choose to misbehave because they are under the mistaken belief that it will get them the recognition they want. Dreikurs refers to such beliefs as "mistaken goals."

All students want to belong, so they try all sorts of behavior to see if it gets them the recognition they want. If they do not get recognition through socially-acceptable means, they turn to unacceptable means. Such behavior reflects the mistaken belief that inappropriate behavior is the only way to get recognition.

Dreikurs identified four mistaken goals: (1) attention getting, (2) power seeking, (3) revenge seeking, and (4) displaying inadequacy. These goals are usually sought in sequential order. When attention getting fails to gain recognition, the student progresses to seeking power, then to seeking revenge, and finally to displaying inadequacy. He recommends a three-step process for teachers in dealing with students' mistaken goals.

Step 1: Identify the student's mistaken goal.

Step 2: Confront the student in a nonthreatening manner.

Step 3: Explore with the student his/her motivation (i.e., mistaken goal).

Key Principles for Teachers

The first thing teachers need to do is identify the student's mistaken goal. Two factors can help the teacher gauge which mistaken goal is operating: the teacher's own reaction to the student's behavior and the student's counter reaction to the teacher's reaction. The teacher's response is an indication of the student's expectation.

If the teacher:	Then the student's goal is:
Feels annoyed	Getting attention
Feels threatened	Seeking power
Feels hurt	Getting revenge
Feels helpless	Displaying inadequacy

If the student:	Then the goal is:
Stops the behavior but then repeats it	Getting attention
Refuses to stop	Seeking power
Becomes hostile	Getting revenge
Refuses to cooperate or participate	Displaying inadequacy

The strategy that Dreikurs recommends for teachers is three-fold. First, the teacher needs to identify the student's mistaken goal. Next, the teacher should confront the student in a nonthreatening way with an explanation of the mistaken goal. Third, the teacher should discuss with the student the faulty logic involved, to get students to examine the purposes behind their behavior. The process calls for teachers to ask students specific questions, in sequential order and to look for reactions that might indicate a mistaken goal. Dreikurs advocates the following questions:

1. Could it be that you want me to pay attention to you?
2. Could it be that you want to prove that nobody can make you do anything?
3. Could it be that you want to hurt me or other students in this class?
4. Could it be that you want everyone to believe you are not capable?

Once the mistaken goals are identified, teachers can begin to take action to defeat the student's purposes and initiate more constructive behavior.

Dreikurs' Guidelines for Teachers

Dreikurs advocates that teachers develop an ongoing relationship that promotes a spirit of cooperation and team effort. Teachers should provide consistent guidance that will facilitate students developing their own inner controls. Discipline is far more than imposing limits at times of stress and conflict. Accordingly, Dreikurs offers the following strategies for teachers.

DOs and DON'Ts for Teachers

DOs   Give students clear-cut directions for expected behavior.

Apply logical consequences rather than arbitrary punishment.

Allow students a say in establishing rules and consequences.

Let students assume responsibility for their own behavior and learning.

Be firm. Let students know that you are a friend, but that you will not accept certain behavior.

Set limits from the beginning, but work toward developing a sense of responsibility.

Teach students to impose limits on themselves.

Close an incident quickly and revive positive feelings.

Forgive and forget.

Mean what you say, but make simple demands.

Always distinguish between the deed and the doer.

Treat students as social equals.

Encourage students' efforts.

DON'Ts   Act in ways that reinforce mistaken goals.

Nag and scold.

Find fault with students.

Threaten students.

Ask students to make promises.

Praise students' work and character.

Point out how much better the student could do.

Encourage comparison with others.

Have double standards—one for you and another for your students.

The following two charts provide elements of Dreikurs' approach both from the student's and the teacher's perspective. The first chart shows, for each mistaken goal, the student's belief and purpose as well as the student's typical behavior and reaction to teacher intervention attempts. The second chart shows the teacher's feelings, typical reactions, and ineffective and effective strategies for each mistaken goal.

Mistaken Goals: The Student's Perspective

Student's Mistaken Goal	Student's Belief	Student's Message/Purpose	Student's Behavior/Action	Student's General Reaction to Teacher Intervention
Attention	I belong only when I'm noticed or served. I'm important only when everyone is paying attention to me.	"Look at me!" Tries to keep teacher busy with him/her.	Pesters, is nuisance. Clowns around, shows off. Constantly disrupts class. Asks endless questions. Is bashful. Uses excessive charm.	Temporarily complies with teacher request to stop behavior. Later resumes same behavior or seeks attention in some other way.
Power	I belong only when I'm in charge or when I'm proving that no one can make me do anything. I'm important only when I'm the boss.	"You can't make me!" Tries to control teacher and/or dominate situation.	Disobeys. Argues. Refuses to follow directions. Has temper tantrums. Tells lies. Does little or no work.	Defiantly continues the behavior. Intensifies action if reprimanded. Submits with defiant compliance.
Revenge	I belong only when I'm hurting others and getting even. I'm important only when I'm fixing my hurt by getting others.	"I'll get even with you!" Tries to compensate for own hurt by hurting others.	Makes mean remarks. Calls others names. Destroys property. Physically attacks others. Is defiant. Runs away.	Becomes violent or hostile. Intensifies the hurtful behavior. Seeks further revenge, retaliation. In retaliation, directs hostility toward the teacher. May become sullen. Rejects efforts made by others (initially).
Display of Inadequacy	I belong only when I convince others that I am unable and helpless. I'm important only when I'm proving I'm a failure.	"I'm no good, so leave me alone!" Feels that he/she can't do anything right so doesn't try to do anything at all.	Rarely participates. Gives up easily. Never gets work done. Keeps to him/herself. Plays "dumb." Has extensive absenteeism.	No response or half-hearted response. Shows no improvement. Becomes more passive, refuses to interact.

Mistaken Goals: The Teacher's Perspective

Goal: Attention

Teacher's Feeling/Thinking	Teacher's Common Reactions	Specific Questions for Diagnosis	Effective Strategies	Ineffective Strategies
Annoyed. Irritated. "This student occupies too much of my time." "I wish he/she would stop bothering me."	Gives service to student. Frequently reminds. Tries to coax. Pays attention by keeping after student. Nags, scolds.	"Could it be that you want me to pay attention to you?" or "Could it be that you want me to do something special for you?"	When possible, ignore the student's bid for attention. Give attention and encouragement at other times. Give attention in unexpected ways. Recognize positive behavior. Walk away when student demands attention. Make a contract (If …, then …). Analyze how your own behavior might be affecting the student. Identify alternatives for the student. Give permission to the student to "bid for attention" with parameters. When not possible to ignore, make eye contact without any comment or call student's name. Follow through by allowing natural or logical consequences to occur.	Showing annoyance. Becoming "bugged." Giving negative attention by nagging, scolding or correcting. Giving attention by answering excessive questions, reminding, coaxing or talking to.

Goal: Power

Teacher's Feeling/Thinking	Teacher's Common Reactions	Specific Questions for Diagnosis	Effective Strategies	Ineffective Strategies
Threatened. Angry. Provoked. Defeated. "He/she can't get away with this." "Who's running this class?"	Fights "power with power." Engages in power struggle. Defends authority. Threatens. Argues. Punishes. Tries to force student. Gives in.	"Could it be that you want to prove that nobody can make you do anything?" or "Could it be that you want to be boss?"	Refuse to engage in conflict. Withdraw as authority figure. Help students use power constructively by enlisting their help. Redirect students by inviting them to participate in decision-making. Give student position of responsibility. Put student in charge of something. Give responsibility for own work by providing options. Give sincere encouragement. Stop entire class and have them wait for student to stop behavior. Make an agreement. Enlist help of class. Remain calm. Speak softly. Provide for cooling off period.	Becoming emotionally involved. Arguing. Threatening. Punishing. Raising voice. Giving in.

Mistaken Goals: The Teacher's Perspective (continued)
Goal: Revenge

Teacher's Feeling/Thinking	Teacher's Common Reactions	Specific Questions for Diagnosis	Effective Strategies	Ineffective Strategies
Hurt.	Retaliates.	"Could it be that you want to hurt me or others in the class?"	Examine behavior that is being interpreted by student as hurtful.	Retaliation.
Angry.	Get even.	or	Try to understand the student's feelings of hurt.	Punishment.
Outraged.	Punishes harshly.	"Could it be that you want to get even?"	Build a trusting relationship.	Acting hurt.
Humiliated.	Yells.		Set up situations for student to exhibit talents or strengths.	Continuing the alienation.
Rejected.	Counterattacks.		Call on class to support and encourage the student.	
"How can I get even?"	Seeks revenge.		Enlist a buddy.	
"How mean can he/she be?"				

Goal: Display of Inadequacy

Teacher's Feeling/Thinking	Teacher's Common Reactions	Specific Questions for Diagnosis	Effective Strategies	Ineffective Strategies
Despair.	Withdraws.	"Could it be that you want to be left alone?"	Stay involved with the student.	Giving up.
Hopelessness.	Gives up helping.	or	Encourage and reward effort, no matter how small.	Pitying.
Discouraged.	"Writes off."	"Could it be that you want everyone to believe you are not capable?"	Demonstrate that the student can be successful.	Doing for the student what he/she can do for self.
Powerless.	Criticizes.		Break difficult tasks into smaller segments.	Giving outward signals of frustration.
"I can't do anything with him/her."			Demonstrate desired behavior.	Criticizing.
"I don't know what to do anymore."			Make student feel worthwhile.	Expecting immediate results.
			Assign student helpers.	
			Trust the student with responsibilities.	

Examples of appropriate teacher reactions to mistaken goals

1. **For attention-getting behavior.** Sometimes it is not feasible for teachers to ignore behavior that is disrupting the class. In such cases teachers need to give attention in ways that are not rewarding to the student. The teacher may call the student's name and make eye contact without any comments. Or the teacher may describe the behavior without any trace of annoyance by saying,

   "I see that you are not finishing your assignment."

   One technique that is sometimes effective is to privately confront the student with his/her goal and ask, "How many times do you think you will need my attention in the next hour?" The student will usually not know what to say. The teacher might then say, "If I give you attention 15 times, will that be enough?" This will sound like an exaggeration to the student. Then when the student misbehaves the teacher responds by saying, "Joel, number 1," "Joel, number 2," and so forth. The teacher does not comment on the behavior or scold, which would give Joel the attention he seeks, but simply lets him know his behavior is being noted.

2. **For power-seeking behavior.** Teachers can also redirect students' ambitions to be in charge by inviting them to participate in making decisions or by giving them positions of responsibility. A teacher might take a student aside and say, "The language during physical education is very unsportsmanlike. The others look up to you. Do you think you could help out by setting an example?" Or in the same situation the teacher might say, "I have a problem. It concerns the language I am hearing. What do you think I should do?" In this way, the teacher gives the student power while avoiding a power struggle.

   Teachers may also confront the behavior openly. When a disruption begins, the teacher could say, "I cannot continue to teach when you are doing that. Can you think of a way you could do what you want and I could still teach?" If students cannot think of any ways, the teacher should be prepared to suggest some alternatives.

   By withdrawing as a power figure, teachers take fuel from a student's fire. Students cannot be involved in a power struggle with themselves. They will not receive status or recognition if they cannot get the best of the teacher. Teachers who withdraw thwart the purpose of power-seeking behavior.

3. **For verbal or physical fighting between students.** The probable goals are: attention, power, or revenge directed at the teacher; attention directed at the rest of the group; power or revenge directed at an antagonist.

   The problem owners are the students involved and/or you, if the fight is disruptive or dangerous, although, the actual disagreement belongs to students. Avoid reinforcing mistaken goals by taking away students' responsibility for solving their own problems. Whenever possible, let students settle their own disputes.

Some other alternatives:

1. **If verbal, and for attention, power or revenge.** Let students who complain about each other settle their own disputes. Tell them to do this only once; ignore future complaints.

2. **If physical, and for attention, power, or revenge.** On the playground, if the fighters aren't attracting a crowd, ignore them and deprive them of an audience. Or establish a "no fighting" rule; students who fight are demonstrating their decision to "sit on the sidelines" until they are ready to stop fighting.

   If students fight in the building, establish a place for them to talk over their conflicts. With young students, designate two chairs the "talk-it-over chairs." Let students work out their problems independently. Stay silent and uninvolved. Your only concern is that they stay away from the group until they're ready to stop fighting.

   Accept any solution (except fighting), including complete silence while they're supposedly "talking it over." If they return too soon, say, "I see you've still not decided how to get along. Please leave the group and decide how you'll get along. I'll come over in a few minutes to see if you've solved your problem and are ready to return." Keep returning students to the negotiation area if fighting continues, gradually increasing the time away.

   Separate students who are too angry to negotiate. Say, "I can see that you two need to cool off. Christine, you go _____ and Geraldine, you go _____. I'll check with you in a while to see if you're ready to talk it over or return to the classroom."

Distinguishing Between Logical Consequences and Punishment

A democratic teaching style calls for teachers to learn to distinguish logical and natural consequences from punishment. According to Dreikurs, while it is quite permissible for the democratic teacher to employ logical consequences or to permit natural consequences following misbehavior, it is not permissible to use punishment. Dreikurs defines punishment as any hurtful action taken by a "superior authority" as a means of coercing an "inferior being" to do the bidding of the authority. Natural and logical consequences replace punishment in the democratic classroom.

Dreikurs advises teachers to first determine which of the four mistaken goals is operating and then to respond to counteract it. For example, when students misbehave to gain attention, teachers should make sure that they do not receive it then, but provide other outlets for gaining attention. When students try to exert power over others, teachers should avoid involving themselves in power struggles, while finding alternative ways to give students power and status. If students seek revenge for real or imagined events, they should be treated in ways that reduce their need to be avenged. When students misbehave out of feelings of helplessness and impotency, then teachers should build up their self-confidence.

Dreikurs recognizes that at times these approaches will be ineffective in redirecting misbehavior, and then students will have to pay the consequences of their misbehavior in order to learn to behave appropriately. At such times, he advises teachers to act democratically, not autocratically, and to use logical, not arbitrary, consequences. He equates arbitrary consequences with punishment.

There are three types of negative consequences: natural, logical, and arbitrary. Natural consequences occur automatically as the result of a particular behavior. They are the unavoidable consequences or inevitable reactions brought about by a student's actions when no one interferes to prevent these consequences from occurring. Natural consequences are based on the natural flow of events, taking place without teacher interference. On the other hand, logical consequences involve teacher intervention. Logical consequences are arranged by the teacher, but are related to the behavior in question. However, while they are structured by the teacher, they must be experienced by the student as logical. Arbitrary consequences are also arranged by the teacher and are not clearly related to the behavior being punished. Some characteristics of logical consequences and punishment are listed below.

Logical Consequences	Punishment
Logically related to the behavior	Arbitrary or contrived
Deliberately planned and delivered	Reactionary
Emotionally neutral	Emotionally charged
Rational and depersonalized	Personalized
Develops self-control	Produces avoidance behavior
Protects self-esteem	Erodes self-esteem

The following examples compare natural, logical, and arbitrary consequences.

Behavior	Consequence		
	Natural	**Logical**	**Arbitrary**
Student teases peers.	Student isn't chosen to be included in game students are playing during recess.	Student is required to play alone during recess.	Student loses points.
Student is late for class.	Student misses information needed for test.	Student is responsible for making up any work missed.	Student is sent to principal's office for rest of class period and then has to make up all work.
Student hits another student during recess.	Student is hit back.	Student misses recess the next day.	Student is kept after school.

Hoover and Kindsvatter (1997) suggest that in democratically conducted classrooms, remediation be applied in accordance with the concept of "reasonable consequences." They define a reasonable consequence as a measure with a developmental focus that targets a personal learning outcome for the student. Ideally, when a reasonable consequence is applied, the student will recognize a connection that goes beyond a simple chronological one between the misbehavior and the consequence. For example, two students who persist in having a private conversation instead of doing their classwork may be separated, but it should be clear that the consequence is being applied because a previous reminder was ignored. A reasonable consequence implies taking action "for" the student, or in the student's interest, rather than "against" the student. A teacher should be the student's advocate in a proactive way. In using a reasonable consequence, the teacher takes into account the overall impact of the disciplinary measure to minimize negative emotional overlay.

A reasonable consequence is based on the assumption that the student can ultimately be persuaded by principles of reason, justice, mutual consideration, fair play, and social responsibility. The idea is to apply a judicious resolution without having a winner and a loser. The principle of restitution may also be included as part of the response. The overall intent is to help the student learn acceptable behavior from the experience. Even though the teacher's intent may be instructional rather than punitive, students may perceive it differently. However, any unintended side effects can be mitigated by determining a reasonable consequence which involves participation, reflection, and understanding on the part of the student. While the outcomes of reasonable and logical consequences are clearly more desirable than the outcomes of punishment, attaining such desirable outcomes is to a large extent dependent on the teacher's manner of delivery.

While, in practice, a punishment and a reasonable or logical consequence may be hard to distinguish, the critical difference is in the spirit and purpose with which each addresses the misbehavior and the underlying message which is communicated to the student.

Underlying Message with Punishment	**Underlying Message with Logical Consequences**
I'll show you who's in charge.	I trust you to make a choice.
You deserve to be punished.	You are worthwhile and responsible.
You can't get away with doing this to me.	You can learn from your experience.
You can't be trusted to make the right decision.	You can act responsibly.

Though this line of reasoning has merit, as Grossman (1995) points out, in some cases the logical consequences of misbehaving may not be enough to counter the intrinsic rewards of students' actions. Telling students who lie that one does not believe them, making a student wash graffiti off the wall, sending a student to the end of the line for cutting when he would have been at the end of the line anyway, and requiring a student who teases others to remain isolated may not affect the student as particularly unpleasant. In such cases, applying logical consequences could be ineffective, and the teacher might have to resort to other kinds of consequences.

For Dreikurs, distinguishing between logical consequences and punishment represents a critical distinction. When applying consequences, teachers should:

1. Pose alternatives that fit the situation and let students decide either verbally or through their behavior.

    "Terry, I'm sorry but throwing the blocks is not permitted. You can play with them correctly or stop playing with them for a while. You decide."

    "If you go to the library, you go to work on your report."

2. Offer choices firmly but respectfully.

    "Either help us out on this project or leave the group."

    "When the books are put away, we can go to lunch."

Sometimes it is effective to state your intentions.

"I'm willing to help you with the project, but only after you've given it your best effort."

To make sure their actions express logical consequences rather than punishment teachers can ask the following questions for self-reflection.

Ask Yourself

1. Am I showing an open attitude?
2. Am I giving students a choice and then accepting their decisions?
3. Am I speaking in a firm but friendly tone of voice?
4. Does my nonverbal behavior match my tone of voice?
5. Are the consequences I devise logically related to the misbehavior?
6. Am I involving students whenever possible?

Summary of Dreikurs' Views

When Dreikurs' principles are implemented effectively they have the potential to bring about genuine attitudinal change among students, so that they eventually behave more appropriately because they choose to do what they think is the right thing to do. Dreikurs refers to his approach as democratic in that teachers and students decide together on rules and consequences and take joint responsibility for maintaining a classroom climate conducive to learning.

Dreikurs' approach requires a commitment over time for its results to become apparent. It also requires that teachers spend considerable time talking to students about their actions. With its emphasis on mutual respect, acceptance, encouragement, student effort, and general responsibility, this approach represents a powerful technique for students' personal growth enhancement.

Dreikurs' greatest contribution to classroom discipline lies not in how to suppress undesirable behavior in the short run, rather in how to build over time an inner sense of responsibility and respect for others.

Albert's Democratic Management: The Three Cs—Capable, Connected, and Contributing

Building on the work of Dreikurs, Albert (1989) and Dinkmeyer, McKay, and Dinkmeyer (1980) point out that intervening to redirect students' disruptive classroom behavior prompted by mistaken goals is only part of the overall democratic management of classroom problems. The need to belong in the classroom is interpreted as a desire to feel significant and important and to find a satisfying place within the classroom or group. Before students can choose more positive forms of classroom behavior as a means of belonging in the classroom setting, they must feel capable, connected, and confident in their ability to contribute to the classroom. Albert called these the three Cs. When these are satisfied, students achieve a strong sense of belonging. To belong, students must feel capable of completing academic and other tasks, believe that they can connect successfully on a personal level with teachers and classmates, and think they can contribute in a significant way to the group or class.

Three factors affect students' abilities to satisfy the three Cs: (1) The quality of the student/teacher relationship; (2) the classroom climate, especially in regard to opportunities for cooperation and success; and (3) the classroom structure for encouraging contributions from all.

Examples of strategies that help students feel more capable include:

1. Communicate to students that it is all right to make mistakes. Teachers can talk about mistakes as being a vital part of learning. They can equate mistakes and effort and generally attempt to minimize any negative effects that might be associated with making mistakes.

2. Build student confidence by focusing on improvements, noticing contributions, acknowledging strengths, and generally showing faith in students. Teachers can also ensure that students are not left to fail at tasks for long periods of time.

3. Assist students in recognizing past successes they have experienced. This can be done by keeping checklists of skills or flowcharts of concepts that track students' progress by recording and displaying what they have learned. Another vehicle is accomplishment albums in which students keep examples of past work that has been done successfully.

4. Recognize success by providing opportunities for students to acknowledge their own and others' accomplishments. This might be accomplished by occasionally assisting students in running their own award assemblies or providing positive "time-outs" which give students opportunities for self-congratulation and selection of self-rewarding activities.

Examples of strategies that help students connect with the teacher and their classmates include:

1. Accept students by showing a willingness to accept differences in students' personal styles, such as personal idiosyncrasies in dress, habits, or mannerisms.

2. Attend to students by greeting them warmly, listening to them, and helping them seek attention in appropriate ways when they desire it.

3. Appreciate students' efforts to contribute positively in the classroom, and to their own and others' learning. Explicit oral or written statements of appreciation can acknowledge a student's actions, the teacher's own positive feelings about these actions, and the benefits accrued when students act in helpful and supportive ways.

4. Show appropriate affection to students, especially when such affection is not contingent on any accomplishment, per se, or when students are upset or troubled by events in their lives, both inside and outside the classroom.

Examples of strategies that might help students think they can contribute include:

1. Invite students' help with daily tasks.
2. Ask students to make choices and give input about classroom practices and curriculum.
3. Encourage students to help each other through peer tutoring, peer counseling, and peer recognition.

By helping students feel capable to connect and to contribute, teachers can help build students' self-esteem so that they will be more likely to pursue their goals of belonging in positive ways that will benefit themselves as well as their classmates.

Learning Practice Task: Case Study of Darryl-the-pain

Activity Directions: Read the case study below. Then, working with a partner, respond to the questions posed.

Case Study. *Darryl entered the classroom and smiled at Ms. Dunn. She smiled back and told Darryl his assignment was at his desk. Darryl then responded, "I ain't got no book." Ms. Dunn gave him a book. "I ain't got no paper" was his next response. Ms. Dunn handed Darryl a piece of paper. Darryl followed with "I ain't got no pencil." Ms. Dunn asked Cindy to lend Darryl a pencil. Finally, Darryl slammed his books on his desk and yelled, "Shit!" He immediately glanced at Ms. Dunn fully expecting an angry response. Ms. Dunn just smiled, shook her head and went on with what she was doing. Realizing his attempt to provoke Ms. Dunn wasn't working, Darryl settled down to work.*

What was Darryl's agenda?

_____

_____

_____

_____

What was Ms. Dunn attempting?

_____

_____

_____

_____

Do you think Ms. Dunn's behavior was appropriate? _____

What would you have done?

_____

_____

_____

_____

Learning Practice Task: Identifying Effective Strategies

Activity Directions: For each of the cases below:

- Identify the student's mistaken goal.
- List two strategies Dreikurs would consider effective.
- List two strategies Dreikurs would consider ineffective.

1. Sarah habitually comes to class late, making sure her arrival is noticed. When Ms. Banner asks her to explain why she is late, she retorts with, "You're always on my case."

   Mistaken goal: _____

   Effective strategies: _____

   _____

   Ineffective strategies: _____

   _____

2. Mario can often be found staring into space. He avoids both the teacher and his classmates. His teacher has made many attempts to get him to work. He rarely does any work at all.

   Mistaken goal: _____

   Effective strategies: _____

   _____

   Ineffective strategies: _____

   _____

3. Mike is always taunting his classmates. Today he has pulled Jessica's hair when she refused to give him a pencil.

   Mistaken goal: _____

   Effective strategies: _____

   _____

   Ineffective strategies: _____

   _____

Learning Practice Task: Considering Mistaken Goals

Activity Directions: Working with a small group, answer each of the following questions.

1. How can determining the goal of misbehavior help teachers choose the most effective approach to discipline? _____

2. What goal(s) is best handled with active listening? _____

3. What goal(s) is best handled with I-messages? _____

4. What goal(s) is best handled with logical consequences? _____

Ginott's Congruent Communication: Sane Teachers, Sane Messages

Haim Ginott is the author of three books that address the relationship between adults and children. In his first two books he presented specific strategies for dealing with parent/child conflict, urging parents to communicate to their children that, while they may disapprove of their behavior at times, they still accept and love them (Ginott, 1965, 1969). In his final book, Ginott (1972) extended his notions of acceptance to the classroom, advocating styles of communication that humanize rather than dehumanize students. He emphasizes the socio-emotional climate of the classroom and calls on teachers to demonstrate concern for students' feelings. Ginott recognized that the messages teachers communicate to students have a significant impact on their self-esteem.

Ginott was the first to emphasize the importance of how teachers talk to students and how teachers' talk is linked to students' behavior. Adult messages are a direct line to a child's self-esteem. Teachers have the power to help construct or to erode a student's self-concept, and that power is wielded largely through their style of talk with students. For Ginott, the two most important factors are the teacher's self-discipline and the communication style the teacher uses. Before teachers can work effectively with students, they must learn to accept, understand, and express their own perspectives and feelings in ways that respect, help, and empower students. Teachers must model what they want to foster in students. Their own behavior should extend empathy, warmth, and genuineness. Student alienation and class disruptions result from a communication style that is characterized by indifference, disrespect, ridicule, sarcasm, stereotyping, and inappropriate displays of personal frustration.

Implicit in Ginott's recommendations for adults dealing with children is the underlying belief that all human beings need to feel respected, understood, and cared for to reach their greatest potential.

Key Principles for Teachers

This section describes the main themes of Ginott's message for teachers.

The Danger of Equating Work with Worth

Most children are socialized beginning with storybook tales, TV programs, and adult talk to accept that the degree to which a person is loved, appreciated, and valued by others depends on how well he or she performs, accomplishes commendable deeds, and achieves desirable goals. Parents often attempt to motivate their children to achieve by displaying greater signs of love and appreciation for their children after they succeed in an endeavor, than they display after they fail. Consequently, many students enter school believing that their personal worth depends on how well they perform in school.

Just as parents need to communicate their love for their children even when they fail, teachers need to communicate that they still accept their students even when they perform poorly. Ginott warns of the danger of continual association between achievement levels and character judgments. For Ginott, it is imperative that teachers distinguish between a student's accomplishments and the value of that student. Rather than view a student's display of off-task or inappropriate behavior as a reflection of a character flaw, the teacher takes responsibility for teaching each student to be on-task to achieve learning goals.

While the promise of approval and respect as a positive reinforcer for on-task and productive behavior can be effective in the short run, it produces undesirable side effects over time. Thus, rewards for achievement or on-task behaviors that communicate, "You are a better, more worthwhile person because you have succeeded or behaved as someone else wants you to behave," are destructive reinforcers. Likewise, withholding affection and displaying personal disappointment after off-task behaviors are destructive punishments.

When students are led to believe that the most successful among them will be accepted and respected more than those who are less successful, their ego defense mechanisms discourage their participation in what can seem like a game with excessively high stakes and few winners. When students believe they are worth less in the eyes of others if they are less successful in school-related activities, they become defensive about participating in such activities. A defensive attitude undermines a cooperative stance (Cangelosi, 1997).

Students Are People Too

For Ginott, an important aspect of the learning environment is the socio-emotional climate in the classroom. His position is that discipline problems will be markedly reduced if teachers create an atmosphere of concern for students' feelings. His main thrust for teachers is that they should deal positively with students' emotions and recognize that their communication pattern will strongly influence students' feelings and, ultimately, their self-esteem.

Ginott also advocates that teachers deal openly with their own feelings. He reminds teachers that "students are people" and should be treated with respect. When conflict arises, teachers often resort to attacking students by putting them down rather than dealing with their feelings.

Guidance via effective communication occurs over an extended period and takes time to take hold. Ginott described this process as "a series of little victories." When teachers influence behavior through compassion, understanding, support, and respect they can turn volatile situations into victories and, over time, develop student self-direction, responsibility, and concern for others. He emphasizes the importance of teachers modeling the behavior they expect of their students by exercising self-discipline. Students observe how teachers handle conflict situations and tend to imitate them.

Teacher Self-discipline

The importance of teachers' self-discipline and maturity is a fundamental premise of Ginott's approach to classroom discipline. These qualities are reflected in their ability to listen sensitively to students' communications and respond to students in positive ways. Teachers should accept the validity of students feelings, assist students to take appropriate responsibility for their actions, and help students engage in styles of conflict resolution and problem-solving that do not lead to power struggles.

Communicating in Sane Messages

Ginott's main message for teachers is to distinguish between the "deed and the doer" at all times. He refers to messages that address the problem situation without attacking the student personally as *sane messages*. Sane messages address the situation that is creating the difficulty, express anger appropriately, acknowledge students' feelings, and invite cooperation. Insane messages go beyond the problem at hand to attack the student's personally. These types of messages tell students to deny their feelings about themselves and to base their sense of self-worth on others' judgments. Congruent messages are communications that allow students to trust their own perceptions and feelings.

Ginott warns teachers of the disabling effect of labeling students and of using sarcasm. Such character assassinations as labeling, diagnosing, and offering prognoses of students' character contribute to negative self-images that often turn into self-fulfilling prophecies. Comments such as the following only serve to limit students' visions of what they can do and be: "You're always so irresponsible."

Similarly, Ginott warns of the danger of sarcasm. While teachers may only be intending to be clever, this form of wit is often at the student's expense. Students often do not understand the intended wit and end up with hurt feelings because they feel they are being put down. It is better to avoid sarcasm than to run the risk of hurting students' feelings.

Furthermore, a sane and congruent communication never denies feelings, whether students' or teachers'. Ginott not only believes teachers have a right to their anger, he also recommends that they express their anger directly. He feels that given the demands put on teachers, it's natural to get frustrated and angry occasionally.

The Perils of Praise

Like many others (e.g., Dreikurs, Brophy, Gordon, Kohn), Ginott takes issue with teacher praise. As with negative comments, praise can have detrimental effects on forming a positive self-image. Ginott warns of the drawbacks of using praise, especially when it is evaluative.

Evaluative praise evaluates students; the teacher becomes a source of approval deciding on a student's worth. Appreciative praise shows recognition for what a student has done, acknowledges the student's effort, and shares the teacher's personal reaction. Rather than evaluative praise, teachers should describe their own feelings and provide honest recognitions and comment on student efforts, as in, "The words you chose really painted a picture for me."

Ginott's specific points about praise are presented in more detail along with other authors' positions on praise in Chapter 4.

Why to Avoid the Why-question

Rather than promoting a helping relationship and building trust, asking *why* hints at criticism. The implicit assumption with the why-question is that the student should have acted differently. This gives the message that you are judging not accepting the student.

For many, the word establishes a mindset of disapproval, e.g., "Why didn't you . . . ?", "Why can't you . . . ?", "Why are you . . . ?", "Why do you have to . . . ?" Thus, feelings of being threatened or judged are often evoked, leading to either withdrawing or the need to rationalize or defend, distracting from the communication process.

As Ginott sees it, why-questions are character assassinations in disguise—just another form of criticism. They tell students they have a problem. These questions don't prompt inquiry, and they don't really call for answers. Such questions as the following are merely hostile inquiries, used primarily to make students feel guilty.

"Why can't you get along with anyone?"

"Why are you always the last one finished?"

"Why can't you ever find your work?"

Ginott's Guidelines for Teachers

Teachers should:

- Model the behavior they want to see from their students.
- Handle conflict reasonably and respectfully by exercising self-discipline.
- When correcting students, send sane messages that address the situation not the student.
- Express anger, but in sane (appropriate) ways.
- Describe the student's behavior and offer acceptable alternatives.
- Use encouragement rather than praise.

Teachers should not:

- Equate work with worth.
- Label students or diagnose their character.
- Use sarcasm.
- Get into arguments with students.
- Preach, moralize, or try to impose guilt.
- Give evaluative praise.

Classroom Strategies and Interventions

Ginott has some important recommendations for teachers. Regarding punishment, he believes punishment only produces hostility and a desire for revenge. It never makes students want to improve. Hence, he suggests teachers find alternatives to punishments. Below are some specific examples of classroom strategies.

Eliminate Labeling

Ginott coined the phrase, "labeling is disabling," believing that it limits students' vision of themselves. Repeated messages over time become self-fulfilling prophecies. Instead, he suggests that teachers make statements that encourage students to set goals for themselves by expressing their belief in students.

"I think you can solve this on your own, but if you need help let me know."

Invite Cooperation

Teachers invite cooperation by describing the situation and indicating what needs to be done. In avoiding direct commands, teachers allow students to decide what they should do.

"This is time to work without any noise. You need to work silently now."

Ginott also suggests another way to invite cooperation. Teachers can decide with the class before an activity what kinds of personal behavior will be needed during the activity.

Express Anger in Sane Ways

When teachers lose control, they tend to communicate with students in ways that blame students for whatever is happening. Their comments are delivered as students personality flaws, rather than as a genuine expression of the feeling they are experiencing. What is called for is a clear distinction between what the teacher is experiencing and what students are doing. Not,

> *"You're always talking when you're supposed to be working. Can't you keep your mouth shut."* or *"I can't believe you are that irresponsible,"*

rather,

> *"I'm so angry right now I want to scream!"* or *"I'm disgusted by that comment you made to Jackie."*

Teachers can also enlist students to communicate their own messages in nonblameful language by facilitating the communication process and asking students to relate their own experiences and reactions rather than blame the other person. So the teacher might say,

> *"Instead of telling us why Manny did what he did, tell us about your own feelings and reasons for doing what you did."*

The teacher can provide further guidance by offering the student a way to start, as in:

> *"Try starting by saying, 'I got angry when . . . ,' and then go on from there."*

Stay in the Present

For Ginott, staying in the present means teachers don't pre-judge or hold grudges. Like Glasser, he thinks teachers' motto should be, "Every day is a new beginning."

> *"Lets start with a clean slate today, Latisha."*

Use Self-discipline

Teachers should refrain from using behaviors they are trying to eliminate in their students, such as raising their voice to stop loud talking, using force to break up a fight, or being rude to students who are showing disrespect.

Accept and Acknowledge Students' Feelings

When students are upset or afraid, telling them not to be afraid, explaining that no one else is afraid, or telling them that they shouldn't be afraid sends the message that their feelings are not real. It doesn't dispel their emotions, rather it causes them to doubt their own inner feelings. The message they get is that the teacher doesn't understand and, therefore, may not be helpful in times of trouble. Ginott cautions teachers to treat children's fears carefully. A better response is to acknowledge what they feel and offer assistance.

> *"I see you're upset. How can I help?"*

With older students, invalidating feelings tells students they are not accepted. Such dismissal implies that students are not entitled to their feelings, and that the teacher knows how they ought to feel.

Use Laconic Language

Laconic language is short and to-the-point. All too often, teachers give long, drawnout directions. Rather than pontificate, teachers should talk sparingly. He suggests they talk like reporters write—in headlines and soundbites. Ginott thinks unnecessary detailed talk about what to do is disrespectful to students. Furthermore, it slows down learning activities, conditions students to tune out, and provokes annoyance.

Direction Rather Than Correction

Misbehavior requires that students be redirected, not reprimanded. Ginott recommends that teachers issue simple requests, just the facts with no editorial commentary. The teacher simply states the facts and lets students decide whether their behavior is in keeping with what they expect of themselves.

For example, the teacher might say:

"I would like you to stop talking, so you can hear the directions."

Considerations and Potential Concerns

Developing the kinds of communication and dialogue Ginott recommends will require a considerable amount of commitment, practice, and effort. Teachers' efforts to communicate empathy and warmth for students will not always be reciprocated by trust and cooperation. The multifaceted nature of the student/teacher relationship make it impossible to prescribe relationships between what and how the teacher communicates and how students will react. A whole host of social and cultural as well as individual differences affect perceptions and interpretations of, and reactions to, any communication.

While using effective communication, displaying empathy, and valuing students' feelings are necessary tools for today's classroom, they may not be sufficient as a total classroom management plan. These strategies may need to be supplemented for dealing with students who display defiant, hostile, or verbally-abusive behavior, at least initially.

The way of interacting with students Ginott espouses involves more than skill, per se—it must be accompanied by a genuine desire to make the classroom experience more positive. Finally, in order for these strategies to work optimally, teachers need to make them their own by integrating them into their own personal style. Direct experience with particular students, groups, and classes will allow teachers to determine what works, in what setting and in what context.

Learning Practice Task: Distinguishing Between the Deed and the Doer

Activity Directions: For each of the following student behaviors, write an alternative statement that rejects the student's behavior but not the student.

Student Behavior	Statement Rejecting Student	Statement Rejecting Behavior Only
Paul won't let Tommy have a turn.	*Nice boys let others have their turn.*	_____ _____ _____
Sally has left the reading center a mess.	*Don't you know any better?*	_____ _____ _____
Jimmy is talking while Sue is giving her answer.	*Don't be so impolite.*	_____ _____ _____
Becky doesn't complete her part of a group assignment.	*You haven't been much help to your group.*	_____ _____ _____
Francisco teases Carla about being fat.	*Other people have feelings, too, you know.*	_____ _____ _____

Learning Practice Task: Case Study of No-work-Kate

Activity Directions: Read the case study below. Then working with a partner, develop some strategies that are consistent with Ginott's ideas about dealing with students.

Kate, a student in Ms. Bee's class, does little socializing with other students and never disrupts class. But Ms. Bee cannot get her to do her work. She hardly ever completes an assignment. She puts forth very little effort.

How would Ginott deal with Kate?

Ginott would advise teachers to use a number of gentle tactics to encourage Kate to do her work.

Give an appropriate example for each of the following:

Sending a sane message. _____

_____

_____

_____

Inviting cooperation. _____

_____

_____

_____

Acknowledging feelings. _____

_____

_____

_____

Correcting by directing. _____

_____

_____

_____

Chapter 6

Managing for Compliance

Using Rewards and Consequences to Modify Student Behavior

Traditional wisdom for managing individual student behavior and maintaining order in the classroom has relied on the use of extrinsic rewards and punishment, praise, modeling, and teacher evaluation of appropriate behavior and acceptable work. When teachers use consequences to manage students' behavior, they are using their authority position to convince students to control their behavior.

For some students, especially younger students still in the early stages of moral development and older students who are testing the waters, teachers will need to apply appropriate consequences. Extrinsic reinforcers are sometimes the only way to get some students to begin to behave appropriately, in particular, those who have a history of unsuccessful school experiences and very limited success with classroom learning tasks. Even for these students, however, once more adaptive behavior is demonstrated, other strategies that help them develop their own self-control need to be introduced.

It may also be necessary to use consequences to suppress, control, and redirect behavior which is aggressive, abusive, or disruptive to learning. For this reason, it is important for teachers to have such strategies in their repertoire. However, teachers should view getting students to behave in a desired way for the moment with extrinsic motivation as only a shortterm goal. Motivating students to want to behave appropriately is the ultimate long-range goal and involves systematically supporting students' independence and self-management. Teachers who are most successful in dealing with students who pose behavior challenges use longterm, solution-oriented approaches rather than shortterm desist and control responses (Brophy & McCaslin, 1992). In so doing, they typically enlist students to become active participants in developing a resolution to the problem.

Basically, teachers either reward students for behaving appropriately or punish them for behaving inappropriately. Research has clearly demonstrated that individuals respond better to positive reinforcement than they do to punishment, thus the emphasis for school-based behavior and classroom management has been on identifying and dispensing rewards that will develop, sustain, or increase behaviors that are deemed appropriate for the classroom setting.

Relying primarily on the behavioral model for classroom management does have certain benefits. The foremost is that it offers teachers alternatives for working with students that are positive and helps them refrain from using reprimands and punishment to control student behavior. Also, the behavioral approach, with its emphasis on rewarding appropriate behavior, helps teachers focus on identifying potentially meaningful reinforcers for students, and thus, is more likely to produce positive and supportive interactions with students. Its focus on actual behaviors also helps teachers to be more objective and refrain from labeling students' character.

For the most part, the behavioral approach does get students to comply with the teacher's demands, but it perpetuates student reliance on the teacher rather than enhances student autonomy. Several issues have been raised by researchers which serve to question the use of rewards and punishment to modify student behavior.

While the behavioral approach has several benefits, it is not without its potential drawbacks. There are some research findings, especially relative to the effects of contingent use of rewards on classroom behavior, indicating that the relationship between rewards and punishment and subsequent individual student behavior is more complex than had been assumed by those advocating primary use of the behavioral approach for managing classroom behavior. Several issues have been raised by researchers which serve to question the use of rewards and punishment to modify student behavior. Extrinsic positive reinforcement doesn't always increase desired behavior. Under certain conditions, positive reinforcement can have detrimental effects. For example, giving expected tangible rewards simply for doing a task, without regard to standard of performance, has a negative effect (Cameron & Pierce, 1994).

Extrinsically-motivated actions are characterized by pressure and tension and can result in low self-esteem and anxiety (Deci & Ryan, 1985). Using rewards for desired behavior and academic performance can erode intrinsic motivation (Dickinson, 1989; Doyle, 1986; Lepper, 1983; Richmond & McCroskey, 1984; Schwartz, 1990; Sutherland, 1993). Students who are already motivated to learn can lose their intrinsic motivation to do so if they become too interested in earning extrinsic rewards (e.g., Condry & Chambers, 1978; DeCharms, 1976; Deci, 1976, 1978; Deci & Ryan, 1987; Lepper & Greene, 1978; Pittman, Boggiano, & Ruble, 1982; Ross, 1976).

Another issue relates to the alignment of teacher intention with actual student effect. Students don't always experience consequences congruent with the teacher's intention. For example, praising certain students in front of their peers can be counterproductive. For some students, teacher attention in the form of recognition or praise is embarrassing or threatening rather than rewarding.

Furthermore, the behavioral change brought about by positive and negative reinforcements in one situation has not been shown to generalize to other situations (e.g., classes, teachers, environments) or to be maintained when the extrinsic reinforcers are dropped (Brophy & Putnam, 1978; Emery & Marholin, 1977). In addition, the effectiveness of positive and negative reinforcements as a classroom management tool varies according to the student's age and developmental level, with the pattern being that it is most effective with younger students, somewhat less effective with upper-elementary and middle school students, and least effective with secondary school students (Brophy & Putnam, 1978; Forness, 1973; Stallings, 1975).

Another important issue is that positive reinforcement can increase students' learned helplessness and dependency if they come to rely excessively on teacher approval in lieu of their own motivation (Ginott, 1972; Weiner, 1979). Similarly, positive reinforcement can discourage creativity if students become more concerned about pleasing their teachers or conforming to their teachers' expectations than on finding their own solutions to problems (Johnson & Johnson, 1987; Soar & Soar, 1975).

Inhibiting behavior should not be confused with instilling attitudes. Student obedience can not be equated with student motivation. Conditions that foster quick obedience do not foster internalization of self-control, and internalized self-control, or self-regulation, is necessary to function adaptively both in classrooms and in society (e.g., Kohn,

1993; Lepper, 1983; McCaslin & Good, 1992). As long as conceptions of classroom management remain rooted in the behavioral paradigm of teaching, the responsibility for student motivation and effort will fall largely on teachers, and outside of students themselves.

Another potential danger with the use of consequences to control students not often considered is that it can serve to insulate teachers from important feedback on their classroom practices. For example, students might disguise the fact that they are bored, frustrated, or even angry because of feared negative consequences. Hence, teachers fail to realize the need to use other strategies that might enhance learning and student-teacher relationships. Such lack of feedback can also serve to sustain inferior or less effective teaching practices (Grossman, 1990; Ryan, 1979).

Skinner's Behavior Modification

The basic principle of reinforcement theory is that voluntary behavior is largely determined by the events or consequences that immediately follow it. That is, behavior is learned, and an individual's behavior is influenced by the consequences that follow it. Hence, what is important is the consequence that the behavior produces because that is what will over time strengthen, maintain, or weaken the occurrence of the behavior in the future.

Overview of reinforcement theory:

- The basic premise for using consequences to effect behavior change is that behavior is influenced by the consequences that follow it.
- Behavior can be developed, maintained, strengthened, or weakened by the consequences which follow the behavior.
- Reinforcement theory, or behavior modification, is based on the notion that behavior that is rewarded will tend to be repeated while behavior that is not rewarded (i.e., ignored or punished) will tend to be weakened or eliminated.
- Research supports that positive reinforcement is a much more powerful behavior modification tool than punishment, hence management strategies advocated for the classroom emphasize using positive reinforcement or rewards to modify student behavior.

This basic principle as applied to teaching, and learning theory has been given a variety of labels by educators. It has been referred to as contingency management, precision teaching, positive feedback, reinforcement theory, operant conditioning, applied behavior analysis, and, most commonly, behavior modification. Regardless of the label, the essence of the approach is that you deal with the student's here-and-now behaviors which are readily observable, rather than look at the student's past history to try to determine the cause of the behavior.

Managing students' behavior by applying consequences has three major benefits.

1. It offers teachers alternatives in working with students that are positive and helps them get away from primarily using reprimands and punishment to control student behavior.
2. The behavioral approach, with its emphasis on rewarding appropriate behavior, helps teachers focus on identifying potentially meaningful reinforcers for students, and thus, is more likely to produce positive and supportive interactions with students.
3. Its focus on actual behaviors helps teachers to be more objective and keep from labeling students' character (e.g., lazy, inconsiderate, manipulative).

In relying primarily on a behavioral approach for classroom management, teachers should consider the following potential drawbacks.

- What the teacher may think is reinforcing may have the opposite effect for some students.
- Becoming too interested in extrinsic rewards can lessen students' intrinsic motivation.
- Students may become dependent on teacher approval.
- Creativity can be discouraged.
- Teachers may be deprived of important feedback if students fear negative consequences.
- Behavior change in one situation does not generalize to other situations.
- Its effectiveness lessens as students get older.

Getting students to behave in a desired way for the moment with extrinsic motivation is only a shortterm goal. Motivating students to want to behave appropriately is the ultimate longterm goal and involves systematically supporting students' in developing internal controls. Nonetheless, teachers will sometimes need to use consequences to ensure a safe and productive learning environment for all students. While using behavior modification techniques can be viewed as manipulative, it is actually not the technique that is manipulative, rather it is the teacher's intention. If these techniques are used solely to ensure mindless compliance or to seek revenge, then they are manipulative. Any technique that attempts to change students' behavior can be used unethically if it is merely self-serving. A more important limitation of management by consequences is that focusing on the obvious and overt behavior can keep the teacher from addressing the underlying motivation for the inappropriate behavior, accommodating basic unmet needs, or discovering the real message being communicated by the inappropriate behavior.

Ideally, students find satisfaction in their learning and the sense of purpose and accomplishment that ensues. Satisfactorily completing learning tasks is essentially its own intrinsic reward. Realistically, this happens only with more capable students who have the greatest opportunity to experience success and the resulting enhanced self-esteem. For many other students, there are few opportunities to experience success simply on the basis of their performance. For these students, the teacher's purposeful and sensitive use of rewards can make a difference. Such rewards may be in the form of extra teacher attention, support and recognition, as well as with appropriate praise and encouragement of incremental gains in learning and performance.

The Four Basic Reinforcement Principles

The following basic principles describe the effect on behavior of four different consequences for behavior.

Positive Reinforcement

The occurrence of a behavior is increased when that behavior is followed by a positive consequence.

If Joey is rewarded with a positive consequence such as verbal praise or a star every time he responds appropriately during group discussion, his appropriate behavior is likely to occur more frequently.

If you want someone to respond in a desired way you should follow the desired response with a positive reinforcer. Using positive reinforcers for appropriate behavior usually generates good feelings on the part of both the giver and the receiver. Positive reinforcers can be tangible, such as food, toys, money, or tokens to be exchanged for other reinforcers, or social, such as adult or peer approval or recognition. Privileges, activities, or responsibilities, or things a person likes to do, can also be used as reinforcers and are especially appropriate for use in the classroom. Reinforcers occurring naturally in the environment, such as free time, extra recess, or special responsibilities in a school setting, should be used as often as possible.

Punishment Type I

Behavior is weakened when that behavior is followed by a negative consequence.

Luis was kept after school for starting a fight in class. His fighting was punished by his being kept after school, a negative consequence.

This type of punishment has been and still is a popular method used by schools to attempt to change and control behavior. However, there are many reasons why it should be applied with caution. Punishment Type I:

- Often only suppresses the punished behavior for a brief period of time.
- Does not weaken behavior in the long run.
- May lead to other inappropriate behaviors.
- May generate negative feelings such as resentment, fear, hostility.
- May be stimulating or reinforcing in that it requires the attention of significant adults, whose presence is often reinforcing.
- May strengthen inappropriate behaviors which remove the punishment, such as pleading, lying, cheating.

Punishment Type II

Behavior is weakened when occurrence of the behavior results in removal of a positive reinforcer. This form of punishment is generally more effective than Punishment Type I. There are basically two forms of Punishment Type II.

1. Time Out. The contingent withdrawal of reinforcement for a specified period of time.

   When Maxine makes disruptive noises to gain attention from her classmates, she is removed for a brief period of time to the hallway. Because Maxine is removed from the available source of positive reinforcement (peer attention) her disruptive noise-making should be weakened.

2. Response Cost. The contingent withdrawal of a specified amount of reinforcement.

   Rafael frequently called out answers before being called on, so his teacher decided to give him five poker chips when he entered the class. Each time he talked without being called on, he "paid" the teacher one chip. At the end of the day, each chip he had left could be redeemed for a specific reward. Rafael's failure to wait to be called on resulted in the removal of a specified amount of reinforcement, i.e., one chip.

Negative Reinforcement

Behavior is strengthened when occurrence of the behavior results in the removal of a negative reinforcer.

For Charlene, doing math is a negative reinforcer. Whenever she got nine of the first ten problems correct, her teacher released her from having to do the last five problems. Completing her math was strengthened because it had the effect of terminating a negative reinforcer, i.e., doing more math.

Five Additional Reinforcement Principles

Extinction

Behavior is weakened and/or eliminated when no reinforcement is given (i.e., behavior is ignored). Teachers often inadvertently extinguish appropriate behavior and strengthen inappropriate behavior by ignoring students when they are working quietly and constructively. By failing to reinforce the constructive work, teachers may weaken appropriate behavior. When the students begin to talk to their neighbors, the teacher starts yelling at them for not working. By attending to this behavior while ignoring constructive work, the teacher may strengthen the inappropriate behavior.

Premack Principle

High frequency behaviors can be used to reinforce low frequency behaviors. If a person's preferred (high frequency/high probability) behavior becomes dependent on the occurrence of a less preferred (low frequency/low probability) behavior, the less preferred behavior will be increased.

Rudine requires an inordinate amount of teacher attention. To try to get Rudine to work for longer periods of time independently, the teacher gave her a red plastic chip for each ten-minute period she worked without seeking the teacher's attention. At the end of the morning, each chip was worth one minute of teacher attention. The preferred behavior (being with the teacher) was used to reinforce the less preferred behavior, working independently.

Other examples of the Premack Principle are:
- "You do what I say before you do what you want."
- "Eat your peas and then you can have your ice cream."
- "If all of you get your books and materials put away, you can leave for recess early."
- "If you work quietly for twenty minutes, you can have free time to talk to anyone you like for five minutes."

Reinforcement of Incompatible Behavior

A behavior is weakened when an incompatible behavior is reinforced.

When students are constantly out of their seats, the teacher could choose to reinforce in-seat behavior rather than punish out-of-seat behavior.

The following are additional examples of an inappropriate behavior and its corresponding incompatible behavior:

Inappropriate Behavior	Incompatible Behavior
Students being late	Students arriving on time
Talking without permission	Raising hand and being called on
Requiring teacher attention to complete work	Working independently

Shaping

Closer and closer approximations to the ultimate desired behavior are reinforced. When a desired behavior does not occur or is at a very low level, shaping procedures can be effective. In shaping, reinforcement and extinction are combined to achieve new behavior. There are two essential aspects of shaping:

1. Differential Reinforcement in which only the responses that meet a certain criterion are reinforced, while those that do not meet the criterion are not reinforced (extinguished);

2. Shifting the Reinforcement Criterion such that the response criterion to be reinforced is gradually changed in the direction of the final desired behavior.

Working longer or faster, paying attention, staying in one's seat, and engaging in desirable social behavior are examples of behavior for which shaping is appropriate.

Sasha's class disturbances were continuous. To begin to modify her behavior, her teacher decided to reinforce her for behaving for fifteen minutes, for half an hour, for one hour, for two hours, and finally for the entire morning. Her appropriate behavior was shaped from a few minutes in duration to all morning.

Satiation

Repeated presentation of a reinforcer results in loss of its effectiveness.

The teacher who says, "Great job," to students over and over again may find that this form of praise becomes ineffective over time.

The type of reinforcement given should be varied to maintain effectiveness. For example, the teacher might keep a variety of treats in a "treasure" box and change the contents frequently so that students never know what treat they might get.

Examples of Decreasing Inappropriate Behavior

Inappropriate Behavior: Students had been several minutes late arriving for class.

Desired Behavior: Arriving on time to class.

Intervention Strategy: Teacher read a short segment of an exciting mystery story for the first few minutes after lunch one day, then announced that it would be continued during the first few minutes of class each morning. Those present would have a chance to hear what happened next.

Reinforcer: Hearing a mystery story.

Inappropriate Behavior: Juan frequently talks without permission.

Desired Behavior: Raising hand and being called on before speaking.

Intervention Strategy: Juan was given five poker chips when he entered the classroom. Each time he talked without permission he "paid" the teacher one chip. At the end of the day, each chip remaining in his possession was worth an allotted period of time to be spent working on the computer.

Reinforcer: Using the computer.

Inappropriate Behavior: Abby requires excessive amount of teacher attention.

Desired Behavior: Longer periods of time working independently.

Intervention Strategy: For each fifteen-minute period that Abby worked independently, she received a token. At the end of a two-hour period each token was worth one minute of teacher attention.

Reinforcer: Having teacher attention.

Inappropriate Behavior: Students were talking out excessively, creating a chaotic learning environment.

Desired Behavior: Keeping talkouts to 5 or less during the 45 minute reading class.

Intervention Strategy: The teacher informed students that she would allow them a special privilege the last 5 minutes of class each day if they decreased talkouts to less than 5 during a class period. The students suggested games, snacks, and free time as special privileges. Talkouts were recorded with a checkmark on the board.

Reinforcer: Special privilege for the last 5 minutes of class.

Examples of Increasing Appropriate Behavior

Desired Behavior: Recognition of sight words.

Intervention Strategy: For each word learned, Maxine received a bead; however, if a word was missed during the review sessions, a bead was returned. When a pre-selected number of beads had been accumulated, the student was given time to string the beads.

Reinforcer: Receiving beads for a necklace.

Desired Behavior: Learning multiplication tables.

Intervention Strategy: One piece of a model car was given for each learned multiplication fact. When all the parts had been earned, the student could assemble the car during free time.

Reinforcer: Earning pieces of a model car kit.

Desired Behavior: For Sam and Micky to complete more of their class assignments.

Intervention Strategy: Since Sam and Micky often did not complete their written assignments, the teacher offered them the opportunity to earn an extra gym period for the class if they completed at least 90% of their written assignments for 1 week.

Reinforcer: Opportunity for class to have an extra gym class.

Desired Behavior: Completing class math assignments.

Intervention Strategy: Since Jeff hated doing his math assignments, the teacher agreed to check his work after he had completed 10 of the 15 problems assigned. If he had got 9 of the first 10 problems correct, he did not have to do the last 5.

Reinforcer: Not having to finish the last 5 problems.

Behavior Modification Principles Simplified: Options for Modifying Behavior

Increasing Desired Behavior

Add (+)

Positive Reinforcement: Add reward or incentive.

Shaping: Reward improvement until desired behavior is reached.

Premack Principle: Contingent pairing of reward with something negative.

Take Away (−)

Negative Reinforcement: Take away something negative.

Decreasing Undesired Behavior

Add (+)

Punishment Type I: Add negative consequence.

Reinforcing Incompatible Behavior: Add reinforcement for opposite behavior while taking away any reinforcement for undesirable behavior.

Take Away (−)

Punishment Type II: Take away positive reinforcer.

Response Cost: Take away contingent amount of reinforcement or something earned.

Time Out: Take away from reinforcing environment.

Extinction: Take away any reinforcement.

Learning Practice Task: Identifying Classroom Examples

Activity Directions: List examples of your use of any of the nine reinforcement principles in your classroom.

Strategies to increase desired behavior: Positive and negative reinforcement, shaping, and the Premack principle.

_____

_____

_____

_____

_____

_____

Strategies to decrease inappropriate behavior: Punishment, time out, response cost, planned ignoring, and reinforcement of incompatible behavior.

_____

_____

_____

_____

_____

_____

Using Punishment Effectively

If and when to punish students has been the subject of wide debate. The effects of punishment are limited and specific. Although punishment can control misbehavior, it does not teach desirable behavior or reduce the desire to misbehave. And punishment has retaliatory side effects that can either be active (spite, revenge, vandalism, assault) or passive (tardiness, truancy, inattention, theft, restlessness). In addition, punishment over time can induce resistance to teacher influence.

Punishment is never a solution by itself; at best it is only part of a solution. In general, punishment should:

- Be used discriminately rather than routinely, combined with positive procedures, and used only when students are not responsive to reward-based interventions or praise/ignore strategies.
- Be used only in response to repeated misbehavior, as a "treatment of last resort" for students who persist in the same kinds of misbehavior.
- Be employed consciously and deliberately, as part of a planned response to repeated misbehavior (i.e., as a logical consequence).

What to Remember about Using Punishment

Characteristics of Effective Punishment

- Is given immediately;
- Makes it clear that it is the behavior that is being rejected, not the person;
- Relies on taking away reinforcers while providing a clear-cut method for earning them back;
- Makes use of a single warning (either a signal or verbal);
- Is delivered in a calm, matter-of-fact manner;
- Is given along with reinforcement for behavior incompatible with the punished behavior;
- Is consistent in that the undesired behavior never receives reinforcement;
- Is logically related to the type of misbehavior.

For Punishment to be Effective It Must

- Prevent avoidance and escape from the source of punishment;
- Minimize the need for future punishment;
- Not provide a model of aggressive behavior;
- Not be excessive in frequency or duration.

Problems Associated with the Use of Punishment

- When punished, children learn to escape and avoid the punisher.
- Whatever removes the punishment will be strengthened. If pleading, false promises, or lying remove the punishment, inappropriate behavior will be strengthened.
- Punishment generates negative emotional feelings.
- Punishment can cause counter-aggressive behavior (i.e., desire for revenge or retaliation).
- Punishment does not teach the correct behavior.
- Punishment suppresses the undesirable behavior temporarily but does not weaken it longterm.
- Punishment can actually be reinforcing in that it requires the attention of significant adults.

Critical Reflection on Practice: Thinking About Punishment

Activity Directions: For this activity, you will be working with 3 to 5 peers.

1. Discuss the following:
   - Remember a time you were punished by your parent(s).
     —What was your initial response? Longterm response?
     —What did you learn? or learn to do?
     —Was it the intended lesson?
   - In your experience, does punishment "work?"
   - How are you still carrying the effects of punishment with you now?

2. As a group, try to get consensus on some beliefs and attitudes about punishment.

Our consensus beliefs and attitudes about punishment:

_____

_____

_____

_____

_____

_____

Using Time Out

The time-out strategy is an acceptable and often effective strategy for calming down a rowdy or misbehaving elementary school child. Basically, the student is sent to a stimulation-free area or time-out room for 2, 5, or perhaps 10 or 15 minutes. The time-out area should be free of high-interest stimulation—no windows; no secretaries to watch; no lunch bags to plunder; no equipment to fiddle with; and no attractive magazines, posters, or calendars. The purpose of time out if for the student to calm down and think about his or her behavior, not earn a refreshing change of scenery.

Many junior and senior high schools have created in-school monitored suspension rooms that are used for short periods during the day, as well as for all-day detentions. The suspension rooms operate in basically the same way as time-out areas, except that teachers or supervisors monitor the room on a rotating basis. The suspended students are expected to continue working as if they were attending their normal classes (Davis & Thomas, 1989).

An important consideration is that if time out is being used as a routine response to student inappropriate behavior, then it should indicate to the teacher the need to try additional strategies.

Guidelines for effective use of time out

The following guidelines are important to follow when using time out (Alberto & Troutman, 1990, pp. 274–275).

A teacher should work through the following sequence of steps in using a time-out room or any of the forms of this procedure.

1. Before beginning to use time out as a management procedure, identify the behavior(s) that will result in use of a time-out procedure. Be sure the students understand the behavior. Explain the behavior expected of students while they are in time out. Tell them how long the time-out period will last.

2. When the misbehavior occurs, re-identify it. Tell the student in a calm manner, "That is fighting. Go to time out for ___ minutes." No other conversation should ensue. Ignore any statements the student may make as an excuse for misbehavior or relating to feelings about time out. If necessary, lead the student to the time-out area. If the student resists, Hall and Hall (1980, p. 11) suggest that the teacher:

   a. Gently but firmly lead the student to time out.

   b. Be prepared to add time to time out if the student refuses to go or yells, screams, kicks, or turns over furniture.

   c. Require the student to clean up any mess resulting from resistance to time out before the student may return to classroom activities.

   d. Be prepared to use a backup consequence for students who refuse time out.

3. Once a student enters the time-out area, the time begins. Check your watch or set a timer. Gast and Nelson (1977a) review three formats for contingent release from time-out rooms:

   a. Release contingent on a specified period (for example, two minutes) of appropriate behavior.

   b. Release contingent on a minimum duration of time out, with an extension until all inappropriate behavior has terminated.

   c. Release contingent on a minimum duration of time out, with an extension (such as 15 seconds) during which no inappropriate responses are exhibited.

4. Once the time interval has ended, return the student to the previous appropriate activity. Do not comment on how well the student behaved while in time out. A student should be returned to the activity he or she was engaged in before time out to avoid negatively reinforcing an escape from that activity.

Monitoring the use of time out

To monitor the effects of time out and to substantiate proper and ethical use of the procedure, records should be kept of each time-out occasion, especially when a time-out room is used.

Records should include at least the following information (Gast & Nelson, 1977b):

1. The student's name.

2. The episode resulting in the student's placement in time out (behavior, activity, other students involved, staff person and so on).

3. The time of day the student was placed in time out.

4. The time of day the student was released from time out.

5. The total time in time out.

6. The type of time out (contingent, exclusion, or seclusion).

7. The student's behavior in time out.

Questions to ask before using time out

Prior to selecting a time-out procedure, the teacher should consider the following questions concerning its use:

1. Have more positive procedures, for example, differential reinforcement strategies, been considered?
2. Have both nonseclusionary and seclusionary time-out procedures been considered?
3. Can time out be implemented with minimal student resistance? Can the teacher handle the possible resistance?
4. Have the rules of appropriate behavior and the results for misbehavior been clearly explained and understood?
5. Have the rules of behavior while in time out been clearly explained and understood?
6. Have district regulations concerning the use of time-out procedures been reviewed and complied with?
7. Will appropriate behavior be reinforced in conjunction with the use of time out?

Types of Reinforcers: The Reinforcement Hierarchy

There are a variety of reinforcers that can be effective for promoting desired behaviors. Effectiveness of a reinforcer will depend on individual student characteristics and preferences as well as the particular setting and the task demands. Factors such as age, social class, learning aptitude, task difficulty, and skill acquisition level will influence reinforcer effectiveness.

Reinforcers can be thought of on a continuum beginning with more tangible rewards and ultimately ending with personal satisfaction. The following continuum represents eight levels of reinforcers.

Reinforcers

Level 1	Level 2	Level 3	Level 4	Level 5	Level 6	Level 7	Level 8
Consumable	Tangible	Token	Activity	Privilege	Peer Recognition	Adult Approval	Self Satisfaction

The continuum is hierarchical, moving from lower-order consumable reinforcers toward higher-order reinforcers that occur naturally in the classroom environment like special privileges, teacher praise, and eventually, self-satisfaction with one's own accomplishments.

There are two principles that apply to this hierarchy of reinforcers.

Principle 1: You should not use lower levels of reinforcement than are actually necessary to initiate or maintain behavior.

Principle 2: You should continually move along the continuum toward higher-order reinforcers that occur naturally in the environment.

Material Reinforcers

Consumable, tangible, and token reinforcers are all material rewards. Consumable reinforcers are edible rewards such as M&Ms, jelly beans, life savers, peanuts, raisins, or chips. Tangible rewards are items such as toys, badges, certificates, stars, or stickers. Although material reinforcers can be quite effective, higher-order types of reinforcers can be just as effective.

Token reinforcers are tangible "place holders" that can be exchanged at a later time for other reinforcers. They work like money in that they can be accumulated and "spent" for something desired sometime in the future. Frequently poker chips, stars, checkmarks, happy faces, or points are used in classrooms as tokens. Token systems are often used in special education classes either for the whole class or for individuals who have not responded to praise, activities, or other reinforcers common to the classroom setting. In general education classrooms, teachers who use points or checks which accumulate toward earning other rewards are using token systems. Token systems are successful partly because they allow the reinforcement to be broken down into small segments thereby providing immediate and frequent reinforcement.

Token reinforcement systems, when properly implemented, can be effective for managing a wide range of behaviors. Token systems usually work best if the class or individual students involved participate in setting up the system and defining the types and costs of the reinforcers to be earned. Token systems should be kept simple so that the record system and the exchange policy are manageable for the classroom teacher.

Sometimes token systems can be used to condition other naturally occurring reinforcers. Students who have not responded to typical classroom reinforcers will work for tokens that allow them to have things they want or to do things they want to do. Pairing adult approval with giving tokens can eventually lead to the withdrawal of the token reinforcer.

Activity or Privilege Reinforcers

Activity or privilege reinforcers are things students like to do, such as playing a game, helping the teacher, having lunch with the principal, taking roll call or collecting materials. Because classroom teachers could find it prohibitively expensive to use tangible reinforcers, activity reinforcers offer an alternative. Among those research has shown to be effective in a school setting are jobs which carry responsibility, such as helping the principal, being a hall monitor or messenger, running AV equipment, or correcting papers.

Social Reinforcers

Social reinforcers include both adult and peer approval and include various forms of attention, praise, and recognition. Using social reinforcers in conjunction with other reinforcers being used will over time lead to being able to give social reinforcement only.

Structured Contingency Systems

While it is usually easier and more natural to arrange contingencies and consequences on an informal basis, sometimes it may be necessary to establish a very structured contingency system in order to increase the likelihood that the behaviors you want to change are clearly defined and the reinforcement contingencies are explicitly specified. Two formalized and systematic ways of linking reinforcement with behavior are contingency contracts and token systems.

Contingency contracts

A structured written contract might be necessary when working with more than one student or when the behavior being worked on is an agreement that either the student or the teacher wishes to keep between themselves. The basic contract is in the form: If . . ., then . . . .

To ensure the effectiveness of a contract it is useful to:

- Meet privately with the student and explain the rationale and procedures for developing the contract.
- Agree on the responsibilities of others (teachers, parents) in helping the student achieve the goals of the contract.
- Agree on a maintenance goal to encourage the learner to sustain his or her progress over an extended period of time.

Token systems

A token is used much like money in that it can be exchanged for a desired object or activity at some future time. A token system is typically used in special education classes and in other special environments.

Ms. Archer's classwide token system below is an example of an effective token system. Note that her approach also incorporates other principles (i.e., self-evaluation, commitment to change).

Case Study: Ms. Archer's Classwide Token System

Ms. Archer used a classwide token system for encouraging appropriate behavior in her third-grade class. Throughout the year she used a system in which the class as a whole earned blue chips for desirable behavior and red chips for undesirable behavior. When a monthly goal for the number of blue chips was reached, the class was rewarded with a special treat or privilege.

Goals and rewards escalated during the course of the year, beginning with a class party at the end of the first month and culminating in a class-selected field trip. During each day blue chips were dropped into a container for various appropriate behaviors—two for transitioning from one activity to the next in a timely fashion, ten for each satisfactory room cleanup, one for each student who at the end of the day had completed all his or her work, and so on. Red chips were dropped into the container for fighting or arguing, excessive noise, throwing trash on the floor, returning late from lunch or recess, or other transgressions.

Shaking the container of chips was often used to signal that there was too much talking or misbehaving and that failure to get quiet would result in another red chip. At the end of the day the blue and red chips were counted and a daily tally was kept. Ms. Archer often used the results of the tally to discuss with the class the kind of day it had been. She would ask students what they thought might have contributed to an especially pleasant or disruptive day. Sometimes during these discussions the class would set goals for the next day (or week). Occasionally she would ask particular students to commit to "a better day tomorrow."

Setting up a contingency contract

The following steps should be included in setting up a contingency contract:
- The student should participate in the development of the contract.
- The task or behavior to be accomplished should be stated in positive terms.
- The performance criteria should be stated in specific terms.
- The contract should extend for a brief but specified time period.
- The contract should be designed to ensure success. The student should be capable of accomplishing the specified task.
- The reinforcement should be mutually determined.
- Reinforcement should be frequent and immediate in the beginning.
- The contract should be signed by all persons concerned with its success.

Setting up a token system

In setting up a token system, the following items will need to be determined ahead of time to insure that the system is manageable.
- The specific behavior(s) which can earn tokens.

- A convenient token.
- How often the tokens will be given.
- When tokens will be given.
- Who will administer distributing the tokens (i.e., teacher, peer, or self-monitored).
- The back-up reinforcer(s) the tokens will earn.
- A reinforcement "menu" for cashing in the tokens.
- When the exchange times will be.

Sample Contract Formats

Social Behavior

A simple contract to change a social behavior could follow the format below.

(Student's name) and (Teacher's name) agree to the following:

If (Student's name) performs the positive behavior(s) listed below, (Teacher's name) will provide the reinforcement listed below:

Positive behavior(s): (List in specific terms the behavior to be performed. Specify the time, place and frequency of performance required. State how and when observations and evaluations are to be made.)

Reward: (State the reinforcement in precise terms. Specify the time, place, frequency, and quantity in which the reinforcement will be provided for satisfactory performance.)

(Student's signature)	(Teacher's signature)
(date)	(date)

Academic Behavior

A simple contract for academic behavior could follow the following format.

I (Student's name), agree to complete the following learning activities, according to the (stated performance criteria) to obtain the (reinforcement listed below):

Learning activities: (List the activity or sequence of activities to be performed.)

Requirements: (List the performance criteria to be used, for example, % correct. Also state the time period allowed.)

Reward: (State the grade or other reinforcer provided upon satisfactory performance.)

(Student's signature)	(Teacher's signature)
(date)	(date)

Determining Effective Reinforcers

The best way to determine whether a consequence is rewarding is to observe its effect on the behavior it follows. Consequences that are rewarding for some students may not be effective reinforcement for others. The teacher may find that Mary will beam and work harder when told, "I'm so proud of you!" while the same statement will cause Tim to wince and result in decreased effort.

Choosing Reinforcers

The following specific strategies can be used to help choose reinforcers:

1. Observe the student. Watching what the student likes to do will often indicate what reinforcers will be most powerful.
2. Ask the student. Reward questionnaires and surveys, both open-ended and structured, can be administered to provide information when necessary.
3. Use novel reinforcers. The surprise element can sometimes be effective.
4. Allow reinforcer sampling. This technique can give students experience with rewards they have not experienced. It also can prevent satiation, or tiring of a reinforcer.

The following chart lists potential activities, privileges and tokens that can be used in the classroom for reinforcers.

Potential Classroom Reinforcers

Activities

Using the computer	Visiting another class	Independent study
Reading a story	Running errands	After-school activity
Assisting the teacher with teaching	Reading chosen book	Helping in the principal's office
Caring for class pets, plants, etc.	Erasing boards	Working in the cafeteria
Collecting materials	Planning daily schedule	Presenting hobby to class
Doing a craft activity	Collecting lunch tickets	Decorating classroom/bulletin board
Helping other students	Helping custodian, librarian	Going to library
Presenting a skit		

Privileges

Taking a short break	Time to work on special project	Listening to music
Choice of seat for specified period	Classroom supervision	No homework on chosen night
Free time	Omitting specific assignments	Team captain
Playing a game with a friend	Talking period	Early dismissal
Extra or longer recess/gym	Removing lowest grade	Lunch with teacher or principal
Being first in line	Leading a class activity	Earning privilege for class
Displaying student's work	Room "manager"	Using media equipment
Pick a partner to work with	Hall monitor	Using teacher's materials
"Citizen of the Day/Week"	Individual conference time	Keep score for class game

Tokens

Badges to be worn for day	Happy face on paper	Noting progress on chart
Special certificate of completed work	Check marks	Reward certificates
Points or chips	Cards	Note to parent about good work
Puzzle piece/model piece	Stars/stickers	Grades

Reinforcer Surveys

Reinforcer surveys can be either open-ended or more structured surveys in which alternatives are provided. They can either be completed by the student independently or can be administered in an interview format where the teacher records the student's responses.

Students could also interview each other. Examples of an open-ended format and a choice format are provided.

The "Student Reinforcement Choice Survey" was adapted from Raschke (1981). These are provided only as suggested formats. Teachers should tailor specific questions and reinforcement menus to their own students.

Student Reward Questionnaire

1. The best thing that could happen to me in school is _____
2. What motivates me the most to do well is _____
3. The most fun I have in school is when I _____
4. If I could do anything in school I wanted, I would _____
5. If I could change a class rule, it would be _____
6. What I like best about school is _____
7. Something I really enjoy doing at school is _____
8. I feel good at school when I'm _____
9. My favorite activity in class is _____
10. What I like least about school is _____
11. The school subject or period I like best is _____
12. The thing I need most in school is _____
13. I would work hard in school for _____
14. When I do well at school, I would like my teacher to _____
15. The person at school I would like most to praise me is _____
16. If I did a good job, the person I would like someone to tell is _____
17. My favorite adult in school is _____
18. The best thing my teacher can do for me is _____

Student Reinforcement Choice Survey

1. The way I best like to learn about something new in this class is:
   a. Lecture and discussion
   b. Guest speakers
   c. Books
   d. Films, tapes, videos
   e. Completing projects
   f. Conducting experiments
   g. Small-group work

2. My favorite seating arrangement in this class is:
   a. Desks in rows
   b. Chairs at small tables
   c. Desks randomly scattered
   d. Study carrels
   e. Desks in a circle

3. The special job I like to help the teacher with the most in this class is:
   a. Handing out or collecting papers
   b. Running errands
   c. Decorating a bulletin board
   d. Running the filmstrip projector, VCR
   e. Writing the assignment on the chalkboard
   f. Helping other students

4. The privilege I would like to earn in this class for doing my best work is to:
   a. Sit anywhere I want in the class
   b. Help the teacher grade papers
   c. Individual conference time
   d. Give the class assignments
   e. Pick a partner to work with

5. When I do well in this class, I like it most when the teacher:
   a. Tells me privately
   b. Tells the class about my good work
   c. Writes a note on my paper
   d. Puts my work on the bulletin board
   e. Puts a sticker on my paper

6. When I work hard in this class I would most like to earn:
   a. Free time
   b. Lunch with the teacher
   c. A favorite activity with a friend
   d. Time with my favorite adult at school
   e. My work displayed on a bulletin board

7. My favorite free-time activity in this class is:
   a. Using the computer
   b. Listening to music
   c. Doing a puzzle or a craft activity
   d. Visiting with a friend
   e. Reading a book

8. What I would like most for doing my best work in this class is:
   a. Receiving an award in front of the class
   b. Receiving an A+
   c. A phone call or note to my parent(s)
   d. Having my work displayed in the hallway
   e. Earning free time for the whole class

Learning Practice Task: Behavior Modification Sample Problems

Activity Directions: Below are some sample cases that require intervention strategies. Try your hand at designing behavior modification programs for these four students. Ask yourself, "What behavior could take the place of the undesirable behavior? What might be reinforcing for the student? What factors might be sustaining the behavior?"

1. Carlos bullies and frightens other students. Three of his classmates are reluctant to go to recess because he picks on them. How would you go about reducing his aggressive behavior? How would you strengthen his cooperative and socially-desirable behavior?

_____

_____

_____

2. Keisha is bright and very verbal. Her relationship with the teacher is excellent, but her relationship with the other students is posing a problem. During recess she prefers talking to her teacher to playing with other students. What can you suggest to increase her approaches toward and involvement with other students?

_____

_____

_____

3. Ronnie swears excessively. "Who the hell cares?" "Screw this work." Not only are these comments disruptive, they are "catching." A few of the other students are beginning to see if they can get away with swearing. As the teacher, what would you do about his swearing?

_____

_____

_____

4. Joanne is an eight-year-old of average intelligence who has just been transferred from a self-contained learning disabilities class to a regular third-grade classroom. However, she seems overwhelmed by the larger class size and the lack of structure in her new learning environment. Joanne is constantly out of her seat, walking around the room and talking to her classmates. How would you decrease Joanne's out-of-seat behavior? How would you improve her ability to remain on task?

_____

_____

_____

Rewards and Motivational Development

Both developmental and individual factors influence the potential effectiveness of different reinforcers (Grossman, 1990). What motivates students to behave appropriately in school depends to some extent on their age (Brophy, 1981; Hartner, 1978; Meyer, Bachmann, Bierman, Hempelmann, Plager, & Spiller, 1979; Walker, 1979). Preschoolers, kindergartners, and students in the primary grades are usually willing to comply with rules just because teachers say so. They will tend to do what they are told in order to obtain smiles, attention, and praise from their teachers and to avoid their teachers' disapproval and lectures. They find such things as candy, stickers, checks, and stars rewarding. At this age, students need immediate reinforcement and gratification.

As they get older, students are less willing to do things just because their teachers say so. This makes their teachers' attention and approval less influential in motivating them, and peer approval becomes more important. Other kinds of material rewards such as trips, food, and special events replace stickers, checks, and smiling faces as effective rewards. They are also better able to accept symbolic rewards that they can turn in for the real thing in the future.

By adolescence, some students may question any rule that seems arbitrary to them. Their teachers' approval can be totally irrelevant compared to the approval of their peers. Rewards that were effective when they were younger may play a much smaller role in motivating them than graduating from school, preparing for a job, or earning a desired grade.

Hartner (1978) provides a theoretical explanation for these observations. According to her, students' motivational systems develop in an orderly way. She suggests that preschool and primary school students are externally oriented; they respond to adult approval of their behavior and use feedback from adults to judge their successes and failures. As a result, they respond positively to being told that they are good students because they raise their hands, wait their turn, and so on. Because of this perspective, they also want to know that their teachers think well of their drawings, writings, stories, and other efforts.

By the time students are in the upper elementary grades though, they can reward themselves for behaving appropriately. Now they tell themselves that they are good students because they raise their hands and wait their turn. Thus, while preschool and primary teachers should praise their students for behaving well, upper elementary and secondary teachers should encourage students to reward themselves for "good" behavior. This means focusing comments more on providing students with factual feedback about how they are doing—their strengths and weaknesses, successes and failures.

Hartner notes that by the time students are in secondary school, they have internalized standards they can use to evaluate their own accomplishments. Accordingly, teachers should reduce the amount of feedback they provide their students and instead encourage students to evaluate themselves. In other words, as students mature, teachers can support them to function independently in order to foster their personal growth.

The First Step in the Behavioral Approach: Describing Behavior in Observable Terms

The behavioral approach is based on the premise that you deal only with those behaviors that you can see and objectively describe.

The first step in applying behavior modification principles is to identify specific behaviors to try to modify. The behavior which needs to be changed is usually labeled the *target* behavior. Before you can modify or improve a student's behavior, you need to determine exactly what he or she is doing. This procedure is generally referred to as "operationalizing" the target behavior, or describing exactly what is and is not included in the target behavior.

When you pinpoint a target behavior you make objective statements about the actual behavior without imposing your feelings or impressions about the behavior. For example:

John hits other children.

> *Not: John is aggressive.*

Kim talks loudly and without being called on.

> *Not: Kim is disruptive.*

Additional examples of behavioral descriptions:

- **Undesirable physical contact.** Hitting, kicking, shoving, pinching, slapping, striking with object, throwing object which hits another person, poking with object, biting, pulling hair, grabbing, or touching
- **Verbalization** (directed toward teacher or classmates). Carrying on conversations with other children when it is not allowed; answering teacher without raising hand or without being called on; making comments or calling out remarks when no questions have been asked; calling teacher's name to get his/her attention; crying or screaming; singing, whistling, laughing, coughing, or blowing loudly.
- **Attending behavior.** Listening to, looking at, or responding to the teacher; reading, writing, or otherwise completing assigned work.

You are merely trying to describe the behavior you observe, rather than projecting your interpretation of why the student is engaging in the behavior. Focusing on "actual" behavior will help you to be more objective and keep from labeling or interpreting students' behavior. Pinpointing a target behavior involves describing the behavior clearly and objectively, that is, things that are said or done. Statements which try to describe an individual's character are not examples of specifying a target behavior.

The following examples represent "interpretations" of behavior, going beyond what is observable.

A person's:

- Attitude toward others (e.g., hostile).
- Mental state (e.g., disturbed, depressed).
- Feeling (e.g., anxious, unhappy).
- Personality or character trait (e.g., lazy, inconsiderate, selfish).
- Motive or intention (e.g., manipulative, poorly motivated).

Learning Practice Task: Describing Behavior

Activity Directions: Write behavioral descriptions for the following types of behavior.

1. Socially-desirable behavior: _____

_____

2. Disrupting others: _____

_____

3. Aggressive behavior: _____

_____

Learning Practice Task: Behavior Description Exercise

Activity Directions: This is an exercise in describing behavior, i.e., specific actions which are observable and measurable. Check the items which you think meet this criterion.

1. Mario is a lazy student.   _____
2. Darius has a hostile attitude toward his classmates.   _____
3. Rebecca comes to school 15 minutes late every morning.   _____
4. Juan kicks Michael during gym class.   _____
5. Brian dislikes other children.   _____
6. Sam moves around the room and disrupts other students in math class. _____
7. Cindy is inconsiderate of other students in the room.   _____
8. Jaime doesn't work very hard on his homework.   _____
9. Lyle is poorly motivated.   _____
10. Carol is a manipulator.   _____
11. Felipe is uncooperative in group work.   _____
12. Ellen does not finish her class assignments.   _____

Recording Behavior

Once a behavior has been objectively described, the next step is to determine the frequency and/or severity of the behavior. It is important to measure and record the behavior for three main reasons. (1) First, it is difficult to be accurate relying solely on memory, especially in a classroom situation. It is important to determine the exact frequency or duration of a behavior so you know the extent of the problem. (2) Secondly, accurate data will allow you to select a reinforcement schedule which is based on reasonable expectations for initial behavior change. (3) Thirdly, it is necessary to keep a record so that you can determine when changes occur or fail to occur.

There are several ways of recording behavior that are simple to use and take little effort. The easiest method is to simply tally the behavior each time it occurs. This method is appropriate for a behavior that can be easily counted. This type of frequency counting is best used in asking the questions, "how often?" or "how many?" as in the following examples.

- *How often does the student hit?*
- *How often does the student call out?*
- *How many math problems does the student complete?*
- *How many homework papers did the student pass in this week?*

When a behavior occurs at very high rates (more than 30–40 times a day) or is difficult to observe during normal classroom activity, the time sample technique can be used. Time sampling involves the recording of behavior only at certain times rather than continuously. You can observe high frequency behaviors during only short periods of time and make projections about the total behavior based on the sample. Predetermined time periods will depend on the behavior to be measured. You might use the first 5 minutes of each hour, 15-minute blocks 4 times a day, or one-half hour once a day. The procedure that you select should ensure that the sample is representative of the actual occurrence of the behavior. Insuring that the behavior is representative might include sampling across times of day, subject areas, lesson formats, assignment difficulty, and so forth.

For behavior that occurs for long periods of time or is hard to break down into smaller units (i.e., in-seat behavior, moving from place to place, getting ready for work), the duration of the behavior should be recorded. The method chosen to record behavior should be manageable in that it should allow the teacher to carry on normal teaching activities. The method should also be nonobtrusive to the extent possible.

Procedures for Observational Recording

Observational recording procedures are used to record behavior as it is actually occurring. Recording behavior helps you to determine the extent of the problem. It also provides a method for you to determine if the behavior is changing as a result of your attempt to modify the behavior. There are several types of observational recording procedures. The appropriate recording method for a specific targeted behavior will largely depend on the type of behavior as well as the time allocation required.

Event recording or frequency count

Teachers interested in knowing the frequency at which a behavior is occurring can simply tally the behavior each time it occurs. Event recording provides an exact record of how often the student engages in the target behavior. This method is appropriate for discrete behaviors that can be easily counted. Discrete behaviors have an obvious beginning and end. This type of frequency counting is best used when the teacher wants to know how often or how many times a behavior occurs.

An advantage of event recording is the relative ease of data collection which does not interfere with ongoing tasks. The teacher need not interrupt the lesson to record the data. Data can be recorded on a card clipped to the teacher's record book or paper clips could be put in a container each time the behavior occurs and recorded at a later time. The data collected can then be transferred to an observation record form similar to the one presented below.

Frequency Observation Record Form

Student:　*Carl P.*

Behavior:　*Disrupting others*

Observations

Date	Subject	Start	End	Time	Tally	Total	Base rate
9/28	math	10:00	10:20	20 min.	/////–//	7	21/hr.
10/3	reading	9:00	9:30	30 min.	////	4	8/hr.
10/5	science	11:00	11:15	15 min.	///	3	12/hr.

Certain behaviors cannot be adequately measured with a frequency count. This procedure is not appropriate if the behavior can occur for an extended time period (i.e., out-of-seat, thumb sucking) or if the behavior occurs at such a high frequency the teacher is not likely to get an accurate count (i.e., eye blinking).

Duration recording

Duration recording allows the teacher to determine the length of time the student spends engaging in some behavior. This procedure is used when it is more important to know how long a behavior lasts than it is to know how often it occurs. For behavior that occurs for long periods of time or is difficult to break down into smaller units, duration recording is more appropriate than event recording. A stopwatch is usually the most efficient tool for recording duration. Clocks and regular watches will usually be sufficient for behaviors recorded in a classroom setting. Generally, the duration of the behavior is recorded to the nearest minute. A sample data collection form to record behavior duration is shown below. Note that this type of data recording also preserves a frequency count for the time period in which the recording was done.

Duration Observation Record Form

Student: *Sally G.*
Behavior: *Out of seat*

Observations

Date	Occurrence	Start	End	Length	Observation Period
11/2	1	10:03	10:05	2 min.	10:00 to 10:30
	2	10:11	10:15	4 min.	
	3	10:24	10:27	3 min.	
11/5	1	9:30	9:36	6 min.	9:30 to 10:00
	2	9:50	9:57	7 min.	

Latency recording

If the teacher is concerned with the length of time it takes a student to begin doing something, then latency recording would be the appropriate procedure. Latency recording measures how much time elapses before a certain behavior is initiated. For example, the teacher may want to know how much time elapses between giving Sue an instruction and when she actually begins working. Another example for which latency recording would be appropriate is recording the time elapsed between asking a student to go to his/her seat and the time he/she returns. As is the case with duration recording, latency recording involves the use of a stopwatch, clock, or wristwatch. The data recording would also be similar to that used for duration recording and would record the time the initial instruction or cue is given and the time the behavior is initiated or completed.

Interval recording

When the teacher wants to know the proportion of time the behavior occurs, either interval recording or time sampling is used. The interval recording method usually requires the undivided attention of the person observing. However, the major advantage of this recording procedure is that it provides both the relative frequency and the duration of the targeted behavior. For some overt behaviors, such as yelling or fighting, the teacher's concentrated attention may not be required.

In interval recording, each observation session is divided into equal time periods. The observer records occurrence/nonoccurrence of the behavior during these intervals. This procedure is frequently used to measure on- and off-task behavior. Interval recording is also useful when recording the behavior of more than one student at a time or more than one behavior. In the example below, the teacher has recorded whether or not the two students observed were attending to the assigned task during one-minute intervals of a ten-minute observation period.

Simple Interval Recording Procedure

Student	Minutes									
	1	2	3	4	5	6	7	8	9	10
Sandy	Y	N	N	Y	Y	Y	N	Y	N	N
Becky	N	N	Y	Y	N	N	N	Y	Y	Y

Key: Y = On-task   N = Off-task

The teacher recorded "Y" during five intervals for both students. The students observed were on-task 50 percent of the 10 one-minute intervals.

Time sampling

This technique is similar to interval recording in that recordings are made only during a specified time. However, unlike interval recording, it does not require continuous observation and therefore is more convenient to use in a class setting. When a behavior occurs at very high rates or is difficult to record while teaching, the time sampling method can be used. The target behavior is recorded only during selected short periods and then the data is projected to estimate the total occurrence of the behavior.

Although time samples are frequently made at equal intervals, it is sometimes desirable to sample at irregular or random intervals throughout the time sampling observation sessions. The length of the intervals between observations should be determined by considering the frequency of the behavior. If the behavior can occur for only a short period of time, such as attending behavior, frequent samples will need to be made to make accurate projections.

Time sampling is most appropriate for measuring ongoing behavior. Because it is often desirable to convert the data to percent of time, usually five or ten samples per observation session are made. In the example below, a 30-minute observation period is divided into six five-minute intervals. The student is observed only at the end of the five-minute interval. The teacher records a "√" if the student is attending at the instant of observation.

Time Sample of a Student's On-/Off-Task Behavior

10:05	10:10	10:15	10:20	10:25	10:30
√	—	√	—	—	—

12:05	12:10	12:15	12:20	12:25	12:30
—	—	√	√	√	√

Key: √ = attending   — = non-attending

The sample observation form shown above for the frequency count procedure also employs a time sampling procedure in that the behavior is observed only during certain times, rather than continuously. Because the behavior is being converted to a base rate per hour for ease of interpretation, 15-, 20-, and 30-minute intervals are used to make conversion easier.

Learning Practice Task: Practicing Recording Behavior

Activity Directions: Working with 1 or 2 peers, use the case study provided or one of your own to describe the student's behavior, select a target behavior, and design an appropriate observation procedure. Follow the 8 steps listed below.

Describing Your Student

Step 1: Write a series of short statements that describe your student. Use whatever available information you have on the student.

____ _____

____ _____

____ _____

____ _____

____ _____

____ _____

____ _____

____ _____

Analyzing Your Student

Step 2: Go back to your descriptions from Step 1 and put a "B" in front of those statements that are actual behaviors.

Step 3: Add an "S" in front of those behaviors that you think are specific enough that they could be modified, and you could actually see a change in during the next month.

Step 4: From your list of specific behaviors, select the one behavior which you would most like to see change in immediately.

Consider the following factors in selecting your target behavior:
- Does the behavior interfere with the student's social interactions with peers?
- Does the behavior interfere with the student's learning?
- Does the behavior interfere with your ability to teach/manage the class?
- Does the behavior interfere with the rights/needs of other students?
- Can the behavior be easily quantified?

Target behavior: _____

Step 5: List the criteria you prioritized to select your target behavior.

_____

_____

_____

_____

_____

Observing Your Student

Now that you have selected a behavior to try to modify, the next step is to observe and record the behavior. Recording behavior will allow you to determine:

- The frequency/severity of the behavior
- A reasonable reinforcement schedule for bringing about initial behavior change
- If your intervention plan is working

Step 6: State exactly what it is you'll be watching for. What kinds of comments and actions are included in the target behavior?

_____

_____

_____

Recording Your Student's Behavior

Step 7: After asking yourself the following questions, determine an appropriate observation procedure and describe it below.

- Will you record actual frequency for the school day or subject area or will you use a time sample?
- If you choose a time sample, consider if it is important to sample across different times of day, subject areas, activity types, or assignment difficulty? Are there any other factors that may be related to the target behavior?
- Is it important to know how long the behavior lasts (duration) or how often it occurs (frequency)?
- Do you want to know how much time elapses before the behavior is initiated (latency)?
- Will you need help to record the behavior? What resources can you use?

_____

_____

_____

Step 8: Design a simple checklist, chart, or other recording procedure that will allow you to record your student's behavior over a 4-week period.

Reinforcement Schedules: How Often and When to Give Reinforcers

Reinforcement schedules determine how often and when a reinforcer is given. Since classroom reinforcement systems should be considered as temporary structures to bring about behavior change, teachers should have a plan to use reinforcers less often and, eventually, move to natural reinforcers. Reinforcement schedules should move through the following three levels:

Level 1: Continuous Reinforcement

Level 2: Intermittent Reinforcement

Level 3: Nonscheduled Delivery of Reinforcement

The process of reducing the amount of reinforcement (e.g., frequency or duration) and the type of reinforcer (e.g., token or social) is generally referred to as thinning or fading. In fading the teacher moves from a frequent schedule of reinforcement to a lesser schedule. The ratio between appropriate responding and reinforcement is systematically increased. Fading the schedule of reinforcement helps decrease dependence on artificial reinforcers. Reinforcement gradually becomes available less often or becomes dependent on greater amounts of appropriate behavior. Increasing the amount of time on-task or the number of examples to be completed for reinforcement to occur are examples of fading the reinforcement schedule. However, it is important not to fade the schedule of reinforcement too drastically. If the student doesn't earn reinforcement often enough to maintain his/her responding, there can be a decrease in the previously established rate of response. In some instances, the student may stop responding altogether.

Alberto and Troutman (1990, pp. 238–239) have noted that fading schedules of reinforcement should have the following desired effects:

1. Higher, steadier levels of responding as a result of moving to variable schedules;
2. Decreasing expectation of reinforcement;
3. Maintenance of the behavior over longer periods of time, as the student becomes accustomed to delayed gratification;
4. Removal of the teacher as a necessary behavior monitor;
5. Transfer of control from the reinforcer to more traditional methods, such as teacher praise and attention, especially if schedule fading is done in conjunction with pairing social reinforcers with tokens or primary reinforcers;
6. An increase in persistence in responding toward working for goals or reinforcers that require greater amounts of work and/or effort.

Continuous Reinforcement

Under a continuous reinforcement schedule, every appropriate response is reinforced. That is, every time the student makes the desired response, the student is reinforced. This reinforcement schedule is best used to develop the acquisition of a new skill or behavior and to initially strengthen a desirable behavior. It is the fastest way to establish a new behavior and is the most effective schedule for shaping a behavior. When a desired behavior does not occur or is at a very low level, shaping procedures can be effective. Closer and closer approximations to the ultimate desired behavior are reinforced. In shaping, the reinforcement criterion is shifted so that the response criterion to receive reinforcement is gradually changed in the direction of the final desired behavior. At each level in the shaping process, only the responses that meet a certain criterion are reinforced. Working longer or faster, remaining in one's seat, or engaging in appropriate social behavior are examples of behavior for which shaping would be effective.

Intermittent Reinforcement

In intermittent reinforcement, only certain responses are reinforced. Reinforcement schedules can either be fixed or variable. In fixed schedules, reinforcement occurs after a fixed number of responses. In a variable schedule, "on the average" every *nth* response is reinforced, but the reinforcement may come at any time, so that the actual number of responses required for reinforcement will vary.

Reinforcement schedules can be determined either on the basis of the number of responses which have been made (ratio) or the passage of time between responses (interval). For example, on a ratio schedule, a student might be reinforced for every five correct answers and, on an interval schedule, for every five minutes the student stays in his/her seat.

Intermittent schedules of reinforcement are more effective and efficient in maintaining behavior once higher rates have been established. An advantage of intermittent reinforcement is that it is more resistant to extinction. That is, if reinforcement stops, the desired behavior will continue for a longer period of time following intermittent reinforcement than it will following continuous reinforcement.

Nonscheduled Delivery of Reinforcement

As schedule shifts are made from a continuous schedule to a fixed schedule to a variable schedule, a point is finally reached where predetermined timing of reinforcer delivery is no longer required. At this point the behavior is under the control of naturally-occurring reinforcers.

DOs and DON'Ts of Behavior Modification Programs

DOs   Be specific about the behavior you want to modify. Not "disturbing class," but "talking out" or "out of seat." Not "getting work done," but "words read" or "problems completed."

Count the behavior long enough to establish a baseline before you introduce your intervention. Sometimes counting alone will extinguish an undesirable behavior or accelerate a desirable one.

Use natural reinforcers whenever possible. Candy, gum, and money are fine if you need them, but five minutes of free time or the chance to work on a favorite project often will work.

Let the student take over the recording of his/her own behavior if possible, and administer his/her own consequences.

Reward approximations at first. Then gradually shift your expectation until the desired behavior is accomplished.

Maintain an air of detachment. If you over-react with praise or disappointment, you will not know whether the student is responding to the consequences or to your behavior. If you want to use praise or disapproval as a consequence, it should be consistent and be recorded as part of the intervention program.

Continue to record. You haven't really modified unless the new behavior continues after the removal of the consequence.

Set your expectations high, but attainable. If you expect too little, you may be keeping the student from reaching his/her full potential.

DON'Ts   Think of behavior modification as a replacement for effective teaching. Behavior modification is an aid, not a substitute.

Start before you've thought about what you want to accomplish in specific terms.

Try to modify more than one behavior for a particular student at one time.

Make more than one change in the arrangement at a time. If you do, you'll never know what worked.

Give up if the first thing you try doesn't work. You may need to increase the frequency or amount of the consequence, or substitute another.

Blame the child if you aren't getting results. Analyze the intervention plan and figure out what you are doing wrong and change it.

Give more than one warning before applying a consequence.

Use verbal reprimands when students misbehave. Avoid name-calling, labeling, lecturing, or preaching. Instead, treat undesirable consequences for inappropriate behavior as logical consequences to be invoked in a calm, matter-of-fact manner.

Reward students only if they reach a specific level of achievement. Effort and improvement should be rewarded.

Let the mechanics of the program get you down. Once you fully understand the system, you will find ways to simplify procedures to fit your needs.

Learning Practice Task: Your Own Problem Case

Activity Directions: Working with a partner, select a problem behavior you are currently encountering in your classroom. In may be with an individual student, a small group, or the whole class. During this activity you will be working with your partner to develop a change procedure for both of your target behaviors. Follow the steps listed below.

1. State the problem (target) behavior.

2. Operationalize the target behavior.

3. Estimate the frequency and/or duration of the target behavior.

4. Set a reasonable goal for the target behavior.

5. Determine an appropriate reinforcer and/or consequence.

6. Develop an intervention program that will gradually modify the target behavior.

Target Behavior: _____

Description of kinds of comments and actions which are included in the target behavior:

_____

_____

_____

Estimated frequency (duration) of target behavior: _____

Goal for the target behavior:

_____

_____

_____

Reinforcer/Consequence:

_____

_____

_____

Intervention program:

_____

_____

_____

_____

Implementing a Systematic Behavior Intervention Program

Fully including students with a wider range of learning and behavior problems means that classroom teachers, in addition to specialists, will also need to be able to implement more longterm intervention procedures. Some students with more intense situational, emotional, or behavioral problems will require individual and systematic attention in addition to group management techniques. For such students systematic behavior change programs might be necessary initially to bring about appropriate classroom behavior.

A systematic intervention program is intended for use with students who exhibit more intense learning or behavior problems.

Steps for Implementing a Systematic Behavior Change Program

The 23-step program presented here outlines a systematic procedure for implementing a change program which includes, identifying and prioritizing target behaviors; describing, observing and recording behavior; developing and implementing an intervention program; and evaluating its effectiveness.

1. **Prepare a behavior profile.** List several behavioral excesses and deficits, as well as student assets. Thinking of assets of the student will help you keep a positive focus.

2. **Prioritize the target behaviors.** For your list of excessive and deficit behaviors, consider the following criteria for prioritizing the target behaviors you would like to try to modify.
   - Impedes the student's learning
   - Effects student's social interaction with peers
   - Disrupts class activities
   - Interferes with other students' learning
   - Requires excessive amount of your time

3. **Select a specific behavior you want to change.**

4. **Operationalize the target behavior.** Operationalize the target behavior by describing the kind of comments and actions which are included in the target behavior.

5. **Prepare a situational analysis.** In order to determine what may be cueing or maintaining the target behavior, it is important to consider those events which both precede and follow the behavior. There are three parts to a situational analysis:
   1. Antecedent
   2. Behavior
   3. Consequence

   The antecedent is what happens just prior to the behavior. The behavior is exactly what the student does. The consequence is what happens immediately following the behavior. Included here is both the other student(s) reaction as well as your reaction.

   Preparing a situational analysis of the target behavior can help you see what might be cueing or maintaining the behavior and help identify what has to be changed in order to modify the behavior.

6. **Identify any consequences that may be reinforcing inappropriate behavior.**

7. **Determine a data collection procedure.** Your data collection procedure needs to identify exactly what kinds of comments and actions you'll be watching for. Determine the factors that may be related to the target behavior (e.g., time of day, activity, task difficulty) and make sure your observation procedure samples adequately across variations of these factors. Determine if you will need help to record the behavior and identify resources you can use.

8. **Design a data collection checklist, chart or other procedure.** Design a simple checklist, chart, or other procedure that will allow you to collect data to establish an accurate "baseline" for the behavior prior to implementing your intervention.

- If you are observing discrete behaviors, record the frequency or number of times the behavior occurs (e.g., calling out, number of homework assignments done).
- If you are interested in the duration of the behavior, record the beginning and ending time for each time the behavior occurs (e.g., out of seat).
- If you want to know "latency," record the amount of time which elapses before the behavior is initiated (e.g., getting back in seat, beginning assignment).
- If you want to know the proportion or percent of the time the behavior occurs, divide the observation into equal time periods and record occurrence/nonoccurrence of the behavior (e.g., on- and off-task).

9. **Observe and record data on the target behavior long enough to get a reliable baseline.**

10. **Establish a procedure for recording the behavior at regular intervals.** You will need to continue to record the behavior at designated intervals (daily, weekly) during the intervention program by keeping an ongoing record so that you can monitor the effectiveness of your intervention.

11. **Record your observations, questions or concerns during the intervention program in an ongoing observation diary.**

12. **Set an initial goal for the target behavior.** Based on your observation data, set a reasonable goal for the target behavior. In order to get your intervention program started, your initial goal should be set at a level which is likely to be attained.

13. **Determine a likely reinforcer or establish a reinforcement menu.** There are several methods for selecting potential reinforcers. Based on past experience with the student or observation you may already have an idea about what your student might be willing to work for.

    You may want to conduct an informal interview with the student or a more formal interview in which you complete a structured reinforcement survey. Or, you could ask the student to complete a reward questionnaire. You may decide on a single reinforcer or you may want to establish a reinforcement menu to provide the student with several options.

14. **Develop an intervention program to change the target behavior.**

15. **Discuss the intervention program with the student.** Arrange a time to discuss the intervention program with the student. Let the student know what you are concerned about. Share the data you have collected. Solicit the student's input about your planned intervention strategy. You may want to modify the plan based on the student's reaction or any suggestions the student might have.

16. **Involve the student in self-monitoring, if possible.** Whenever possible the student should be involved in monitoring his/her own behavior. Try to devise a way you can involve the student directly, either from the beginning or after the program is established.

17. **Implement the intervention program.** During the implementation of the intervention program, continue to record the student's behavior on a regular basis (Step 10) and make entries in your observation diary weekly (Step 11).

18. **Record progress on a graph to see if the program is working.**

19. **If the intervention program isn't working, determine what may be going wrong.** If your intervention isn't working, consider the following:

- Have you adequately identified and defined the target behavior?
- Have you selected the right kind of reinforcer? Is it reinforcing to the student?
- Are you providing reinforcement soon enough?
- Are you reinforcing too often?
- Are you being consistent in your implementation of the intervention program?
- Have you made the intervention program more complicated than it needs to be?
- Are others involved following through (e.g., principal, parent, "buddy")?
- Is social reinforcement by peers outweighing your reinforcement?

20. **If necessary, make modifications.**

21. **Once the program is working, begin reducing the frequency and amount of reinforcement.** Decide on a plan to reduce the schedule of reinforcement, including the frequency as well as the amount of reinforcement.

22. **Move to reinforcers that are natural to the classroom.** Develop a longterm plan to move to natural reinforcers. Change the type of reinforcement to higher-order reinforcers by moving along the continuum from tangible, to activity or privilege, to peer recognition or adult approval, to self-satisfaction.

23. **Fade out the intervention program.**

This systematic behavior change program is basically teacher-directed, but it can be augmented to allow for greater student involvement at every step. The following section describes specific ways to increase student involvement.

Student Self-managed Behavior Intervention Programs

When systematic reinforcement programs are necessary to help students learn to control their behavior, teachers can support students in managing their own intervention programs to a great extent. With student-managed rather than teacher-managed intervention programs, students are in charge of the consequences and apply positive and negative reinforcements to their own behavior. Initially, students will have to be taught how to get started and will require monitoring to make sure they know what to do and are following through and doing it correctly. Helping students use self-management effectively will take a collaborative effort between the teacher and the student.

Effectively implementing self-management approaches begins with motivating students to want to modify their behavior through active listening, reasoning with them, and other respectful, interactive behaviors so they will cooperate voluntarily. Together the teacher and the student identify the inappropriate behavior which is interfering with the student's learning and productive behavior. The teacher makes sure that the student understands why the behavior is causing a problem.

Including the following steps will help ensure successful self-managed programs. Students can be helped to:

1. Establish a baseline of how often, how long, and in which situations they behave unproductively.

2. Identify an appropriate behavior that the student can substitute for inappropriate ones, if possible.

3. Set realistic goals for behavior change.

4. Establish consequences that are significant to them and are positive if possible, negative if necessary.

5. Develop a manageable and unobtrusive system for self-observation and record-keeping.

6. Record their observations on charts or graphs so they can monitor their behavior.

7. Evaluate their behavior to determine the kinds and amounts of positive and/or negative consequences they have "earned" during each observation period.

8. Administer their own reinforcement.

9. Evaluate their progress periodically.

10. Modify their program when necessary (goals, consequences, observation, and reinforcement schedules).

11. Generalize their improved behavior to other situations and in relationships with other people.

12. Reinforce themselves with internal satisfaction such as thinking about how much better they feel, how much better they get along with others and how they are staying out of trouble.

13. Eliminate the extrinsic reinforcements.

14. Determine whether their behavioral improvement is maintained in the absence of extrinsic consequences.

Below is an example of a summary of a structured intervention program. A summary format such as this one is a useful record keeping procedure to document specific interventions that have been tried with a particular student. A blank format is also provided.

Sample Behavior Intervention Program Summary

Student:	*Amy T.*
Description of target behavior:	*Talking-out without teacher permission: making comments or calling out remarks when no questions have been asked, or answering teacher without raising hand or without being called on.*
Observation Procedure:	*Frequency count of talkouts kept by teacher each day for one week during social studies period.*
Baseline data:	*Observed 40 times over a period of 5 days for a total of 300 minutes. (5 hours)*
	Rate of occurrence of target behavior: 8 times per hour.
Description of intervention program:	*Amy agreed to try to refrain from talking-out during social studies to earn the privilege of visiting Mr. Thompson, the school counselor, once a week for 20 minutes.*
Reinforcer:	*Amy would visit Mr. Thompson on Friday afternoons if she had not talked-out more than twenty times that week.*
Program adaptation (if necessary):	*Amy was able to meet the criteria to receive her reinforcer, so no program modification was needed.*
Results:	*Amy's talkouts average one per class, or five per week presently.*
Program maintenance/fading out:	*After two weeks of the intervention program, Amy agreed that she would have to keep talkouts below ten per week to visit Mr. Thompson. After four weeks the criteria was raised to five or less per week.*
Total length of program:	*Six weeks.*

Behavior Intervention Program Summary

Student: _____

Description of target behavior: _____

_____

_____

_____

Observation procedure: _____

_____

_____

_____

Baseline data:

Observed _____ times over a period of _____ days for a total of _____ minutes.

Rate of occurrence of target behavior: _____

Description of intervention program: _____

_____

_____

_____

_____

_____

Reinforcer: _____

_____

_____

Program adaptation (if necessary): _____

_____

_____

_____

Results: _____

_____

_____

_____

_____

_____

Program maintenance/fading out: _____

_____

_____

_____

_____

Total length of program: _____

Assertion: Standing Up for Your Rights and Needs

Assertion is the ability to stand up for your rights in ways that help insure that others won't ignore or circumvent them. Responding assertively means stating your needs and wants without deriding, attacking, or making another person responsible for your reaction or feelings. Being assertive means letting others know what you want, need, like, don't like, and how their behavior affects you.

Unassertive people have trouble initiating conversations, often readily accommodate others' requests, accede to inappropriate demands, and are unable to ask others to respect their rights and needs. For those who are unassertive, before they can respond assertively they will have to first confront the negative thought patterns and beliefs that interfere with asserting their rights and impede assertive responses. Those who fail to act assertively typically hold nonassertive beliefs about their rights and those of others (Jakubowski, 1977). Four of those beliefs are discussed below.

1. *I do not have the right to place my needs above those of others.*

   Rebuttal: Healthy people have needs and strive to fulfill those needs. Your needs are as valid as others' needs. It's not your needs *or* my needs, it's your needs *and* my needs. The way to handle conflict over need satisfaction is negotiation and compromise. One of the negative consequences associated with not validating your own needs is often passive-aggressive behavior. Unable or unwilling to express your feelings of resentment or anger directly can lead to dealing with your anger in subtle and indirect ways. In the long run, if you frequently deny or ignore your own needs, you may come to feel a growing loss of self-esteem and an increasing sense of hurt and anger. It can be a double-edged sword in that you not only fail to get your needs met, but you feel bad about yourself as well.

2. *I do not have the right to feel angry or to express my anger.*

   Rebuttal: Life is made up of trivial incidents, and it is normal to be irritated occasionally by seemingly insignificant events. You have a right to feel angry and to express your anger in ways that don't infringe on others' rights.

3. *I do not have the right to make requests of others.*

   Rebuttal: You have a right to ask others to change their behavior if their behavior has an adverse effect on you. A request is not the same as a demand. However, if your rights are being violated and your requests for a change are being ignored, you have a right to make demands.

4. *I do not have the right to do anything which might hurt someone's feelings.*

   Rebuttal: It's undesirable to deliberately try to hurt others. However, it is impossible as well as undesirable to try to govern your actions so as to never hurt anyone. You have a right to express your thoughts and feelings, even if someone else's feelings occasionally get hurt. To do otherwise would be inauthentic and deny others an opportunity to learn how to handle their own feelings. Some people get hurt because they're unreasonably sensitive and others use their hurt to manipulate others.

Comparing Nonassertive, Aggressive, and Assertive Behavior

In responding to a given situation, you have three behavior choices. You can respond nonassertively, aggressively, or assertively. The following sections describe each of these three types of behavior.

Nonassertion

Nonassertion is the inability to express your thoughts or feelings when necessary. This type of behavior exemplifies lack of respect for your own right to express your ideas and opinions, needs and wants, and feelings.

Behavior in conflict or problem situations

Behavior when a conflict arises takes the form of two different types of denial:

- Denying your own needs, or
- Ignoring your needs.

In both cases your response is to do nothing. In the first, case you choose to forget about your own needs and satisfy the other person's needs. In the second case, you pretend nothing is wrong, that is, you claim no problem exists. In either case, you allow others to behave in ways that show no regard for your needs.

Typical behavior is to:

- Deny
- Ignore
- Flee
- Forget
- Overlook
- Surrender

Advantage

The advantage this type of behavior offers is that it avoids conflict. However, there are several disadvantages associated with nonassertive behavior.

Disadvantages

- You won't get what you want or need.
- You may experience feelings of inadequacy.
- You may get angry at others for taking advantage of you.
- You encourage others to take advantage of you, treat you with disrespect, or pity you.

Aggression

Aggression is expressing your thoughts or feelings in a way that disregards another person's right to be respected. Aggressive behavior is self-enhancing at the expense of others.

Behavior in conflict or problem situation

The aggressive person tends to do the following when dealing with a problem:

- Attack
- Threaten
- Put down
- Hurt

Advantage

While you generally get what you want, there are other costs.

Disadvantages

- Causes others to feel hurt or humiliated.
- Causes others to feel angry or defensive.
- Produces negative consequences, such as counter-aggressive behavior or desire for revenge.
- Closes off communication channels.

Assertion

Assertion is expressing your needs, thoughts, or feelings clearly and directly without judging, dictating or threatening. You honestly state your feelings without either denying your own right to express yourself (nonassertion) or denying the rights of others to be treated with respect (aggression).

Behavior in conflict or problem situations

When a conflict situation occurs, the assertive response is to confront the behavior by:

- Stating your needs.
- Making your own intentions clear.
- Expressing your feelings.
- Describing the impact of the person's behavior.
- Making your position clear (taking a stand).
- Asking for a behavior change.
- Interpreting behavior in nonjudgmental ways.

Advantages

- Generates positive feelings for both the sender and the receiver.
- Maintains the self-respect of both parties.
- Usually resolves the conflict or problem.
- Leads to compromise when necessary.
- Is honest.
- Avoids feelings of resentment, anger, or guilt.

Disadvantages

- Doesn't guarantee you'll get what you want.
- The other person may feel hurt.

Responding assertively will not guarantee that you will always get what you want. However, behaving assertively offers the best chance of getting your needs met. Also, while aggressive behavior is far more likely to cause hurt feelings, behaving assertively will not ensure that the other person will not feel hurt. Some people actually use their hurt to manipulate others.

Below are examples of the kinds of responses which are typical of nonassertive, aggressive, and assertive approaches to dealing with students (Silberman & Wheelan, 1980).

Nonassertive	Aggressive	Assertive
Plead	Blow up in anger	Persist, insist
Worry about upsetting students	Get into power struggles	Give brief reasons
Evade problems and issues	Endlessly argue	Make clear, direct requests

Example: *Angie, a terribly disorganized student in your class, can seldom find her books or work when needed. She comes to you with a look of frustration and reports that she can't locate a book report due that day.*

Response Options	Category
Say nothing and look exasperated.	Nonassertive
Sternly lecture Angie about the importance of keeping track of her things.	Aggressive
Empathize with her frustration and insist on an agreement as to how this might be avoided in the future.	Assertive

Assertive Responses

Teachers need to recognize that asserting their right to maintain a classroom atmosphere conducive to teaching and learning should not interfere with respecting the rights and needs of their students. Advocating for using assertive behavior is not synonymous with promoting an authoritarian stance. Developing assertion skills enables teachers to directly and honestly express themselves without attributing blame to students or denying students' rights and needs.

The key characteristics of assertive responses are:

- Nonjudgmental
- Take a clear stand
- State personal needs

Assertive responses express your needs and desires directly and nonjudgmentally. Teachers sometimes need to be proactive in approaching students rather than always being reactive, or responding after a misbehavior occurs. For example, it is important to confront (approach) a student who is doing minimal or poor-quality work.

Appropriate responses could take any of the following forms:

Assertive Response	Assertive Language
Request a Behavior Change	I'd like you to put that away now.
	I would like you to tell me when I do something you don't like.
Express a Need	I need to leave by 3:00.
	I need everyone in their seats now.
State an Intention	When this happens I will . . . .
Make your Position Clear	This is really important to me.
	I want you to know how much this worries me.
Take a Stand	I'm not willing to do that, but I would . . . .
	You're not allowed to do that here.
Describe the Impact	I can't give everyone a chance to answer when you are calling out the answer.
Express a Feeling	I'm feeling sad.
	I get pretty angry when I see that.

Although developing assertion skills is important for efficiently managing the learning environment and dealing with student inappropriate behavior, it is also a valuable skill for effectively communicating in a variety of school situations. Assertion skills can support collaboration efforts among general education teachers and other special service support staff in that they provide a means for clearly communicating your needs in a manner that does not deny the needs of other involved parties. These skills can be helpful in:

- Parent conferences and confrontations;
- Letting administrators and supervisors know where you stand;
- Working with peer teachers and support staff.

Personal Entitlements

The list of personal entitlements below are some of our basic human rights. As such, they are rights of both teachers and students. Teachers should assert these rights for themselves while simultaneously honoring, supporting and helping students assert their rights.

1. I am entitled to be treated with respect.
2. I am entitled to say no and not feel guilty.
3. I am entitled to make mistakes.
4. I am entitled to experience and express my feelings.
5. I am entitled to fulfill my needs.
6. I am entitled to take time and think.
7. I am entitled to change my mind.
8. I am entitled to do less than I am humanly capable of doing.
9. I am entitled to ask for what I want.
10. I am entitled to feel good about myself.

Learning Practice Task: Recognizing Assertive, Aggressive, and Nonassertive Responses

Activity Directions: Below are some situations you are likely to encounter. Read each situation and response and decide whether the response is assertive, aggressive, or nonassertive. When you have finished, find a partner and share your answers. If you have different answers for any of the items, discuss how you categorized the response and try to reach consensus.

Situation 1:   You are at a faculty meeting and are making a point about the new school discipline policy. Before you have a chance to finish your comment, Steve, who has a habit of interrupting, begins to make his point. You respond with,

Response: "You make me mad when you always butt in."

Response Category: _____

Situation 2:   Your principal is walking down the corridor, your classroom door is open, and he steps in and says, "Your class is making too much noise." Your response,

Response: "Sorry sir. I really am awfully sorry."

Response Category: _____

Situation 3:   You are team teaching but you're doing all the planning, teaching, interacting and evaluating students. You say,

Response: "We're supposed to be team teaching, and yet I see that I am doing all the work. I'd like to talk about changing this."

Response Category: _____

Learning Practice Task: Practicing Assertive Behavior

Activity Directions: You will be working in groups of three. Each person will take a turn playing the role of the teacher in responding assertively to a specific situation. You will also play the role of student and the role of observer. When you are serving in the role of observer, you will give structured, constructive feedback to the person playing the role of teacher, and you will complete a feedback checklist to help you give feedback relevant to use of assertive behaviors.

Use the situation provided below for this activity. Follow the sequence of steps listed.

Case Study: *During your lesson, a student gives a note to another student and then starts to chuckle. Other students are watching for your reaction.*

Guidelines for the Role Play:

A. It is not necessary to continue the role play to complete resolution of the situation. The purpose is only to provide experience in enacting assertive behaviors.

B. The person playing the student role should respond as naturally as possible.

C. The observer should keep the feedback focus on the use of assertive behavior.

Step 1: Divide into groups of three for this activity. Then, individually write out a statement that describes the problem clearly and/or that insists that your rights be respected. When each person has finished, compare and contrast your statements. After discussion, if you think it is necessary, make appropriate revisions on your original statement.

Step 2: Use role playing to portray the situation, with each person taking a turn in the role as teacher, student, and observer. Before you begin role playing, review the Peer Task Sheet: Assertion Feedback Checklist and clarify any behaviors you may have questions about. During the role play, when you are playing the teacher you will be trying to use the assertive verbal and nonverbal behaviors listed. The person acting as observer will be watching you and completing the checklist in order to give you specific feedback on your performance. Decide who will play the teacher first and begin your first round of role playing.

Step 3: Get feedback on your use of assertive behaviors. The observer should follow the procedures outlined in Peer Task Sheet: Guidelines for Structured Feedback during the feedback session. Discuss any discrepancies between your perceptions of your behavior and the observer's feedback. Also discuss any problems you experienced when attempting to take an assertive stance.

Continue Steps 2 and 3 until each person has had a chance to play each role.

Peer Task Sheet: Assertion Feedback Checklist

Verbal Behavior	Presence of Behavior		
	Yes	Somewhat	No
Statements were direct and to the point.	___	___	___
Statements accurately reflected the teacher's goals.	___	___	___
Statements were firm yet not hostile.	___	___	___
Statements showed some consideration, respect, or recognition of the student.	___	___	___
Statements left room for escalation.	___	___	___
Statements included sarcasm, name-calling, or threatening.	___	___	___
Statements included preaching or lecturing.	___	___	___
Statements included pleading.	___	___	___
Statements blamed the student for the teacher's feelings.	___	___	___

Nonverbal Behavior	Assertive	Nonassertive	Aggressive
Eye Contact	__ Maintained eye contact	__ Avoided eye contact	__ Glared, stared-down
Voice Volume	__ Appropriate loudness	__ Too soft	__ Too loud
Voice Tone	__ Natural sounding	__ Whiny, tremulous	__ Shouting, yelling
Voice Fluency	__ Fluent, even speed	__ Hesitant, pauses, filler words	__ Fast speed, "jackhammer"
Facial Features	__ Confident, engaged look	__ Nervous twitches, inappropriate smiling	__ Impassive, stony look; contorted, disgusted expression
Body Language	__ Alert, confident posture	__ Nervous gestures, trembling, fidgeting, shifting body	__ Rigid posture, pointing, shaking fists
Touch	__ Comforting, encouraging touch	__ None or erratic touching	__ Poking, grabbing, pushing

Peer Task Sheet: Guidelines for Structured Feedback

Stage 1: Begin with the strengths of the assertion (see above). State exactly which behaviors were appropriate.

Stage 2: After you have exhausted all positive feedback, offer feedback in the areas where improvement could be made.

Guidelines for Constructive Feedback

Step 1: Describe the specific behavior without labeling it.
> Give objective rather than judgmental feedback.
> Avoid blaming, name-calling, preaching, or lecturing.

Step 2: Offer possible ways to improve.
> Alternate ways of behaving should be expressed in a tentative rather than an absolute manner.
> Do not impose a suggestion.

Step 3: Ask the person for a reaction to the suggestions.
> Allow the person to accept, refuse, or modify the suggestion.

During the feedback session, keep the focus on assertion issues. Do not get involved with lengthy descriptions of the problem or anticipated negative reactions.

Canters' Assertive Discipline

"Assertive discipline," as popularized by the Canters (1976, 1992), is only one application of the basic principles of assertion to the classroom setting. Assertion is a broader concept than is typically applied to classroom discipline (e.g., Bower & Bower, 1991; Jakubowski, 1977; Jakubowski & Lange, 1978; Lange & Jakubowski, 1976; Silberman & Wheelan, 1980). The notion of assertion applied to the classroom setting means that teachers assert their right to establish an optimal environment for teaching and learning, but they do not treat students with hostility, and they respect students' rights as well. The goal for developing assertion skills is to:

Enable teachers to express themselves directly and honestly without attributing blame or denying students their rights and needs.

Assertive discipline espouses that teachers have the right to establish classroom control by setting limits on student behavior. However, they should not meet their needs in ways that disregard students' needs and feelings; both teachers and students have rights.

Teachers have two fundamental rights:

1. The right to establish a learning environment that maximizes student potential for learning, and
2. The right to expect students to behave in ways that are conducive to teaching and learning.

When students behave in ways that interfere with teachers' rights to maintain an orderly, safe, and productive environment for students, teachers need to confront student misbehavior and enforce limits on acceptable student behavior.

Students also have basic rights in the classroom, including the right to have teachers who:

1. Hold positive expectations for student performance,
2. Establish supportive, safe environments for learning,
3. Communicate clear expectations for appropriate behavior, and
4. Hold students accountable for their behavior.

Key Concepts for Assertive Classroom Discipline

The following elements represent the key principles that form the basis of the Canters' system of assertive discipline.

- Teachers must insist on responsible behavior from their students.
- Students make a choice. When they choose to behave, they enjoy the rewards; when they choose to misbehave, they pay the consequences.
- Teachers have basic educational rights in their classrooms including:
  —The right to establish optimal learning environments.
  —The right to ask for and expect appropriate behavior from their students.
  —The right to receive support from administrators and parents when necessary.
- Students have basic rights in the classroom including:
  —The right to have caring teachers who help them limit their inappropriate, self-destructive behavior.
  —The right to have teachers who provide a positive learning environment that is safe and conducive to learning.
  —The right to choose how to behave, with full understanding of the consequences that will follow their choices.

These rights are best met through assertive discipline in which the teacher clearly communicates expectations to students and consistently follows up with appropriate actions that are in the best interests of students.

Assertive discipline enables teachers to:

1. Say no, without feeling guilty.
2. Express thoughts and feelings that others might find intimidating.
3. Stand up for feelings and rights when under fire from others.
4. Comfortably place demands on others.
5. Firmly influence students' behavior without yelling and threatening.

Assertive discipline consists of the following elements:

1. Employing assertive response styles, as distinct from nonassertive or aggressive response styles.
2. Establishing and communicating clear expectations for desired student behavior.
3. Refusing to accept excuses students offer for their misbehavior.
4. Following through with promises (reasonable consequences, previously established) rather than with threats.
5. Using hints, questions, and I-messages rather than demands for requesting student behavior.
6. Being assertive in confrontations with students, including statements of expectations, consequences that will occur, and why the action is necessary.

Implementing the Basic Principles of Assertive Discipline

The underlying premise of assertive discipline involves both caring about oneself as well as caring about students. Teachers need to care about themselves to the point of not allowing students to take advantage of them or interfere with their educational agendas. Students don't have the right to interfere with the rights of others or to interfere with others' learning.

Teachers need to care about students to the point of not allowing them to behave in ways that are damaging to themselves or impede their learning. An assertive teacher clearly and firmly communicates needs and requirements to students and follows through consistently with appropriate actions to support student compliance with established expectations.

When students fail to behave in acceptable ways, teachers have three options:

1. They can give in to students, allowing them to engage in inappropriate behavior (nonassertion).
2. They can respond with hostility and anger, attacking and putting down students (aggression). This behavior frequently causes students to counter-react.
3. They can calmly insist that students fulfill their expectations (assertion).

Implementing an Assertive Discipline Plan

Teachers should prepare an action plan in advance. This discipline plan should include explicit statements of their expectations, routines, and rules as well as the intervention approaches they will use when students misbehave.

The following steps are offered by Charles (1996) for implementing the basic principles of assertive discipline.

1. Develop an awareness of the roadblocks to assertive discipline.
2. Recognize and eliminate these roadblocks.
3. Practice using assertive response styles.
4. Establish behavior limits.
5. Follow through on the established limits.
6. Implement a system of positive consequences.

Verbal Limit-setting Technique for Dealing Effectively with Noncompliance

One helpful approach the Canters recommend is the broken record technique. This technique is similar to Glasser's reality therapy technique in which, faced with diversion attempts, the teacher continuously asks, "What did *you* do?" The broken record technique involves insistent repetition of the original message. Often students try to divert teachers from their intended message. This technique is especially effective in these cases as the following example illustrates.

Teacher: *Harry, fighting is not allowed in this class.*
Student: *It wasn't my fault. He hit me first.*

Teacher: *That might be the case, but you cannot fight in class.*
Student: *Well, he started it. I was just sitting there.*

Teacher: *I understand you may not have started it, but I will not accept fighting in this class.*

Some Cautions

Assertive discipline does help teachers examine and clarify their expectations for behavior, establish rules for expected student behavior, and systematically apply rewards, consequences, and punishments. However, the model has several drawbacks.

Following are some cautions concerning Canters' assertive discipline.

- The Canters' model of assertive discipline should not be conceived as a total discipline plan because it does not deal with other elements which have a direct impact on expected student behavior.
- A comprehensive classroom management plan would include consideration of preventive planning strategies, overall structural and organizational factors, curriculum and task demand issues, and teaching style as well as interpersonal relationships, both between teachers and students and among students.
- While the model addresses the notion that both students and teachers have rights, student rights are defined from the teacher's perspective.
- Canters' model of assertive discipline over-emphasizes student control, potentially at the risk of inhibiting student personal growth toward establishing self-discipline.

Comparing the Major Paradigms for Classroom Management and Discipline

In order to summarize the main concepts of the major paradigms for discipline, the following chart is provided. For each of the five approaches, the basic theory, key principles, classroom intervention strategies, strengths, and issues are included. This chart furnishes the reader with a quick reference to compare and contrast these different approaches to managing classrooms and student behavior.

Comparison of Major Approaches to Classroom Management

Glasser's Managing Without Coercion	Dreikurs' Democratic Discipline	Ginott's Congruent Communication	Skinner's Behavior Modification	Canters' Assertive Discipline
Basic Theory				
Students can control their behavior and choose whether to behave appropriately. Schools should be structured to meet students' basic needs for belonging, power, freedom, and satisfaction. Discipline problems will be minimal if teachers support and expect quality work.	All human beings strive for recognition. This model is based on the belief that acting-out students make poor choices based on inappropriate notions of how to meet their basic need to be accepted.	Teachers have a significant impact on student's self-esteem through the messages they send. This communication model emphasizes the use of congruent communication between teachers and students.	Behavior is learned according to principles of reinforcement and punishment. Behavior can be developed, maintained, strengthened, weakened or eliminated by the consequences which follow the behavior.	This model is based on the principles of assertiveness training. When students misbehave, teachers can react (1) nonassertively and surrender to students' wants, (2) aggressively and respond hostilely or (3) assertively and calmly insist that students meet their expectations. Students make a choice to behave and enjoy the rewards or misbehave and pay the consequences.
Key Principles				
Students are responsible to make successful choices. Teachers should help students learn to make better choices. Teachers formulate a series of questions to direct students to consider their behavior. Teachers should lead not boss. Teachers should establish warm, noncoercive relationships with students.	All behavior, including misbehavior, is purposeful, and directed toward achieving social recognition. The four mistaken goals that subconsciously motivate misbehavior are attention-getting, power, revenge and helplessness or inadequacy. Teachers determine which goals are motivating students' behavior through observation and questioning.	The teacher's behavior is the most important element in maintaining discipline. Teachers encourage students to behave appropriately by treating them appropriately. Teachers should continually convey helpfulness and acceptance. Teachers need to address the situation rather than the student's character.	Students will work to seek pleasurable experiences and avoid negative experiences. Targeted undesirable behaviors are replaced with acceptable behaviors. Appropriate behavior is reinforced with rewards and incentives. Inappropriate behavior is ignored or punished.	Teachers have a right to determine the environment, structure, routines and rules that will facilitate learning. Teachers have a right to expect and insist that students conform to their standards. Teachers use consequences—positive if possible, negative if necessary—to convince students that it is to their advantage to behave appropriately.
Strategies/Interventions				
Teachers focus students' attention on their undesirable behavior and develop a plan with students for more productive behavior. Teachers help students solve problems, avoid punishment and retribution. Classroom meetings are held to focus on problems and solutions. Classrooms should be structured around cooperative learning teams.	Basic guidelines include: Focus on the behavior, not the student. Take charge of negative emotions. Avoid escalating the situation. Allow students to "save face." Model nonaggressive behavior. Provide encouragement. Use natural and logical, not arbitrary, consequences.	Teachers should: Send sane messages. Express anger appropriately. Avoid labeling students. Convey to students how they feel. Listen empathetically to students.	Procedures include: Identify target behavior. Identify antecedents and consequences. Gather baseline data. Use reinforcement. Use punishment sparingly. Institute token economy. Develop level systems. Use group contingencies. Write contingency contracts.	Procedures include: State clear general behavioral expectations. Insist on correct behavior with verbal confrontations that call for follow-through. Develop a plan for discipline with limit-setting consequences that can easily be enforced. Provide group reinforcement for on-task behavior. Encourage responsible behavior with praise and other positive consequences.

Comparison of Major Approaches to Classroom Management (continued)

Glasser's Managing Without Coercion	Dreikurs' Democratic Discipline	Ginott's Congruent Communication	Skinner's Behavior Modification	Canters' Assertive Discipline
Strengths				
Students take responsibility for their behavior and develop plans aimed at altering unproductive behavior.

Teachers don't accept student excuses.

Stresses discipline without resorting to punishment.

Conveys cooperative, democratic values. | Teachers relate respectfully to students and emphasize improvement over perfection.

Students learn the value of equal rights and human dignity.

Students develop a sense of compassion and community spirit.

Stresses cooperation over competition. | Deals openly and honestly with students.

Provides prosocial modeling.

Builds self-confidence to make decisions and solve problems.

Provides positive climate where students feel safe to express rights, needs and feelings. | By focusing on actual behaviors, it helps teachers be more objective.

Offers positive alternatives to reprimanding and punishing students.

With its emphasis on rewarding appropriate behavior and identifying meaningful reinforcers for students, it is likely to produce supportive interactions with students. | Offers well-organized, highly-structured and easy to implement set of procedures.

More efficiently uses class time by effectively stopping misbehavior.

Helps teachers examine and clarify their expectations for behavior.

Presses students to consider their own behavior. |
| **Issues** | | | | |
| Students may not be capable of devising a meaningful plan to improve their behavior.

Extensive time commitment to persevere with students.

Requires high degree of teacher patience.

Has greater potential for effectiveness if used as a schoolwide system requiring relative consensus which may be difficult to acquire. | It can be difficult to determine goal of students' behavior, because they often send false or mixed signals.

Strategies may not be sufficient for addressing aggressive or violent student behaviors.

It is sometimes difficult to establish logical consequences.

In some situations, logical consequences may not be enough to counter the intrinsic rewards of students' actions. | Requires substantial commitment to master and use tools of effective communication.

Teacher efforts to communicate empathy and warmth may not be reciprocated with student trust and cooperation.

Strategies may not be sufficient to deal effectively with students who display defiant, hostile or verbally abusive behavior.

Students' language capacity may diminish effectiveness of communication. | Focuses on controlling behavior with little concern for students' emotions.

Limits student choice and development of problem-solving strategies.

Can increase learned helplessness, dependency and extrinsic motivation.

Can decrease student creativity and teacher spontaneity.

Reduces willingness to do more than what is expected. | Over-emphasizes student control inhibiting development of self-discipline.

Unidirectional mode of communication denies reciprocal interaction.

Establishes authoritarian climate in which students' rights are minimal.

Development of student responsibility, consensus building, decision making and problem solving is lacking.

Harsh, demeaning and disrespectful communication style. |

Chapter 7

Managing for Enhanced Support

by Amy Duncan

Support for Students with More Challenging Behaviors

It is after school in the teacher's lounge. Two colleagues are deep in conversation. With their heads together, they share an event that occurred earlier in the day. This scenario is repeated almost daily, each educator finding solace in being able to tell yet another story about his or her most challenging student. As they talk, each teacher focuses on a different young face. The stories, however, are remarkably the same; days filled with defiant words, angry gestures, physical aggression, and very little learning.

You may see yourself and members of your school community reflected in this scenario. The increasing number of students that display seriously disruptive behaviors may cause you to question the fundamental elements of your educational beliefs. How can you maintain authentic interactions with students who defy your requests? How can you develop a sense of community with students who, on the surface, seem unmotivated by relationships with their peers or with you? How can you make effective decisions about ways to support these students in educational environments when they demand so much of your energy?

The student who verbally defies requests, responds with physical aggression to peers, threatens adults, and destroys classroom materials both disrupts the learning process for your students and erodes your sense of professional competence. And so, you find yourself in search of a magic set of practices, that, when discovered and implemented, will bring about immediate results.

This challenge is compounded by commonly-held beliefs and practices about which behavior management strategies are most appropriate for students with more extreme behavior problems. Because they don't respond to punishment, teachers react by providing more severe consequences for their behavior. Because they are defiant, teachers react by imposing authority over them. Because they don't get along with other students, teachers react by isolating them. Because they refuse to complete assignments, teachers react by limiting their access to school experiences. Because they are angry, teachers react in anger in return.

The remarkable truth about students who demonstrate serious behavior challenges is this: they can be successful when provided with a classroom environment that invites communication, compliance, and self-reflection while incorporating effective escalation and conflict intervention strategies—the same structures for classroom management that are being advocated in this text.

To envision these concepts working effectively with students with behavior disorders, however, it may be helpful to think of the process of classroom management as a continuum of intervention levels. Students who present more significant challenges require strategies that are designed and implemented using an increased level of insight, planning, and structure.

This chapter provides a framework for designing such strategies. The framework acts as a guide to facilitate awareness of the function oppositional, defiant, and aggressive behaviors serve for the student, integrating concepts within this text to implement a comprehensive plan of behavior support.

Factors Influencing More Serious Behavior Problems

Documented evidence and conventional wisdom suggest that the number of students who fall into the category of "seriously disruptive" is increasing. The content in Chapter 2 invites an examination of the biological, environmental, and psychological factors influencing this growing problem. Students whose behavior is defiant and combative may reflect a devaluing of the educational process by society, an increase in biologically-based mental illnesses, affective disorders in younger individuals, and the increase of special education students having identified emotional disturbances fully included in their neighborhood schools.

Issues for Schools

As concern about these students has elevated, schools have struggled to integrate proactive plans within classrooms due to the fact that a number of perplexing issues remain unresolved:

- Who is accountable for the behavior of seriously disruptive students?
- How can other students be protected from physical and psychological harm?
- How can teachers balance the needs of one student with the needs of the rest of the class?
- How can educators find the time necessary to develop effective intervention plans?
- How can teachers become sensitive to the cultural issues that filter perceptions surrounding conflict and aggression?
- How can teachers demonstrate respect for students while intervening to stop behavioral disruptions?

In addition, as they face of changing populations of student behavior patterns, schools have continued to respond within old paradigms. Past practices in managing students whose behavior is routinely defiant and aggressive have been based on the following filters of perception:

- Maintaining order and meeting the needs of teachers for compliance is the most important purpose for responding to students' misbehavior.
- Punishment is efficient because it sends the most direct message to the student and appears to change surface behavior.
- The role of the educator is to determine the behaviors that need changing, then design the strategies that will manipulate the student to produce more "positive" behavior.
- Students with serious behavior problems don't really belong at their neighborhood school. They are someone else's concern.

- Suspension and expulsion are effective tools for managing students with behavior disorders.
- The home environment is the most significant contributor to student misbehavior.

These perceptions do little to empower educators to take ownership and identify the resources necessary to meet the needs of these students. Too often the result is to teach students to do three things well: (1) say you're sorry; (2) say what the teacher wants you to say; and (3) do your time (detention) if you break a rule (Gossen, 1992).

And so educators continue to wrestle with many options for "coping" with challenging behaviors. Behavior contracts, behavior plans, suspension, and a reduced instructional day are all ways that individual teachers and schools have sought to bring these students into compliant patterns of behavior. While these ways of managing the surface behavior of aggression and defiance may show sporadic changes, they do not produce consistent results and do not result in more self-generated behavior on the part of students.

Impact of Clinical Procedures

As educators have attempted to design and implement more traditional "behavior plans," they have found them to be cumbersome and time-consuming. Based frequently on clinical methods and procedures, behavior plans are developed using "specialists," "diagnosis," "prescription," and "treatment" with the students as "cases." This filter of perception keeps students at arm's length and may create a barrier to truly understanding the motivation behind aggressive outbursts and oppositional responses. While practices articulated in this text encourage a responsibility-building model for the general population of students, there remains a tendency to impose a stimulus-response structure on our most challenging students.

Framing a New Response

The good news is that when behavior-disordered students are viewed through new lenses, structures of support can be built that will create both systematic and efficient practices for schools. Teachers are empowered to respond in new ways, decreasing the levels of burnout and frustration. Parents/guardians will experience a stronger partnership with their child's school. Students will experience a school community in which they learn more efficiently, expand the quality of their life experiences, and be encouraged to develop responsible patterns of interacting with others. To achieve this outcome, the new lens must focus initially on the sources of more challenging student behaviors.

Sources of More Challenging Behaviors

Teachers make countless decisions each day, many of these in response to the variety of explosive behaviors acted out in classrooms. At what point should I intervene? What type of action should I take right now? How can I de-escalate this angry outburst? An extensive body of information about the fundamental causes of serious behaviors in students is available, contributing to your ability to make informed decisions about the type of response you make.

Unmet Human Needs

Many defiant and aggressive behavior patterns can be understood through the concepts of human development outlined in Chapter 2. Students who have had limited exposure to nurturing relationships, loving environments, and learning experiences will be less likely to have their basic human needs fulfilled. They lash out in anger and frustration in an attempt to meet those needs. In addition, they will have limited access to models of personal skills that will guide them toward resiliency and resourcefulness. Glenn and Nelson (1989) characterize these missing skills as: weak perceptions of personal capabilities, weak perceptions of self-significance, weak perceptions of personal influence over life, weak interpersonal skills, weak systemic skills (the ability to respond to the limits and consequences of everyday life), and weak judgmental skills (the ability to make wise decisions based on a moral framework).

Neurological Factors

Medical research is now able to access information about the human brain as it relates to behavioral functions. Through the use of neuroimaging techniques, theoretical models of how the brain works with identifiable disorders can be constructed. Specifically, the research on Attention Deficit/Hyperactivity Disorder has provided insight into the neurological sources of disruptive behavior. It is most helpful to understand that many students may have behavioral challenges due to a dysfunction in the proactive processes of executive functioning. According to Denckla and Reader (1993), executive functioning can be characterized as anticipatory control, utilizing a working memory to reflect and generate strategies to acquire what is needed to set and monitor goals. A more specific understanding of the impact of disorders of executive function comes from the work of Russell Barkley (1996). The student's physiological inability to inhibit behaviors (interference control) creates challenges for the student in:

1. Working memory (nonverbal)—the ability to use self-awareness, sense of time, forethought, and hindsight to manipulate or act on events or imitate behavior patterns.
2. Internalization of speech (verbal working memory)—the ability to use self-reflection, problem solving, and moral reasoning to be receptive to rule-governed behavior.
3. Self-regulation of affect/motivation/arousal—the ability to use emotional self-control and motivation to integrate objectivity and social perception to make appropriate goals and provide direction.
4. Reconstitution—the ability to analyze and synthesize behavior; to develop verbal and behavioral fluency, creativity, and goal direction.
5. Motor control/fluency/syntax—the ability to inhibit irrelevant responses, execute novel and complex motor sequences, reengage in a task following disruption, maintain sensitivity to response feedback for the purpose of maintaining persistence toward goals, and behavioral flexibility.

These factors directly impact the student's ability to internalize, regulate, and reproduce acceptable behaviors and inhibit unacceptable ones.

For students experiencing the physical, emotional, and learning impact of Traumatic Brain Injury, neurological factors may also contribute to disorders of behavior. The neurodevelopmental dysfunction of attention, memory, language, organization, neuromotor functions, cognitive, and social cognition limit the student's ability to construct prosocial interactions (Levine, 1995).

Cognitive Delays

Students with cognitive delays will also experience challenges in retrieval and use of skills essential for effective classroom and social behaviors. The developmental level of these students is incongruent with their chronological age and unrealistic expectations may be a factor in ineffective management strategies. In addition, structures of oral and receptive language may be inefficient. Many students with cognitive delays may have behaviors reflective of their inability to adequately express basic human needs and preferences.

Impact on Classroom Practice

These research findings identifying sources of behavior disorders support two concurrent themes that can be applied to work with students in the classroom.

1. Students may act out in extreme ways because their basic human needs have not been fulfilled.
2. Students may be unable to produce prosocial patterns of behavior because they lack the requisite neurological structures.

More specifically, students with significant behavioral challenges will require educational strategies that support them in acquiring:

- Internal motivation structures,
- Self regulation skills,
- Skills in decoding social interaction patterns,
- Skills in predicting and performing social interaction patterns,
- Strategies to access rules and apply them to their behavior, and
- A perception of personal significance and influence.

The information available to teachers on the sources of more severe behaviors can be used to build a new foundation of classroom practice. Effective educational environments are ones that are responsive to the unique emotional and neurological needs of students with behavioral challenges. Comprehensive strategies designed to motivate and directly teach the skills necessary for acceptable behavior, will have more likelihood of success than teacher responses that only reward and apply consequences.

Current Perspectives on the Impact of Students Exhibiting Disruptive, Oppositional, and Aggressive Behaviors

The journey toward developing classrooms that support students with challenging behaviors begins when you examine your intentions for them. What do you want them to achieve in your classroom? What types of adult and peer interactions do you want them to have? What do you want them to know about themselves as learners? What skills do you want them to have when they leave school? How do you want them to experience community? When you have a student who continually defies your authority and is aggressive toward you and other students, it is difficult to keep these intentions clear. The following activity encourages you to examine some of your intentions for students.

Learning Practice Task: Clarifying Intentions

Activity Directions: Respond to items 1 through 6. After reviewing your answers, use the Questions for Self-reflection as sources for discussion and/or journal writing.

1. After handing back test results, a student who has received an F, screams at you that the test was unfair and stupid. In this situation, I am most likely to:

_____

_____

2. Confident that he has done a good job, a student who you know to be aggressive when frustrated shows you art work he has just completed. He asks you if you like it. You don't like it and believe that he could have done a better job. In this situation, I am most likely to:

_____

_____

3. A student who consistently shouts out when he wants your attention, screams that he wants help on his math assignment. Your patience has worn thin. In this situation, I am most likely to:

_____

_____

4. A student with a developmental delay gets up from his seat and runs out of the room. I this situation, I am most likely to:

_____

_____

5. In the middle of a soccer game during PE, a fight breaks out between two students. In this situation, I am most likely to:

_____

_____

6. You have made a request to a student to get back on task and complete an assignment. He stands up and yells an abusive retort in your face. In this situation, I am most likely to:

_____

_____

Questions for Self-reflection

What do my responses reveal about my intentions for the student in each scenario?

What will each student likely learn from the response I have indicated?

What have I learned about my intentions for students with severe behavior problems?

What changes do I want to make so that my good intentions will become a reality in my classroom?

Once you have the opportunity to examine and then determine your intentions for students with the most severe behavioral challenges, you will establish a supportive and proactive point of reference as you interact with them and plan for their needs. If your intention is to create lifelong learners who make responsible choices in their lives, then you will want to give them opportunities for practice in choice-making, learning from mistakes, and recognizing the impact their behavior has on others. The decisions that you make about managing challenging behavior will be driven by these intentions, and your actions will be characteristically different. As you respond to the internal pressure to do something different, you will need to have access to resources and innovative ideas as well as an environment that supports risk taking and collaborative planning. You then have the rationale necessary to make the significant change, from a set of random techniques that merely manipulate behavioral change, to a plan that supports positive behavioral growth in the classroom.

The Need for a Behavior Support Plan

The most effective plan is a highly organized synthesis of strategies identified throughout this text that are successful with the general population of students, in conjunction with uniquely designed classroom supports that fulfill the needs of highly disruptive students. Because these students are resistant to more traditional approaches, a more comprehensive plan will require additional commitment to a more complex and time-intensive process. The Intensive Behavior Support Plan presented in this chapter has been designed to impact the student's behavior in a constructive way, while maintaining realistic classroom application. The building blocks of the Intensive Behavior Support Plan include many elements of the "Systematic Behavior Change Program," presented in Chapter 6, and are a synthesis of the following research perspectives:

1. The theories of basic needs (Maslow, Glasser, Driekurs) are addressed in the plan by articulating "What needs are not being met for this student?" "What does their behavior communicate about what they need?" "What changes can be made in the school classroom environment so that those needs can be met?"

2. The theories of functional analysis/reinforcement (Skinner) are addressed in the plan by identifying, "What function does a certain behavior serve for this student?" "What seems to prompt the behavior?" "What consequence seems to maintain it?" "How can the student be taught an alternative behavior that serves the same function as the unacceptable behavior?"

Adding to the practicality of the Intensive Behavior Support Plan, each step is guided by the following perspectives unique to the students with the most severe behavior issues:

- They have an increased need for access to feelings of community and relationships with adults.
- They need an external motivation structure to support their attention to learning tasks and to peers.
- They have an increased need to see themselves as significant and contributing members of their community.
- They have a greater need for predictable patterns and choices within their learning environment.
- They require direct instruction and practice to integrate social skills.
- They require logical consequences and opportunities for self-reflection.

As the plan is constructed, you will consider methods to support positive behaviors using lifestyle and health enhancements, technological and instructional factors, environmental designs, and direct instruction of skills. A highly disruptive student will have a higher likelihood of changing when his/her needs are addressed strategically and comprehensively by individuals who truly care about them.

The Intensive Behavior Support Plan will be outlined in the form of a mediating structure to guide your thinking and planning. The following information is provided to enhance your understanding of each plan component.

Tools for Understanding Behavior As a Function of Communication

All human beings have important things to say. We use our verbal skills to tell others about our physical needs, our perspectives, and our emotions. Our verbal skills, however, are not the only ways we communicate. Our observable behavior also communicates many of these same needs. Facial expressions, gestures, movement, and actions are ways that all human beings reveal essential aspects of who they are. An important view to hold about behavior is that it is, in essence, communication.

Once you widen your perception about extreme behaviors to take in the view that this behavior is not only related to the context in which it occurs but also serves a function for the student, you are well on your way to developing a powerful partnership with the student. You, indeed, may develop that sixth sense that will allow you to listen to students in

Possible Communicative Functions of Behavior

If I:	If I:	If I:
• distract teachers or peers when the focus is on someone else; • make loud noises when people stop interacting with me; • do annoying things because others tell me to do them; or • talk about having no friends to play with at recess;	• become confrontational and aggressive; • become angry when a favorite activity is taken away; • question why "we always have to do it this way"; • become "compliant" when I get my way; • passively resist following classroom rules; or • need to win in competitive situations;	• procrastinate and fail to complete assignments; • say "I can't and I don't know how"; • complain of physical ailments; or • become defiant when I'm given a time limitation on an activity;
Then I might be saying: **I need a sense of belonging.**	Then I might be saying: **I need to control my environment.**	Then I might be saying: **I need to escape or avoid.**
If I: • become aggressive with other students during high activity times in the classroom; • become verbally defiant during testing or other demanding situations; • become frustrated when the classroom routine changes; or • use angry outbursts during large group activities like assemblies;	If I: • make silly noises during quiet work times; • hit other students after long periods of seat work; • complain about being bored"; • fidget during periods of long listening; or • do self-stimulation activities when asked to work independently;	If I: • become frustrated when I want something but can't find the word for it; • hit other students to let them know I want to play with them; • attempt to injure myself when I can't tell the teacher what I want or need";
Then I might be saying: **I need to reduce sensory stimulation.**	Then I might be saying: **I need to increase sensory stimulation.**	Then I might be saying: **I need a communication system.**

this new and different way. Educators often assume that children who are verbal are capable of communicating feelings and needs adequately. Cognitive delays, learning disabilities, and emotional overlays can inhibit these processes. Student behavior communicates the desire to obtain something (validation, an object, sensory stimulation, control over their environment) or to avoid something (tasks, attention, stimulation, interactions with specific peers or adults).

Students lash out in angry and hurtful ways because they have needs that are not being met in their home and/or classroom setting. The practice of dealing with challenging behavior effectively involves understanding the whole child, examining and understanding the communicative function of the behavior, encouraging successful behaviors, intervening effectively, and teaching more positive behaviors so that they can become more prosocial in their interactions with others and more efficient learners. The chart on the previous page reflects a variety of possible communicative functions of student behavior.

Critical Reflection on Practice: What Does this Behavior Tell Me about Student Needs?

Activity Directions: Think about a student who presents severe behavioral challenges in your classroom. Respond to the following questions:

1. As you work with this student, what behaviors do you see that are most disruptive?

_____

_____

_____

2. What do you think the student is trying to say about what he/she needs by behaving in that manner?

_____

_____

_____

3. In what ways are those needs not being met in your classroom?

_____

_____

_____

4. What are some ways these needs are being addressed in your classroom?

_____

_____

_____

5. What are you realizing about this student now?

_____

_____

_____

Determining what a student may be trying to communicate when he/she engages in oppositional, explosive, or aggressive behavior is essential for effective intervention. This model of management views all behavior as a communicative function and, if the needs of the student can be identified through analysis of the "communicative intent," more prosocial behaviors can be integrated into the student's repertoire of responses. The goal then, is to replace the challenging behaviors with positive ones that meet the same need(s) thereby reducing reliance on the challenging behaviors to satisfy the identified need.

Developing Understanding through Observation and Documentation

The purpose of data gathering is to know the student—to understand the student in meaningful ways. Through observation and information gathering you can watch for patterns that help you to discover new insights about what the student may be saying through his/her behavior.

In order to translate what you may observe and anticipate what that surface observation might be saying about what the student needs, you will want to determine ways to uncover sequences and patterns that the student exhibits.

Structures and methods of observation and data collection have their foundation in clinical literature and applied behavior analysis. The methods you choose can result in useful data that will help you to make effective decisions about ways to accommodate, adapt, support, or prevent the most challenging of behavior patterns. This information is essential baseline data; a point of comparison that articulates what a behavior looks like before and after your plan has been implemented. When you understand what a behavior looks like, sounds like, and feels like, clearly you will be able to see whether the support plan you develop is successful in replacing challenging behaviors with more productive ones for the student.

In addition to the formats for data collection provided in Chapter 6, you may wish to design your own forms and procedures, personalizing the process for you and the student you are working with. The following options for data gathering will provide you with an overview of methods that you and/or a team of individuals can use to inform your perception(s) of a student:

Method 1: Understanding the Source of the Behavior

Collecting information from files, teacher reports, work samples, parent and student interviews helps to answer the following questions:

- What is this child's story (family structure, health and developmental information, educational experiences)?
- What are the student's interests and goals?
- What are the family's hopes and dreams for this student?
- What are this student's gifts and strengths?
- In what ways does this child's behavioral issues impact their learning, friendships, lifestyle and home life?
- What type of instructional modifications are necessary for this student?

Method 2: Uncovering Predictable Patterns

Charting the frequency, intensity, and duration of a behavior provides a visual map describing the circumstances under which the behavior worsens (increases) or improves (decreases). It is helpful to consider data that allow you to see the behavior as it is connected to various settings, learning tasks, peers, adults, times of day, and other circumstances. More specific areas to consider might be: attending to task, managing self-control, accessing social skills, adjusting to change, responding to adult requests, cooperating, and participating in group activities, accepting feedback, using unstructured time, managing frustration, caring for school and personal property, responding to the needs of others, adult attention, organizational skills, and social language skills.

Charting the events that occur just prior to and following the challenging behavior (using antecedent analysis), will provide information about the environment, events, persons, instructional activities, times of day, physical and medication needs, and other factors. necessary to reliably predict when both acceptable and unacceptable behaviors are most likely to occur. Antecedent patterns can be the signal that alerts the teacher that the explosive behavior is imminent. Choosing to intervene early in the antecedent sequence is a powerful tool in eliminating the unwanted behavior. Chapter 2 provides additional strategies for determining when to intervene.

Method 3: Assessing Function

Collecting information through observation, student interviews, parent questionnaire, and file documentation assists in identifying functions that the challenging behavior could be serving for the student. Essential questions would be:

1. What is the student seeking to obtain? You might want to consider interactions, attention, types of tasks, environmental needs, physical needs, sensory stimulation, specific objects, feelings, and food items.

2. What is the student seeking to avoid? You might want to consider specific individuals, specific tasks, environments, sensory overload, teacher expectations, fears, and setting demands.

3. What is the student's ability to express wants and needs? You might want to consider the existence of oral and receptive language abilities, the sophistication of social language, the ability to make requests, and the ability to express emotions verbally.

These three methods make the process of data gathering a functional one for the teacher. When it is completed, you will know the source of the behavior, predictable patterns from which to intervene, and the function that the behavior serves for the student. This vital information, in summary form, is utilized as the foundation for the Intensive Behavior Support Plan in Part 1: Understanding the Behavior.

Developing an Effective Behavior Support Plan

The following template can be used as a planning format to generate the necessary support structures for a student with significant behavioral challenges. It has been designed for you to duplicate and use as an individual providing positive behavioral supports or as a framework for a team to use. In addition, it can be used as a map to guide your thinking as a reflective practitioner, seeking to refine your skills with students who present the most significant challenges. In the section immediately following the template, each element will be clarified as to its purpose and significance. Each element has been designed to align with the components for successful strategy development previously identified in this chapter.

Intensive Behavior Support Plan

Student's Name _____

Birth Date ____ / ____ / ____

Parent(s)/Guardian(s) _____

Challenging Behavior(s)
Brainstorm behaviors and describe in operational terms.

Today's Date ____ / ____ / ____

Team Members

Part 1 – Understanding the Behavior

Learner Characteristics
Consider special talents, preferred activities, academic skills, etc.

Factors That Impact the Behavior
Clarify behavior based on observation, consider time, environment, specific tasks, proximity of teachers and others.

The behavior increases when:

The behavior decreases when:

Possible Communicative Functions
Consider what the student may be obtaining or avoiding through the behavior.

I _____ (behavior) _____ because I:

Functional Alternatives
Behavioral assets: Consider behavior that serves the same functions as the challenging behavior.

Skill inefficiency: Social/communication skills needing direct instruction.

The Rationale for Intensive Behavior Support Plan Components

Part 1 – Understanding the Behavior

Challenging Behaviors

These behaviors must be stated in clear, observable language so that the behavioral challenge is clarified and focused.

Learner Characteristics

A student whose behavior is especially difficult will challenge you to feel positive about him/her. A well rounded description of this student, including important data collected, allows you and all team members to see this child in a new light—an individual with dreams, preferences, strengths, and loves. Your plan will be stronger when these factors are taken into account.

Factors that Impact the Behavior

This is the section that synthesizes the vital assessment information gathered so that it can be effectively utilized. When you can articulate the conditions under which the behavior increases and decreases, you can predict the strategies that will be the most effective. When you can anticipate the antecedents surrounding the behavior you can intervene and de-escalate unacceptable behaviors.

Possible Communicative Functions

Based on what you know about the student from the assessment process, what do you and other team members think the student is communicating through the challenging behaviors? These guesses are what will inform your choice of strategies. Indeed, the strategies must be directly related to one of these functions to be successful. Chapter 2 can provide additional insights.

Functional Alternatives

Determine the social and learning behaviors or skills that the student performs that may be ways of achieving the same function as the behaviors you are concerned with. These skills that are already in the student's repertoire can be powerful additions to the plan.

Part 2 – Plan Development

Consider ways to meet the student's communicative function in positive ways including behavioral assets and strategies to teach needed skills.

Developing Relationships and a Sense of Significance	Creating Home/School Partnerships	Designing Motivation Supports
Adapting Curriculum and Instruction	**Developing Interpersonal Communication Skills**	**Encouraging Self-regulation Skills**
Structuring Setting Modifications	**Supporting the Student in Other Settings** *Consider ways to encourage behavioral change across all settings.*	**Response Plan** *What intervention can you use to encourage the student to return to more prosocial behavior?*

Part 2 – Plan Development

Developing Relationships and a Sense of Significance

Because these students have few positive relationships and do not perceive themselves as a person of influence, it is important that you provide experiences that communicate: "I care. You are important to me." "I will not give up on you." "You have choices, and you have the power to make positive ones." The desire to belong is a fundamental human need.

Creating Home and School Partnerships

Parents of highly disruptive students tire quickly of responding to concerns from school. They often feel judged by educators and powerless regarding their impact on their child. However, their support and participation is essential to their child's success. Strategies that encourage rapport-building and positive communication invite them rather than require them to be partners in this unique plan.

Designing Motivational Support

The neurodevelopmental structures of students with behavior disorders can predispose them to challenges in self-regulation, motivation, and arousal. They may require an external motivation system to encourage their attention to learning tasks and successful social interaction. It is important to involve the student in the design of this system because novel reinforcement opportunities must be provided. As the over use of extrinsic rewards may erode intrinsic motivation, a method of weaning the student away from external motivation structures toward more self-management is important to include in this part of the plan. This will encourage the development of more internalized motivation responses within the individual student.

Adapting Curriculum and Instruction

Students who have difficulty organizing information, initiating activity, and completing tasks require a framework that provides frequent feedback, creates alternative ways for responding to task completion, and matches workload to the attentional capacity of the student.

Developing Interpersonal and Communication Skills

The impact of poor executive functioning can be seen as the underlying cause of difficulties in this area. If a student is challenged in recognizing, predicting, and applying appropriate social skills in a given setting , then opportunities for observation, direct instruction, coaching, and practice are necessary for success.

Encouraging Self-regulation Skills

The systems needed to respond efficiently to the environment are not accessible to these students. External structures that reinforce, directly teach, then move toward internal regulation are beneficial. Designing opportunities for choice, movement, self-reflection, and self-monitoring in a variety of settings meet that need.

Structuring Setting Modifications

These students struggle with sensory information that limits their ability to respond to learning tasks and social relationships. They may receive an excess of information or it may come in fragmented pieces. We can help them by providing a school environment that

(Part 2, continues)

Part 3 – Plan Implementation

Action Plan	Person(s) Responsible	Date to be Completed
Sequence of steps, methods, resources, and materials needed to make the plan successful.		
1. _____	_____	_____
2. _____	_____	_____
3. _____	_____	_____
4. _____	_____	_____
5. _____	_____	_____
6. _____	_____	_____
7. _____	_____	_____
8. _____	_____	_____
9. _____	_____	_____

Part 2 – Plan Development (continued)

supports their sensory management and responses. A structured classroom environment that is stable and has predictable routines and boundaries gives students an opportunity to develop the spatial and temporal organization that they lack and facilitates self-dependence (Gothelf, Rikhye, & Silberman, 1988).

Supporting the Student in Other Settings

Students who begin to demonstrate productive social and learning behaviors in the classroom must be directly encouraged to transition those skills to other settings in the school, i.e., playground, break time, other classrooms, PE, and integrated settings. Without a clear plan, generalized success will be limited.

Response Plan

Although your hope is to always have a plan that is effective, it must be remembered that human beings are mercurial. Having a back up system or "Plan B" available and planned for if the student has a crisis or reverts to a previous behavior allows you to feel confident about all aspects of your interactions.

Part 3 – Plan Implementation

A well-designed plan has little opportunity for success unless a clear outline of the action sequence is articulated. Identifying the individuals responsible for carrying out each task adds a level of accountability and communicates commitment to the student.

Part 4 – Summary and Evaluation of the Action Plan

Evaluation

Summary

Adapted from: FOCUS: Facilitating Organized Change through Unconventional Strategies. West End SELPA, San Bernardino County Superintendent of Schools. San Bernardino, CA, 1998.

Part 4 – Summary and Evaluation of the Action Plan

Once a plan is implemented, new insights may be gained that will generate new strategies. It is important to identify the specific actions that have taken place so that growth can be acknowledged and successes celebrated.

There are many factors that are essential in carrying out this plan. The completed plan included here on the following pages will provide you with ideas that will be helpful to your own designs. As you review each section you may synthesize the concepts learned previously and integrate your own ideas.

Intensive Behavior Support Plan

Student's Name Jason Sommers	**Today's Date** 02/14/98
Birth Date 06/15/87	**Team Members** Ms. Avery (Jason's teacher)
Parent(s)/Guardian(s)	Mr. & Mrs. Sommers (Jason's parents)
Sharon and Everett Sommers	Mr. Coffelt (Resource Specialist)
	Mrs. Alvarez (Assistant Principal)
	Mrs. Yip, Facilitator (Counselor)
	Mr. Jackson (1st grade teacher)

Challenging Behavior(s)
Brainstorm behaviors and describe in operational terms.

Talks back and makes threats to the teacher when reminded to stay on task with written assignments.

Hits peers at recess during games and when lining up.

Part 1 – Understanding the Behavior

Learner Characteristics
Consider special talents, preferred activities, academic skills, etc.

- He is the youngest child of four.
- His parents are divorced; he sees his Dad on alternate weekends.
- He is the goalie for his soccer team.
- He is skilled at the computer.
- He excels in math.
- He is challenged by language arts activities, especially writing.
- He is a gifted artist and likes to sketch.

Factors That Impact the Behavior
Clarify behavior based on observation, consider time, environment specific tasks, proximity of teachers and others.

The behavior increases when:

- He is near James during recess.
- He has to do written assignments.
- After recess and lunch.
- On Mondays after he has visited his Dad.
- He makes a transition from one activity to the next.

The behavior decreases when:

- The teacher is in close proximity.
- He is involved in group projects.
- He is doing a "hands on" activity.
- He is playing with primary-age students.

Possible Communicative Functions
Consider what the student may be obtaining or avoiding through the behavior.

I talk back and threaten others because I:

- Want adult attention.
- Want to be accepted by my peers and have friends.
- Need extra help during written assignments.
- Want to avoid doing written assignments.
- Don't feel smart.
- Don't know more positive ways to express my anger or frustration.
- Want to be told I'm doing a good job.

Functional Alternatives

Behavioral assets: Consider behavior that serves the same functions as the challenging behavior.

I can get positive attention when I:

- Create an art project.
- Play soccer.
- Help someone on the computer.
- I am smart in math and computer skills.

Skill inefficiency: Social/communication skills needing direct instruction.

- I need to learn conflict resolution skills.
- I need to learn alternative ways to deal with anger and frustration.
- I need to learn positive responses to feedback.
- I need to learn ways to ask for help.

The Process of Plan Development

As the rationale for each section has been outlined, the necessary components of the Intensive Behavior Support Plan have been articulated. To ensure the success of one teacher seeking to create a more comprehensive system of support or a team of educators and parents working together on behalf of the student, the following section provides the step by step process needed to design the plan.

Part 1 – Understanding the Behavior

Step 1. Identify the challenging behavior(s) that you want to address. Articulate these in operational terms, so that the behavior can be seen and heard. Examples of this might be: looks away from written assignments 20 times in a 30 minute period, or hits other students with a closed fist. It is important to be as descriptive as possible not only so that a quality plan can be developed but also so that you can see qualitative and quantitative success upon implementation.

Step 2. Develop your plan for gathering information with the purpose of understanding the behavior. If you are utilizing a team, identify and clarify who will be gathering what information.

Step 3. Implement your data gathering procedures, until you are confident that you have a clear picture of the source, the patterns, and the function of the behavior.

Step 4. Initiate your plan design process. If you are utilizing a team it is most helpful to use a group memory process. This is achieved by graphically displaying the plan so that all group members can see it. This may be done by duplicating the plan on a chart for each group member or by projecting the plan on a screen through computer or overhead projector. Through the use of a recorder, the plan can be viewed by the team as it is being developed. It is also helpful to use a facilitator to encourage good ideas and monitor the group process.

As you begin, utilize the concepts of brainstorming: (1) suspend your judgment of your own or another group member's ideas (no evaluative comments); (2) let the ideas flow freely; (3) generate as many ideas as possible; (4) utilize a recorder to document information for the group.

The facilitator will direct the group's attention to the beginning of the template. Using each section as a prompt, he/she will guide the process toward completion making use of the following suggestions.

Learner Characteristics

Paint a picture of the student in the clearest terms possible. This will assist everyone in having a holistic construct of the student as a unique human being.

Factors that Impact the Behavior

Utilize assessment data to answer two questions. Under what conditions does the behavior increase (worsen) or decrease (improve)? You are asked to look at all possible factors that you gleaned through the assessment process and in addition, identify specific intervention strategies to use when the challenging behavior escalates.

Possible Communicative Functions

Articulate all possible functions that this behavior could be communicating. It should be emphasized that these are guesses and as such the brainstorming process is especially helpful. When these functions are shared they are done so by following the format: I _____ because I _____. The use of the pronoun "I" encourages a vision of the student as a whole person, with unique needs.

Functional Alternatives

Identify all possible behaviors and skills that the student already has in his/her repertoire that can be reinforced as ways of meeting the same function as the behavior you are concerned about. These can be identified as replacement behaviors.

Part 2 – Plan Development

Consider ways to meet the student's communicative function in positive ways including behavioral assets and strategies to teach needed skills.

Developing Relationships and a Sense of Significance

- Jason will be a special assistant at recess. He will hand out equipment and teach soccer skills to younger students.
- Jason will be an instructional assistant in the special education class each day, and will assist with art activities once a week.
- Jason will assist Mrs. Alvarez each month in designing the display case at the school entrance.

Creating Home/School Partnerships

- Invite Dad to come into class two times a month to help support an art or PE activity.
- Use a daily "success report" where Ms. Avery indicates positive experience for the day, Jason adds his comments, and it is sent home (Mom or Dad can respond back).
- Mrs./Mr. Sommers can reserve 15 minutes of special time with Jason playing a game or doing an interactive activity of his choosing.

Designing Motivation Supports

- Jason and Ms. Avery will develop a "menu" of activities selected by Jason that he can do when assignments are completed. These might be:
  - play time
  - monopoly
  - other games on the computer
  - listen to taped stories
  - read a soccer magazine
  - have time to sketch.
- Jason will add additional items to the list.

Adapting Curriculum and Instruction

- Establish an interactive journal where Jason will write about a topic of his own choosing and Ms. Avery will write back without corrections.
- Jason can work with the writing group Mrs. Coffelt teaches in his classroom.
- All reports and projects will be completed on the computer.

Developing Interpersonal Communication Skills

- Give Jason the role of "observer" in the cooperative group, recording positive comments made in his group.
- Jason will become part of the peer mediation team, learning mediation skills and acting as a "conflict manager" at recess two times a week.
- Jason will role play problem situations in class, demonstrating prosocial alternatives.

Encouraging Self-regulation Skills

- Jason will have a daily schedule of activities on his desk so that he can predict what is happening next.
- Ms. Avery will "frame" all new activities by clarifying the expectations personally with Jason.
- Ms. Avery will develop a "silent signal" using a gesture to let Jason know when he is on target and to prompt a change of behavior.
- Jason will use a silent signal to indicate he needs help from Ms. Avery.

Structuring Setting Modifications

- Give Jason seating close to Ms. Avery and away from James.
- Mrs. Yip will reserve special time to touch base with Jason before school starts on every Monday he returns from his Dad's home.
- Jason can have 2 seats during written assignments and he can move between them.

Supporting the Student in Other Settings

Consider ways to encourage behavioral change across all settings.

- Lunch supervisors will give a positive ticket to Jason when he has participated positively and avoided hitting at recess.
- Mrs. Alvarez and Mrs. Yip will give special citations to Jason when they see him on school ground.

Response Plan

What intervention can you use to encourage the student return to more pro-social behavior?

The sequence of response will be:
1. Ms. Avery will quietly remind Jason of the behavior she would like to see.
2. Ms. Avery will offer Jason a choice: "You can do ___ or ___."
3. Ms. Avery will quietly ask Jason to go outside to talk with her.
4. Jason will take his work and go to another classroom.
5. Jason can return to class after a conference time to re-establish the relationship and review alternative choices.

Part 2 – Plan Development

As you begin to design strategies, be certain that each strategy meets the communicative function of the behavior and, in essence, replaces the unacceptable behavior. The strategies should be articulated so that they can be implemented. They should be stated in a positive way and should meet the following criteria:

1. They are within the student's developmental ability to perform.
2. They are as powerful and serve the same function as the nonproductive behavior.
3. They are within the student's repertoire of actions.
4. They are incompatible with unacceptable behavior.

Developing Relationships and a Sense of Significance

Identify activities and individuals that will provide opportunities for the student to contribute to his/her school and community. You might consider including in this section:

1. Peer teaching opportunities with younger students or students with disabilities.
2. Special time with a significant adult, 5–10 minutes playing a game or doing an activity chosen by the child.
3. Meaningful community-based service or special jobs within the school.

Creating Home and School Partnerships

Identify specific ways that the school community can reach out to include parents/guardians in the success of their child. By having the parent(s)/guardians involved in the development of the plan, they will have an opportunity to make commitments to follow-up on strategies requiring health and reinforcement support at home. You might consider including in this section:

1. Calling the parent with positive information and compliments.
2. Creating a home-school report card that will encourage rewards at home.
3. Encouraging the parents to participate in meeting by bringing their own observation information.
4. Inviting the parents to share a unique talent or interest with their child's class.

Designing Motivation Supports

Generating ideas that create a complete system beginning with external motivation strategies and extending through self-motivation strategies are essential in assisting this student towards self-regulation. Additional information in Chapter 6 can be integrated into this section of the plan. To be successful, all reinforcement should be provided frequently, have variety, be highly desirable, and provided immediately in response to the student's acceptable behavior. In this section you may want to consider:

1. The development of a reinforcement "menu" of items available within the school setting, such as computer time or games, that can be exchanged for points. This list should be developed through the collaboration of the teacher and student. Identifying approximately ten different activities available to the student within the school environment, this "menu" can be revisited to provide the needed variety.
2. Using a silent signal (like a hand gesture) previously agreed upon with the student is a quiet, personal, and effective way to provide reinforcement and social feedback. The student can add points to their own chart when they see the signal.

(Part 2, continues)

Part 3 – Plan Implementation

Action Plan *Sequence of steps, methods, resources, and materials needed to make the plan successful.*	Person(s) Responsible	Date to be Completed
1. Set up aide activities at lunch and recess with lunch supervision.	Mrs. Alvarez and Lunch Supervisor	2/17/98
2. Set up instructional aide time in special education class.	Mrs Alvarez and Mr. Thomas (Special Education Teacher)	2/16/98
3. Interview Jason for motivation menu. Initiate interactive journal, instructional strategies, and silent signals.	Ms. Avery and Jason	2/16/98
4. Determine counseling dates.	Parents and Mr. Yip	2/16/98
5. Begin parent communication system and special time at home.	Parents and Ms. Avery	2/16/98
6. Invite Jason to Peer Mediation meetings.	Mr. Yip and Mediation Team	2/18/98
7. Meet to discuss plan success and needed changes.	Mr. Yip	2/15/98
8.		
9.		

Adapting Curriculum and Instruction

Identify learning experiences and methods of imputing information that will match the student's interest and learning style. In this section, you may want to consider:

1. Cooperative group structures with strategic placement of this student in a meaningful role.
2. Providing a faster pace of delivery of instruction.
3. Adjusting the length of the assignment.
4. Using numbered or different colored folders to assist assignment organization.
5. Provide the student with two chairs. They may have the choice of seating.

Developing Interpersonal and Communication Skills

Identify methods for providing the student with lessons and experiences that will allow him/her to learn necessary social skills. In this section, you may want to consider:

1. Cooperative group structures where the student plays the observer role and must collect examples of positive statements by other students.
2. Using video tape (with parental permission) of positive behaviors. Review these with the student encouraging a dialogue about what caused this positive response and ways that it can continue.
3. Use of literature as a foundation for discussion about social interaction concerns.
4. Role-play of social entry skills, initiating play, verbal reciprocity, social style interaction, and expressive language organization.

Encouraging Self-regulation Skills

Identify methods for teaching the student self-reflection and self-management strategies. In this section you may want to consider:

1. Methods for the student to see and participate in charting progress.
2. Opportunities for self-reflection through journaling and/or dialogue that focuses on finding and articulating solutions, i.e., What did I learn? What will I do next time that will be different?
3. Work areas that are well organized with accessible and well-labeled items.
4. A classroom that has a variety of visual and auditory opportunities for those needing sensory stimulation or less variety for those needing less sensory stimulation.
5. A space that students can use for a "cool down" area.
6. Areas and opportunities for movement.
7. A visible schedule of classroom activities.

Supporting the Student in Other Settings

Identify strategies that will extend the plan to support the student's behavioral success beyond the classroom. In this section you may want to consider:

1. Framing the expectations for the student and articulating the reinforcement that can be expected.
2. Using a peer to provide verbal and nonverbal reminders to the student.
3. Using community and business partnerships to involve the student in activities away from school. Frame the expectations and provide options for rehearsal.
4. Providing role play situations to experience alternatives to use in generalized settings.

(Part 2, continues)

Part 4 – Summary and Evaluation of the Action Plan

Summary	Evaluation
1. Jason has been trained and participates as a special assistant at recess, an instructional aide, and has designed one display case.	Jason has shown initiative in preparing the display case. His outbursts of hitting at recess have reduced from 4 incidents per week to one.
2. Mr. Sommers has come to class once and consistently uses "special time" at least 3 times per week. The home/school report card has been sent home each day. Jason did not deliver it to his parents twice.	Jason's behavior is positive when his father visits. Jason will earn points toward his menu rewards by delivering the home/school report card consistently.
3. The reinforcement menu has been developed and altered each week with Jason's input.	Jason has earned consistent points for work completion. Threats have been reduced by 60%. Jason continues to show agitation with longer written assignments.
4. Jason has used the computer to complete three reports and meets with the writing group daily. He makes three journal entries per week.	Jason will be taught additional writing strategies. The computer will be made available to him for all written assignments. Oral tests and alternative projects will be offered as an alternative.
5. Jason has joined the Peer Mediation training.	Jason will continue with training and classroom instruction of prosocial behaviors will begin this week.
6. Jason and Ms. Avery have developed a silent signal and when he has completed a task on his schedule, he checks it off.	Jason will be encouraged to use the silent signal when needing assistance.
7. Ms. Avery has not been able to set up a special time on Monday mornings to meet with Jason. He has been moved away from James.	Jason has continued to have consistent difficulties on Monday mornings. Ms. Avery will be released to spend special time with Jason each Monday.
8. Only one noon supervisor has been approached about giving Jason "positive tickets."	All lunch supervisors will be given positive tickets and encouraged to use them. Ms. Avery reports that the sequence of interventions in the response plan.

Adapted from: FOCUS: Facilitating Organized Change through Unconventional Strategies. West End SELPA, San Bernardino County Superintendent of Schools. San Bernardino, CA, 1998.

Response plan

A set of strategies needs to be in place so that there will be an effective response to the student in an unexpected crisis situation or, if the plan is not successful, in redirecting the student's behavior. As you review the information in Chapter 8 on escalation intervention, it is important to be reminded of additional considerations to be taken into account with this special group of students:

- All interventions should be directed to the student in a personal and private manner (private signal, pre-agreed upon silent signal).
- All requests should be formulated to direct the student toward the more acceptable activity. "What you need to be doing now is . . . ."

The language that you use should be simple and direct. You may consider options from the following sequence:

1. Use a silent signal to redirect the student.
2. Offer a replacement activity.
3. Provide a reminder to the student about the expectation.
4. Provide a choice: "you can do this or this"; "which would you like to do?"
5. Provide the option of an alternate task, i.e., working briefly from a special work folder that has less taxing tasks then returning to regular class work.
6. Provide an alternative location for the student to complete work.
7. Redirect the student to a "cool down" area of the room.

As you can see in this sequence, the use of the term "time out" is replaced with the term "cool down." In the traditional framework of time-out procedures, time-out is frequently used as a punishment. Its use with highly disruptive students is complicated because the act of being sent to the time-out area usually results in an additional power struggle. An already explosive situation becomes escalated when the student won't go and you can't make him without the use of physical intervention. When time-out is redefined as a "cool down" period, the teacher sends the following message: "I want you to learn. You are not ready to learn now."

Part 3 – Plan Implementation

Action Plan. The Action Plan section is designed to ensure that all dimensions of the support structure will be carried out. It clarifies responsibilities and articulates mutual accountability. As you design this section you may want to think about other individuals and environments that surround the student during the day. Are there other factors that need to be brought into focus to guarantee success?

In this section you may want to consider the following factors:

1. What do you want other staff members to know that will help them to provide behavioral supports for this student?
2. What types of professional development experiences might be beneficial for them?
3. What can you do to encourage support from other students?

Part 4 – Summary and Evaluation of the Action Plan

After the plan has been designed and implemented, it is important to summarize what has happened as a result and what successes have been realized. As areas needing further refinement are identified, the plan can be revised.

Learning Practice Task: Analyzing the Plan

Activity Directions: As you review the sample plan, respond to the following questions:

1. Based on Jason's learner characteristics and the factors that impact his behavior, what communicative functions did you find to be particularly meaningful? What are some you would add if you were a member of the team?

   _____

   _____

   _____

2. Are there any additional assets or skill deficits that you might predict Jason to have?

   _____

   _____

   _____

3. As you look at the communicative functions, identify the strategies that have been designed to meet each one.

   _____

   _____

   _____

4. Which of the strategies do you find particularly significant?

   _____

   _____

   _____

5. What are some strategies that you would add as a member of the team?

   _____

   _____

   _____

6. As you look at the Response Plan, are there additional steps you would add?

   _____

   _____

   _____

7. As you evaluate the Action Plan, are there any steps that you would add to guarantee the plan's success?

   _____

   _____

   _____

8. What did you learn from this evaluation that you would want to use in your own plans?

   _____

   _____

   _____

Quality Indicators in Plan Implementation

In analyzing the sample plan, you can identify many factors that are essential for creating a plan that produces results for a student. Plans are more likely to have success when:

1. They make use of a team including the student, educator and the parent.
2. They utilize assessment data to inform strategy development.
3. All team members have a positive intention for the student.
4. All strategies are designed to address the communicative function of the behavior and replacement behaviors are integrated.
5. All of the factors of the plan are articulated in an action plan.
6. Logical consequences are used rather that punishment.
7. There is continuity of plan implementation across all settings of the environment.
8. The level of success is carefully articulated, reviewed and redesigned when necessary.

The template for the Intensive Behavior Support Plan can also be used as an efficient way to review strategy elements and, when necessary, reformat them so they are in alignment with new insights or information that the team has about the student. Such self- and team-reflective practices will provide the additional tools needed to have fresh insights. Students with challenging behaviors have the ability to be effective teachers for all educators. The challenge of aligning authentic practices with your management of students who seem to be unmanageable, draws forth creativity, dedication, and persistence.

Critical Reflection on Practice: My Self-renewal Plan

Activity Directions: Think about your work with a particularly challenging student. Reflect on the actions that you will take to maintain your effectiveness in the classroom.

1. What are the skills that you bring to your relationship with highly disruptive students?
2. What are the skills that you want to develop?
3. What are materials and resources that you would like to look for that will assist your awareness?
4. What colleagues would you like to collaborate with?
5. What types of classrooms would you like to visit?
6. What types of informal connections would you like to make with parents?
7. What activities will you choose to do that will provide you with rest and renewal?

Chapter 8

Making the Management/Control/Leadership Connection

Teachers are placed in the role of managing student behavior in order to maintain an environment conducive to teaching and learning. When attempting to change or deal with students' inappropriate behavior, the typical teacher response is to try to control deviant behavior by exercising power and control, rather than consider the appropriateness of the learning context for accommodating individual student needs. Teachers can choose to manage student behavior by using their authority and exercising direct control by dispensing rewards and punishment, or they can choose not to use their power in favor of strategies that empower students to make their own choices.

Authority Structures

Traditionally, effective classroom management has been largely viewed as tantamount to controlling student behavior, keeping students on-task and maintaining lesson flow, calling for constant teacher vigilance and appropriate teacher intervention. Furthermore, student behavior is judged to be inappropriate irrespective of consideration of individual student characteristics, performance expectations, or appropriateness of the learning task. The implicit assumption is that students are unable or unwilling to exercise control and/or solve their problems. Hence, teachers may impose their requirements for order without relating them to student requirements for learning.

The concept of control is equated with the teacher's perception of the student's ability to behave appropriately or solve problems. Teachers' belief systems about their primary role with respect to classroom management influence their behavior control styles, and their use of power and control (Larrivee, 1995).

- When teachers believe students *choose* not to provide an appropriate solution, they impose a solution.
- When teachers believe students are *not capable* of providing a solution, they may provide an adaptation, either in task structure or performance expectation.

Although teacher perception of student needs relative to classroom control are viewed quite differently in these two approaches, in both cases the teacher takes responsibility either by exercising control or applying structure. In the first case teachers see students as needing to be disciplined, whereas in the second case they see students as needing to be helped. While the latter approach may be more humane, both of these approaches socialize students to expect to have problems solved for them. These views relative to classroom management may be appropriate for classroom organizations in which instruction is primarily teacher-directed and where the teacher is the primary decision-maker, however, these approaches do not hold students responsible and thus are not likely to build student competence and/or autonomy for eventual self-management.

The recent shift in classroom management focus from obedience to responsibility calls for the teacher to foster student autonomy. The shift from authoritarian hierarchy of authority to democratic community also redefines the concept of control from control of students to helping students develop internal control and exercising teacher self-control in conflict situations.

Sources of Power

The teacher has four power bases from which to operate. The chart below defines each of these types of power and lists corresponding key characteristics of classroom organization and management.

Characteristics of Power Bases

Power Type	Power Base	Characteristic Classroom Organization and Management
Coercive	Authority by virtue of power to reward and punish.	Dictates rules and procedures. Uses system of incentives and punishments. Requires careful teacher surveillance.
Legitimate	Authority by virtue of appointed position.	Clearly communicates delineation of teacher and student role. Prescribes standards for appropriate behavior. Reminds students of their position of authority.
Expert	Authority by virtue of knowledge/expertise.	Centers around content. Focuses on keeping students on-task. Uses procedures that redirect students to the learning task. Carefully monitors student progression through the lesson.
Referent	Authority by virtue of relationship power.	Establishes democratic procedures. Respects students' rights. Negotiates mutual solutions to problems.

Expert Power

Expert power is attributed to one who has a specialized body of knowledge. Teachers are attributed expert power by students when they view them as knowledgeable, competent, and in charge. Students are usually willing to follow the teacher's direction because they feel confident that the teacher knows what he/she is doing.

Teachers who value management by expert power usually show great enthusiasm for the subject, have subject matter command, exercise academic leadership, establish orderly procedures, and actively involve students. These teachers know how to make involvement with the learning activity much more interesting than off-task or disruptive behavior. They inspire and challenge students to excel.

Teachers with an expert power base orchestrate learning tasks to keep students interested, ground activities in sound rationale, give clear directions, ensure that students know what is expected, and monitor for individual and group progress. They also consider individual learning style differences in their planning and are able to gauge the appropriate level of structure for a particular lesson goal. Teachers with expert power act with authority, although their power is subliminal.

Referent Power

Referent power is the power that comes from connecting with students in authentic and humane ways. Referent power is power teachers have based on students' admiration and respect. Teachers who have referent power elicit expected behavior from students because their students like them. Relationship with students is more personal and is characterized by nurturing, supportive, and caring behaviors. These teachers exhibit genuine concern for students and place high value in cultivating human relationships. Fostering the personal growth of their students and helping them feel good about themselves are high on their agenda. They value student opinions and trust students to make appropriate choices and to be accountable when they don't.

Teachers who manage by referent power command rather than demand respect. They do not assume that their position gives them any right to treat students differently from anyone else. They use power judiciously and involve students in setting reasonable and ethical expectations for acceptable behavior. For these teachers, their job is to be "of service" to students.

When teachers have referent power, students are willing to adjust their behavior to maintain the teacher's respect. Power is implicit and based on influence and positive identification with the teacher. Students want to maintain a positive relationship because they identify with the teacher as a role model.

While referent power is often associated with teacher charisma, it can be developed by any teacher. The route to establishing referent power is through treating students with dignity and respect. A teacher doesn't lose power when assuming a nurturing posture, in fact he/she may gain it (Gootman, 1997). Several studies examining the effectiveness of various power bases have shown referent power to be the most effective, and coercive and legitimate power as the least effective (Golanda, 1990; McCroskey & Richmond, 1983; Stahelski & Frost, 1987).

Teachers who use referent and expert authority bases are concerned with facilitating student development, encouraging intrinsic motivation, and supporting the development of self-esteem by increasing student competence and power. These teachers are also less likely to suffer from high stress level or burnout.

Coercive Power

Teachers acting with coercive authority demand compliance, exercise rigid control, deny students a role in decision-making, and set arbitrary limits on acceptable behavior. Their foremost concern is with maintaining order, and they often view order and control as ends in themselves rather than means to an end.

Coercive power is exemplified by systems of imposed rules of order and standards of acceptable behavior with contingencies attached. Often the rules are posted in large print as commandments in front of the class as constant reminders. These are the rules which the system is ready to enforce with sanctions ranging from verbal reprimands, point losses, time outs, and referral to higher authority in the chain of command.

Legitimate Power

Legitimate power is power granted to teachers due to their position as the teacher. Teachers who manage by this type of authority believe it is there rightful role to prescribe standards. They typically operate in a businesslike fashion, maintain distance from students as a symbol of their unequal power base, and frequently remind student who's in charge.

This management style might be thought of as the default posture. Teachers who use this type of power believe they have the right to exert authority over students because of the authority vested in them as part of their role. They feel they are sanctioned by society by virtue of their teaching certification to run the classroom the way they see fit.

In relationships such as student/teacher in which the distribution of power is unequal, coercive and legitimate power are readily available and easy to wield. Yet use of these types of power over students generally alters behavior only temporarily and largely fails to induce longterm change, growth, and learning.

Legitimate and coercive power bases exercise overt control over students and decrease student self-control. These management types encourage extrinsic motivation and afford fewer opportunities for developing self-esteem. In addition, these management strategies are more effective at the primary level. They lose their effectiveness as students get older and are relatively ineffective by the secondary level.

Teachers who manage by attempting to control students are also more likely to experience high stress levels, precipitate more student confrontation and aggressive behavior, and suffer from teacher burnout.

At one time, teachers could depend primarily on legitimate power by virtue of their title. However, changes in our society have lessened the effectiveness of this type of authority. Where in the past, most students tacitly agreed to be managed by the teacher, today's students are more likely to challenge the authority of the teacher. Role models available from sports and via the media promote confrontation not obedience.

While teachers have a primary power base from which they operate, a total management plan represents a coalescence of several forms of power. Teachers who effectively manage their classrooms do so by skillfully conjoining forms of influence and judiciously using the power vested in them. They weave in and out of various modes of authority. Having expert or referent power doesn't preclude them from using other types of authority when they deem it necessary. Although creating a democratic community, maintained by a mutually agreed-upon code of conduct, is a worthy pursuit, it does not negate the teacher's right to, on occasion, exercise more direct control. There are situations which arise where the ethical use of authority does not rule out unilateral social control. Noblit (1993) used the term *moral authority* to refer to the type of authority where a teacher develops classroom procedures and routines, engages in reciprocal negotiation, yet still retains the right to steer the curriculum and interactions toward goals deemed worthwhile for students. Each teacher will need to seriously consider what constitutes ethical authority and how and when shared responsibility and negotiation serve the needs of both the teacher and students; and conversely, when it does not.

Management versus Leadership: Bossing or Leading?

Classroom management has long been the metaphor for establishing relations of authority in the classroom. The very use of the term management carries with it assumptions about power and purpose. As McLaughlin (1994) notes, the term classroom management accurately reflects a "preoccupation with scientific efficiency and bureaucratic political control at the school level."

Management is a relationship based on authority; leadership is a noncoercive relationship of influence (Rost, 1991). Managers have a relationship of authority over their subordinates. Glasser (1990) makes a clear distinction between the teacher role as manager, or as he refers to this role, as boss, and the teacher role as leader.

Comparison of Characteristics of a Boss and a Leader

Boss	Leader
Drives	Leads
Relies on authority	Relies on cooperation
Says "I"	Says "We"
Creates fear	Creates confidence
Knows how	Shows how
Creates resentment	Breeds enthusiasm
Fixes blame	Fixes mistakes
Makes work drudgery	Makes work interesting

Leaders go beyond stopping behavior to guiding and showing students what to do. The teacher who leads is more thoughtful, helpful, and responsive to students.

Leadership requires a clear vision of what a classroom could become. The leader translates this vision into goals and expectations that reflect their mutual purposes. Shared leadership is based on assumptions that students will exercise self-direction and self-control in service of what they are committed to. Effort is motivated by achieving, not solely by external rewards or the threats of punishment.

In the classroom, both teachers and students are able to influence others for the common purpose of making a better classroom. Leaders and followers enjoy a multidirectional relationship of potential influence. Leaders influence followers, and followers influence leaders as well as other followers. The leader/follower relationship is also unequal because leaders commit more effort and resources to influencing followers than vise versa. Hence, a teacher who sees a student abusing another student must act with authority. Leadership is not sacrificed by exercising the authority of one's position. The teacher who is in charge can exercise more or less control as the situation demands.

Authority is the right teachers have to make decisions that affect the choices available to students. It is the right vested in them as teachers. Power is how they use it. Teachers use their authority when they assign work to students. Power is what they use to get students to complete their assignments.

Choice and Voice: Fundamentals of Leading a Democratic Learning Community

While teachers may operate from a primary power base, a total management plan calls for joining forms of influence and using power judiciously. The teacher needs to be able to move in and out of various modes of authority as he/she deems necessary. Maintaining a democratic learning community does not preclude the teacher's right to exercise more direct control as situations arise. The teacher needs to strike a balance between exercising too much control, which propagates student dependence, and not exercising enough control, thereby jeopardizing a safe and productive learning environment.

Teachers will need to consider what constitutes judicious authority and how and when they can enhance student autonomy through shared decision-making, negotiation, and problem solving. In the democratic learning community, power *over* students is transformed into power *with* students. Adjusting the power-status dynamics to turn more power over to students, means giving students a voice in classroom practices.

The teacher can still maintain some control, yet give students a sense of power and freedom by giving them choices among acceptable options. Students have a choice but the options offered are within defined parameters which the teacher deems appropriate to the learning goals. The following choices empower students to have some voice, while still meeting the teacher's objectives.

Greater involvement in general and procedural choices:

- The order in which students do their assigned classwork.
- Where to sit, or if they sit for certain activities.
- Which field trip they would like to take.
- Which community service project they would like to adopt.
- Which classroom activities should require silence.
- When they need a break from their work.

Greater involvement in curriculum and learning task choices:

- Which book to read from a list of suggested books.
- What to write about given some general guidelines.
- Which of several suggested topics they would like to study.
- How they would like to study the topics and in which order.
- How they present a project, e.g., oral report, video, visual display, play, poem, song.

These options vary in the degree of control given over to students. Teachers who are most comfortable managing the classroom by "keeping the lid on" can begin to involve students to a greater extent by turning over less significant decisions, such as where to go on a field trip. Eventually, they can work their way up to sharing decision-making power in more significant matters.

Teachers can begin to wean students from unilateral control by gradually increasing the degree of involvement and participation students have in decision making. Teachers can devise their own sequence for relinquishing more and more control to students. A sample continuum is presented below. In this continuum, for example, teachers who are comfortable at the level of presenting students with a tentative decision and then getting student input can move to actually sharing with students their thinking process along with any dilemmas and trade-offs they have concerns about.

- Teacher makes decision and announces to students what they will do.
- Teacher makes decision and provides students with rationale for decision to enlist buy-in.
- Teacher presents tentative decision, subject to student input.
- Teacher presents ideas and invites questions and comments prior to making a decision.
- Teacher defines limits and asks students to make decision.
- Teacher allows students to make decisions which are only confined by school policies.

Critical Reflection on Practice: Balancing Conformity with Autonomy

Activity Directions: Reflect on all the activities students experience and the requirements placed on students in your classroom. If you have more that one class, select one class for this activity. Then complete steps 1 to 8.

Step 1: List all the rules, procedures and/or activities that control students and require them to conform (e.g., line up, fold papers, have only four people at learning center at a time).

_____

_____

_____

_____

Step 2: List all the procedures and activities that allow students some choice and self-management (e.g., choose activity, get a drink without permission).

_____

_____

_____

_____

Step 3: Describe ways in which the choice and self-management list can be extended and still maintain learning and behavior goals.

_____

_____

_____

_____

Step 4: Which of the conformity requirements you listed in Step 1 could be eliminated or altered?

_____

Step 5: What did this exercise tell you about how you promote student autonomy and support self-management? _____

_____

Step 6: What did you learn about your management style from this exercise? _____

_____

Step 7: Are you satisfied with the balance of control with freedom in your classroom? _____

Step 8: What did this exercise cause you to question about your current classroom policies and procedures?

_____

Another way teachers share power is by giving students more opportunities to manage their own behavior. When problems occur, teachers use intervention strategies that focus not on what they need to do *to* students, rather on what they can do *for* students to help them make better choices. The following section describes ways teachers can intervene to deal with student behavior that is problematic and unproductive by supporting students in using self-control.

Intervention Escalation

The idea of intervention escalation is to move systematically, sequentially, and progressively "up the ladder of escalation." Without specific intent to promote student self-management and self-control, teachers often move very quickly up the intervention ladder. Many teachers virtually skip Level 2 interventions, those most critical to helping students develop self-management. You should have several intervention options in your repertoire at each level. Your escalation pattern needs to strike a balance between moving too slowly, failing to assert your expectations, and moving too rapidly, not allowing students an opportunity for regulating their behavior on their own.

Intervention Escalation Hierarchy

Level 1 Interventions

Maintain the lesson flow
Deter a minor problem from escalating into a major one
Occur before the teacher begins to harbor negative feelings

Level 2 Interventions

Reduce student anxiety
Keep students working productively
Address motive underlying the misbehavior

Level 3 Interventions

Maintain positive relationship, restore if necessary
Create window of opportunity
Allow students to save face

Intervention Options

Level 1: When student starts to stray.

Planned ignoring	Eye contact
Signal interference	Proximity control
Touch	Task engagement feedback
State positive expectation	Provide rationale
Brief directive	

Level 2: When student persists.

Invite cooperation	Statement of value
Express your needs	State your disappointment
I statement	Impact statement
Simple request	Direct appeal to values
Request that student change behavior	Request that student make a better choice
Ask what student needs	Ask student to make value judgment
Ask student to empathize with others' feelings	Ask student to consider others' needs
Quiet correction	
Enlist group feedback	Redirect by asking for help
Redirect with humor	Redirect by restructuring task
Provide hurdle help	Provide personal support
Acknowledge student's challenge	Accept student's feelings
	Appeal to future reward
Offer incentive	Suggest better alternative
Gentle reminder	Rule reminder

Level 3: When student decides not to cooperate.

Reminder of consequence	Antiseptic bounce
Ask student to make choice	Give range of choices
Warning	Give either/or choice
Thinking time	Separation
Isolation	Student conference
Logical consequence	Restoration
Send to office	In-school suspension
Limited time suspension	Suspension

Intervention Escalation Levels

Listed above are many types of interventions for dealing with student behavior as it becomes more serious. By intent, the list of options at Level 2 is the longest. This is because supporting students in making a better choice is a core belief driving this approach to classroom management.

Learning Practice Task: Developing Your Ladder of Escalation

Activity Directions: Develop your own ladder of escalation by planning 10 steps of progressive escalation.

Step 1: _____

Step 2: _____

Step 3: _____

Step 4: _____

Step 5: _____

Step 6: _____

Step 7: _____

Step 8: _____

Step 9: _____

Step 10: _____

Question for Self-reflection

At what point in my current escalation sequence, do I want to expand my intervention options?

Teacher Emotional Escalation in Reacting to Challenging Student Behaviors

Teachers can't control how students act and react, but they can exercise control over their own actions and reactions to students' behavior. Often teachers automatically react to a student's inappropriate behavior rather than consciously deciding how best to respond to the student and/or the situation. Teachers can get drawn into situations with students that quickly escalate into no-win episodes. By becoming more aware of how students can, and do, push their emotional buttons, teachers can develop more supportive and effective strategies to deescalate conflicts.

Dealing with Student Defiance

Responding to direct student defiance is an especially difficult situation for teachers to deal with effectively. Such situations are usually emotional encounters for both teachers and students. Colvin (1988) notes that teacher defiance involves a sequential chain of events that are relatively trivial early in the chain (questioning, arguing), but that culminate in very serious behaviors at the end (verbal and physical abuse, threats). He has developed a procedure for anticipating and preventing direct teacher defiance that relies on careful situational analysis and teacher self-control. The key is to anticipate and exercise control during the trivial behaviors early in the chain, so that escalation does not occur and you can prevent more serious behaviors.

Situations that are likely to escalate quickly often begin when the student is in an agitated emotional state (angry, frustrated) and engages the teacher in a confrontational interaction through a question-asking strategy in response to the teacher's requests or directives. Once the engagement process begins, the teacher and student are usually log-jammed in a power struggle that quickly escalates into explosiveness and defiance.

A typical chain proceeds like this:

- Student is in agitated state.
- Teacher makes request or issues a directive.
- Student asks resisting question.
- Teacher repeats directive.
- Student gives excuse, argues or complains.
- Teacher continues to press for compliance.
- Student "blows" resulting in verbally and/or physically aggressive behavior.

The following dialogue illustrates this chain (Walker & Walker, 1991).

Example of Teacher/Student Escalation Chain

Context: Eric comes into Mr. Damon's 10th-grade history class 10 minutes late and in a surly mood. He takes his time getting to his desk and engages several students in conversation along the way. An argument develops with one of the students who resents Eric's intrusion. Angry words are exchanged.

(Student is in agitated state.)

Mr. Damon: "Eric, go to your desk, now! You're always trying the patience of this class and you're running out of rope with me, fast."

(Teacher gives a direct terminating command.)

Eric: "Jason borrowed my history book yesterday and he left it home. So what am I supposed to do? I can't work."

(Student asks question in an attempt to deflect teacher command.)

Mr. Damon: "Bringing your work materials and books to class is not Jason's responsibility or mine. It's yours! I'm telling you for the last time to sit down!"

(Teacher reissues command.)

Eric: "Look, I can't work if I don't have the materials to work with, now can I? Any fool can see that." [Under his breath to a peer, Jason refers to Mr. Damon as a stupid jerk, which Mr. Damon overhears.]

(Student offers an excuse.)

Context: Mr. Damon ignores the insult but continues to insist that Eric sit down, stop disturbing the class, and occupy himself. He approaches Eric in an authoritative manner. Both are very angry and have the attention of the most of the class.

Mr. Damon: "For the last time, Eric, you'd better sit down if you know what's good for you! If you want to stay in my class, you'd better do what I say."

(Teacher continues pressure for compliance.)

Eric: "I don't give a _____ about this class. _____ you!" [Eric storms out and slams the door. Mr. Damon calls the office and reports the incident.]

(Student has tantrum and defies the teacher.)

As can be readily seen, the teacher is not in control and has lost the opportunity to teach the student. The student rather than the teacher is in control of the situation. As long as the teacher responds in a stepwise fashion to each increment (question, argument) in the student's pattern of escalating behavior, the interaction is very likely to result in the student exploding.

The Basic Rule in this Situation

When a student in an agitated state begins to actively resist teacher demands and attempts to engage the teacher in an interaction about the directive, the teacher should immediately begin disengaging.

To avoid this chain reaction, there are three ground rules.

1. Do not make demands on students when they are in an agitated state.
2. Do not allow yourself to become "engaged" in the student's question-and-answer agenda.
3. Do not attempt to force the student's hand.

The teacher should attempt to wait out the mood before initiating a direct demand. A student in this state will likely interpret a teacher demand as a provocative event, especially when it is delivered with an audience of peers. In certain situations it might be appropriate to inquire about what's going on with the student, but it should not be followed with a demand at the time.

It is especially important for teachers to recognize the student's "engagers" such as questions, disagreements, contradictions, arguments, and counterarguments. The teacher needs to refrain from responding to the student's questions and, above all, not get caught up arguing with the student. Instead the teacher should ignore the student's bait and restate what the student needs to do. If the student refuses, the teacher should leave the student alone while the student is in the agitated state. The teacher should not try to coerce the student through such tactics as hovering and waiting, using social punishment (glaring, verbal reprimands, social intimidation), or making threats about future consequences. Never touch the student in this state; leave the student's presence and end the interaction. If there is a set consequence for this type of behavior, such as loss of points or privileges, it should be applied promptly with a minimum of verbalization.

Dealing with Students under Stress

The conflict cycle paradigm developed by Long (1996) offers a way to understand why and how competent teachers can find themselves in self-defeating struggles. Students under stress behave emotionally because they are controlled more by feelings than by logic. They will protect themselves from pain and perceived or actual attack by being defensive, primitive, and regressive. When the teacher reacts to this type of behavior with righteous indignation, a power struggle ensues in which the teacher's primary objective is now "winning" rather than resolving the conflict.

According to the conflict cycle paradigm, the interaction between a student and a teacher follows a circular pattern in which the attitudes, feelings, and behaviors of the teacher and the student mutually influence each other to create the conflict cycle. Once this cycle is set in motion, the negative interplay between the teacher and the student is very difficult to interrupt. When teachers react emotionally, they invalidate the feelings and deny the issues behind the student's behavior and become part of the problem rather than part of the solution.

The conflict cycle depicts the circular and escalating nature of student/teacher conflict and how troubled students create counteraggressive feelings in teachers which frequently lead to a mutual, self-defeating power struggle. Enacting the cycle serves to reinforce the student's "irrational" beliefs. (Irrational beliefs as well as strategies for helping students deal with them are also discussed in Chapter 9.)

The Conflict Cycle Paradigm

- Stressful incident occurs which activates student's irrational belief (e.g., all adults are hostile).
- These negative thoughts determine and trigger the student's feelings.
- The student's negative feelings drive inappropriate behavior.
- The inappropriate behavior incites the teacher.
- The teacher mirrors the student's behavior.
- This adverse reaction increases the student's stress and triggers more intense feelings and drives more inappropriate behavior.
- More severe inappropriate behavior causes even more teacher anger and denunciation.
- The student's irrational belief (all adults are hostile) is reinforced.
- The student has no reason to change either the irrational belief or the inappropriate behavior.

Even if the student loses the initial battle by the teacher winning and dispensing punishment, the student wins the psychological war. The irrational belief is perpetuated and serves as a self-fulfilling prophecy.

It is important to note that in this model, a stressful incident is an event that the student perceives as threatening and serves to activate the student's irrational belief. The student's internal process for deciding whether an event is stressful is based on the meaning the student attributes to the event. An ordinary request to share an answer could be the stressful triggering event, if it brings up an irrational belief such as "If I don't get it right everyone will think I'm stupid."

The cycle begins with a student's eroded sense of self-esteem that plays a central role in determining how the student thinks about him/herself, relationships with others, and beliefs about what will happen in the future (i.e., self-fulfilling prophecy). Developmentally, a child's sense of self is formed by the nature of relationships with significant adults and, later, peers in the child's life which provide ongoing feedback about the child's character and behavior. When a child receives primarily negative feedback that tells the child he/she is difficult, stupid, hopeless, or weak, over time the child internalizes a deprecating self-perception. How a child learns to think about him/herself becomes the prevailing element in determining feelings and, ultimately, behavior. In other words, the child's behavior will be consistent with this internalized self-image, regardless of the real data or facts.

In addition to developing a set of personal beliefs, the child also develops beliefs about the world and other people. If the adults in the child's world are hostile, rejecting, and hopeless, the child learns to mistrust adults. Personal beliefs and beliefs about the way the world works merge sometime in the early elementary school years and form the child's emerging personality. Now the child has a characteristic way of perceiving, interpreting, feeling, behaving, and responding to life events.

As Long notes, troubled children need to explain why they were abused, neglected, or rejected. The search for an explanation does not take place in reality, rather in their "irrational" beliefs that form to explain their painful life experiences. This means all life events are filtered and evaluated by the student's belief system, activated by the student's irrational thoughts. Initially, the student's negative beliefs about others represent an accurate assessment of the student's experiences. What moves these reality-based beliefs to irrational status is the projection to all situations and relationships in the future. The following is an example of how an irrational belief forms.

My mother neglected me [fact].

I can't count on her to meet my needs [fact].

All adults I'll ever meet will neglect me and my needs [irrational belief].

These irrational beliefs are maintained because they provide troubled students with a sense of security and control by making their world predictable. But most importantly, these irrational beliefs protect students from experiencing the underlying feeling of rage. The way they maintain these beliefs is to project their internal worldview on others by engaging them in endless power struggles. This process of getting others to confirm their irrational beliefs becomes the student's self-fulfilling prophecy.

The following case illustrates the self-fulfilling prophecy of a passive-aggressive student.

Student belief	*Direct expression of anger is dangerous so I better disguise my feelings. If the teacher ever found out how I really feel, terrible things would happen.*
Learned behavior	*Student learns to express anger in passive-aggressive, or indirect, ways.*
Classroom behaviors	*When the teacher asks student to do something he doesn't like, he does it in a way that disappoints and frustrates the teacher.*
	When he's angry at the teacher, he will get back at her by stealing her keys or messing up the room when she's gone.
Impact on teacher	*As all the little things add up, the teacher over time gets on "emotional overload." But the teacher is unaware of the accumulated anger toward the student.*
Precipitating incident	*At the end of a particularly tiring day, the student falls out of his chair, "accidentally" ripping off part of the teacher's new bulletin board display. When the student ignores her first two requests to get back in his seat, the teacher "loses it" and yells, threatens the student, and throws a tantrum.*
Student response:	*"Gee, I didn't mean to do it."*
Teacher thinks:	*Boy, I shocked myself by the amount of anger I expressed. Maybe I did overreact. That's not like me, I own him an apology.*

Teacher says:	*"I'm sorry I yelled at you."*
Student says:	*"That's OK."*
Student thinks:	*Look at how crazy people get when they show their anger. It's a good thing I don't act like that! Ms. Lee needs to change, not me.*
Result:	*The student's self-fulfilling prophecy stays in place.*

One of the most significant insights of understanding the conflict cycle is how a student can recreate their own negative feelings in the teacher. Aggressive students create counteraggressive feelings, depressed students create feelings of helplessness, and so forth. The teacher usually acts on these feelings by mirroring the student's behavior. For example, if the student yells, the teacher yells. Once the teacher behaves like the student, the cycle is set in motion. The teacher feels unjustly attacked by an aggressive student act and becomes flooded by feelings of outrage. Because the teacher feels totally justified in a retaliatory reaction, he/she doesn't acknowledge a role in escalating the conflict which makes the cycle extremely difficult to stop. Teachers do not have control over how students behave and react, but they do have control over how they react to students. They can become more aware of how students push their emotional panic buttons and develop more supportive and effective strategies to interrupt the conflict cycle.

Breaking the Cycle of Reacting

It is important to remember that once the conflict escalates into a power struggle, there are no winners. At this point, there is very little chance that the student is going to act more maturely while in such an intense state of arousal. The greatest hope for change lies in the teacher's ability to respond in a way that can break the cycle. When teachers know how students in conflict think and feel and understand how they can provoke them into acting in hostile and rejecting ways, they recognize that managing student behavior begins with self-control when their buttons are pushed. But teachers also have to move beyond understanding the dynamics that suck them into mirroring the student's behavior to learning to avoid such power struggles.

In order to help students, teachers need to identify and address the important and underlying issues in a student's life, rather than mere knee-jerk reactions to provoking behavior. Teachers can use the insight the conflict cycle offers to recognize and accept the counteraggressive feelings often evoked in conflicts with students and refrain from sending blaming you-messages such as the following:

Don't you dare do that with me!

Can't you ever use your head?

Why don't you act your age for a change.

The blaming you-messages the student receives only serve to support the student's view of him/herself and confirm the student's self-fulfilling prophecy. It fuels the fire by creating more stress, leading to more inappropriate behavior and greater teacher disgust. For the student, the teacher is now part of the problem, and for the teacher, having the last word and winning overrides all else.

In such situations where the teacher feels upset and angry in response to student behavior which is aggressive, hostile, and defiant, what is called for is an authentic message which expresses the teacher's feelings. When the message is about the teacher's feelings, not about the student's shortcomings, it will be delivered in I-language not blame-attributing you-language, as the following message illustrates.

> *"I really get angry when you come into my room, kick stuff around, and yell in my face. I can see you're upset, but that kind of behavior doesn't help me understand why you're angry or make me want to help you."*

Such an honest response also helps limit the teacher's impulse to retaliate and keeps the focus on what the student needs to do to regain control. When the response doesn't imply right or wrong, it keeps the communication channels open. Most importantly, such responses model exercising control over angry feelings while simultaneously accepting and acknowledging the teacher's right to experience and express negative feelings. (Using I-language is also discussed in Chapter 4.)

When teachers consciously choose to express their anger, it helps them replace destructive words about the student with constructive words about what needs to happen. Being able to identify why student behaviors may trigger your reactions can help you begin to make better choices as you work with students.

Learning Practice Task: Becoming Proactive – Breaking the Cycle of Reacting

Activity Directions: Working with a partner, take turns sharing answers to the following questions.

What behaviors push your buttons?

_____

_____

_____

Which of the following behaviors frustrate you or make you angry?

☐ Hoarding materials _____   ☐ Talking all the time _____

☐ Sulking _____   ☐ Demanding attention _____

☐ Talking back _____   ☐ Bullying smaller students _____

☐ Constantly asking questions _____   ☐ Showing an angry temper _____

☐ Not beginning work on time _____   ☐ Always moving around _____

☐ Taking others' things _____   ☐ Disrupting the group _____

☐ Not following directions _____   ☐ Challenging you _____

For those you identified, put them in priority order.

For your top priority, consider why this behavior might be difficult for you. List reasons that come to mind for why this behavior causes you to react.

_____

_____

_____

Do you react overtly or do you usually try to hold yourself in check? _____

What are some ways you can separate your own issues from what your expectations are for your students?

_____

_____

_____

Considering disciplinary interactions only, what would you consider to be a good day?

_____

_____

_____

Part III

Promoting Student Self-management and Responsibility

Chapter 9

Supporting Student Self-assessment, Self-management, and Self-reflection

Because students have typically been socialized to a classroom environment in which the teacher directs activities, manages student behavior, and evaluates student performance, asking students to be responsible for their own behavior requires a shift in student-acquired expectations and ways of behaving. Teachers can initially facilitate this shift by asking students to engage in self-diagnosis of the appropriateness of their behavior. This changes the student/teacher interaction pattern from one in which the teacher evaluates students' behavior to one in which students provide their own assessment of their actions. The notion of self-assessment is a key concept for establishing shared responsibility for maintaining a supportive learning community.

Often students fail to act in appropriate ways not because of lack of motivation, conscious choice, or unwillingness, rather because they have not learned what constitutes acceptable ways of behaving or under what circumstances a behavior would be appropriate or inappropriate. Specific strategy instruction and structured learning experiences can enable students to learn social and self-management skills that will help them develop positive peer relationships, work cooperatively in learning groups, and participate productively in classroom activities. Crucial to this learning is the modeling provided by the teacher.

Developing Collaborative Problem-solving

If teachers want to move away from a teacher-controlled environment and call on students to be active participants in making choices and solving problems, they may have to (at least initially) engage in strategy building to teach students the strategies they may be lacking in areas such as decision-making, problem-solving, self-control, and conflict resolution. If students are lacking the necessary repertoire to make appropriate choices, then it is incumbent on teachers to teach students strategies so that they will eventually become more capable of making better choices in the future. Thus the teacher may need to provide sequenced lessons and structured experiences to teach students strategies so that in time the teacher can turn over responsibility to students and function in a more facilitative role where students are expected to make choices and find solutions and, in fact, have a response repertoire for making appropriate choices.

Using Classroom Meetings to Develop Decision-making Skills

To encourage ongoing communication between teachers and students, regularly scheduled class meetings are one vehicle. Like any community, a class has goals to achieve, problems to resolve, opportunities to assess, interpersonal conflicts to work out, and decisions to make. All of these issues can be handled through class meetings.

Topics for class meetings can range from individual concerns which the whole group can help solve to whole-group concerns. Topics may be brief and informational or may require lengthy discussion. In addition to the term class meeting, circle time, weekly meeting, problem solving, shared decision making, or any suitable name can be used. Teachers who have made the class meeting an integral part of their program most typically hold class meetings weekly.

Some teachers like to chair meetings, others prefer a rotating chair in which students take turns running the meeting and have the opportunity to practice leadership skills. Some teachers have students submit ideas beforehand, while others encourage students to raise issues at the meeting. Another option is to post a folder marked "Next Class Meeting" to allow students to participate who might not otherwise initiate a topic for consideration.

Sometimes the teacher may want to call everyone together again and ask, "Are you still satisfied with our solution?" It's important to communicate the message that decisions are not chiseled in stone and that they can be discarded in search of a better solution. Also, this reinforces the value of students' solutions. By beginning each meeting with a discussion of the results of the solutions developed at the previous meeting, students feel their solutions are useful and important. Class meetings are designed for the purpose of teaching problem-solving so reinforcing students' successful efforts, analyzing failures and helping them develop increasingly more effective solutions is integral to the process.

Glasser's Suggestions

Glasser suggests the classroom meeting as an effective vehicle for attending to matters such as class rules, behavior, and discipline. He recommends two basic ground rules to set the stage for students and teachers to interact without finding fault, placing blame, or seeking to punish or retaliate. The ground rules should be established in the first meeting, kept to a minimum (2 or 3) and stated in positive terms. Glasser's two major ground rules are:

1. Class members deal with each other with mutual respect, and
2. Meetings are established for class members to help each other.

He also recommends the following general procedures.

General Procedures

1. Meetings should be held at a consistently scheduled time or times each week.
2. The established time should never be canceled as a punishment.
3. Topics for the meeting may be placed on the agenda and/or introduced by the teacher or by class members.
4. All topics relative to the class as a group or to any individual class member can be discussed in the class meeting forum.
5. Brief minutes should be kept including only lists of options generated and final decisions. This provides a record which may be referred to should the class decide to reconsider their decision some time in the future.

Guidelines

1. Don't expect effectiveness of the classroom meeting format to be immediate. Social problem solving is a complex process and will require practice to be successful.
2. The role of the teacher is to serve as a facilitator to keep students focused on the topic, ensure a democratic atmosphere where everyone is listened to, and reflect student comments back to the group.

3. Teacher input as a facilitator may need to be extensive at initial class meetings; however, the teacher should diminish his/her role and remain in the background as soon as the students have learned the problem-solving process.

The Process

Conducting class meetings involves the following systematic problem-solving process.

Step 1: Establishing a climate of warmth and trust.

Step 2: Exposing and clarifying the problem.

Step 3: Making the personal value judgment.

Step 4: Identifying alternate ways to act.

Step 5: Determining an appropriate consequence.

Step 6: Making a commitment.

Step 7: Following up with an evaluation of effectiveness.

According to Glasser, classroom meetings should do the following:

- Provide a stable way to bridge the gap between school and life.
- Help students believe they can control their own destinies and that they themselves are a vital part of the world they live in.
- Keep a class together because the more and less capable can interact.
- Promote involvement because students can always succeed in a meeting—no one can fail.
- Help motivate students to do some of the less exciting fact-finding that may evolve from the meetings.
- Reduce isolation and failure so that a spirit of cooperation can exist.
- Help students gain confidence when they state an opinion before a group, thus helping them prepare for the many opportunities in life to speak for themselves.
- Increase responsibility for learning and for the kind of learning that is fostered by and shared with the entire class.
- Provide for the kind of involvement, value judgments, plans, and commitments that produce changes in behavior.

Increasing Students' Involvement in Class Meetings

A major goal in implementing class meetings is teaching students the skills involved in functioning effectively in a problem-solving group. With this goal in mind, teachers need to consider gradually increasing student responsibility for facilitating class meetings. Jones and Jones (1998) note that this is difficult to do with primary-grade children, but third-grade students can be taught to run their own class meetings successfully. They offer the following four steps for having students take over the class meeting.

1. After leading approximately 10 class meetings, present students with a handout describing the major functions a leader serves when facilitating a group meeting (see chart, Class Meeting Jobs). Discuss each function and behavior with the class and inform them that they will soon be asked to lead their own meetings by having students serve these important functions.

2. Introduce an agenda item or classroom problem. While the class discusses this situation, point out and define each intervention you make. Because you continue to serve all three functions, the discussion will be interrupted on numerous occasions. Students are usually excited about learning the new skills, however, and enjoy your instructional interventions.

3. After running three or four actual class meetings in which you consistently point out the function of each intervention, meet with and teach one student the role of discussion leader. At the next meeting, this student serves as the discussion leader while you maintain the other roles. Prior to the next meeting, you meet with another student who learns the role of task observer. At the following meeting, the student serves this function. After this meeting, you instruct a third student in the role of behavior and feeling observer, and at the following meeting you become a group member who abides by the group responsibilities, while the students run the meeting.

4. Each student should function in a role for five or six meetings, so that he or she can master the skills associated with the role and effectively model it for other students. If a student has difficulty with a role, take time between meetings to instruct the student in the skills associated with the role. Providing students with this type of experience requires a small amount of time and considerable restraint and patience, but students respond to their new skills by becoming more positive, productive class members. Indeed, problem students often respond especially well, for they gain self-esteem and peer acceptance when serving as productive participants in class meetings.

Class Meeting Jobs

Discussion Leader

1. Make sure everyone is comfortable and all distracting things are out of the way.

2. Make sure everyone can see all others in the circle.

3. Give the speaker time to get his or her point across.

4. Give the speaker a nod or a smile.

5. Ask clarifying questions:
   a. Are you saying that . . . ?
   b. Do you feel that . . . ?

6. Summarize:
   a. "Is there anything else you would like to say?
   b. Would someone briefly summarize what has been said?

Task Observer

1. Make sure the task gets finished on time.

2. Watch the time.

3. Make suggestions of alternatives to solve the problem.

4. Point out behaviors that don't help in solving a problem.

5. Listen carefully and understand what the discussion leader is doing.

6. Understand the agenda and call out each agenda item.

Behavior and Feeling Observer

1. How did this discussion make you feel?

2. What could we do now? What might help us?

3. Was anything asked that caused you _____ (name of person) to be concerned?
   Can you tell us what it was and how you felt about it?

4. _____ (person's name) you usually help us out. Do you have any ideas for this problem?

5. Has anyone thought of new ideas for improving our discussions?

6. How many of you feel that the discussion was of value to you? Why?

Topics for Class Meetings

Many different kinds of issues can be raised at class meetings. Below are some examples to suggest the wide variety of topics possible (adapted from Kirschenbaum, 1995).

- The teacher is concerned about students frequently interrupting each another.
- Several students have complained that things have disappeared from their desks.
- A student wants to suggest to the class that they raise money for famine relief in Africa.
- Some students are concerned about the cliques in the classroom.

- The teacher is concerned that white and black students always sit separately in the classroom.
- The class needs to decide what service project it is going to do.
- The teacher would like some ideas for the next unit she is planning.
- A student thinks the teacher is being unfair in applying one of the class rules.
- A student has an idea for a class trip.
- Several students think a new rule is needed to solve a problem they are having.
- The teacher wants the class's feedback on the unit they just completed.
- The solution from a previous class meeting is not working. It needs to be reexamined.

Purposes for Class Meetings

Lickona (1991) has identified purposes the class meeting can fulfill:

- Deepen students' sense of shared ownership of the classroom.
- Improve students' moral reasoning, including their ability to take the perspective of others.
- Develop their listening skills and ability to express themselves in a group.
- Develop their self-worth by providing a forum in which their thoughts are valued.
- Teach the skills and attitudes needed to participate effectively in democratic decision-making.

A Sample Problem-solving Class Meeting

Weinstein and Mignano (1997) provide the following example of a teacher using a class meeting to solve a problem her students were experiencing at the end of recess each day. Note how she makes certain that everyone agrees on what the problem is, that she does not allow students to evaluate suggestions during the brainstorming phase of the activity, that she herself speaks against suggestions she doesn't like, and that she doesn't allow students to vote on the solution.

Teacher: *A few weeks ago, you were very upset about what was happening when you came in from the playground at the end of recess. We let it go for a while to see if the problem would go away by itself, but lately people have been telling me that things are still pretty bad out there.* [Students begin to murmur in agreement and to comment on what is happening.] *Can you tell me exactly what happens? After all, I'm not out there, so I don't really understand what's going on.*

Student: *When the aide blows the whistle to come in, everyone gets in a big clump in the little alleyway by the door and then everybody pushes and shoves, and people start to fight, and then the aides get mad, and people get sent to the office, and ...* [she talks so fast it's hard to understand].

Teacher: *Wait—you have to help me.* [She draws a map of the playground and the school on the board.] *Now let's see if I understand. Everyone clumps up right here?* [She points to an area on the map.] *Okay, so this is the problem. We're all agreed on what it is?* [There are signs of agreement.] *Now, let's brainstorm some solutions. Remember, when we brainstorm, we let everyone have their say without evaluating. We'll evaluate all the suggestions at the end.*

Student: *We come in a double door, and the doors are always kept closed until after we're lined up, and everyone gets smushed in so then it's hard to open the doors. If they were left open all the time, we could get in easier.* [Teacher writes on board: "#I. Leave doors open all the time."]

Teacher: *Another idea?* [She continues to solicit ideas and to write down each suggestion in a numbered list on the board.]

Student: *Open the doors right before the whistle is blown.*

Student: *Call students to line up by class.*

Student: *Line up by class and the quietest two classes go in first, one through each door.*

Student: *Two classes line up by the fence, and two classes line up by the brick wall.*

Student: *Get more aides. Right now there are only two.*

Student: *Line up in one long line by the fence.*

Student: *The classes play until the teachers come and get them.*

Student: *The teachers wouldn't agree to that.*

Teacher: *We're not discussing now, we're thinking of solutions. Then we will evaluate.*

Student: *Have a different whistle signal for each class, one whistle for one class, two for another, etc.*

Student: *Line up the way we do in the morning, each class in a different place.*

Student: *Have an aide bring each class to their classroom.*

Student: *Have classes go in different doors.*

Teacher: *Are there any more ideas?* [Suggestions seem to be at an end.] *Okay, our next job is to quietly read these suggestions and think about them. Take two or three minutes to discuss the suggestions with your table group. Then I'll call you all back together again and we'll begin to evaluate as a whole class.* [Students discuss the suggestions in their small groups.] *Okay, what we'll do now is discuss each one and decide what we think about each suggestion. What I'd like to do is come up with a few suggestions to present to Mr. Fehn* [the principal]. *We'll decide how we want to present these later—if we'll write, or invite him to come to our class, or if I'll represent you. Okay, anyone want to react?* [As students state positive or negative reactions, the teacher puts a plus or a minus sign by each suggestion that is mentioned.]

Student: *I like the idea of using more doors because that way kids would be separated and there wouldn't be so much pushing and shoving.* [The teacher acknowledges this comment and puts a plus sign by that suggestion.]

Student: *I like the one about more aides. If there were more aides, then they could stop kids from pushing.*

Student: *I don't think that's a good idea because it would cost money and the school doesn't have the money.*

Teacher: *I'm going to write a dollar sign next to this one so you can think about the issue of money.*

Student: *I like the idea of the teachers picking up the classes, but I don't think the teachers would like it.*

Teacher: *Let me give you my perspective on that. My lunch time is from 11:57 to 12:37. I will tell you frankly and honestly that even though I adore you, my lunch time is very precious to me and I would not appreciate giving up part of that time every day to come pick you up.*

Student: *Our table likes the idea of having two classes by the wall and two by the fence.*

Student: *Our table likes #2, open the doors just before the whistle.*

Teacher: *Sometimes people line up to go in before the aides blow the whistle. If people are already smushed in there, would opening the doors before blowing the whistle help?* [There's some general discussion of the teacher's comment and this suggestion.]

Student: *I like the idea of lining up by class in different places. It works in the morning, so it would probably work in the afternoon.*

Student: *I don't really like the idea of two classes lining up by the wall and two by the fence. Kids would still be too close, and they would still push. It might be better if they were farther apart, like maybe two classes could line up here and two could line up on the other side of the playground.*

Teacher: *So you're really saying you like the idea of having classes line up in designated places.* [Student agrees.]

Student: *I don't like the ones that say line up because we're supposed to be doing that now and it doesn't work.*

Teacher: *Do you think it would help if you lined up in designated areas and used more doors?* [The student agrees.]

Student: *Why don't we vote?*

Teacher: *I don't want to vote because then there are winners and losers. But let's see if there are some we can eliminate. Let's sift out the ones that we think won't work. For example, I'm telling you that the one about having the teachers pick up the classes won't work because the teachers won't want to give up lunch. Let's look at the suggestions that have no marks next to them and the ones that have minus signs next to them.* [She points to each one and asks, "Do you think this would work?" For each, the class says "no," and she erases.] *Okay, let's see what's left.* [There are only three left: use more doors; have classes assigned to different doors; have an aide assigned to each door.] *Does anyone have any objection to these three?* [One girl has reservations about one of the three and explains why.] *Do you think you could live with it?* [Girl indicates that she is willing to go along with the class.] *Well, I think these three make a good package that we can present to Mr. Fehn. Let's talk tomorrow about how we want to present these ideas.*

The Define, Personalize, and Challenge Procedure

Class meetings, like other group participation formats, require judicious planning to achieve the desired results. Even though class meetings are more open-ended, they should be structured while remaining open and sufficiently flexible to entertain unexpected events. One way to prepare for class meetings is to prepare questions that can steer the meeting. One specific questioning format provides a progressive procedure to advance to more thoughtful and insightful development of a topic. Below specific elements of the define, personalize and challenge procedure are described (Froyen, 1993).

Defining questions

These questions explore the meaning of an idea or issue. The emphasis is on gathering information. Using this format invites all students to contribute something without the fear of evaluation.

- Why do we have rules?
- What is an important rule?
- What does it mean to say "Those are the rules of the game." or "You have to play by the rules to get ahead in life."

Personalizing

Questions in this stage ask students to personalize what has been contributed in stage one. Students are asked to make personal connections to experience the topic as less abstract and impersonal. Here they associate feelings with the topic or issue. This stage also calls for examining the topic in light of experiences common to others. The intent is for students to begin to see that common experiences are interpreted in different ways and have different effects on individual's beliefs and behavior.

- How do rules affect your life?
- When do you want to make rules?
- How do you feel when you break a rule?
- Have you ever tried to get someone to break a rule?
- What are the "rules" at your dinner table?

Challenging

In this last stage, students are asked to do something about the problem or with the ideas that have emerged. Students are asked to exercise judgment and arrive at conclusions. The questions are designed to engage students in analysis and evaluation thought processes.

- What would happen if we didn't have rules?
- If you could make just one rule, what would it be?
- Are there times when rules should be broken?

Community Meetings

Community meetings serve the same purpose as classroom meetings, only for a larger cohesive group. The community meeting can serve as a forum for teaching students critical skills and attitudes for democratic citizenship. In this format, entire grades or the school as a whole come together to discuss issues, solve problems, and make decisions as a community.

Modeled on the traditional town meeting, community meetings give everyone the opportunity to speak. There is no single method that works best in all types of communities; each school will need to find its own best approach to community meetings. It will be important to clarify what problems and issues they are willing to allow community decisions on.

Initially, the principal or a teacher lead the meeting in order to model practices that facilitate broad-based participation, encourage and respect divergent viewpoints and achieve fair decisions. At one school, the principal helped students establish four criteria for considering decisions (Kirschenbaum, 1995).

- Is it fair?
- Is it consistent?
- Is it safe?
- Is it necessary?

A community meeting by definition includes the whole community. This means janitors, nurses, cafeteria workers, bus drivers, and anyone else who is a part of the school. Everyone has a voice, and teachers can have an influential voice at the meeting while also being conscious of their status. Participating judiciously is a fine line teachers will need to walk.

Development of Moral Judgment and Problem Solving

Most students realize the need to work collaboratively in the classroom between the ages of 7 and 11, according to Kohlberg (1975). Kohlberg's six stages of moral judgment offer a model for understanding the types of moral thinking students are capable of at various developmental stages. Teachers can play an important role in guiding their students toward functioning at higher levels of moral judgment if they consider students' moral development as well as their conceptual and affective development in their choice of potential solutions to classroom and group functioning management issues. The chart on the following page identifies stages that typify moral development.

While moral development follows a path similar to that of cognitive and psycho-social development, progression from birth through adolescence is not as certain or as rapid. Although Kohlberg (1975) originally proposed an invariable and universal sequence for developing moral judgment, more current thinking recognizes the influence of environmental and cultural factors. Many factors affect the pace and culminating level of moral judgment achieved by an individual. The age level at which a child passes through the various stages will vary with individual differences and life experiences as well as opportunity to test out and contemplate moral dilemmas.

Piaget (1965) put the onset of moral development at the age of six; Kohlberg posited three levels with typical ranges. The preconventional level is usually operating up until the age of 7 or 8, progressing to the conventional level typically between the ages of 7 and 11, and reaching the potential for the postconventional level somewhere in the early teen years, though not everyone will reach the highest level.

Kohlberg's Stages of Moral Development

Moral Stage	Moral Development	Characteristic Behavior
Preconventional Orientation		
Stage 1 – Punishment and obedience	Measures right and wrong based on physical consequences; avoids pain; fears getting caught; sees the world from personal perspective only.	Obeys those with power to avoid punishment; acts according to pleasure-pain principle; doesn't see that others have rights too.
Stage 2 – Instrumental-relativist	Satisfying personal needs and desires determines rightness of an act; aware of needs of others; begins to understand concepts of sharing and fairness.	Does things for others if it will fulfill personal needs.
Conventional Orientation		
Stage 3 – Good boy–nice girl	Bases what is right on the approval of others; begins to understand importance of intention; thinks in terms of distinct stereotypes; develops empathy and affection and appreciates such from others; clear assessment of right and wrong.	Pleases others; seeks others' approval; conforms to what dominant group defines as acceptable; applies the Golden Rule; identifies with significant others.
Stage 4 – Law and order	Underlying ethic is to act within legal guidelines to protect the group/society; laws and legal sanctions are the basis for legitimate action; laws are rigid and have to be followed to maintain society; develops sense of shared responsibility and loyalty to community.	Respects authority; does one's duty; acts to protect and guarantee rights of others; acts for common good; acts on allegiance to more than one group; can step into others' shoes and see how their own actions affect others.
Postconventional Orientation		
Stage 5 – Social contract	What is right is determined by society, such as laws made in a democracy; moral dilemmas necessitate an ability to reason abstractly and to consider arguments and consequences in relation to democratic principles.	Acts in accordance with standards, requirements and rights of the individual; considers various positions; considers situational context.
Stage 6 – Universal ethical principle	Decides what is right by making conscious choices based on a set of self-chosen ethical principles; ethical principles must be logically consistent and broadly applicable; principles are not dependent on written formulas.	Acts according to principles of justice, reciprocity, and equality of human rights.

According to George (1980), the development of a child's moral code reflects progressive changes in judgment and vantage point from which the child looks at moral predicaments. The sequence is noted below.

Moral Judgment	Decision-making Criteria
Ethical absolutism (self-interest)	Moves from succumbing to outside authority in Stage 1 to personal gratification in Stage 2.
Ethical relativism (others' acceptance)	Moves from approval from significant others in Stage 3 to maintaining group solidarity in Stage 4.
Ethical reciprocity (personal values)	Moves from democratically agreed-upon rights in Stage 5 to equality of all in Stage 6.

Teachers can make use of Kohlberg's moral development sequence to both design disciplinary measures and develop problem-solving strategies in alignment with students' logical abilities. Teachers can use their influence to maximize the development of moral judgment. Throughout the lower primary grades, students begin to understand the concept of fairness and to appreciate the natural consequences that follow from sharing and cooperating. Relative to classroom management, this means that teachers need to explain why certain rules and procedures are necessary to assure fair treatment of all students, and to give their rationale in ways the students can see and appreciate.

During the primary elementary grades, most students internalize the need to work collaboratively toward common goals in the classroom setting. They also come to understand relationships and how their behavior affects others. At the same time they see that some rules are necessary for order and smooth functioning of the group, they simultaneously recognize that other rules are arbitrary and don't serve a meaningful purpose. They are less willing to do things just because the teacher says so and may question why they are expected to behave in certain ways. They reason that chewing gum or wearing a hat doesn't infringe on anyone's rights, and therefore shouldn't be prohibited. Because they can distinguish between necessary and arbitrary rules, see others' points of view, and empathize with the feelings of others, teachers are able to expand moral consciousness at this level by involving students in setting class rules and consequences.

As all teachers know, not all students within this age range have reached this level of moral functioning for a multitude of reasons, which might include poor modeling, not having the benefit of an explanation for behavior expectations from primary caretakers (i.e., they learn to obey but not reason), failure to identify with their class, or immaturity. Teachers can help counteract lack of opportunity to learn by modeling, explaining the reasons behind expected behavior, using role playing to help students see the effects of their behavior on others, engaging students in cooperative learning experiences, and finding ways to foster group identification (Grossman, 1995).

At the primary level, children learn by example, so teachers will need to show them how to act in concrete ways. Children learn situation-specific rules before they are able to grasp universal principles of justice. When students consistently see the teacher listening respectfully to everyone's point of view, they are more likely to adopt this practice than if they are constantly reminded to listen.

Teachers can also help students develop moral reasoning by asking them to think about the implications of their actions for the group by responding to "What would happen if . . . ?" questions such as:

"What would happen if everyone called out whenever they wanted."

"What would happen if no one picked up after themselves and put things back where others could find them."

To learn the principle of reciprocity in relationships, teachers can explain to students the kinds of reactions their behavior evokes in others, ask students to consider how they would feel, what they would think, and how they would react if someone behaved the same way toward them. For example, the teacher might ask "If you had been waiting for a long time and someone cut in line ahead of you, how would you react (feel)?"

Students functioning at the conventional level behave responsibly because they're involved with people who matter to them. As long as class and teacher relationships are positive and rewarding, students act according to class norms. However, if the relationship between teacher and student or between student and other students deteriorates, a student may revert to thinking he/she has only him/herself, then it's logical to act in self-interest only. If the communication channels break down, the teacher loses the opportunity to impact the life of the student. As a reaction to the student's self-serving behavior, the teacher may revert to using power over the student causing a conflict between the developmental level of the student for more mature treatment and the use of teacher control through punishment.

At higher stages, students have moved from being concerned about what the teacher might do to them, or what other students might think of them, to basing their decisions on their own values. They behave appropriately because it's the right thing to do and they can feel good about themselves. Using higher-order principles of justice involves cognitive, affective, and behavioral components, and hence most educators believe that all three areas need to be incorporated for bringing about change. Typically, the recommendation at this level is to present moral dilemmas for students to solve and to engage students in values clarification exercises. However, such cognitive approaches alone will likely be insufficient; what is needed to enhance moral judgment is to motivate students to want to behave for the good of all. One approach is for you as the teacher to tell students how and why you live by the principles you do or, if such self-disclosure seems inappropriate, to use other public figures as examples. Another approach in the affective arena is to give students the chance to help others so they can learn from experience how helping can make them feel good about themselves.

Teachers can influence the moral judgment of students at this level by pointing out lack of congruence between values and actions, although some adolescents may resist and assume a defensive posture. Teachers can also engage in rational discussions about their behavior and appeal to social responsibility and orchestrate class discussions about moral issues. Teachers might also engage students in taking part in school and community projects that right injustices and inequity. After all, a democratic society is predicated on its citizens reaching this highest stage of moral justice.

Teachers can also engage students in self-reflective questioning to facilitate their thinking about decision-making criteria. Following are some appropriate questions at each of the six stages for influencing a student's moral reasoning regarding respecting others' property offered by Froyen (1993).

Stage 1: What do you think I should do when I see someone taking another student's backpack?

Stage 2: When you are tempted to help yourself to something that belongs to someone else, what can you ask yourself to reconsider that decision?

Stage 3: What can you do so that your classmates will think you are someone who respects their right to decide who can use their stuff?

Stage 4: What can you do if you see a classmate being forced to relinquish a personal possession to someone else?

Stage 5: What would life be like if people disregarded other's property rights?

Stage 6: How would your view of yourself as a responsible person be affected if you were told that you behaved in ways that others saw as inconsiderate of their property?

The reference points for determining what represents justice one applies in decision-making do not remain stable. The degree of complexity of a situation may constrain a child from applying the cognitive reasoning he/she has developed in intellectual functioning in a given moral dilemma. On the other hand, children often select a solution when presented with a moral dilemma that represents one stage higher than their current level of thinking, indicating that they are able to recognize a better solution than they might generate on their own (Froyen, 1993).

Under one set of conditions a student may use Stage 1 criteria and in another set of circumstances adopt a Stage 3 perspective. Likewise, a teacher may choose to reinforce Stage 2 conceptions of justice or challenge students to function at Stage 6 by questioning the congruence between their values and their actions. Unless, or until, students have opportunities to test ideas, it is unlikely that moral reasoning will match cognitive capacity at the upper stages of moral development. In adolescence, the student has the cognitive capacity for reflectively viewing values and society, although not many students actually reach the highest stage of moral development during their school years where they base decisions on equity of human rights.

The Cultural Assimilator

The Cultural Assimilator is an intercultural training strategy intended to help students understand the perspectives of persons from another culture and to teach them about the other's subjective culture (Albert, 1983). Teachers can devise a variety of their own ways they might use appropriate cultural assimilators in their classrooms to enhance moral judgment, cultural awareness, and acceptance of differences.

The Cultural Assimilator consists of a number of situations, episodes, or critical incidents depicting interactions between persons from two cultures, followed by alternate attributions or explanations of their behavior. Each incident presents typical interaction situations in which misunderstandings are likely to occur. The four alternate attributions presented are all plausible interpretations of the situation, three of them fitting best the assumptions of the learner's culture, the fourth being a typical attribution of the other (target) culture. Learners read the incident and the alternative attributions and select the one attribution they believe members of the other culture typically choose. After each choice, learners receive culturally relevant, misperception-correcting feedback.

The example, The Rock Concert, giving culture assimilator critical incidents, alternative attributions, and corrective feedback illustrates this approach.

Cultural Assimilator: The Rock Concert

Judy is a 15-year-old U.S. high school student spending a month in Mexico as part of an international living program. She lives with a middle-class Mexican family and has become a good friend of the 14-year-old daughter, Rosa, and through her, her circle of girlfriends. Judy finds life in Mexico interesting because of the novelty of the situation but feels a little frustrated at the restricted range of activities she is permitted to indulge in, compared with her life back home. Whenever she suggests they do something a little different or daring, the others seem very uncomfortable and refuse to discuss it.

She was thus excited to learn that a popular American rock group was to play in the city next week and suggested to Rosa and her friends that they should all go. Although they admitted they would like to go, the others looked very apprehensive and said they could never get permission to attend such an event. Judy then proposed that they should pretend to visit someone else and sneak off to the concert. The group refused even to consider the idea, and Judy concluded exasperatedly that they were a very unadventurous lot.

What is the source of the Mexican girls' reluctance to consider Judy's proposal?

1. They are much more conscious of conforming to social norms than Judy.
2. They resent Judy (a foreigner) trying to tell them what to do.
3. They do not really want to go to the rock concert and are just making excuses so as not to offend Judy.
4. They are scared of what might happen at the concert but do not wish to admit their fears.

Rationales for the alternative explanations:

1. This is the most probable explanation. In Latin cultures the socialization of children is strictly controlled (especially for girls), and they learn early the value and necessity to conform to social norms. Behavior that might be viewed in more individualistic (and less conforming) societies as simply adventurous or explorative is regarded in conformist societies with apprehension and as potentially disruptive of the close, interdependent social network. Rebelliousness or delinquency amongst the young is thus rare in such societies. The Mexican girls are thus much more conscious than Judy of the need to strictly adhere to social norms and expected behavior, and they fear dire consequences and shame if they do not. Sojourners should be aware of the social pressures to conform in such cultures and should not place hosts in situations where they are asked to go against social norms.
2. There is little indication that this is the case. They seem to accept Judy as part of their group and while they may not be willing to take up her suggestions they do not resent them. There is a more probable explanation.
3. This seems unlikely. They are probably as interested in rock music as Judy, and would probably not see the need to fabricate excuses to Judy if they were not. There is a better explanation.
4. They are not afraid so much by what might happen at the concert as the consequences of what might happen if it is found out that they did attend.

From R. W. Brislin, K. Cushner, C. Cherrie, and M. Yong. *Intercultural interactions: A practical guide.* Newbury Park, CA: Sage Publications, 1986, pp. 82, 105, 106. Reprinted by permission.

Strategies for Teaching Social Skills

Often students will need to increase their repertoire of skills in order to make more appropriate choices to regulate their own behavior. Students need to be taught strategies for dealing more effectively in trying situations which evoke such feelings as hurt, anger, disappointment, frustration, and so forth. This section offers specific strategies which teach students alternative behavior and decision-making strategies.

Social skills training is an umbrella that includes a variety of skills. Generally, it refers to teaching students coping skills for dealing with situations which pose problems for many students. Social skills training includes helping students learn to manage their own impulses, control anger, and cope with disappointment and frustration. It also helps students build positive relationships, deal with the unreasonable behavior of others, and learn problem-solving strategies.

Basically it can involve any skill or strategy that helps students manage their behavior in a way which is productive to learning and adaptive to the demands of the classroom setting. Attempts to modify behaviors, cognitions (beliefs and attitudes), and emotions are included. Specific intervention strategies can be behavioral, physiological, or cognitive. Labels such as problem-solving, self-instructional training, self-control, cognitive and metacognitive strategies, aggression replacement training, anger and stress management, coping skills, and life skills have all been used to describe types of social skills training.

Different approaches to social skills training involve variations in levels and intensity of training. Alternatives available range from traditional lessons, which create an awareness and/or offer specific strategies, to structured learning which involves teaching a series of steps or subskills to mastery, to longterm processes, which involve modifying basic beliefs and inner language (cognitive/metacognitive strategies).

Teaching social skills is not different from teaching other skills in that effective instruction involves using direct instruction including explaining, demonstrating, and providing opportunities for performance feedback. Modeling is especially important in teaching social skills as is engaging in role playing. As with other complex skills, teaching social skills may involve braking down the desired skill into components which may need to be taught separately.

Strategies for Social Skill Enhancement

Specific skill instruction and structured learning experiences can enable students to learn social and coping skills that will help them develop positive peer relationships, work cooperatively in learning groups and participate productively in classroom activities. Because many of today's students are deficient in desired social and self-management skills, there is need to teach these skills, not only in special settings such as special education classes or counseling sessions, but as part of the mainstream curriculum.

Many strategies advocated for effectively teaching social skills are the same as those for teaching academic skills, such as direct instruction, specific learning strategies, cooperative learning groups, and skill sequencing. Strategies emphasize teacher modeling of self-questioning (e.g., "If I do this what is the worst that can happen?"), and providing examples from the teacher's own life experiences. Students are prompted to "think ahead." Specifically, students might be prompted to:

- Think of a number of different alternatives to solve particular problems.
- Determine what is likely to happen when a particular strategy is chosen.
- Compare results of similar strategies.
- Contrast results of different strategies.

- Compare a strategy that is likely to produce a positive consequence with one that will likely produce a negative consequence.
- Analyze best and worst that could happen.
- List pros and cons of alternative choices.

Goldstein and his colleagues (1983) advocate structured learning as a method for teaching social skills. Characterized by regular and systematic direct instruction, structured learning incorporates four methodological elements: modeling, role playing, performance feedback, and transfer of training. Structured learning is best conducted in groups of five to eight students. The approach has been adapted for use in the general classroom setting as well as the special class and is generally recommended for students in the upper elementary grades through senior high. In structured learning a single skill is taught following a sequential order of presentation involving moving from a modeling phase to a transfer phase.

Modeling

The teacher exposes the group to examples of the skill by presenting several different examples of the skill being used in different settings with different people. The teacher breaks down the skill into specific behavioral steps which are demonstrated in the modeling displays followed by group discussion. The focus of the discussion is on the personal impact of the modeling on each member of the group.

Role Plays

Role plays are developed from the examples generated by students in the discussion. Each student is given an opportunity to role play (or practice) the skill following the behavioral steps which comprise the skill. The teacher's role is to provide support in the form of suggestions and coaching throughout the role play.

Performance Feedback

Following the role play, the teacher asks for performance feedback such as praise, constructive criticism, or approval from the main actor and the other group members. The goal is to provide the main actor with support, as well as suggestions on how to become more effective in using the given skill.

Transfer of Training

The final phase of structured learning is generalization of the skill beyond the classroom setting to enhance the probability that the skill will transfer into the student's real-life behavior repertoire. To facilitate transfer of learning, overlearning and real-life reinforcement are used. Overlearning occurs when the student is given the opportunity to practice the skill in different situations and over a long period of time. Real-life reinforcement occurs when teachers give students feedback and recognition whenever they see the skill being applied. They might also make suggestions on when the student can use a given strategy.

The following strategies enhance the transfer and maintenance of social skills in the structured learning approach (McGinnis & Goldstein, 1984).

1. Providing instruction in natural environments where the skill is actually needed or in a setting that is similar to those environments where the skill is to be used.
2. Teaching the skill in the context of a variety of situations and settings by multiple role plays with different persons.
3. Overlearning the skill by practicing several times in different sets of circumstances.

4. Planned withdrawal of instruction with periodic review and reteaching of the skills as needed.

5. Teaching students to use the skill when conditions indicate the skill would be useful.

6. Planning for opportunities where students can practice the skills they learned in the teaching session.

Structured learning can be integrated into the teacher's behavior management system such that when potential problems arise in the classroom, the teacher elicits a prosocial response from the student by suggesting that the steps to a particular skill be used. This provides a positive alternative to reprimanding the student for having the problem, as well as a means for teaching the student when to use a given skill. In so doing, the teacher is reminding the student what to do rather than what not to do. Such an approach turns naturally occurring problem situations into learning opportunities and provides an environment in which a positive emphasis is placed on learning how to deal with interpersonal problems.

Role reversal can be a useful technique in structured learning, especially with older students. It can be especially helpful when a student's performance anxiety creates difficulty in role playing his/her own role. The teacher or even a peer can act out the main actor role, while the main actor takes on the role of the person with whom he/she has the problem. In this case, role reversal assists the student by having another person model the behaviors the student him/herself needs for dealing with the specific problem. Role reversal may also contribute to the student's empathy or understanding of the other person's position.

Below is an example of a structured learning sequence for the skill of dealing with an other's anger.

Skills for Dealing with Feelings: Dealing with an Other's Anger

Steps	Trainer Notes
1. Listen to what the person has to say.	Discuss the importance of not interrupting or becoming defensive. If needed, the student should say to himself/ herself, "I can stay calm."
2. Think about your choices: 　a. Keep listening. 　b. Ask why he/she is angry. 　c. Give him/her an idea to fix the problem. 　d. Walk away for now.	Discuss the possible consequences of each choice. If the student begins to feel angry too, he/she should walk away until he/she calms down.
3. Act out your best choice.	If one choice doesn't work, the student should try another one.

Suggested Content for Modeling Displays:

A. School: The teacher is angry at you for not doing well on a test.

B. Home: Your parents are angry because you didn't clean your room.

C. Peer group: Another student is angry at you because you didn't choose him/her to play a game.

From A. P. Goldstein. *The prepare curriculum: Teaching prosocial competencies.* Champaign, IL: Research Press, 1988, p. 182. Reprinted by permission.

Using the Role Play Effectively

Role playing is a creative series of enactments and reenactments in which students have the opportunity to analyze a problem, explore their feelings about it, and then consider many different alternatives and the consequences of those alternatives. In role playing, students experience situations in an environment that is safer than real-life situations. Role playing can be used to enact a wide variety of school situations for the group's input and to provide opportunities for class members to give feedback and discuss their perceptions of the situation.

Role playing is especially useful in solving relationship problems among students. It is a valuable intervention for helping students stand back and look at their problems through the eyes of others. It can help students understand the situation of another who might be feeling rejected, unwanted, or unable to handle frustration in an acceptable manner.

Morgan and Reinhart (1991) describe three uses for role playing as an effective intervention strategy.

Clarifying a Problem

This intervention is used to enact an incident that needs clarification, such as a fight. It brings out not only the details of the incident but the emotions that precipitated the event as well. The incident (the fight) is acted out only up to the point of contact.

This type of role playing serves several purposes for both the teacher and the students. The teacher does not have to try to figure out who did what to whom first and does not have to serve as the judge and jury. The teacher will not have to lecture, reprimand, or pass judgment. Instead, the students observe the role play, discuss it, and then they decide. To begin the role play, the teacher insists that the students show, not tell, what happened.

It is helpful for the students because they gain insight into their own behavior. In time, they learn to recognize what starts conflicts, how they become involved, and how they often create their own problems.

When the role play is finished, the teacher recounts the details observed and turns it over to the group. The following types of questions can be asked:

"Now, what did you all notice?"

"How did that make _____ feel?"

"What about _____'s feelings?"

"What really happened here?"

"What could be done?"

Finding Solutions

This type of role play is used to demonstrate to and impress upon the students that many problems have more than one solution. It is important for the students to see how others feel in certain situations and to discover for themselves that certain behaviors do not solve some problems. In this type of role play, the event or problem is acted out more than once.

For the first enactment, the involved students make a report of what happened. Then actors are assigned (*not* the students involved), and they act out the incident exactly as it was described. A group meeting follows where the teacher asks several questions to get everybody involved in finding optional solutions to the problem. The teacher might start by saying, "Let's discuss what you liked about the way this problem was handled. Were there any mistakes made? Was there a solution? How many think they could handle this situation in a better way?"

For the second enactment, the teacher designates a new set of actors who act out the same situation, but this time they must come up with a different solution. This is followed with another group discussion asking the same questions. Also, the group is asked to compare the two solutions and determine which one was most helpful.

Getting in Touch and Developing Empathy

This type of role play is used to help students become aware of their feelings and to recognize the impact that their emotions have on their bodies and how it affects their behavior. Empathy for others does not come about until students are in touch with their own feelings first. There are a number of situations and problems that almost all students experience that can be used to help students get in touch with their own feelings and begin developing empathy for others' feelings. Following is a list of ideas that can be used.

- Someone told a lie about you.
- Someone tore up your paper.
- Someone shoved your books off the desk.
- Someone called you a name.
- Someone told you to shut up.
- You have just failed a test.
- You stole something and now you have to face up to it.

The teacher begins by inventing situations that cause emotional reactions. Then the students are asked to "freeze" their facial expressions. For younger students, a mirror can be passed around so that they can see how they are affected by their emotions. The teacher points out all of the outward signs of emotion such as frowning, twisting their eyes, and turning their mouths.

This is followed by having them "freeze" their whole bodies and describe where they feel tension. Next they should improvise a dialogue with another person and act out the situation. As in the other types of role play, the group observes and provides other alternatives to the actors' solutions.

In designing a role play experience, teachers need to prepare students to participate, engage students in warm-up activities, structure the actual role playing, and provide for adequate closure to help students integrate the experience. The following guidelines will help teachers develop role plays which are meaningful to students and promote personal reflection and growth.

Setting the Stage

It is important that the teacher convey to the students that there are many problems that are not easily solved. The teacher should emphasize that there are many solutions to most problems and that everyone has difficulty from time to time.

In setting the stage for the role play, the teacher presents the problem the students are going to act out and gives them time to think about the problem beforehand. To set the tone for the role play, students should be warmed up to the characters by teacher questioning such as:

- What is _____ like?
- How does _____ feel?
- What do you think _____ thinks about?

The teacher should be careful not to typecast a particular student who frequently engages in aggressive behavior, fighting, swearing, yelling, crying, and so forth.

Warm-up

Because role playing may be a new experience for many students, they may be uncomfortable at first. Initial warm-up activities for younger students might include asking them to pretend that they have just won a ball game and then that they have just lost. They might also be asked to act as if they were walking home on a cold day. The teacher should continue with additional exercises of this sort until the students understand the difference between being oneself and acting like someone else, between actor and audience roles, and until the students show the ability and interest to perform in front of their classmates.

The Role Play

The teacher decides when to stop the role play. If the role play gets off focus, the teacher stops the role play and asks questions such as:

- Are you really playing the character?
- What kind of person is ____?
- Are we working on the problem?
- Does this seem like something ____ would really do?

It should be noted that this is not a time to reprimand or allow other members of the group to tell one of the actors what to do. The student should be allowed to work out his/her own idea of the role.

The teacher should instruct the audience to watch how the different characters act in the situation and be prepared to make suggestions for alternate solutions.

One type of situation in which it is preferable for a teacher to play a part is when inappropriate behaviors must be enacted as part of the role-play situation. A student should not be placed in the position of exhibiting inappropriate behaviors even when the goal is to create a realistic role-play situation. Often the students enjoy the part of tormentors, and this is easily carried too far, with the main point of the role play being lost. In addition, you do not want students to act in the role-play setting in ways you do not want them to act in real-life settings. It is also beneficial to have the teacher participate in a role when it is crucial to have an adult role realistically portrayed.

Discussion/Closure

The class should evaluate how well each part was portrayed and how each could have been more effective. The teacher can structure the discussion by asking probing questions such as:

- What was the solution?
- Was the problem solved?
- How do you suppose ____ felt?
- What would you have done?
- Where could you use what you have learned today?

The teacher should try to bring about an awareness that each individual performed the part differently and encourage discussion of individual differences in student styles, background, and experiences. It is important to bring closure to the experience to help students process the role play and make personal connections.

Learning Practice Task: Designing a Role Play

Activity Directions: Working with a small group, design a role play experience to address a class/ group/individual problem area (i.e., excessive peer criticism, group exclusion, lack of consideration for others' feelings). First define the problem, then create a structured role play scenario.

Problem to be addressed:

_____
_____
_____
_____
_____
_____

Role play experience:

_____
_____
_____
_____
_____
_____
_____
_____
_____
_____
_____
_____
_____
_____
_____
_____
_____
_____
_____
_____
_____
_____
_____
_____

(Include a warm-up activity, guidelines for the role play, a selection procedure for the actors and audience, and a closure activity.)

Learning Practice Task: Developing Strategies for Teaching Social Skills

Activity Directions: Working with a small group, use the Case Study: Defiant Marvin to complete the following steps.

Case Study: Defiant Marvin

Situation: *Marvin is a middle school student with a pattern of oppositional and sometimes defiant behavior. He is academically deficient, poorly motivated, has little respect for authority, and is very skilled at provoking teachers. Marvin is in a running power struggle with his teacher, Mr. Paul. They have had many confrontational episodes. Now they are quick to engage each other in angry exchanges. Marvin often responds with either sullen noncompliance or outright defiance to Mr. Paul's commands and directions. Mr. Paul has difficulty extending himself to instruct or assist Marvin.*

Step 1: Identify Marvin's social skill deficits.

_____

_____

_____

_____

_____

_____

Step 2: Identify Marvin's skills.

_____

_____

_____

_____

_____

_____

Step 3: Select one social skill area and develop specific steps for teaching the skill.

_____

_____

_____

_____

_____

_____

Step 4: List general strategies the teacher could use to teach and reinforce the skill.

_____

_____

_____

_____

_____

_____

Teaching Cognitive Behavior Management Strategies

Recent developments for modifying student behavior focus more on internalized behaviors such as thoughts and feelings as powerful mediators for behavior. Such intervention strategies are generally referred to as cognitive or metacognitive strategies. Attempts to modify behavior are directed toward the covert behaviors of thinking and feeling as the primary vehicles for appraising and interpreting events.

Our beliefs (cognitive structures) strongly influence both the way we think about something (cognitive processes) and our self-talk (inner speech or covert self-instruction). Our thinking process which materializes in our inner speech form the basis for our behavior. This position is represented in a category of interventions labeled *cognitive behavior modification* as distinguished from conventional behavior modification which focuses on environmental changes primarily externally directed.

Cognitive behavior management intervention strategies are: self-administered, emphasize self-control, involve self-talk, and use modeling. The characteristics which distinguish cognitive behavior management from other forms of behavior management used to modify student behavior are:

1. Students themselves rather than the teacher serve as the primary change agents (if not initially, at least by the end).
2. The focus is on helping students gain self-control.
3. Verbalization is a primary component. The student talks to him/herself, first out loud, then on a covert level (silently).
4. Modeling is an essential element.

Three cognitive behavior management strategies have been used successfully for promoting positive behavior change in school settings: cognitive restructuring, self-instructional training, and stress inoculation.

Cognitive Restructuring: Changing Irrational Beliefs which Lead to Maladaptive Behavior

Cognitive restructuring simply means modifying one's beliefs. The basic theory underlying cognitive restructuring training is:

> Behavior is a manifestation of the feelings produced by what we are thinking. The way to change maladaptive behavior is to modify the irrational thinking that led to the behavior.

Cognitive restructuring is a strategy applied to modify irrational beliefs. An irrational belief is one which (1) has no factual basis or is illogical and (2) is harmful to the person holding the belief (Ellis, 1974). Examples of common irrational beliefs many children and youth hold include:

- I must be stupid if I make mistakes.
- Everything must go my way all the time.
- I never have any control over what happens to me.
- I must be good at everything I do.
- If people do things I don't like, they must be bad and need to be punished.
- Everyone should treat me fairly all the time.
- I should not have to wait for what I want.
- I should not have to do anything I don't want to.

Belief systems develop through modeling and reinforcement. This is why many children use only aggressive behaviors when they are frustrated or want something—it is the only behavior they have experienced.

Because beliefs are learned, they can also be unlearned through the process of restructuring. Many of our basic beliefs we learned in childhood are actually irrational beliefs (Ellis & Harper, 1975). As a child grows, the child begins to incorporate a sublanguage which serves to attribute meaning to the events occurring in the child's life. This sublanguage eventually becomes the child's belief system which develops as does language, primarily through modeling.

The belief system of the significant person(s) in the child's life will largely determine whether the child thinks rationally or irrationally about the events in his or her life. If, for example, the child misbehaves and the parent(s) says "You know better than to do that!" the child will most likely come to believe "It's bad to make a mistake, I am bad because I make mistakes and because I'm bad I should be punished." The more rational belief is that mistakes are a normal part of learning and that making a mistake doesn't make me bad. If I didn't learn this as a child, I will probably continue to interpret my mistakes as intolerable unless I am able to dispute and change my belief. If I hold onto this belief, I am likely to set unrealistic expectations for myself and others.

Ellis (1974) takes the position that much of our behavior is influenced by the way we feel and that our feelings are a product of our beliefs. When individuals hold an irrational belief they are likely to behave inappropriately because the irrational thinking produces a negative emotional state (e.g., anger, anxiety). An event triggers a counterproductive belief, often at an unconscious level, and strong emotions surface, generally manifesting in a maladaptive behavior.

Ellis developed an intervention program called Rational Emotive Therapy based on the premise that it is not life events that cause a person distress, rather it is the way a person views the events that cause the emotional reaction (Ellis & Bernard, 1984). The main strategy in Ellis' brand of therapy is "disputing irrational beliefs." Here the student either goes through a structured process alone or with the help of the teacher. Disputing irrational beliefs has students go through the following process:

1. Describe the event eliciting a behavior,
2. Identify their thoughts and feelings,
3. Describe their response,
4. Provide support for their thoughts,
5. "Dispute" their thoughts by providing counter evidence, and finally,
6. Replace their irrational thoughts with more productive thoughts.

The process involves the following seven steps.

Step 1: Describing the event associated with the inappropriate behavior.

Step 2: Identifying the thinking triggered by the event. What does the student usually think or say to him/herself? This is difficult for students because they don't actually "speak to themselves." If students get stuck here they may need some prompting, such as providing a list for the student to choose from. Or, the teacher may provide a scenario to illustrate the irrational thinking.

Step 3: Describing the feeling the student has when he/she thinks about the belief and the event. Here the teacher may need to use role playing or guided imagery to help the student identify the feeling.

Step 4: Describing the behavior. The teacher may need to ask leading questions such as "What did you do when . . . ?"

Step 5: Providing evidence (facts) to support the student's belief.

Step 6: Giving evidence that his/her belief might not be true. The teacher needs to be prepared to cite such evidence if the student denies any evidence. If the student persists in his/her denial, the teacher might ask the student to collect evidence that his/her belief is true while the teacher collects evidence that it is false. Then the teacher sits down with the student to compare data.

Step 7: Thinking of a rational belief or thought to take the place of the irrational belief. The teacher should prompt the student to practice saying the new belief to him/herself or tape it and play it frequently. Or, the student might read the statement from a card he/she carries around. Since changing a student's thinking is a longterm process, the teacher should periodically have the student review with the teacher ahead of time what he/she plans to do if an event likely to trigger the old thinking occurs.

This strategy can be used in a group or with an individual student, either verbally or in writing, with or without the teacher's help. Roush (1984) offers an alternative approach which is more appropriate for use with younger students. He recommends that students become familiar with the following six types of irrational thinking so that they recognize them in others and in themselves.

Roush's common classes of irrational thinking.

1. Robot thinking ("It's not my fault.")
2. I Stink thinking ("It's all my fault.")
3. You Stink! thinking ("It's all your fault.")
4. Fairy Tale thinking ("That's not fair!")
5. Namby Pamby thinking ("I can't stand it!")
6. Doomsday thinking ("Woe is me!")

He uses the following five questions for challenging beliefs, and teaches the acronym "A FROG" to help students remember them.

A – Does it help keep me alive?
F – Does it make me feel better?
R – Is it based on reality?
O – Does it help me get along with others?
G – Does it help me reach my goals?

In Roush's approach to cognitive restructuring, the teacher cues students with comments like "It sounds like you're doing some 'You stink!' thinking. Are you?" If the student agrees, the teacher directs the student to consider each of the five questions. Obviously, the task of cognitive restructuring is a difficult one. Teachers can help students learn to use the following progression:

• Use a logical argument.
• If necessary, move to an empirical argument where the student looks for physical evidence of the validity or fallacy of his/her belief.
• If this fails, move to a functional argument in which the student is asked to examine whether the thinking makes him/her feel better or worse.

The following two illustrations provide examples of the three argument types for "You stink!" and "Doomsday" irrational thinking (Kaplan, 1995).

"You stink!"

Logical: *Do you do bad things* (or things others don't like) *sometimes? Are you a bad person? Should you always be punished for doing something that others don't like?" Have the student try to give you an example of doing something to someone that he/she didn't like or thought was bad (e.g., calling someone a name or taking something away from someone, or disappointing another person). The point you want to get across is that people are fallible and often do things that hurt or disappoint others; if we do such things and we don't consider ourselves bad or deserving of punishment, why should we consider others bad and deserving of punishment?*

Empirical: *Have the student collect data to support* (or disprove) *his/her argument. For example, if the student believes that all teachers are always picking on him/her, have the student collect data for a few days on positive and negative comments teachers direct at him/her; hopefully, these data will show that not all* (but some) *of the student's teachers pick on him/her some* (not all) *of the time.*

Functional: *Simply ask the student if his/her thinking makes him/her feel better or worse: "How do you feel when you think that all of your teachers always pick on you? Does that make you feel good or bad? Do you like feeling bad? Maybe if you changed your thinking you might start feeling better—would you like to feel better?"*

"Doomsday"

Logical: *"Bad things are always happening to good people; if they worried about that prospect all the time, they would never experience any joy in their lives. It doesn't pay to worry about things over which you have little control."*

Empirical: *Have the student collect data about good or positive things that happened to him/her over a one-week period.*

Functional: *The same as for "You stink!"*

Cognitive restructuring involves developing an awareness in students of those events and thoughts associated with negative feelings and resulting inappropriate behaviors. Students need to first be in touch with their feelings, then reflect on the event or action which led to the feeling, before they can identify the thinking that mediated between the event and the feeling. For some students, this awareness will need to be developed at length prior to the use of other higher-order skills.

Teachers interested in implementing cognitive restructuring strategies can combine aspects of both of the approaches described, develop their own lessons and procedures to match their students' developmental levels, and/or use the approaches suggested in the commercial materials available. A "positive thinking" worksheet is a typical mode used with these strategies. The following Angry Thinking/Positive Thinking Worksheet is an application of Ellis' disputing irrational beliefs. It simplifies the seven-step process into five steps. Think about how you may want to infuse this or similar worksheets into classroom practices.

Angry Thinking/Positive Thinking Worksheet

Directions: Write down the situation and your thoughts and feelings about the situation. Then write down a different, more positive thought and the different feeling you would have.

What happened:

_____

_____

_____

What I was thinking:

_____

_____

_____

How I felt:

_____

_____

_____

A different, more positive thought:

_____

_____

_____

_____

The new feeling:

_____

_____

_____

Self-instructional Training Strategies

Self-instructional training is based on the work of Luria (1961) and Vygotsky (1962) whose research on socialization and language development suggests that young children go through three stages where others' speech initially controls their behavior, then their own overt speech, and eventually their own inner speech governs their behavior. The basic theory that underlies self-instructional training is:

> Language and socialization skill development is based on children moving from a self-talk stage to an inner-speech stage. Self-instructional training involves recreating this progression.

Meichenbaum (1977) developed a practical program based on this theory to self-instruct impulsive children to control their behavior. His strategy has the following five steps.

1. Cognitive modeling in which the teacher performs the task while talking to him/herself out loud.
2. Overt external guidance in which the student performs the task under the teacher's guidance.
3. Overt self-guidance where the student performs the task while instructing him/herself aloud.
4. Faded overt self-guidance where the student whispers the instructions while performing the task.
5. Covert self-instruction where the student performs the task while using inner speech.

The following example illustrates Meichenbaum's self-instructional strategy for self-control (Kaplan, 1995).

Self-instructional Strategy for Self-control Example

Step 1: Teacher models and talks out loud while student watches and listens.

    a. Teacher imitates student doing work and starting to get upset. Teacher says out loud, "My muscles are getting tense and my face feels hot. I must be starting to get upset. What am I supposed to do when I get upset about my work?"

    b. Teacher says out loud, "First, I'm supposed to take a few deep breaths."

    c. Teacher models diaphragmatic breathing.

    d. Teacher says out loud, "That feels better. What should I do next?"

    e. Teacher says out loud, "I'll raise my hand and ask for help."

    f. Teacher models hand-raising and waiting-for-attention behavior.

    g. Teacher says out loud, "Good! I controlled my behavior. I can do it!"

Step 2: Student performs tasks while teacher gives instructions out loud.

    a. Student role plays self doing work and starting to get upset. Teacher says out loud, "My muscles are getting tense and my face feels hot. I must be starting to get upset. What am I supposed to do when I start to get upset about my work?"

    b. Teacher says out loud, "First, I'm supposed to take a few deep breaths."

    c. Student does diaphragmatic breathing.

    d. Teacher says out loud, "That feels better. What should I do next?"

    e. Teacher says out loud, "I'll raise my hand and ask for help."

    f. Student models hand-raising and waiting-for-attention behavior.

    g. Teacher says, "Good! I controlled my behavior. I can do it!"

    (Steps a through e are repeated within each step.)

Step 3: Student performs tasks while repeating steps out loud.

Step 4: Student performs tasks while whispering steps.

Step 5: Student performs tasks while thinking them.

The *Think Aloud* (Camp & Bash, 1981) materials available commercially are based on Meichenbaum's work. Self-instructional strategies can be used to help students work on a variety of academic behaviors (e.g., paying attention, writing a report), social behaviors (e.g., reducing aggressive behavior, building tolerance for frustration), and self-control (e.g., dealing with anger, provocation). The idea is that the student would eventually be able to talk him/herself through the situation by going through the steps without teacher assistance. Sometimes cue cards are used to act as a reminder. Other helpful strategies include using peer modeling, cueing and prompting, rehearsing meaningful self-talk translated by the student into his/her own words, and encouraging and reinforcing use outside of the classroom.

Below are some descriptions and examples of specific strategies. Examples of self-statements for dealing with anger and stress are included to help you get started using self-talk to manage your own behavior and to present as illustrations for your students.

Self-statements for Dealing with Anger and Stress

Preparing for an Anger-provoking Situation

- *I won't let this get me down.*
- *I'm ready. I know how to deal with this.*
- *I can follow my plan.*
- *I know what to do.*
- *I can do this.*
- *I know it's all up to me.*
- *I can handle my anger.*
- *I will not argue.*
- *I can control my thoughts.*
- *It won't be easy, but I'm confident.*
- *Don't take yourself too seriously.*

Reacting During the Encounter

- *Nothing can discourage me.*
- *Stay cool.*
- *No one else can control me.*
- *I don't have to prove myself.*
- *I'm not going to let this get to me.*

Accentuate the Positive.

- *Keep things in perspective.*
- *Don't blow this out of proportion.*
- *It's not that important.*
- *I've got a handle on this situation and I can control it.*
- *Keep smiling. Hang in there.*
- *Keep a sense of humor.*

Coping with Anger Symptoms

- *I'm determined to handle this.*
- *I can feel my muscles starting to get tight.*
- *It won't get me anywhere to get angry.*
- *Getting upset won't do any good.*
- *I'm going to hold my ground, but I'm not going to get crazy.*
- *Be respectful—don't accuse.*
- *Be constructive, not destructive.*
- *Remember, I'm in control.*
- *I'm upset, but I'm handling myself pretty well.*
- *Take it easy, don't counter-attack.*
- *I can't expect others to act the way I would.*
- *Try to relax. Take a few deep breaths.*

Reflecting on the Encounter

Unresolved Conflict

- *I did not argue—that's progress.*
- *Don't take it to heart.*
- *Forget about it.*
- *This will take time to work out.*
- *Remember to relax.*
- *I'm not going to worry about it.*
- *I won't take it personally.*
- *I'll think positive thoughts.*
- *It's not that serious.*
- *I'm not going to let this get me down.*

Resolved Conflict, Successful Coping

- *I did it!*
- *I'm proud of myself.*
- *I really handled that well.*
- *It wasn't as bad as I thought.*
- *I kept myself from getting angry.*
- *I can control myself.*
- *I'm getting better at this all the time.*

The "Sample Cue Card: Keeping Out of Fights" is an example of a self-control strategy tailored to a particular student. It includes a self-evaluation format, so the student can evaluate his/her own performance. If these cards are completed on a regular basis, they can also provide evaluative data for the teacher to use to determine if modification is warranted.

Sample Cue Card: Keeping Out of Fights

1. Stop and count to 10.
2. Think about why you want to fight.
3. Decide what you want to happen.
4. Think about other choices beside fighting.
   a. Walk away from the situation.
   b. Talk to the person in a calm, non-hostile way.
   c. Apologize.
   d. Ask someone for help solving the problem.
5. Do what you think is your best choice.

How did you do? Great _____ OK _____ Not so good _____.

"Skill Alternatives to Aggression: Using Self-control" is an example of a structured sequential program which is more general. It incorporates stress inoculation by paying attention to body signals and connects the event with the feeling, a cognitive restructuring strategy.

Skill Alternatives to Aggression: Using Self-control

Steps	Trainer Notes
1. Tune in to what is going on in your body that helps you know that you are about to lose control of yourself.	Are you getting tense, angry, hot, fidgety?
2. Decide what happened to make you feel this way.	Consider outside events or "internal" events (thoughts).
3. Think about ways in which you might control yourself.	Slow down; count to 10; assert yourself; leave; do something else.
4. Choose the best way to control yourself and do it.	

Suggested Content for Modeling Displays

A. School or neighborhood: Main actor controls yelling at teacher when teacher criticizes harshly.

B. Home: Main actor controls self when parent forbids desired activity.

C. Peer group: Main actor controls self when friend takes something without asking permission.

Comments

It is often helpful to discuss various ways of controlling oneself before role playing the skill. The list of self-control techniques can be written on the board and used to generate alternative tactics youngsters can use in a variety of situations.

From A. P. Goldstein. *The prepare curriculum: Teaching prosocial competencies.* Champaign, IL: Research Press, 1988, p. 118. Reprinted by permission.

The addresses for several of the major publishers of materials that teach social and self-management skills are provided below.

Aspen Publishing, Inc.
1600 Research Blvd.
Rockville, MD 20850

Institute for Rational Emotive Therapy
(formerly Institute for Rational Living)
45 E. 65th St.
New York, NY 10021-6593

PRO-ED, Inc.
8700 Shoal Creek Blvd.
Austin, TX 78758

Research Press
2612 Mattis Ave.
Champaign, IL 61820

Timberline Press
Box 70071
Eugene, OR 97401

Learning Practice Task: Developing an Individualized Cue Card

Activity Directions: Working with a small group, follow the steps below to develop a cue card for a specific student's problem behavior.

Step 1: Decide on a problem behavior.

Step 2: Review the following strategies before beginning to plan your cue card.

- ☐ Cognitive restructuring
- ☐ Identifying irrational thinking
- ☐ Challenging beliefs
- ☐ Disputing irrational beliefs
- ☐ Stress inoculation
- ☐ Physiological stress management
- ☐ Self-instructional training
- ☐ Self-control/self-talk
- ☐ Assertion statements
- ☐ Stress scripts
- ☐ Defusing/reflecting
- ☐ Generating alternatives

Step 3: Decide which of the above concepts you want to include.

Step 4: Develop your cue card.

Step 5: Incorporate an evaluation component.

Chapter 10

Teacher and Student Conflict Management Strategies

In conflict situations, students often use strategies that have negative consequences and are either aggressive or passive. Students frequently resort to verbal or physical abuse, retreat from the situation, or tattle or attempt to enlist others to solve problems for them.

Most students need help in building a repertoire of effective strategies for managing conflict. In order to learn new strategies, students will need to experience the results of using positive approaches and discover workable strategies through structured learning experiences which give them opportunities to practice more effective strategies for solving conflicts.

Conflict Management Strategies

The following section describes some strategies that students can be taught to use. They will also need to be taught decision rules for determining when a procedure is likely to result in a positive outcome. Though each is listed separately, they will often be used in combination. Some strategies involve individual decisions and self-control while some require the cooperation of others. Some strategies are for immediate problem resolution while some offer defusing or delaying tactics.

Strategies 1 to 5 require cooperation from all of the parties involved. Strategies 6 to 11 are strategies which provide immediate defusing of the situation in which conflict resolution is delayed for the time being. Strategies 12 to 15 involve structured language and implementation of effective communication techniques. Strategies 16 and 17 are assertion strategies and involve making direct statements expressing the person's position. Strategies 18 and 19 are self-control strategies and involve impulse control. Strategy 20 involves seeking assistance.

20 Conflict Management Strategies

Strategy 1: Negotiating

In negotiating, students express their individual positions in the conflict and try to decide what can be done. Negotiating can be a simple discussion or a more structured step-by-step approach. The idea is to break down the points of the conflict and examine each aspect. In negotiation a period of discussion occurs for the purpose of bringing about a resolution that is mutually agreed to. Other, less involved strategies which immediately diffuse the situation may need to be taught first to pave the way for the process of negotiation.

Strategy 2: Compromising

Compromise not only requires mutual cooperation but also a period of negotiation to establish that compromise will be used to resolve the problem. In a compromise, everyone agrees to give up a little. It allows both students to save face while each gets some of what he/she originally wanted. The concept of giving up something to get something back is often a difficult concept for children to grasp.

Strategy 3: Sharing

In sharing, individuals decide to share for mutual benefit. Inherent in the sharing process are the notions of reciprocity and equality. These are both difficult concepts for children to understand because their world is the here and now.

Strategy 4: Taking Turns

Taking turns is one of the simplest strategies. The key to teaching turn-taking is getting students to recognize that whoever goes second needs some kind of face-saving for giving up the first turn. Although a student could act alone by relinquishing his/her turn, the strategy is more effectively used when students decide who will have the first and second turn.

Strategy 5: Chance

Using chance generally moves the conflict toward resolution and offers face-saving for everyone. In using chance, those involved need to agree to use it and to the consequences of the outcome. Any method that leaves the resolution to chance such as flipping a coin, drawing straws, or picking a number can be used.

Strategy 6: Distracting

This strategy offers a way to defuse a potentially volatile situation by diverting attention. It allows a cooling off period and can also be a face-saving tactic. When used appropriately it is not a cop-out but a temporary move that leaves the door open for conflict resolution at a later time.

Strategy 7: Postponing

Postponing conflict resolution to a more appropriate time often allows the problem to be handled more successfully. Postponement strategies are useful when one or both persons are not up to handling the conflict situation at the time.

Strategy 8: Exaggerating

In this strategy, the involved parties engage in an exaggerated interpretation of the issue. Exaggeration often helps students put their issues in perspective.

Strategy 9: Humor

Humor is used to diffuse the angry feelings associated with conflict. Quick wit, the "saving remark," laughing at oneself, or poking fun at one's own expense take the pressure off a situation. If the other person can begin to look at things from a different perspective, he or she can be more objective. There is risk involved in using this strategy because students sometimes misinterpret humor as making fun of them, hence humor works best when it is self-directed. It can "seize the moment" by helping students recognize the awkwardness of the moment. It can also serve to mask real feelings, make someone a scapegoat, or cause hurt and should be used with these cautions in mind.

Strategy 10: Abandoning

This strategy involves moving away from a situation and is appropriate when the person cannot handle the situation. When the student comes to the realization that nothing but harm is likely to result or he/she needs to exercise self-control, this strategy is appropriate.

Strategy 11: Apologizing

Apologizing can mean admitting responsibility when the student recognizes his/her behavior was wrong. It can also be a simple way of saying you are sorry that the other person feels hurt without accepting responsibility for why the person feels hurt. Such recognition of the other person's feelings can often serve as a tension defuser.

Strategy 12: Blame-free Explanation

Expressing anger by attacking or blaming others elicits angry retaliation. Expressing your position or feelings in a way that does not blame the other person will elicit a more positive reaction.

Strategy 13: Sending an I-message

In this strategy you refrain from blaming the other person or evaluating the person's behavior and simply state the concrete effect of the behavior and your feelings about the behavior.

Strategy 14: Making an Impact-statement

Here you state the effect of the behavior and why it is causing a problem for you. This is similar to the previous two strategies, however here you limit your comments to the consequences of the behavior.

Strategy 15: Active Listening

This is the most difficult of the structured language strategies and is a strategy that necessitates highly developed skill. Active listening involves listening to what the other person is saying, trying to grasp the feelings the other person is having, and sending back a message that communicates to the person that you understand what they are feeling. The process involves learning to listen not only to what the person is saying in words but also what message is being communicated by other signals such as voice intonation or nonverbal signs. Conflicts are often the result of not listening or misinterpreting what is being said. Even young children can be taught to listen by using such phrases as "Go ahead, I'm listening to you," "You talk first, then it will be my turn," and "You said . . ., is that what you meant?"

Strategy 16: Stating Your Intention

This strategy is an assertion strategy and involves stating exactly what you intend to do either right now or the next time the behavior occurs.

Strategy 17: Making a Request

This is another assertion strategy and involves making a direct request for the other person to change his/her behavior. It could also be a request for the other person to take a specific action.

Strategy 18: Passive Listening

This strategy is an impulse-control strategy in which the person remains silent for a time. It may involve a self-instructional strategy such as counting to 10 to keep from interrupting the other person, arguing, or becoming defensive.

Strategy 19: Self-talk

This strategy is a self-control strategy which involves positive self-talk in an attempt to reduce stress and keep oneself under control by engaging in rehearsed self-dialogue.

Strategy 20: Seeking Assistance

This strategy should be reserved for situations that cannot be handled without outside help. It should be used when additional information or knowledge is necessary or the situation is too complex, involved, or volatile.

Third-party Facilitation: Arbitration and Mediation

There are two processes for third-party dispute resolution. One involves relinquishing responsibility for the resolution process, the other is a participatory process. In arbitration, a dispute is turned over to an impartial third party who considers all the positions, needs and wants of the parties involved and makes a final and binding judgment as to how the conflict will be resolved. In agreeing to use the arbitration process, the involved parties have decided to abide by the decision of the "arbitrator" rather than resolve the conflict themselves.

In mediation, a neutral third party facilitates the process by actively assisting the involved parties to work out a resolution that both or all parties can agree to. In this process, the mediator typically acts as the "gate keeper" to monitor the use of effective communication skills. Effective mediation involves listening, paraphrasing, clarifying, and assertion skills.

Many schools are now using peer mediation as a way to resolve conflicts. In most programs, select students receive training in the communication skills involved and disputing students agree to the mediation process. An example of a teacher mediation and a peer mediation process are described in the next section.

Teacher Mediation

Teachers spend a lot of their energy handling hassles students have with one another. They often get "sucked into" their students' battles. Teachers often act as arbitrators and offer solutions or attempt to determine who is at fault. As soon as the teacher becomes involved, he or she has taken on the ownership of the problem which really belongs to the students.

Teacher mediation is a process that keeps teachers out of student battles and helps students take responsibility for working out their problems. In teacher mediation, the role of the teacher is to use active listening to feed back the message and feelings of each of the students so that each feels that his/her position has been heard. This process lets the students take responsibility for working out the problem.

Teacher Mediation Process

In teacher mediation, the teacher:
- Has students talk directly to one another, not through the teacher.
- Uses door openers (e.g., "What seems to be the problem?") rather than probing questions (e.g., "Why did you do that?").
- Uses active listening to help students clarify feelings and uncover their needs.
- Does not buy into their problem.
- Stays nonjudgmental rather than attributes blame.
- Refuses to sanction either student's position.
- Does not become the enforcer.
- Refrains from "rescuing" the students, rather allows them to come up with their own solution.

Peer Mediation

Below is an example of a peer mediation process taught to students (Sunburst Communications, 1996). In this program students receive training in active listening skills as part of learning to be a mediator.

The Mediation Process

Step 1: Introductions and Ground Rules
- Make introductions.
- Explain mediation.
  - a. Mediators don't take sides, blame, or judge.
  - b. Mediators assure confidentiality, except for weapons, drugs, and abuse.
  - c. Mediators help disputants reach their own agreement.
- Ask disputants to agree to the ground rules.
  - a. To work to try to solve the problem.
  - b. To listen without interrupting.
  - c. To treat each other with respect.

Step 2: Getting the Story
- As each disputant tells his/her story, use "active" listening.
  - a. Concentrate on the words, feelings, and body language.
  - b. Ask questions.
  - c. Paraphrase what you heard.
- Try to identify each disputant's needs.
- Clearly state the problem.

Step 3: Brainstorming for Solutions
- Ask disputants:
  - a. What each is willing to do to resolve the problem.
  - b. To say any idea that comes to mind.
  - c. To come up with as many ideas as possible.
- Ask questions to encourage ideas.
- Do not criticize or judge ideas.
- Keep track of all ideas.

Step 4: Choosing Solutions
- Ask disputants to select the solutions that best meet the needs of both parties.
- Ask disputants if they agree to accept the solution.

Step 5: Closing the Session
- Summarize the agreement.
- Write the agreement.
- Ask disputants to sign the agreement. Then sign it yourself.
- Congratulate everyone for a successful mediation and shake hands.

Adapted from: *Student workshop: Mediation skills.* Pleasantville, NY: Sunburst Communications, 1996.

Learning Practice Task: Practicing Teacher Mediation

Activity Directions: This activity provides an opportunity to practice mediation, using participant-generated student problems. Follow the sequence of steps listed.

Step 1: Divide into groups of four for this activity. As a group, decide on a student-student problem situation to work on.

Step 2: Use role playing to portray the situation, with each person taking a turn in the role of mediator, student, and observer. Before beginning the role play, review the Teacher Mediator Feedback Checklist and clarify any behaviors you may have questions about. During the role play, when you are playing the mediator you will be trying to engage in the behaviors listed. The observer will be completing the checklist in order to give you specific feedback. Decide who will play the mediator first and begin your first round of role playing.

Step 3: Get feedback on your performance as mediator. The focus of the feedback should be the items on the checklist. Discuss any discrepancies between your perceptions of your behavior and the observer's feedback. Also discuss any problems you experienced while trying to be a mediator.

Continue role playing until each person has had a chance to play each role.

Teacher Mediator Feedback Checklist

	Presence of Behavior		
Behavior	**Yes**	**Some-what**	**No**
Teacher refrains from sanctioning either student's position	____	____	____
Teacher refrains from using probing questions	____	____	____
Teacher keeps students talking directly to one another	____	____	____
Teacher is nonjudgmental	____	____	____
Teacher uses opening questions to invite students to discuss the issues	____	____	____
Teacher uses active listening:			
Reflection (empathic listening)	____	____	____
Paraphrasing (restating)	____	____	____
Perception checking (paraphrasing/requesting feedback)	____	____	____
Clarifying (restating/clarifying confusions)	____	____	____
Teacher facilitates students coming up with their own potential solutions	____	____	____

Negotiation

Negotiation is an alternative to arbitration and mediation. In negotiation, there is no third party; the involved parties try to come to a mutually-acceptable resolution to the conflict. The process is based on the premise that the parties want to be fair and equitable and consider the needs and wishes of everyone involved.

Conflicts are usually emotional affairs and those involved often react defensively by acting aggressively and counter attacking when they perceive an attack. In order to negotiate a resolution, the cooperation of both individuals is required. You can't negotiate with someone whose agenda is to win by defeating you.

Win-win Negotiation

Negotiations in which no one loses are referred to as win-win negotiations. When two individuals work through their differences and end up with a solution that meets the needs of both, resentment is minimized and the relationship is usually strengthened. Negotiation is a method of resolving conflicts in which the persons involved discuss specific alternatives in order to arrive at a mutually-acceptable agreement. Successful negotiating can bring about solutions that improve the situation for both parties.

Basically, win-win negotiation is a cooperative process where two or more individuals work through their differences and come up with a resolution that meets the needs of everyone involved. Many students simply can't perceive any alternatives other than aggressive behavior in a conflict situation. Teaching students a problem-solving process can help students think of their own solutions to effectively solve their problems.

The win-win negotiation process can be used to resolve an individual teacher/student conflict or a teacher/class conflict, or it can be used as a decision-making process to ensure that the needs of all involved parties are met. It can also be taught to students as a strategy for student-managed problem resolution.

The win-win negotiation technique is a highly structured six-step process for resolving conflicts in which all involved parties participate in the generation of possible solutions. The process can be used in an obvious conflict situation or in a situation in which one person owns the problem and is proactive in confronting the other person. The process is initially presented as a step-by-step approach to be implemented in the sequence presented until the approach becomes familiar; then individuals can fit the approach to their own natural style.

Steps in win-win negotiation

1. Make a date acceptable to both parties.
2. Describe the problem and your needs.
3. Solicit the other person's perspective and needs.
4. Generate alternative solutions that meet both sets of needs.
5. Evaluate the solutions and select one both parties can support.
6. Follow up the solution to make sure it is working.

In negotiation, both persons commit to the process and cooperate in mutual problem-solving to end up with a solution that satisfies the needs of each. Individuals avoid trying to win at the other's expense and seek a solution that takes into consideration each person's wants and needs. The win-win approach to negotiation doesn't call for compromises in which individuals give up something they really want or need.

The process calls for both parties to agree to a time to discuss the problem, commit to the negotiation process, try to resolve the problem by considering the other person's needs as well as his/her own, and arrive at a solution that meets both sets of needs.

Win-win six-step plan application

Teachers may want to introduce the six-step process on specific problems such as where to go on a field trip or how to study the next science unit. As they become more comfortable with the process, they can include more student participation in more complex class problems. All issues are eligible for win-win problem-solving that are within the teacher's area of freedom—what to study, how to study, how to evaluate classroom tasks and give teacher feedback, as well as matters of classroom behavior.

The Rule-setting Class Meeting is a special use of the win-win problem-solving process that involves the class and teacher working together in setting the rules needed by the class (Burch & Miller, 1979).

Win-win Six-step Problem-solving Process – Setting Class Rules Lesson Plan

Step 0: Setting the Stage

1. Tell the class the purpose of the meeting.

   "The purpose of this meeting is for us to develop mutually agreed-upon rules for how we will work and be together in here."

2. Describe Methods I, II & III.

   "One way for us to set rules is for me to tell you what they will be and punish you if you violate them. In this way I might get my needs met and feel like a winner, but you would probably feel like you lost. (Method I)

   "Another way would be for me to say nothing when your behavior became a problem to me. You might feel like a winner, but I sure wouldn't. (Method II)

   "A third way would be for us to search together for rules that we mutually agree we need. That way we could all win (Method III)."

3. Ask the students if they would be willing to try Method III.

   Allow for discussion and answer their questions. After obtaining consensus to try Method III, write the six steps (below) on the blackboard or, if appropriate, hand out copies. Say that you would like to begin with Step 1, defining needs.

   Explain the concept of area of freedom and give examples of issues that lie outside the freedom of the group (i.e., smoking in class) and those within (i.e., how to study the unit on the American Revolution).

Step 1: Defining Needs or Problems

1. Hand out worksheets with the heading, "What Makes an Effective Class?"
2. At the blackboard, write the word "Effective" and the definition, "to have a positive influence on others."
3. Instruct them individually to think of and list for 3 minutes what they have personally found to be the ingredients of a good class—characteristics that made the class effective for them.

   (Note. Use language appropriate to the age of the students. Also, it is very important that student discussions not evolve into negative evaluations of you or your colleagues. If this should begin, send a clear "I" message, such as "I'm not comfortable with that. I want to talk about rules and policies, not personalities.")
4. Next, ask the students to pair off and share their lists with each other. Allow 3–5 minutes for this discussion.

5. Ask the students to tell you their characteristics and record them on the board or chart pad. Use active listening to clarify; avoid listing the same characteristics more than once. Make certain your needs as a teacher are appropriately included.

Step 2: Generating Possible Solutions

1. Tell the class you now want to do Step 2 of the process. Ask them to turn to the back side of their worksheet and write the heading: "Rules I Want."
2. Tell the students to take a few moments to individually list rules that they think could best achieve the characteristics of an effective class.
3. Next, have them pair and discuss their rules with a partner for a few minutes.
4. Ask the class to tell you the rules they would like. List them on the board.

Step 3: Evaluating the Solutions

1. Ask the class to look at the list of effective characteristics and the list of suggested rules. "Which rules (solutions) do you think would have the best chance of meeting these characteristics (needs)?"

Step 4: Decision Making

1. Work with the students to facilitate consensus about the final classroom rules.
2. Point out that if anyone discovers that a solution hasn't worked well, it could be changed at a later meeting.

Step 5: Implementing the Decision

1. Obtain clarity about who will do what, and when, for each of the rules.
2. Write the agreed upon rules on the Rules Poster and post it in the room.
3. Ask each student to sign her/his name on the Rules Poster indicating agreement about those rules. Actively listen to resistance. Encourage but don't coerce them to sign.

Step 6: Following-up on the Success of the Solution

1. Decide on a future time to have a class meeting for the purpose of evaluating how well the Rules for Class are working.
2. Make the time appropriate (i.e., two weeks after initiating the rules) or when it is obvious one or more rules are not working.
3. Tell students that this follow-up re-evaluation meeting will handle the question of "What do we do if someone breaks the rules?"

Below is an example of the sequential steps for teaching the skill of negotiating. It offers an alternative to the more complex win-win negotiation process, but is similar in its orientation to consider the needs of each party in the compromise solution. This is part of a structured social skills curriculum and is meant to be taught to individuals and small groups of students with specific skill deficits.

Skill Alternatives to Aggression: Negotiating

Steps	Trainer Notes
1. Decide if you and the other person are having a difference of opinion.	Are you getting tense or arguing?
2. Tell the other person what you think about the problem.	State your own position and your perception of the other's position.
3. Ask the other person what he/she thinks about the problem.	
4. Listen openly to his/her answer.	
5. Think about why the other person might feel this way.	
6. Suggest a compromise.	Be sure the proposed compromise takes into account the opinions and feelings of both persons.

Suggested Content for Modeling Displays

A. **School or neighborhood.** Main actor negotiates with neighbor a fee for after-school chores.

B. **Home.** Main actor negotiates with parents about curfew.

C. **Peer group.** Main actor negotiates with friend about what recreational activity to participate in.

Comments

Negotiating is a skill that presupposes an ability to understand the feelings of others. We suggest this skill be reviewed prior to teaching negotiating. Negotiating is also similar in some respects to the skill of convincing others. Negotiating, however, introduces the concept of compromise, a concept that is often worth discussing before role playing this skill.

From A. P. Goldstein. *The prepare curriculum: Teaching prosocial competencies.* Champaign, IL: Research Press, 1988, p. 117. Reprinted by permission.

If students are having difficulty evaluating solutions, the teacher may need to provide some structure. Once students are able to generate a number of alternative solutions to a problem, the process calls for evaluating each solution. Students can be taught to use the criteria of efficacy and feasibility to provide a systematic procedure for evaluation (Kaplan, 1995).

- The efficacy criteria asks: Will this solution help me get what I want, without creating new problems for myself?
- The feasibility criteria asks: Is it likely that I will be able to actually do it?

Teachers can help students apply the criteria to each alternative generated by prompting students with questions such as: "Would this work?" "Would you get what you want?" "Would you create new problems?" Teachers should help students follow the process only, not evaluate solutions. Students should arrive at their own evaluations. Teachers can initially go through each alternative with students, applying the criteria to identify solutions which are both effective and feasible. Teachers can then help students generate more alternatives if those generated do not meet the criteria. Eventually, students will be able to go through this process on their own.

A Problem-solving Process for Teacher-owned Problems

The problem-solving process often moves through the following sequence:

Step 1: Validate student's feelings.

Step 2: Connect with the student.

Step 3: Express your feelings and/or assert your needs.

Step 4: Make a transition to problem-solving.

Step 5: Facilitate the problem-solving process so that the solution mutually satisfies everyone involved.

Step 6: Restore relationship (if necessary).

The following student/teacher dialogue is an example of problem solving in which the teacher respectfully confronts the student and invites the student's participation in arriving at a mutually-agreeable solution.

Teacher: *Mark, when we talked on Tuesday, you said you were going to take your small-group project seriously.* [statement of agreement]

Mark: *Yeah, I know.*

Teacher: *Since then, I've been impressed with how you've worked—that is, up to today. Today, I think you slipped back to old behaviors.* [stating concern]

Mark: *I guess I did.*

Teacher: *What happened?* [exploring]

Mark: *I don't know. I just couldn't get into it today.*

Teacher: *What do you think was different today?* [inquiring]

Mark: *I just think I didn't push myself today.*

Teacher: *What do you think I should do about that?* [soliciting]

Mark: *Give me another chance.*

Teacher: *If I gave you another chance, what could I expect from you?* [soliciting]

Mark: *I'll be serious. I won't act up.*

Teacher: *That sounds good. What should I do if you slip again?* [soliciting]

Mark: *I won't. But, if I do, then call my parents. They'll probably ground me.*

Teacher: *OK. I'll give you a chance. If you stick to our agreement, I won't do anything. If you don't, I'll call your parents. Agreed?* [summarizing]

Mark: *Agreed. By the way, thanks.*

Teacher: *You're welcome.*

Individual Problem-solving Conference

In this example, the teacher moves through a six-step process with the student beginning with describing the problem, moving to brainstorming solutions, to both the teacher and student evaluating the potential solutions, then to selecting, trying out and deciding on the solution (adapted from Gootman, 1997).

Example. *Andy uses profanity when he gets frustrated with school work.*

1. **Describe the problem.** The teacher uses a pattern of asserting and soliciting to get the student to accept ownership of the problem. Whether or not the student

sees it as a problem, the teacher lets him know firmly that it is a problem for others. Living in a community means making compromises for the good of everyone.

Teacher: *Those words are offensive to me and to others in the classroom. [asserting] I've reminded you several times not to use them and it doesn't seem to help. [accepting ownership] We can't allow them in the classroom. [asserting] I notice that when things don't go right with your work, you use cuss words to express your anger. [sharing information] How can you help yourself not use those words in school when you're frustrated? [soliciting]*

Andy: *But I don't think anything's wrong with them. That's how I feel. Besides, my dad uses those same words when he's driving.*

Teacher: *You must decide for yourself what you do out of school but in school, it's against the rules. Besides, it's offensive to others and me. [asserting] The next time you feel frustrated, what could you do that would not offend other people? [soliciting]*

2. **Brainstorm solutions with student.** Both the teacher and student offer solutions.

Andy: *You could ignore me and pretend you don't hear it.*

Teacher: *What else?*

Andy: *I could say a different word instead.*

Andy: *You could wash my mouth out with soap; that's what my friend's mom does.*

Andy: *I could whisper it to myself*

Teacher: *You could miss recess every time you say a cuss word.*

3. **Evaluate solutions with student.** Both teacher and student assert needs and wants.

- Ignore.   Teacher: *I can't live with that. The words are offensive and I can't ignore them.*

- Different word.   Andy: *Maybe that would work if I found a word that really made me feel good getting it out.*

- Wash with soap.   Teacher: *I won't do that to you. That's not healthy.*

- Whisper.   Andy: *That might work, but I might forget and say it out loud. I'm not sure I can remember to keep it down.*

- Miss recess.   Teacher: *I don't want you to miss recess. It's important for you to get exercise and associate with other kids.*
    Andy: *I sure don't want to miss it.*

4. **Select a solution.** The student chooses a solution that both the teacher and student agree on.

Andy decided to try out a different word. He and his teacher tossed around several suggestions and he finally chose to say "phooey" when he was tempted to say the cuss word.

5. **Try out the solution.**

Andy was "phooeying" all over the place.

6. **Evaluate and decide.**

Andy had just about quit using the cuss words, so he and his teacher decided that the problem was almost solved. If he had still been swearing frequently, then they would have had to go back to either Step 2 or 3 and settle on another solution. Perhaps the next time they might try the whispering technique.

The following section provides some more examples of this process.

———————————

Example. *When students are not likely to develop a relationship and the goal is for mutual tolerance or agreeing to disagree.*

Teacher: *You're both very angry.*

Student 1: *That's for sure!*

Student 2: *You'd be mad too if you had to put up with him all day.*

Teacher: *Rather than continue yelling at each other, I'd like you to talk about what each of you did that makes the other mad. After you do that, we'll try to see how we can come up with a solution that will satisfy both of you.*

Example. *Consider the following middle school situation in which a teacher finds herself mediating a conflict between two students who belong to two competing cliques. Her intervention is complex because combatants are "playing" to separate audiences and are unresponsive to her direct overtures.*

Gail: *If you had a brain in your head, you would not act so dumb.*

Chris: *You and your friends would not have a brain if you put your heads together. How can you call me dumb? You've got to be halfway intelligent to know whether I have a brain and you're not even a half-wit.*

Teacher: *Whoa! You two are about to erupt. I want to know what set each of you off. Gail, tell me what upset you first, then Chris, tell me what upset you. I want you both to close your eyes while I listen to what each of you have to say.*

Gail/Chris: *Why do we have to close our eyes?*

Teacher: *It will be easier for me to hear what each of you have to say if I can focus on your words rather than how you treat each other. OK, Gail, what did Chris say or do to upset you and when did she do it? ... OK, Chris, what did Gail say or do to upset you and when did he do it? ... I can see that you both are upset and both of you believe that you have a legitimate reason for feeling the way you do. So, what do we do about your conflict? Since you can't shout one another down and we don't allow fighting in school, what do you want to have happen?*

Chris: *I'd feel a lot better if I could tell Gail off and never see or hear him again.*

Gail: *Me too.*

Teacher: *Is one of you going to transfer to another school tomorrow? Because you both are shaking your heads no, I guess that won't be happening. Since you are going to see and hear each other and I won't let you yell or fight, what else can you do?*

At this point, the teacher has identified the trigger event, calmed the situation, established boundaries for interaction (i.e., no shouting and no fighting), and has started working toward solution generation. The plan that results may be no more than a truce in which students agree to avoid each other or "turn the other cheek" rather than "attack" at the mere sight of one another. The teacher probably would not attempt to have the students become friends. Rather, she would attempt to resolve the open conflict and have the students behave in an acceptable manner.

———————————

Developing Skills to Directly Confront Students

Teachers are faced with many situations in which they need to be proactive and confront students as well as peers, and even supervisors. The goal for this section is to extend basic assertion skills to application in more difficult situations such as confrontation, giving effective criticism, and dealing with persistence. This section presents specific strategies for using assertion and applying these strategies to situations warranting direct confrontation.

There are a variety of ways to assert yourself. Assertion involves direct, honest and appropriate expressions of your thoughts and feelings. Five specific strategies are presented below with examples of how and when to use each strategy appropriately. General guidelines and specific steps are provided for approaching others when their behavior is causing a problem for you. The idea is to deliver criticism in a constructive way and still deal with others' persistence.

Types of Assertion

Simple Assertion

A simple assertion is a direct statement in which you stand up for your rights by stating your needs, wants, and/or intentions. In a simple assertion you express personal rights, beliefs, feelings, or opinions. Examples of simple assertions are:

When being interrupted:

I'd like to finish what I'm saying.

When being asked an important question for which you are unprepared:

I'd like to have a few minutes to think that over.

When telling a student you don't like his/her behavior:

I don't want to see that again.

Acknowledging Assertion

An acknowledging assertion involves expressing affection and appreciation toward others. Some examples are:

I'm so glad you decided to join the group today.

Having a friend like you is very important to me.

I really appreciate the way you helped Maria with her work today.

Validating Assertion

The validating assertion involves making a statement that conveys recognition of the other person's situation or feelings, followed by another statement which stands up for your rights. Examples of validating assertions are:

I know you're angry at James, but I want you to stop yelling so we can get started.

When two people are chatting loudly while a meeting is going on:

You may not realize it but your talking is making it hard for me to hear what's going on in the meeting. Please keep it down.

Often other people more readily respond to assertion when they feel that they have been recognized. However, the validating assertion should not be used as a manipulation merely to gain your own ends without genuine respect for the other person. Habitually saying, "I understand how you feel but …" can be just mouthing understanding and conning others into believing that their feelings are really being taken into account, when in fact their feelings are actually being discounted.

One advantage of a validating assertion is that it allows you a moment to try to empathize with the other person's feelings before reacting. This can help you keep perspective on the situation and reduce the chance of aggressively overreacting when you are irritated.

Escalating Assertion

An escalating assertion involves an increase in intensity or forcefulness of the assertion, moving from request to demand or from preference to refusal.

It starts with a "minimal" assertive response that can usually accomplish your goal with a minimum of effort and negative emotion. When the other person fails to respond to the minimal assertion and continues to behave inappropriately, you gradually escalate the assertion, becoming increasingly firm. Usually it's not necessary to go beyond the initial minimal assertion, but when it is, the idea is to be increasingly firm without becoming aggressive. The escalating assertion can move from a request to a demand, from a preference to an outright refusal, or from a validating assertion to a firm simple assertion. The following example illustrates an escalating assertive response.

A student continues to read a magazine during class.

I know that's much more interesting, but it's time for math.

This is not the time for that.

Put that away now.

It is often effective when using an escalating assertion, just prior to making the final escalated assertion, to offer a "contract option." Here the other person is informed of what the final assertion will be and is given a chance to change behavior before it occurs. For example, the teacher might say "I have no alternative other than to send you to the office if you don't calm down. I'd prefer not to do that, but I will if you continue."

Whether the contract option is simply a threat depends on how it is delivered. If it is said in a threatening tone of voice which relies on emotion to carry the argument, it is a threat. When the contract option is carried out assertively, it is said matter-of-factly, simply giving information about the consequences which will occur if the situation is not resolved.

Confrontive Assertion

A confrontive assertion is used to confront a person with his or her failure to follow through on an agreement, or when the other person's words contradict his or her actions. This type of assertion involves objectively describing what the other person said would be done, what the other person actually did, and what you want done. The following is an example of a confrontive assertion a principal might use with a teacher.

"I thought we'd agreed that you were going to be more considerate toward students. Yet, I noticed today that when two students asked for some information you said that you had better things to do than babysit. As we discussed earlier, I see showing more consideration as an important part of your job. I want to see you interacting more positively with students."

The above are examples of initial confrontive assertive statements. In most cases the ensuing conversation would be an extended interaction between the two people, hopefully resulting in problem-solving dialogue.

Dealing with Persistence by Using Different Types of Assertion

Even though you behave assertively and stand up for your rights, the other person may persist in trying to get you to change your mind. When faced with persistence, a frequent reaction is to either:

1. Discount your personal rights (e.g., "Maybe I don't have the right to . . ."), or
2. Question your original response (e.g., "I guess my explanation really is not good enough. I need an even better justification for my refusal.")

The following five additional techniques are recommended for dealing with persistence.

1. **Broken-record.** This technique involves continuous repetition of the same position (e.g., "I'm not willing to accept . . ."). Rather than provide additional justification, the same message is repeated.
2. **Content-to-process shift.** In this strategy you move from trying to deal with the actual request to dealing with the behavior the person is engaging in (e.g., persistence or redefining of your behavior).
3. **Direct request.** In this strategy you simply ask the person to stop persisting. You may also add how their behavior is affecting you.
4. **Statement of what you will do.** Here you reinforce what you are not willing to do by offering what you would agree to do. This may be a compromise, but it does not have to be.
5. **Counteracting response.** In this strategy you do the opposite of what the other person is doing. For example, if the student raises his voice, you speak more softly; if he gets in your face, you step back; if he blames you, remind him that you are not blaming, you just want a solution.

Dealing with Specific Types of Resistance

Even though you're inviting communication by the language you use, the other person won't necessarily respond appropriately, or in a way that moves the issue toward resolution. And sometimes, the other person doesn't respond at all. In that situation, you will need to be proactive in order to keep the interaction moving toward problem resolution. When the other person fails to respond or responds with resistance you can take the responsibility to make the next move as in the following situations (Jalongo, 1991).

When the other person . . .

Behavior	Appropriate Response
Looks disgusted	*"It seems to you that I'm making a big thing out of nothing and you don't like me bringing this up. Is that what that look means?"*
Leaves	*"You really want to get away from me right now, but that won't solve the problem."*
Is silent	*"I see you're overcome by what I just said. I'd like to hear what you're thinking."*
Laughs	*"This all seems pretty silly to you I guess, but it is really important to me."*
Cries	*"This is really upsetting for you. I thought it was important to be honest."*

Learning to appropriately apply these types of assertions to initiate criticism and respond to persistence will take substantial time and effort, as well as considerable behavioral rehearsal in structured settings in order to enable teachers to become proficient.

Suggestions for enhancing skill in using these strategies:

- Try using each strategy to identify those strategies for which you have a reasonable "inner comfort level."
- Devise your own series of steps or "personal escalation."
- Practice with peers in role-play situations of both potential and actual situations.
- Develop written dialogues and then engage in behavioral rehearsals.
- Establish an ongoing support group to provide a forum for sharing experiences while trying to master these techniques.

Questions for self-reflection when confronting students:

- Was there a direct or implied message of blame?
- Did I describe rather than label the behavior?
- Did I clarify the impact the behavior had on me?
- Did I take responsibility for my own feeling?
- Did I express how I was feeling?

Assertive Confrontation Guidelines

When confronting students with problem behavior it is important to be honest and not demeaning, so that the student will take the problem seriously and yet not become discouraged or antagonistic. Following are some guidelines for acting assertively in situations that warrant confrontation.

Get immediately to the point. Don't "beat around the bush." Such behavior will make the student suspicious of your ulterior motives and will arouse defensiveness. Resist the temptation to ask a stream of incriminating questions. The student will quickly surmise that your questions are intended to bring out a confession. This approach will cause the student to feel under personal attack, and he/she is likely to counterattack or grow increasingly rigid in denying the blame. Come quickly to the point and let the student know the behavior that is a problem. Do not overwhelm the student with a flow of criticism.

Be specific. Do not use labels in describing the student's undesirable behavior (e.g., careless, lazy, irresponsible). Clearly describe the problem behavior and show how it has a concrete effect on you, the student him/herself and/or others. Send an "impact-message." For example, "I've noticed that you've been late three days this week. When you're late, others have to take over for you, and I have to stop and make out a tardy slip and that wastes everyone's time."

Create a positive climate. Communicate to the student that you're providing constructive feedback rather than personal attack. This can be accomplished by giving a brief rationale so that the student can see it's to his/her advantage to change the behavior. However, such rationales should be sincere. For example, "I know you're trying hard to pass this class, and when you're late it makes it harder."

Get a reaction to your criticism. When you ask for a reaction, the student is less likely to feel that he/she has been dumped on and that you're being judgmental. You might simply say, "What's your reaction to what I've said?" When you ask for a response, you need to be open to the possibility of countercriticism, e.g., "All you ever do is criticize." Often there is some truth to countercriticism, and it's important to acknowledge valid criticism.

Ask for the student's suggestions and determine if there's an obstacle to the student's changing his/her behavior. Asking for suggestions enhances the possibility of mutual problem-solving. Any obstacles offered will need to be dealt with.

Get a commitment to change. Ask for a verbal commitment to change. You might also ask for suggestions on what you should do if the student fails to change the behavior.

---

10 Steps for Effective Confrontation

1. Get immediately to the point. Do not ask a series of intimidating questions. Stick with a single problem behavior.
2. Clearly and specifically describe the problem.
3. State how the problem tangibly affects you, the student, or others.
4. Provide a brief and sincere rationale so the student can see that it's to his/her advantage to change the behavior.
5. Ask for a reaction from the student.
6. Acknowledge any objection from the student which seems valid.
7. Ask for suggestions on how to deal with the problem.
8. Determine if there is a realistic obstacle to the student's changing his/her behavior. If so, deal with it.
9. Ask for a verbal commitment to change.
10. Ask for suggestions on what you should do if the student fails to change the behavior.

Critical Reflection on Practice: Using Assertive Confrontation

Activity Directions: During the next week, select someone (e.g., student, peer, colleague, supervisor) who is currently engaging in behavior which is causing a problem. Using the Assertive Confrontation Guidelines, prepare for delivering the confrontation in a constructive way. Then, actually confront the person following the 10-steps. Record the following information.

Brief situational description.

_____

_____

_____

Ineffective behaviors you used.

_____

_____

_____

Problems you encountered.

_____

_____

_____

Successes you had.

_____

_____

_____

Your thoughts/feelings about the encounter.

_____

_____

_____

The focus of the following exercise is on the frequently occurring situation where someone makes a request which you assertively reject, then the person persists with greater efforts to change your mind. In this situation, often you may engage in questioning or discounting of your personal rights. The person refusing renews the request with greater strength and you find yourself questioning whether your explanation really is not good enough, and you begin to scramble for an even better justification for refusing. The focus of the exercise is on recognizing any limiting thinking and unassertive behaviors which arise in response to an other's persistence.

Learning Practice Task: Practicing Dealing with Persistence

Activity Directions: For this role play, generate an actual case that is relevant to your school setting. Working in triads, take turns in the role of the persistent person, the person making the assertive refusal, and the observer.

1. The observer should try to list the types of assertions used as well as the sequence and complete the Peer Task Sheet: Guidelines for Structured Feedback (below). Feedback from the observer should be given after all three group members have taken the role of the persistent person, rather than after each person.

2. It is not necessary to continue the role play to complete resolution of the situation.

During the role-play situation, try to progressively move through the following types of assertions, as appropriate.

1. Validating assertion (statement including recognition of the other person's situation/feelings)
2. Acknowledging assertion (expression of appreciation toward other person)
3. Simple assertion (direct statement expressing your needs)
4. I-message (description of concrete effect of behavior without ascribing blame)
5. Broken-record technique (continue to repeat your original assertion)
6. Escalating assertion (increase level of assertion, e.g., from request to demand, from preference to outright refusal)
7. Confrontive assertion (confronting behavior which contradicts verbal statements)
8. Shift from content to process (i.e., shift from the actual request to the person's persistent behavior, or process)
9. Direct request that person change his/her behavior
10. Define clearly what you are willing to do

During this exercise, try to be aware of:
- Any questioning brought on by the person's refusal to accept your assertion.
- Any discounting of your own personal rights because of persistence of the person's refusal.

After the role-play, discuss:
- Any irrational thinking engaged in,
- Any discounting of personal rights,
- Typical reactions to persistence,
- Strategies most difficult to use,
- Strategies easiest to use,
- Strategies you want to become proficient in,
- Situations in which you might use these strategies during the coming week.

Complete the statements:
- "What I like about my confronting is . . . ."
- "What I want to improve about my confronting is . . . ."

Peer Task Sheet: Guidelines for Structured Feedback

Stage 1: Begin with the strengths of the confrontation. State exactly which behaviors were appropriate.

Stage 2: After you have exhausted all positive feedback, offer feedback in the areas where improvement could be made.

Guidelines for Constructive Feedback

Step 1: Describe the specific behavior without labeling it.

Give objective rather than judgmental feedback.

Avoid blaming, name-calling, preaching, or lecturing.

Step 2: Offer possible ways to improve.

Alternate ways of behaving should be expressed in a tentative rather than an absolute manner.

Do not impose a suggestion.

Step 3: Ask the person for a reaction to the suggestions.

Allow the person to accept, refuse, or modify the suggestion.

Sending Decisive Messages: The Interpretation-Impact-Instead (III) Format

One method for effective confrontation is the decisive message format, or Interpretation-Impact-Instead (III). It provides a way to express yourself clearly and directly, while ensuring that others understand exactly why you have a problem. Sending decisive messages lets the other person know you want to do more than describe the problem, you want to solve the problem. Also, decisive messages are less likely to cause a defensive reaction and shut down communication altogether. A decisive message has four components: A clear description of the problem, your interpretation, the impact, and what you would like instead. Each is described below.

Clear Description

A clear description of an action, event or situation which is causing a problem for you. A clear description is objective and doesn't include any value-laden or emotionally-charged words, such as always, never or ever.

> **Example:** *"When you start to talk before I've finished ..."* rather than *"When you always butt in ...."*

Your interpretation

The personal meaning you attach. Interpretations are subjective, hence there is more than one interpretation of an action, event, or situation.

The impact

Describes what happens as a result of the behavior, or situation created by the behavior. An impact statement might also include how you're acting or feeling because of the behavior or situation.

Impact statements serve the important function of helping you understand more clearly why you were affected by an other's behavior and what impact it is having on you. Although you may think the other person should be aware of the impact of his/her behavior without being told, this is often not the case. It's important to explicitly state the impact of the behavior, so the other person knows exactly why you are concerned.

What you'd like instead

What you would like the other person to do or know. This would include stating where you stand on an issue or how important something is to you, as well as what you'd like to happen next. Telling others what you'd like to happen lets them know what they might do about the problem and helps move toward resolution, rather than let the situation fester.

Example: *"When you got in my face, [description] I thought you were trying to intimidate me. [interpretation] Now, I find I'm just waiting for you to do something wrong. [impact] I'd like to talk with you to see if we can get back on the right track."* [instead]

Learning Practice Task: Identifying Components of the III Decisive Message Format

Activity Directions: Identify which part of a decisive message is being used in each statement listed below. Use the following key: INT = interpretation, IMP = impact, and INS = what you'd like instead.

_____ I'm avoiding you because I'm angry.

_____ When you were late, I missed an important meeting.

_____ I'd like to talk to you about what happened.

_____ I guess you're anxious to get started.

_____ You don't value my opinion.

_____ I feel like you're not listening.

_____ I think you don't care about this class.

_____ I see you're not ready.

_____ I think you were trying to embarrass me.

_____ Ever since then I've been avoiding you.

_____ After our talk last week you seemed to withdraw.

_____ I feel you're wrong.

_____ From now on I would like you to speak respectfully to me.

_____ The next time this happens, I want you to come to me first.

_____ You must have forgotten our agreement.

_____ You're acting like something is bothering you.

The RRRR Process for Openly Confronting Students

Small irritations can accumulate, building into resentments and becoming potential sources of hostility. To prevent a stockpiling of resentments, it is helpful to deal with an annoying incident as it occurs by sharing your feelings with the student who is causing a problem for you.

In actual classroom situations, it can be difficult to deal with problems openly and positively. The pressure of the situation and the presence of other students sometimes mitigate against dealing spontaneously with your feelings. Hence, it is easy to either ignore situations and let resentments slowly build into potential hostility or to attack students by putting them down in some way. Either of these responses might alleviate the situation for a time, but they usually do little to solve the problem in the long run. Positively confronting students can lead to open communication between you and your students so that negotiation and compromise can be used to solve conflicts.

Strategies such as the RRRR Confrontation described in this section offer a process for both teachers and students to express their feelings. It provides a vehicle for open communication so that negotiation and compromise can be used for mutual problem-solving. Using the RRRR process to confront students with teacher concerns allows both teachers and students to express their feelings openly and honestly. The following are benefits of this confrontation process.

- Neither the teacher nor the student attacks the other.
- Both teacher and student respond honestly.
- Each considers the other's request as a viable option.
- A compromise is reached which resolves the problem for both the teacher and the student.

The RRRR Student Confrontation Process

Step 1: Relate

The teacher relates what he/she is concerned about to the student by stating only the behavior or situation of concern and the reason for concern. Next, the student responds similarly by relating to the teacher how he/she felt about the teacher's behavior and the reason for the reaction.

Step 2: Restate

To assure understanding, the student restates the teacher's concern to the satisfaction of the teacher. The teacher then restates the student's concern to the satisfaction of the student.

Note: This step may take several rounds to ensure that both are clear about each other's perception of the problem.

Step 3: Request

The teacher makes a request of the student and then the student responds with a request for the teacher.

Step 4: Resolve

Once the requests are clearly stated and restated, the teacher and student negotiate until both have decided to do something which each is comfortable with that addresses the concern. They then negotiate and compromise, if necessary, until they reach a mutually-agreeable resolution.

The following example of the RRRR Confrontation will help clarify the specific steps.

———————————

Related Concerns

Teacher: *I was annoyed when you were reading another book while I was lecturing because I thought you didn't consider what I was saying important.*

Student: *I got mad when you kept asking me to put the book away and pay attention because it embarrassed me.*

Restated Concerns

Student: *You were annoyed when I was reading another book while you were lecturing because you thought that I didn't consider what you were saying important.*

Teacher: *You didn't like it when I kept asking you to pay attention because it embarrassed you.*

Requests

Teacher: *I would like you to pay attention when I am lecturing.*

Student: *I would like you to let me read when I am bored with your lecture.*

Resolve

Teacher: *I can't let you do something else during my lecture because it sets an example for others. Besides, the information might be important to the unit.*

Student: *I can see your concern, but why should I have to pay attention if I already know the material? I'd like you to let me work on something else if I do it so no one sees when I know the material. That way no one will notice.*

Teacher: *I think that would be hard to do, but I can see that you will be bored if you are already familiar with the material. I can let you know just before class what the lecture will be about. If you feel you are familiar enough with it, you can go to the library. You can keep this privilege as long as you maintain your present academic level.*

Student: *That sounds good. And if I do decide to stay in class, I won't do other work during your lecture.*

Restated Resolution

Student: *You said that I may go to the library if I feel that I would be bored during the lesson because I'm familiar with the material already.*

Teacher: *You said that you'd like that arrangement and that if you decide to stay in the class, you won't do other work.*

———————————

In this example, both the teacher's and the student's issues were stated clearly so that teacher and student understood exactly what each other's concern is. Neither the student nor the teacher attacked the other. Both maintained a high level of honesty and openness. Each considered the other's request and reacted to it as a real possibility. In the end, they reached a mutually-agreeable solution that was reasonable for each of them, a solution that might never have been considered without the confrontation.

Learning Practice Task: Practicing the RRRR Confrontation

Confronting students openly and allowing students the reciprocal right to confront the teacher with their issues will take some practice because it is an unfamiliar format. The following activity is intended to provide practice in developing the necessary skills before transferring them to the classroom.

Activity Directions: To practice this confrontation process you need a group of six or more people, preferably about ten. One person volunteers to be "teacher," one person volunteers to be "coach," and the rest are "students." Each member of the group should have a chance to be teacher, coach, and student in successive rounds. The teacher separates from the students and prepares a ten-minute lesson in any subject for an appropriate age group. The students, meanwhile, plan to role-play different "student types." The types can include a students who is bored, argumentative, arrogant, brown-nosing, or any type of student behavior that might be found in a classroom. (In role-playing students, it is helpful not to get so locked into the role that you do not react normally to responses from the teacher or other students. The quiet student, for example, should speak if he/she has something to say. The argumentative students should behave if the teacher effectively does something to cause him/her to settle down.) The coach at this time reviews the RRRR process to become familiar with the steps.

1. When everyone is ready, the teacher begins the lesson with the students role-playing at the age level suggested by the teacher and the coach observing the process.
2. After about ten minutes of the lesson, the teacher chooses one student who made him/her the most uncomfortable to engage in the student confrontation. The two, teacher and student, sit face to face and engage in the RRRR confrontation process following the prescribed steps. Now the coach plays the important role of keeping the confrontation positive by not allowing destructive statements (personal attacks), by making sure each step is followed, and by ensuring that each person has an equal opportunity to speak.

Questions for Self-reflection

What would keep you from using this process?

What do you know about yourself that might make it difficult to implement this procedure?

What difficulties would you anticipate in using this type of encounter?

For what type of situation do you think this procedure would be likely to be most effective?

How can you best use confrontation with your students?

What is the most efficient way for you to become familiar with this procedure?

Stress Management Strategies

While there is much information and training available for adults on how to cope with and manage stress, children and youth generally get little help in dealing with the stress in their lives. School-age children face increased emotional strain with the demise of the family support structure putting many families in upheaval as they try to cope with the effects of poverty, transience, and divorce. Students have the additional pressure to be accepted, to succeed in school, and peer pressure to belong.

Students have fewer support systems and coping skills and thus are more likely to respond in inappropriate ways to stress, such as using drugs or alcohol, committing crimes, withdrawal, or self-destructive behavior. In the classroom setting, stress reactions can include irritability, low frustration levels, underachievement, bullying, and hostility.

Some strategies teachers can use to enhance the probability that students will actually use cognitive behavior management strategies include:

- Be a model for your students. Use cognitive behavior management strategies yourself and share with your students how you are using and have used these strategies to help you cope with stress.
- Be authentic and disclose your thinking process. Use problem-solving skills in front of your students, even enlist their help.
- Keep in mind that you are a coping model not a mastery model. Mistakes are valuable learning tools and should also be shared with your students.

Techniques available to help students manage stress include some previously discussed such as self-control strategies and social skills training, as well as strategies to help students deal with the physical reactions the body has to stress. Coping strategies for stress management attempt to minimize the effects of stressful situations, so that students can cope more adequately with stressors. Techniques available can be:

Physiological	Cognitive	Behavioral
Diaphragmatic breathing	Self-instruction training	Behavioral self-control
Progressive relaxation training	Cognitive restructuring	Assertiveness training
Exercise		Social skills training

While teaching social skills in general should serve to reduce stress, some simple physiological techniques are also effective in reducing stress. Physiological stress coping skills produce a direct effect on the body. They are the easiest for students to learn and produce the fastest results. Three techniques that can help students cope with stress are described below.

Diaphragmatic Breathing

This technique is easy to learn and requires the least amount of discipline to master. For younger students, you can refer to it as "belly breathing." Simply, the belly pushes out when you inhale and pulls in when you exhale. Students should practice this regularly, if possible, while lying on the floor.

Progressive Relaxation Training (PRT)

PRT is more difficult to learn, but it produces a deeper and longer-lasting state of relaxation. It involves alternately making your muscles tense and then relaxed. The idea is to learn the difference between these two states so that you can more easily recognize tension in your body and use PRT to achieve relaxation. This technique generally follows a script which takes 15–20 minutes. Daily practice for several weeks would be required to achieve results. PRT has been demonstrated effective in helping youths reduce and control nonattending behaviors (Redfering & Bowman, 1981), decreasing test anxiety in middle-school students (Smead, 1981), and calming anxious, mildly handicapped youths (Morganett & Bauer, 1987).

Exercise

There is evidence that aerobic exercise has a tranquilizing effect in reducing stress and can lead to reduction in maladaptive behavior (Allen, 1980; Shipman, 1984). Jogging, roller skating, cycling, or fast walking can readily be done at school and can be incorporated as part of the physical education program.

The following specific relaxation training exercises described by Morgan and Reinhart (1991) are exercises that will help get students in a relaxed state. It is important to realize that all of these techniques require practice, like anything you do that is new to you and new to your students. Students may frustrate you in the beginning by acting silly or being uncooperative. It may seem like chaos at first and you may experience the feeling of not having control of your class. But be persistent and keep working on these interventions until they become as natural as teaching any other lesson.

Tense and Relax. To know what relaxation feels like, students must first be able to recognize their tensions. Although many are already tense, they must experience (in a conscious way) extreme tension so they can feel truly relaxed. Following are a few exercises you can use in the classroom.

Begin by having the students sit up straight at their desks, feet flat on the floor, arms to their sides, and chin resting on their chests. Now, curl the toes under and squeeze tight; now let go. Then squeeze the muscles in the calves; now let go. Follow through with the thighs, buttocks, and tummy, each time letting go. Then pull the shoulders up tight around your neck; let go. Now, make your hands into tight fists; let go. Then tense the arms; let go. Finally, the face muscles: Squeeze the eyes tightly shut; purse the lips together tightly; clench the teeth; now let go.

Follow this with stretching exercises. Stretch the muscles out as far as possible: The feet, legs, arms, and facial muscles. Hold the eyes open very wide, stretch open the jaw, stick out the tongue and stretch; now relax everything. When this exercise is finished, students should know what real tension feels like and how it feels to relax.

Breathing. Have the students practice breathing exercises for 2 or 3 minutes. This is simple and involves taking in a deep breath until the stomach is extended, holding it for 3 or 4 seconds. Then let all the air go rushing out while telling them to blow out all the bad feelings: Angry feelings, scary feelings, sad feelings, nervous feelings. They will probably act silly on you the first few times you do this; remind them what they are supposed to do. Keep bringing them back to the task. Once this has become a daily routine, the silliness will stop.

Now, practice rhythmic, steady, even, deep breathing. Tell your students to close their eyes and begin concentrating on breathing. Do it with them to show what you mean.

The Rag Doll. This is a short, simple exercise that can be used after the students have practiced and incorporated the basic skills of relaxation such as tension/release and breathing.

For a few minutes have them begin with tension/release and steady, deep breathing. Then tell them they are going to let each part of the body imitate a rag doll bit by bit. Give the following directions: First, sit up and let your legs go loose and limp. Now, the body and the arms: Let them go loose and limp; let your head droop down, or back, or to the side, loose and limp just like a rag doll. Keep up your steady, deep breathing. Do this for about 10 minutes.

Using Clay. Give the students a lump of clay and have them hold it for awhile and enjoy its feel. Tell them to rub it around in their hands, kneading, pressing, folding, and squeezing it so that it oozes between their fingers. Ask them to close their eyes and imagine all of the things that they could mold out of the clay. Give them about a minute to imagine these things. Then tell them to select one of those figures and mold what they want. This is a very relaxing exercise for young children.

Behavioral and Cognitive Stress Coping Strategies

Behavioral strategies include verbal and other overt behaviors required by students to manage stress through the manipulation of their environment. They could include some social skills such as responding appropriately to criticism, name-calling, or peer pressure, or time management techniques involving setting longterm and shortterm goals, monitoring time spent, and prioritizing activities.

Cognitive stress coping strategies are the most difficult to learn. In cognitive restructuring, students learn how their beliefs and inner speech can cause anxiety and how to use disputing irrational beliefs and positive self-talk to change their behavior patterns. Meichenbaum (1985) has proposed an integrative strategy combining several skills and involving five stages. His integrative strategy for stress inoculation combines a number of techniques including relaxation, cognitive restructuring, and behavioral rehearsal. These stages are:

1. The "conceptual framework stage" where the student is taught basic concepts regarding stress and stress management.
2. The "relaxation training stage" where the student learns to master some form of relaxation training, usually PRT.
3. The "cognitive restructuring stage" where the student disputes any irrational beliefs that might be contributing to his/her high levels of anxiety or anger.
4. The "stress script stage" where the student writes down everything he/she needs to say or do to manage stress before, during, and after being exposed to the stressor.
5. The "inoculation stage" in which the student uses his/her stress script as he/she is gradually exposed to larger and larger "doses" of the stressor.

The stress script consists of everything the student says and does before, during, and after encountering the anger-provoking stressor. The following is an example of a stress script a student might use to cope with anger provoked by peer teasing (Kaplan, 1995).

Before Confrontation	*"What do I have to do? Take a few belly breaths to get ready. This is going to be hard but I can do it. I just have to remember to take deep breaths and keep telling myself the magic words, 'saying it doesn't make it so.' Here they come. I'm ready for them."*
During Confrontation	*"Stay cool. Saying it doesn't make it so. Take some deep breaths. Saying it doesn't make it so. Just ignore them. Look away. Saying it doesn't make it so. Saying it doesn't make it so."*
After Confrontation	*"I did it! I kept myself from getting angry. It worked. I can control myself. They didn't tease me as much as they usually do. Pretty soon they won't tease me at all. Now let's see ... was there anything I could improve on for next time?"*

Examples of Self-statements for Coping with Stress

Preparing for a stressor:

- What is it you have to do?
- You can develop a plan to deal with it.
- Just think about what you can do about it. That's better than getting anxious.
- No negative self-statements; just think rationally.
- Don't worry; worry won't help anything.
- Maybe what you think is anxiety, is eagerness to confront the stressor.

Reacting During the Stress-Producing Situation:

- Just "psych" yourself up—you can meet this challenge.
- You can convince yourself to do it. You can reason your fear away.
- One step at a time; you can handle the situation.
- Don't think about fear; just think about what you have to do. Stay relevant.
- This anxiety you feel is a reminder to use your coping exercises.
- This tenseness can be an ally; a cue to cope.
- Relax; you're in control. Take a slow, deep breath.
- Ah, good.

Coping with the Feeling of Being Overwhelmed:

- When fear comes, just pause.
- Keep the focus on the present; what is it you have to do? Label your fear from 0 to 10 and watch it change.
- You should expect your fear to rise.
- Don't try to eliminate fear totally; just keep it manageable.

Reflecting on the Experience:

- It worked!
- It wasn't as bad as you expected.
- You made more out of your fear than it was worth.
- Your damn ideas—that's the problem. When you control them, you control your fear.
- It's getting better each time you use the procedures.
- You can be pleased with the progress you're making.
- You did it!
- You're doing better all the time.

From D. Meichenbaum. Self-instructional methods: How to do it. In A. Goldstein and F. Kanfer (Eds.), *Helping people change: Methods and materials.* Elmsford, NY: Pergamon Press, 1975. Reprinted by permission.

Critical Reflection on Practice: Helping Students Deal with Stress

Activity Directions: Follow the steps below to begin planning to implement stress-reducing strategies for your students.

1. Devise a way to identify the sources of stress your students encounter.
2. How might you go about matching causes of stress with strategies for dealing with stress?
3. What factors do you want to consider in devising your program for stress-reduction?
4. What are the major concerns you want to keep in mind?
5. What preventative measures and what coping strategies fit with your teaching and interaction style?
6. What strategies could be readily integrated into your existing program without much additional time commitment?
7. How will you determine the effectiveness of your stress-reducing activities?
8. What will you consider as evidence of positive effects?

Chapter 11

Building Your Personal Management Plan

Teaching requires that you continually challenge your established patterns of behavior, institute new practices, implement new strategies, and develop new tools on an ongoing basis to build and sustain the kind of classroom and personal relationships you want. This section provides a variety of formats and structured forms for assessing and building your personal management plan. It consolidates the key concepts presented in earlier chapters into a framework for reflecting on aspects of your teaching that you would like to improve. Also included is a six-stage process that you can use to structure and monitor a systematic intervention strategy to adapt teaching behaviors and practices.

Developing a personal system of classroom management involves considering instructional factors, management issues, discipline strategies, as well as interpersonal relationships. Effectively managing the classroom setting requires balancing these multiple layers while simultaneously sustaining three critical conditions:

1. A challenging and nourishing environment for learning to occur.
2. Teacher expectations formulated to meet students' basic needs.
3. Opportunities for all students to receive recognition and experience success.

The teacher's capacity for self-reflection and self-analysis is an essential element in the ongoing challenge to balance these interfacing roles and responsibilities. The following sections invite you to reflect on daily practice, assess areas you want to improve, and take action to create the kind of classroom that produces lifelong learners.

Responding Authentically to Students

Teachers' communication styles can be either inauthentic or authentic. Inauthentic responses to students are:

- Indirect, and can be dishonest
- Disrespectful
- Impersonal
- Evaluative

On the other hand, authentic responses to students are:

- Honest and direct
- Respectful
- Personal
- Nonevaluative

The following rating forms ask you to rate your frequency of use and then your level of personal concern for both breaking destructive habits of language and building more productive habits of language.

Habits of Language to Break

Language Habits	Frequency of Use Rating High, Medium, Low	Personal Concern Rating High, Medium, Low
1. You-language	_____	_____
2. Evaluative statements about students	_____	_____
3. Judgmental feedback	_____	_____
4. Nonspecific and personality praise	_____	_____
5. Moralizing by using should and ought	_____	_____
6. Globalizing by using always, never, and ever	_____	_____
7. Asking why questions	_____	_____
8. Telling students what they need	_____	_____
9. Having the last word	_____	_____
10. Hedging with tag-on questions	_____	_____
11. Third-party talk	_____	_____
12. Ultimatums disguised as choices	_____	_____
13. Directives disguised as optional for students	_____	_____
14. Directives disguised as request for students' opinion	_____	_____
15. Sarcastic questions	_____	_____

Habits of Language to Build

Language Habits	Frequency of Use Rating High, Medium, Low	Personal Concern Rating High, Medium, Low
1. Using I-language	_____	_____
2. Making impact-statements	_____	_____
3. Giving encouragement rather than praise	_____	_____
Supporting student self-evaluation by:		
4. Describing rather than evaluating student behavior	_____	_____
5. Giving personal reaction without value judgment	_____	_____
6. Sharing personal position	_____	_____
7. Describing emotional reaction evoked by the student	_____	_____
Fostering student self-reflection by:		
8. Posing questions that help students consider others' perspective	_____	_____
9. Asking questions which expand students' thinking	_____	_____
10. Requesting self-assessment	_____	_____

Incorporating Community-building Experiences

Building a sense of community involves orchestrating community-building activities at two levels. One level is teacher bonding with students and the other level is nurturing thoughtful and considerate interactions among students.

Building a Sense of Community Among Students

In order to build community, teachers need to infuse the classroom with community-building experiences and create a safe place where students feel secure enough to disclose and share what has purpose and meaning for them. Creating such a community involves:

- Fostering a sense of connectedness,
- Building trust,
- Honoring multiple voices, and
- Modeling responding with acknowledgment and acceptance.

Ask Yourself

What experiences do I want to incorporate into daily practice that will build student-to-student connections?

Teacher Practices that Nourish Students and Build Community

Cultivating the classroom as a community means instituting policies, practices, and routines that involve real connections with students that solidify student/teacher alliances. Relating with students as an ally might include the following:

- Having a vehicle for open and ongoing dialogue with students.
- Getting to know students and their backgrounds.
- Making personal connections with one-on-one time with students.
- Developing rituals and traditions.
- Sharing what's important to you.
- Creating networks outside the school walls.

Ask Yourself

What practices do I want to incorporate into daily practice that will strengthen my connections with students?

Personal Attributes

Several personal attributes also contribute to feelings of connectedness, security and belonging. The following five characteristics are important attributes.

Members of the community should be:

- Respectful
- Authentic
- Thoughtful
- Emotionally honest
- Trustworthy

Ask Yourself

How do I demonstrate to my students that I value these attributes?

Creating a Need-satisfying Classroom Environment

The classroom should provide a safe haven for students and meet their basic needs. Ensuring a nurturing and caring climate, involves creating a sense of belonging, importance, and personal power. Creating such an environment involves meeting the following nine needs.

9 Needs of a Learning Community

A Sense of Belonging	A Sense of Importance	A Sense of Power
1. Status among peers	4. Positive identity	7. Competency
2. Safety, both emotional and physical	5. Recognition	8. Control
3. Affection	6. Attention	9. Freedom

Ask Yourself

How am I meeting my students' needs in each of these areas?

Engaging Students in Mutual Problem Solving

Below the skills needed to invite students to engage in a mutual problem-solving process are briefly summarized. They include skills that take the process from listening, to connecting to problem solving.

Skills for Inviting Communication: Listening, Connecting, and Problem Solving

Listening to Students

Opening	Inviting students to share their concerns
Exploring	Open-ended questioning to extend the student's perception
Reflecting	Responding to expressed or implied emotions
Paraphrasing	Repeating message in your own words
Clarifying	Requesting restatement for understanding
Perception Checking	Offering alternative interpretations and asking for clarification

Connecting with Students

Encouraging	Valuing students' effort and competence
Acknowledging	Accepting students' rights, needs, and perspectives without judgment
Validating	Communicating acceptance, understanding or concern for students' feelings
Appreciating	Noticing what students do and what's important to them

Problem-solving with Students

Inviting Cooperation	Asking for help and cooperation
Requesting	Asking for input or advice
Enlisting	Asking what the student wants, needs, or feels
Soliciting	Asking what the student would like to happen
Inquiring	Questioning to move toward problem resolution
Summarizing	Pulling together what has been covered
Sharing Information	Sharing ideas, information, and personal experience
Suggesting	Posing options to try
Challenging	Confronting students about their actions
Asserting	Expressing your rights and needs
Restoring	Intervening to keep on track
Stating Concern	Expressing your concerns

Ask Yourself

At which level, listening, connecting, or problem solving, do I need to begin to invite communication with my students?

Which specific skills do I need to develop or enhance?

What action plan will I implement to develop these skills?

Addressing Student Unproductive Behavior

Considering if, when, and how to intervene is a critical management decision. When deciding to intervene, you will need to address two fundamental questions.

Ask Yourself

Will the intervention:

- Help the student learn better, not just eliminate the disruptive behavior?
- Help the student learn a new way of behaving?

When you identify a student behavior as unacceptable, you have three variables to work with: self, student, or environment. You can:

- Modify the student's behavior.
- Modify the learning context or environment.
- Modify your own reaction to the behavior.

It is important to keep in mind that changing the student's behavior is not your only option and that combining modifying the student's behavior with changes in both your attitude and the learning environment is likely to produce maximum results.

There are three primary alternatives for addressing student behavior that is problematic. Within these primary alternatives, nine options are available to the teacher. Each of these categories is briefly summarized below.

Alternatives for Addressing Student Behavior

Allow   The teacher makes a conscious choice to allow the behavior.

    Permit Allow behavior that is generally accepted for all class members.

    Accept Accept unalterable aspects related to students' personality traits and cultural and social backgrounds.

    Tolerate Allow behavior temporarily when students can't help themselves at the moment.

              Toleration is warranted when behavior is symptomatic of:

- Learner's leeway—student is learning new concept or behavior.
- Developmental stage—age-typical behavior likely to change as the student matures.
- Illness, disability or undeveloped skill—behaviors students can not control.
- Situational stress or emotional state—behavior due to extenuating circumstances.

Intervene   The situation requires that the teacher intervene to attempt to alter the situation.

    Change Teach and model alternative behaviors.

    Modify Deal with behavior without using authoritarian power or consequences.

    Control Stop misbehavior for the moment by applying consequences.

Accommodate   The teacher takes primary responsibility for making adjustments to accommodate students' academic as well as emotional needs.

    Adapt Make contextual and individual adaptations.

    Support Provide personal and/or emotional support.

    Prevent Develop procedures to avoid problems.

Ask Yourself

In what situations do I intervene, when allowing or accommodating student behavior might be more conducive to maintaining a productive learning environment?

Criteria for Assessing Your Intervention Pattern

While there is no objective standard that can be applied to all interactions and responses to students and classroom situations, considering the following eight criteria can help you broaden your response options when addressing unproductive student behavior.

Criteria for Assessing Interventions

Criteria	Self-reflective Questions
Escalating	Am I following a sequence beginning with an unobtrusive response and escalating progressively?
Respectful	Does my response maintain my dignity and treat students respectfully?
Contextual	Does my response take into account the effect of the instructional context and setting on the student's behavior?
Instructive	Do I provide students with guidance in accomplishing the desired behavior change?
Facilitative	Do I provide students with assistance in learning more appropriate ways to behave?
Reflective	Does my response consider how my reaction to the student may have an impact on the student's behavior?
Responsive	Does my response consider that the student's behavior might be a reaction to a personal or academic need not having been met at the time?
Preventive	Does my response go beyond a single episode to anticipating and planning for the future?

The Change Process

The process of change takes you through a series of stages, beginning with self-awareness. At this stage, you examine your ways of behaving and start to question what a particular way of behaving is getting you. You begin to challenge whether your way of behaving is getting you what you want and explore the real "cost" attached to your current behavior. This behavior could be any behavior that you are bringing into question, such as getting angry, engaging in power struggles, or withdrawing. Realizing that your way of behaving is sustaining a state you want to change, such as frustration, discomfort, or stress, leads you to want to change.

Acting on this desire to change will not be quick and easy. Changing classroom patterns of behaving is a process, not an event. Any change creates some level of discomfort. You can't change or grow without experiencing some degree of inner conflict. Often, instead of allowing yourself to be uncertain and confused for awhile, to find your way through, and let go of the old ways of reacting, you rush to get some closure, to "do something" to make the discomfort of not knowing what to do go away. If this uncertainty brings about too much fear and doubt, you may close down the process and either stay with the old way of behaving or seek a quick fix. You look for a ready-made solution, a "prescription" for change. If instead, you change through a personal process of exploration, you subsequently formulate new behaviors that lie within your own comfort zone and are aligned with your own style of relating. When you tap your own resources, you experience an "ah ha" and no longer need to take on others' solutions. You bring who you are based on your beliefs into balance with how you act in the classroom.

Implementing a Systematic Change Process

Making a conscious attempt to change your classroom behavior may initially require devising a specific strategy, technique, or series of steps designed to systematically alter a specific behavior. At first, it may be helpful to have a more structured intervention process for yourself to get you in the habit of self-reflection and self-analysis. Such a process typically involves a variety of active practice techniques along with some way to monitor the change to evaluate progress. Active practice techniques are specific strategies to overtly practice new ways of behaving and responding, often coupled with explicit self-prompting or cueing strategies.

Actually collecting data will help you test out some of the assumptions you may be unwittingly making. Generating a variety of alternative approaches to the problem will help you to take responsibility for what you can control—your behavior.

The following multi-stage process is an example of a process that can be used to structure and monitor an intervention strategy to modify a specific teaching behavior, communication pattern, or way of responding to and interacting with a particular student who poses a problem.

Six-stage Process for Implementing Change in the Classroom

Stage One: Defining the Problem

State the problem, concern or need you have identified. What is it that needs improvement or that might be developed as a new approach or solution? Describe the problem in specific terms. Describe anything you are aware of that has an impact on the problem.

Stage Two: Data Collection

Determine a procedure for collecting data that can be used to analyze the present status of your behavior and the behavior of the your students, or a particular student you want to focus on. At this step, the data collected should be objective, nonevaluative, and provide a means for comparing actual behavior with desired behavior.

Stage Three: Data Interpretation and Pattern Identification

Use this data to try to identify patterns or relationships. Are there certain situations in which the behavior is more or less effective? Consider the interaction effect of the behavior on your teaching function role (e.g., ability to teach, lesson format and structure), your managerial role (e.g., order, organization), as well as your human role (e.g., personal comfort zone, interpersonal relationships with students, affective climate of the classroom).

Stage Four: Generating Alternatives

Once you have looked at your data and discovered areas in which you might want to implement change, generate alternatives for experimentation. Then choose one alternative for implementation. It is important to be specific in describing your alternatives.

Consider all the approaches you could use to deal with the problem behavior or situation. This process might include:

- Listing areas of concern.
- Establishing criteria for prioritizing areas of concern.
- Generating alternatives.
- Predicting possible ramifications or side effects of each alternative.
- Selecting the alternative you think is most likely to bring about a change.

Stage Five: Implementing a Plan of Action

Establish a plan of action and a timetable for implementing your plan. Decide on your first step and then continue developing a schedule of planned steps. Consider including a procedure to get both ongoing feedback and reinforcing support. Include a monitoring procedure (either self or other) that will help you follow through on your action plan. You may want to organize your plan as follows:

Specific Action Steps	Time Period Allocated	Resources Needed	Authority Required	Obstacles to Address

Try your plan long enough to give it a fair chance. Don't give up too easily. On the other hand, as soon as it becomes obvious that any aspect of your plan is not working, figure out what's going wrong and change it.

Stage Six: Evaluation

To engage in data-based decision making you need to decide how you will evaluate the effectiveness of your intervention plan. To determine whether the intervention was successful you need to assess the impact of your intervention. Establish the criteria you will use for evaluation. Devise a measurement technique that will provide objective data. Also consider your own feelings and assessment of the effectiveness and utility of the intervention as well as student feedback and perceptions in the decision-making process.

After considering the results, you may decide to:

1. Adopt the new strategy because it is more congruent with your view of your teaching role and has a positive impact on students, or

2. Modify the new strategy to better fit your style and your ideals, and/or to have a more positive response from students, or

3. Reject the new strategy because you have determined that it is not a preferable option. Now you will need to recycle through these steps and try a different approach.

Because growth involves perpetual change, any change you make is not permanently adopted, modified, or rejected. Further input, new insights and changing perspectives alter your considerations, causing a decision to be changed or reconsidered at any time.

References

Albert, L. (1989). *A teacher's guide to cooperative discipline: How to manage your classroom and promote self-esteem.* Circle Pines, MN: American Guidance Service.

Albert, R. D. (1983). The intercultural sensitizer or culture assimilator: A cognitive approach. In D. Landis & R. W. Brislin (Eds.), *Handbook of intercultural training* (vol. 2). New York: Pergamon.

Alberto, P. A., & Troutman, A. C. (1990). *Applied behavior analysis for teachers.* Columbus, Ohio: Merrill.

Albion, F. M. (1983). A methodological analysis of self-control in applied settings. *Behavior Disorders, 8,* 87–102.

Allen, J. (1980). Jogging can modify disruptive behaviors. *Teaching Exceptional Children, 12,* 66–70.

Anderson, L. M., Evertson, C. M., & Brophy, J. E. (1979). An experimental study of effective teaching in first-grade reading groups. *Elementary School Journal, 79,* 193–223.

Argyris, C. (1990). *Overcoming organizational defenses.* Boston, MA: Allyn & Bacon.

Arndt, R. C. (1994). *School violence in American cities: NLC Survey Overview.* National League of Cities: Washington, DC.

Aronson, E., & Patnoe, S. (1997). *The jigsaw classroom: Building cooperation in the classroom* (2nd ed.). New York: Longman.

Bandura, A. (1993). Perceived self-efficacy in cognitive development and functioning. *Educational Psychologist, 28* (2), 117–148.

Barkley, R. (1987). *Defiant children: A clinician's manual for parent training.* New York: Guilford Press.

Barkley, R. A. (1996). Linkages between attention and executive function. In G. R. Lyon & N. A. Krasnegor (Eds.), *Attention, memory, and executive function.* Baltimore, MD: Brooks.

Battistich, V., Solomon, D., Kim, D., Watson, M., & Schaps, E. (1995). Schools as communities, poverty levels of student populations, and students' attitudes, motives, and performance: A multilevel analysis. *American Educational Research Journal, 32,* 627–658.

Beck, L. (1994). *Reclaiming educational administration as a caring profession.* New York: Teachers College Press.

Bernstein, D. A., & Borkovec, T. D. (1973). *Progressive relaxation training: A manual for the helping professions.* Champaign, IL: Research Press.

Blase, J., & Kirby, P. (1991). *Bringing out the best in teachers: What effective principals do.* Newbury Park, CA: Corwin.

Bolle, J., & Duncan, A. (1992). *Focus: Facilitating organized change with unconventional strategies.* West End Special Education Local Plan Area, San Bernardino County Schools. San Bernardino, CA.

Bornstein, P. H. (1985). Self-instructional training: A commentary and state of the art. *Journal of Applied Behavior Analysis, 18,* 69–72.

Bower, S. A., & Bower, G. H. (1991). *Asserting yourself: A practical guide for positive change.* Reading, MA: Addison-Wesley.

Bowlby, J. (1982). *Attachment and loss* (vol. 1). New York: Basic Books.

Boyer, E. (1983). *High school: A report of the Carnegie Foundation for the Advancement of Teaching.* New York: HarperCollins.

Boyer, E. (1995). *The basic school: A community for learning.* Princeton, NJ: The Carnegie Foundation.

Brandt, R. (1988). On students' needs and team learning: A conversation with William Glasser. *Educational Leadership, 45* (6), 38–45.

Brendtro, L. K., Brokenleg, M., & Van Bockern, S. (1990). *Reclaiming youth at risk: Our hope for the future.* Bloomington, Indiana: National Educational Service.

Brislin, R. W., Cushner, K., Cherrie, C., & Yong, M. (1986). *Intercultural interactions: A practical guide.* Newbury Park, CA: Sage.

Brookfield, S. D. (1995). *Becoming a critically reflective teacher.* San Francisco, CA: Jossey-Bass.

Brophy, J. (1979). Teacher behavior and its effects. *Journal of Educational Psychology, 71,* 733–750.

Brophy, J. (1981). Teacher praise: A functional analysis. *Review of Educational Research, 51,* 5–32.

Brophy, J. (1983). Classroom organization and management. *Elementary School Journal, 83,* 265–285.

Brophy, J. (1987). Synthesis on strategies for motivating students to learn. *Educational Leadership, 45,* 40–48.

Brophy, J. (1988). Educating teachers about managing classrooms and students. *Teaching and Teacher Education, 4* (1), 1–18.

Brophy, J., & Evertson, C. (1974). *Process-product correlations in the Texas Teacher Effectiveness Study: Final report* (Research Report No. 74-4). Austin: University of Texas, Research and Development Center for Teacher Education (ERIC ED 091 094).

Brophy, J., & Evertson, C. (1981). *Student characteristics and teaching.* New York: Longman.

Brophy, J., & Good, T. (1974). *Teacher-student relationships: Causes and consequences.* New York: Holt, Rinehard & Winston.

Brophy, J., & Good, T. L. (1986). Teacher behavior and student achievement. In M. C. Wittrock (Ed.), *Third handbook on research on teaching* (pp. 328–375). New York: Macmillan.

Brophy, J., & McCaslin, M. (1992). Teachers' reports of how they perceive and cope with problem students. *Elementary School Journal, 93,* 3–68.

Brophy, J. E., & Putnam, J. C. (1978). *Classroom management in the elementary grades.* ERIC ED 167, 537.

Bryk, A., & Driscoll, M. (1988). *The high school as community: Contextual influences and consequences for students and teachers.* Madison Wisconsin Center for Education Research, University of Wisconsin-Madison.

Bullough, R. V. (1994). Digging at the roots: Discipline, management, and metaphor. *Action in Teacher Education, 16* (1), 1–10.

Burbules, N. C. (1993). *Dialogue in teaching: Theory and practice.* New York: Teachers College Press.

Burbules, N. C., & Rice, S. (1991). Dialogue across differences: Continuing the conversation. *Harvard Educational Review, 61,* 264–271.

Burch, N., & Miller, K. (1979). *Teacher effectiveness training workbook.* Solana Beach, CA: Effectiveness Training.

Cameron, J., & Pierce, W. D. (1994). Reinforcement, reward, and intrinsic motivation: A meta-analysis. *Review of Educational Research, 64* (3), 363–423.

Camp, B. W., & Bash, M. A. (1981). *Think aloud: Increasing cognitive skill, a problem-solving program for children.* Champaign, IL: Research Press.

Cangelosi, J. S. (1997). *Classroom management strategies: Gaining and maintaining students' cooperation* (3rd ed.). White Plains, NY: Longman.

Canter, L., & Canter, M. (1976). *Assertive discipline: A take-charge approach for today's educator.* Seal Beach, CA: Lee Canter and Associates.

Canter, L., & Canter, M. (1992). *Assertive discipline: Positive behavior management for today's schools* (rev. ed.). Santa Monica, CA: Lee Canter and Associates.

Capra, F. (1983). *The turning point: Science, society, and the rising culture.* New York: Bantam.

Carlson, J. (1978). *The basics of discipline.* Coral Springs, FL: CMTI Press.

Carpenter, R. L., & Apter, S. J. (1987). Research in integration of cognitive-emotional interventions for behavioral disordered children and youth. In M. C. Wang, H. J. Walberg, & M. C. Reynolds (Eds.), *Handbook of special education: Research and practice.* Oxford, England: Pergamon.

Cautela, J. R., & Groden, J. (1978). *Relaxation: A comprehensive manual for adults, children, and children with special needs.* Champaign, IL: Research Press.

Charles, C. M. (1996). *Building classroom discipline* (5th ed.). White Plains, NY: Longman.

Children's Defense Fund (1994). *The state of America's children yearbook 1994.* Washington, DC: Children's Defense Fund.

Cicchetti, D. (1989). How research on child maltreatment has informed the study of child development: Perspectives from developmental psychopathology. In D. Cicchetti & V. Carlson (Eds.), *Child maltreatment: Theory and research on the causes and consequences of child abuse and neglect* (pp. 377–431). New York: Cambridge University Press.

Cole, M., & Cole, S. R. (1989). *The development of children.* New York: Scientific American Books.

Colvin, B. (1988). *Procedures for preventing serious acting out behavior in the classroom.* Unpublished manuscript, Lane Education Service District. Eugene, OR.

Condry, J., & Chambers, J. (1978). Intrinsic motivation and the process of learning. In M. R. Lepper & D. Greene (Eds.), *The hidden cost of reward: New perspectives on the psychology of human motivation.* Hillsdale, NJ: Erlbaum.

Cooperman, M. (1975). Field-dependence and children's problem-solving under varying contingencies of predetermined feedback. *Dissertation Abstracts International, 35,* 2040–2041.

Cormier, W. H., & Cormier, L. S. (1997). *Interviewing strategies for helpers.* Monterey, CA: Brooks/Cole.

Crocker, R. K., & Brooker, G. M. (1986). Classroom control and student outcomes in grades 2 and 5. *American Educational Research Journal, 23,* 1–11.

Csikszentmihalyi, M. (1993). *The evolving self: A psychology for the third millennium.* New York: HarperCollins.

Curtis, J. D., & Detert, R. A. (1981). *How to relax: A holistic approach to stress management.* Mountain View, CA: Mayfield.

Curwin, R. L., & Fuhrmann, B. S. (1975). *Discovering your teaching self: Humanistic approaches to effective teaching.* Boston, MA: Allyn & Bacon.

Curwin, R. L., & Mendler, A. N. (1988). *Discipline with dignity.* Alexandria, VA: Association for Supervision and Curriculum Development.

Davis, G., & Thomas, M. (1989). *Effective schools and effective teachers.* Boston, MA: Allyn & Bacon.

Davis, M., McKay, M., & Eshelman, E. R. (1982). *The relaxation and stress reduction workbook* (2nd ed.). Oakland, CA: New Harbinger.

De Charms, R. (1976). *Enhancing motivation: Change in the classroom.* New York: Irvington.

Deci, E. L. (1976). *Intrinsic motivation.* New York: Plenum.

Deci, E. L. (1978). Applications of research on the effects of rewards. In M. R. Lepper & D. Greene (Eds.), *The hidden costs of reward: New perspectives on the psychology of human motivation.* New York: Erlbaum.

Deci, E. L., & Ryan, R. M. (1985). *Intrinsic motivation and self-determination in human behavior.* New York: Plenum.

Deci, E. L., & Ryan, R. M. (1987). The support of autonomy and the control of behavior. *Journal of Personality and Social Psychology, 53,* 1024–1037.

Deiro, J. A. (1996). *Teaching with heart: Making healthy connections with students.* Thousand Oaks, CA: Corwin Press.

Denckla, M. B., & Reader, M. (1993). Education and psychological interventions: Executive dysfunction and its consequences. In R. Kurlan (Ed.), *Handbook of Tourette's syndrome and related tic and behavioral disorders* (pp. 431–451). New York: Marcel Dekker.

Dewey, J. (1963). *Experience and education.* New York: Collier Books. (Original work published 1938.)

Dickinson, A. M. (1989). The detrimental effects of extrinsic reinforcement on "intrinsic motivation." *The Behavior Analyst, 12,* 1–15.

Dill, V. S., & Haberman, M. (1995). Building a gentler school. *Educational Leadership, 52* (5), 69–67.

Dinkmeyer, D., McKay, G. D., & Dinkmeyer, D. Jr. (1980). *Systematic training for effective teaching: Teacher's handbook.* Circle Pines, MI: American Guidance Service.

Doyle, W. (1986). Classroom organization and management. In M. C. Wittrock (Ed.), *Third Handbook of research on teaching* (pp. 392–431). New York: Macmillan.

Dreikurs, R. (1968). *Psychology in the classroom: A manual for teachers* (2nd ed.). New York: Harper and Row.

Dreikurs, R., & Cassel, P. (1972). *Discipline without tears.* New York: Hawthorn.

Dreikurs, R., Grunwald, B., & Pepper, F. (1982). *Maintaining sanity in the classroom.* New York: Harper and Row.

Dunham, J. (1984). *Stress in teaching.* New York: Nichols.

Elam, S. M., Rose, L. C., & Gallup, A. M. (1994). The 26th annual Phi Delta Kappa/Gallup Poll of the public's attitudes toward the public schools. *Phi Delta Kappan, 76,* 41–56.

Ellis, A. (1974). *Humanistic Psychotherapy: The rational-emotive approach.* New York: McGraw-Hill.

Ellis, A., & Bernard, M. E. (1984). *Rational-emotive approaches to the problems of childhood.* New York: Plenum.

Ellis, A., & Harper, R. A. (1975). *A new guide to rational living.* No. Hollywood, CA: Wilshire Book Company.

Emery, G., Hollon, D. S., & Bedrosian, R. D. (1981). *New directions in cognitive therapy.* New York: Guilford Press.

Emery, R., & Marholin, D. (1977). An applied behavior analysis of delinquency: The irrelevancy of relevant behavior. *American Psychologist, 32,* 860–873.

Emmer, E. T., Evertson, C. M., & Anderson, L. M. (1980). Effective classroom management at the beginning of the school year. *Elementary School Journal, 80,* 219–231.

Erikson, E. H. (1980). *Identity and the life cycle.* New York: Norton.

Erikson, E. H. (1991). *Childhood and society.* New York: Norton.

Evertson, C. M. (1985). Training teachers in classroom management: An experimental study in secondary school classrooms. *Journal of Educational Research, 79,* 51–58.

Evertson, C. M. (1989). Improving elementary classroom management: A school-based training program for beginning the year. *Journal of Educational Research, 83,* 82–90.

Evertson, C. M., Anderson, C. W., Anderson, L. M., & Brophy, J. E. (1980). Relationships between classroom behaviors and student outcomes in junior high mathematics and English classes. *American Educational Research Journal, 17,* 43–60.

Evertson, C. M., & Emmer, E. T. (1982). Effective management at the beginning of the school year in junior high classes. *Journal of Educational Psychology, 74,* 485–498.

Evertson, C. M., Emmer, E. T., Clements, B. S., & Worsham, M. E. (1997). *Classroom management for elementary teachers* (4th ed.). Boston, MA: Allyn & Bacon.

Evertson, C. M., Emmer, E., Sanford, J., & Clements, B. (1983). Improving classroom management: An experiment in elementary classrooms. *Elementary School Journal, 84,* 173–188.

Evertson, C. M., & Weade, R. (1989). Classroom management and teaching style: Instructional stability and variability in two junior high English classrooms. *Elementary School Journal, 89* (3), 379–393.

Fagen, S. A., & Hill, J. M. (1977). *Behavior management: A competency-based manual for in-service training.* Burtonville, MD: Psychoeducational Resources.

Fagen, S. (1979). Psychoeducational management and self-control. In D. Cullinan & M. Epstein (Eds.), *Special education for adolescents: Issues and perspectives.* Columbus, OH: Merrill.

Fagen, S., Long, N., & Stevens, D. (1975). *Teaching children self-control.* Columbus, OH: Merrill.

Farber, B. A., & Miller, J. (1981). Teacher burnout: A psychoeducational perspective. *Teachers College Record, 83* (2), 235–243.

Feindler, E. L., & Fremouw, W. J. (1983). Stress inoculation training for adolescent anger problems. In D. H. Meichenbaum & M. E. Jaremko (Eds.), *Stress reduction and prevention.* New York: Plenum.

Forehand, R., & McMahon, R. (1981). *Helping the non-compliant child.* New York: Guilford Press.

Forman, S. G. (1980). A comparison of cognitive training and response cost procedures in modifying aggressive behavior of elementary school children. *Behavior Therapy, 11,* 594–600.

Forness, S. R. (1973). The reinforcement hierarchy. *Psychology in the Schools, 10,* 168–177.

Freiberg, J. (1996). From tourists to citizens in the classroom. *Educational Leadership, 54,* 32–36.

Freire, P. (1993). *Pedagogy of the oppressed* (rev. ed.). New York: Continuum.

Friesen, D., Prokop, C., & Sarros, J. (1988). Why teachers burn out. *Educational Research Quarterly, 12* (3), 9–19.

Froyen, L. A. (1993). *Classroom management: The reflective teacher-leader.* New York: Merrill.

Gage, N. (1978). *The scientific basis of the art of teaching.* New York: Teachers College Press, Columbia University.

Gallagher, P. A. (1995). *Teaching students with behavior disorders: Techniques and activities for classroom instruction* (2nd ed.). Denver, CO: Love.

Garmezy, N. (1984). Children vulnerable to major mental disorders: Risk and protective factors. In L. Grinspoon (Ed.), *Psychiatric update* (vol. 3, pp. 91–104, 159–161). Washington, DC: American Psychiatric Press.

Gast, D., & Nelson, C. M. (1977a). Legal and ethical considerations for the use of timeout in special education settings. *Journal of Special Education, 11,* 457–467.

Gast, D., & Nelson, C. M. (1977b). Time out in the classroom: Implications for special education. *Exceptional Children, 43,* 461–464.

George, P. S. (1980). Discipline, moral development, and levels of schooling. *Educational Forum, 45,* 57–67.

Gersten, R., Woodward, J., & Darch, C. (1986). Direct instruction: A research-based approach to curriculum design and teaching. *Exceptional Children, 53* (1), 17–31.

Ginott, H. (1965). *Between parent and child.* New York: Avon.

Ginott, H. (1969). *Between parent and teenager.* New York: Macmillan.

Ginott, H. (1972). *Teacher and child.* New York: Macmillan.

Glasser, W. (1965). *Reality therapy: A new approach to psychiatry.* New York: Harper and Row.

Glasser, W. (1969). *Schools without failure.* New York: Harper and Row.

Glasser, W. (1974). A new look at discipline. *Learning, 3* (4), 6–11.

Glasser, W. (1977). 10 steps to good discipline. *Today's Education, 66,* 60–63.

Glasser, W. (1978). Disorders in our schools: Causes and remedies. *Phi Delta Kappan, 59,* 331–333.

Glasser, W. (1986). *Control theory in the classroom.* New York: Perennial Library.

Glasser, W. (1990). *The quality school: Managing students without coercion.* New York: Harper and Row.

Glasser, W. (1993). *The quality school teacher.* New York: Harper Perennial.

Glenn, H. S. (1982). *Developing capable people* (Learner's guide). Fair Oaks, CA: Sunrise Press.

Glenn, H. S., & Nelson, J. (1989). *Raising self-reliant children in a self-indulgent world.* Rocklin, CA: Prima Publications.

Gmelch, W. (1983). Stress for success: How to optimize your performance. *Theory Into Practice, 22* (1), 7–14.

Golanda, E. (1990). *The importance of the source of power in an educational setting.* Paper presented at the annual meeting of the Southern Regional Conference of Educational Administration, Atlanta, GA.

Gold, Y. (1988). Recognizing and coping with academic burnout. *Contemporary Education, 59* (3), 142–145.

Goldstein, A. P. (1991). *Delinquent gangs: A psychological perspective.* Champaign, IL: Research Press.

Goldstein, A. P. (1988). *The prepare curriculum: Teaching prosocial competencies.* Champaign, IL: Research Press.

Goldstein, A. P., Sprafkin, R. P., Gershaw, N. J., & Klein, P. (1983). Structured learning: A psychoeducational approach for teaching social competencies. *Behavioral Disorders, 8* (3), 161–170.

Goleman, D. (1995). *Emotional intelligence.* New York: Bantam.

Good, T., & Brophy, J. (1997). *Looking in classrooms* (7th ed.). New York: HarperCollins.

Goodlad, J. (1990). *Teachers for our nation's schools.* San Francisco, CA: Jossey-Bass.

Gootman, M. E. (1997). *The caring teacher's guide to discipline: Helping young students learn self-control, responsibility, and respect.* Thousand Oaks, CA: Corwin Press.

Gordon, T. (1974). *T.E.T. Teacher effectiveness training.* New York: David McKay.

Gordon, T. (1989). *Teaching children self-discipline at home and at school.* New York: Times.

Gossen, A. C. (1992). *Restitution: Restructuring school discipline.* Chapel Hill, NC: New View Publications.

Gothelf, C. R., Rikhye, C. H., & Silberman, R. K. (1988). *Working with students who have dual sensory impairments and cognitive disabilities: Handbook for special education teachers and related services personnel.* Albany: New York State Education Department, Office for Education of Children with Handicapping Conditions, Title VI-C.

Grant, G. (1988). *The world we created at Hamilton High.* Cambridge: Harvard University Press.

Grossman, H. (1984). *Educating Hispanic students: Cultural implications for instruction, classroom management, counseling, and assessment.* Springfield, IL: Charles C. Thomas.

Grossman, H. (1990). *Trouble-free teaching: Solutions to behavior problems in the classroom.* Mountain View, CA: Mayfield.

Grossman, H. (1995). *Classroom behavior management in a diverse society* (2nd ed.). Mountain View, CA: Mayfield.

Hall, J. (1971). Decisions, decisions, decisions. *Psychology Today, 5* (6), 51–54, 86, 88.

Hall, R. V., & Hall, M. (1980). *How to use time out.* Lawrence, KS: H & H Enterprises.

Halliger, P., & Murphy, J. (1986). The social context of effective schools. *American Journal of Education, 94,* 328–355.

Hamburg, D. A. (1992). *Today's children: Creating a future for a generation in crisis.* New York: Times Books.

Hartner, S. (1978). Effective motivation reconsidered: Toward a developmental model. *Human Development, 21,* 34–64.

Harvey, J. (1988). *The quiet mind: Techniques for transforming stress.* Honesdale, PA: Himalayan International Institute.

Hawkins, J. D., Catalano, R., & Miller, J. Y. (1992). Risk and protective factors for alcohol and other drug problems in adolescence and early adulthood: Implications for substance abuse prevention. *Psychological Bulletin, 112* (2), 64–105.

Herman, J. L. (1992). *Trauma and recovery.* New York: Basic Books.

Hodgkinson, H. (1992). *A demographic look at tomorrow.* Washington, DC: Institute for Educational Leadership/Center for Demographic Policy.

Holt, P., Fine, M. J., & Tollefson, N. (1987). Mediating stress: Survival of the hardy. *Psychology in the Schools, 24,* 51–58.

Hoover, R. L., & Kindsvatter, R. (1997). *Democratic discipline: Foundation and practice.* Columbus, OH: Merrill.

Hyman, I. A. (1990). *Reading, writing, and the hickory stick.* Lexington, MA: Lexington Books.

Hyman, I. A., Dahbany, A., Blum, M., Weiler, E., Brooks-Klein, V., & Pokalo, M. (1997). *School discipline and school violence: Teacher variance approach.* Boston, MA: Allyn & Bacon.

Jakubowski, P., & Lange, A. J. (1978). *The assertive option: Your rights and responsibilities.* Champaign, IL: Research Press.

Jakubowski, P. A. (1977). Assertive behavior and clinical problems of women. In D. Carter & E. Rawlings (Eds.), *Psychotherapy with women.* Springfield, IL: Charles C. Thomas.

Jalongo, M. R. (1991). *Creating learning communities: The role of the teacher in the 21st century.* Bloomington, IN: National Educational Service.

Jenkins, S., & Calhoun, J. F. (1991). Teacher stress: Issues and intervention. *Psychology in the Schools, 28* (1), 60–70.

Johns, B. H., & Keenan, J. P. (1997). *Techniques for managing a safe school.* Denver, CO: Love.

Johnson, S. M. (1990). *Teachers at work.* New York: Basic Books.

Johnson, D., & Johnson, R. (1987). *Learning together and alone: Cooperative, competitive, and individualistic learning.* Englewood Cliffs, NJ: Prentice-Hall.

Johnson D. W., & Johnson, R. T. (1995). Why violence prevention programs don't work-and what does. *Educational Leadership, 52* (5), 63–67.

Johnson, D., Johnson, R., Holubec, E., & Roy, P. (1984). *Circles of learning: Cooperation in the classroom.* Alexandria, VA: Association for Supervision and Curriculum Development.

Jones, F. (1987). *Positive classroom discipline.* New York: McGraw-Hill.

Jones, V. F., & Jones, L. S. (1998). *Comprehensive classroom management: Creating communities of support and solving problems* (5th ed.). Boston, MA: Allyn & Bacon.

Kagan, S. (1990). *Cooperative learning: Resources for teachers.* San Juan Capistrano, CA: Resources for Teachers.

Kaplan, C. (1992). Teachers' punishment histories and their selection of disciplinary techniques. *Contemporary Educational Psychology, 17,* 258–265.

Kaplan, J. S. (1995). *Beyond behavior modification: A cognitive behavioral approach to behavior management in the school* (3rd ed.). Austin, TX: Pro-Ed.

Kasl, E., Dechant, K., & Marsick, V. (1993). Living the learning: Internalizing our model of group learning. In D. Boud, R. Cohen, & D. Walker (Eds.), *Using experience for learning.* Bristol, PA: Open University Press.

Katz, N. H., & Lawyer, J. W. (1994). *Preventing and managing conflict in schools.* Thousand Oaks, CA: Corwin Press.

Keane, R. (1987). The doubting journey: A learning process of self-transformation. In D. Boud & V. Griffin (Eds.), *Appreciating adults' learning: From the learners' perspective.* Toronto: Ontario Institute for Studies in Education Press.

Kendall, P., & Braswell, L. (1984). *Cognitive-behavioral interventions with impulsive children.* New York: Guilford.

Kerr, M. M., & Nelson, C. M. (1998). *Strategies for managing behavior problems in the classroom* (3rd ed.). Upper Saddle River, NJ: Merrill.

Kirschenbaum, H. (1995). *100 ways to enhance values and morality in schools and youth settings.* Boston, MA: Allyn & Bacon.

Knowles, M. (1975). *Self-directed learning: A guide for learners and teachers.* New York: Cambridge.

Knowles, M. (1992). *The adult learner: A neglected species.* (4th ed.). Houston, TX: Gulf.

Kohlberg, L. (1975). The cognitive-developmental approach to moral education. *Phi Delta Kappan, 56,* 670–677.

Kohlberg, L. (1984). *The psychology of moral development.* San Francisco, CA: Harper and Row.

Kohlberg, L., & Gilligan, C. (1972). The adolescent as a philosopher: The discovery of the self in a postconventional world. In J. Kagan & R. Coles (Eds.), *12 to 16: Early adolescence* (pp. 144–179). New York: Norton.

Kohn, A. (1993). *Punished by rewards: The trouble with gold stars, incentive plans, A's, praise and other bribes.* New York: Houghton Mifflin.

Kohn, A. (1996). *Beyond discipline: From compliance to community.* Alexandria, VA: Association for Supervision and Curriculum Development.

Kounin, J. S. (1970). *Discipline and group management in classrooms.* New York: Holt, Rinehart & Winston.

Kreidler, W. J. (1984). *Creative conflict resolution: More than 200 activities for keeping peace in the classroom.* Glenview, IL: Scott, Foresman.

Kroth, R. L. (1985). *Communicating with parents of exceptional children* (2nd ed.). Denver, CO: Love.

Kyriacou, C. (1987). Teacher stress and burnout: An international review. *Educational Research, 29,* 146–150.

Ladson-Billings, G. (1994). *The dreamkeepers: Successful teachers of African American children.* San Francisco, CA: Jossey-Bass.

Ladson-Billings, G. (1995). Toward a theory of culturally relevant pedagogy. *American Educational Research Journal, 32*(3), 465–491.

Lange, A. J., & Jakubowski, P. (1976). *Responsible assertive behavior.* Champaign, IL: Research Press.

Larrivee, B. (1985). *Effective teaching for successful mainstreaming.* New York: Longman.

Larrivee, B. (1991). Social status: A comparison of mainstreamed students with peers of different ability levels. *Journal of Special Education, 25,* 90–101.

Larrivee, B. (1992). *Strategies for effective classroom management: Creating a collaborative climate.* Boston, MA: Allyn & Bacon.

Larrivee, B. (1995). Reconceptualizing classroom management. In B. G. Blair & R. Caine (Eds.), *Integrative learning as the pathway to teaching for holism, complexity and interconnectedness.* Lewiston, NY: Edwin Mellen Press.

Larrivee, B. (1996). *Moving into balance.* Santa Monica, CA: Shoreline.

Larrivee, B. (1997). Restructuring classroom management for more interactive and integrated teaching and learning. In T. Jennings (Ed.), *Restructuring for integrated education: Multiple perspectives, multiple contexts.* In the Henry A. Giroux Critical Studies in Education and Culture Series, Westport, CT: Bergin & Garvey.

Lee, J. L., Pulvino, C. J., & Perrone, P. A. (1998). *Restoring harmony: A guide for managing conflicts in schools.* Columbus, OH: Merrill.

Lepper, M. (1983). Extrinsic reward and intrinsic motivation: Implications for the classroom. In J. Levine & M. Wang (Eds.), *Teacher-student perceptions: Implications for learning.* Hillsdale, NJ: Erlbaum.

Lepper, M. R., & Greene, D. (Eds.). (1978). *The hidden costs of reward: New perspectives on the psychology of human motivation.* New York: Erlbaum.

Levine, M. D. (July, 1995). Childhood neurodevelopmental dysfunction and learning disorders. *Harvard Mental Health Letter, 12*(1), 5–7.

Lieberman, A., & Miller, L. (1984). The social realities of teaching. In A. Lieberman (Ed.), *Teachers: Their world, their work* (pp. 1–16). Alexandria, VA: Association for Supervision and Curriculum Development.

Lightfoot, S. (1984). *The good high school.* New York: Basic Books.

Long, N. (1996). The conflict cycle paradigm on how troubled students get teachers out of control. In N. Long & W. Morse (Eds.), *Conflict in the classroom: The education of at-risk and troubled students* (5th ed., pp. 244–265). Austin, TX: Pro-Ed.

Long, N., & Morse, W. (1996). *Conflict in the classroom: The education of at-risk and troubled students* (5th ed.). Austin, TX: Pro-Ed.

Long, N., Morse, W., & Newman, R. G. (1976). *Conflict in the classroom: The education of emotionally disturbed children* (3rd ed.). Belmont, CA: Wadsworth.

Long, N. J., & Newman, R. G. (1961). A differential approach to the management of surface behavior of children in school. *Bulletin of the School of Education* (Indiana University, Bloomington), *37,* 47–61.

Lortie, D. C. (1975). *Schoolteacher: A sociological study.* Chicago, IL: University of Chicago Press.

Luria, A. R. (1961). *The role of speech in the regulation of normal and abnormal behaviors.* New York: Liveright.

Lynch, J. (1989). *Multicultural education in a global society.* London: Falmer Press.

Lynch, M., & Cicchetti, D. (1992). Maltreated children's reports of relatedness to their teachers. In R. Pianta (Ed.), *Beyond the parent: The role of other adults in children's lives* (pp. 81–108). San Francisco, CA: Jossey-Bass.

Marshall, H. H. (1992). *Redefining student learning: Roots of educational change.* Norwood, NJ: Ablex.

Martin, J. R. (1992). *The schoolhome.* Cambridge, MA: Harvard University Press.

Maslach, C. (1982). *Burnout: The cost of caring.* Englewood Cliffs, NJ: Prentice Hall.

Maslow, A. (1968). *Toward a psychology of being.* New York: Van Nostrand Reinhold.

Masten, A., & Garmezy, N. (1985). Risk, vulnerability, and protective factors in developmental psychopathology. In B. B. Lahey & A. E. Kazdin (Eds.), *Advances in clinical child psychology* (vol. 8, pp. 1–52). New York: Plenum.

McCaslin, M., & Good, T. L. (1992). Compliant cognition: The misalliance of management and instructional goals in current school reform. *Educational Researcher, 21* (3), 4–17.

McCroskey, J. C., & Richmond, V. P. (1983). Power in the classroom I: Teacher and student perceptions. *Communication Education, 32,* 175–184.

Mc Ginnis, E., & Goldstein, A. P. (1984). *Skillstreaming the elementary school child: A guide for teaching prosocial skills.* Champaign, IL: Research Press.

McKay, M., David, M., & Fanning, P. (1981). *Thoughts and feelings: The art of cognitive stress intervention.* Oakland, CA: New Harbinger.

McLaughlin, E. J. (1994). From negation to negotiation: Moving away from the management metaphor. *Action in Teacher Education, 16* (1), 75–84.

McLaughlin, M. (1991). *Strategic sites for teachers' professional development.* Paper presented at the annual meeting of the American Educational Research Association, Chicago, IL.

McLaughlin, M. (1993). What matters most in teachers' workplace context? In J. Little & M. McLaughlin (Eds.), *Teachers' work.* New York: Teachers College Press.

McLaughlin, M. W., & Talbert, J. (1990). Constructing a personalized school environment. *Phi Delta Kappan, 72* (3), 230–235.

McMillan, D., & Chavis, D. (1986). Sense of community: A definition and theory. *Journal of Community Psychology, 14,* 6–23.

McNabb, W. H. (1990). *The developing capable people parenting course: A study of its impact on family cohesion.* Unpublished doctoral dissertation, Pepperdine University, Malibu, CA.

Medley, D. (1977). *Teacher competency and teacher effectiveness: A review of process product research.* Washington, DC: American Association of Colleges for Teacher Education.

Meichenbaum, D. (1975). Self-instructional methods: How to do it. In A. Goldstein & F. Kanfer (Eds.), *Helping people change: Methods and materials.* Elmsford, NY: Pergamon.

Meichenbaum, D. (1977). *Cognitive behavior modification: An integrative approach.* New York: Plenum.

Meichenbaum, D. (1979). Teaching children self-control. In B. B. Lahey & A. E. Kazdin (Eds.), *Advances in clinical child psychology,* (vol. 2). New York: Plenum.

Meichenbaum, D. (1980). Cognitive behavior modification: A promise yet unfulfilled. *Exceptional Education Quarterly, 1* (1), 83–88.

Meichenbaum, D. (1985). *Stress-inoculation training.* Elmsford, NY: Pergamon.

Meichenbaum, D., & Cameron, R. (1983). Stress-inoculation training: Toward a general paradigm for training coping skills. In D. H. Meichenbaum & M. E. Jaremko (Eds.), *Stress reduction and prevention.* New York: Plenum.

Meier, D. (1995). *The power of their ideas.* Boston, MA: Beacon Press.

Merz C., & Furman, G. (1997). *Community and schools: Promise and paradox.* New York: Teachers College Press.

Merzfeld, G., & Powell, R. (1986). *Coping for kids: A complete stress-control program for students ages 8–18.* West Nyack, NY: Center for Applied Research in Education.

Meyer, W. U., Bachmann, M., Bierman, U., Hempelmann, M., Plager, F. O., & Spiller, H. (1979). The information value of evaluative behavior: Influences of praise and blame on perceptions of ability. *Journal of Educational Psychology, 79,* 259–268.

Mills, R. A., Powell, R. R., & Pollack, J. P. (1992). The influence of middle level interdisciplinary teaming on teacher isolation: A case study. *Research in Middle Level Education, 15* (2), 9–25.

Morgan, D. P., & Jenson, W. R. (1988). *Teaching behaviorally disordered students: Preferred practices.* Columbus, OH: Merrill.

Morgan, S. R., & Reinhart, J. A. (1991). *Interventions for students with emotional disorders.* Austin, TX: Pro-Ed.

Morganett, R. S. (1990). *Skills for living: Group counseling activities for young adolescents.* Champaign, IL: Research Press.

Morganett, R. S., & Bauer, A. M. (1987). Coping strategies in mainstreaming educable mentally handicapped children. *Indiana Counsel for Exceptional Children Quarterly, 36,* 20–24.

Morrow, G. (1987). *The compassionate school: A practical guide to educating abused and traumatized children.* Englewood Cliffs, NJ: Prentice Hall.

Moskovitz, S. (1983). *Love despite hate: Child survivors of the Holocaust and their adult lives.* New York: Schocken.

National Center for Children in Poverty (1995). *National Center for Children in Poverty: A program report on the first five years.* New York: Columbia University School of Public Health.

Noblit, G. (1993). Power and caring. *American Educational Research Journal, 30,* 23–38.

Noddings, N. (1992). *The challenge to care in schools.* New York: Teachers College Press.

O'Donnell, J., Hawkins, D., Catalano, R., Abbott, R. D., & Day, L. E. (1995). Preventing school failure, drug use, and delinquency among low-income children: Long-term prevention in elementary schools. *American Journal of Orthopsychiatry, 65,* 87–100.

Oldfather, P. (1993). What students say about motivating experiences in a whole language classroom. *The Reading Teacher, 46* (8), 672–681.

Peck, M. S. (1987). *The different drum.* New York: Simon & Schuster.

Pederson, E., Faucher, T. A., & Eaton, W. W. (1978). A new perspective on the effects of first grade teachers on children's subsequent adult status. *Harvard Educational Review, 48,* 1–31.

Perls, F. (1976). *The Gestalt approach and eyewitness to therapy.* New York: Bantam.

Piaget, J. (1965). *The moral judgment of the child.* New York: Free Press.

Pittman, T., Boggiano, A., & Ruble, D. (1982). Intrinsic and extrinsic motivational orientations: Limiting conditions on the undermining and enhancing effects of reward on intrinsic motivation. In J. Levine & M. Wang (Eds.), *Teacher-student perceptions: Implications for learning.* Hillsdale, NJ: Erlbaum.

Polsgrove, L. (1979). Self-control: Methods for child training. *Behavior Disorders, 4,* 116–130.

Purkey, S. C., & Smith, M. S. (1983). Effective schools: A review. *Elementary School Journal, 83,* 427–452.

Queen, J. A., Blackwelder, B. B., & Mallen, L. P. (1997). *Responsible classroom management for teachers and students.* Columbus, OH: Merrill.

Randolph, C. H., & Evertson, C. M. (1994). Images of management for learner-centered classrooms. *Action in Teacher Education, 16* (1), 55–63.

Randolph, C. H., & Evertson, C. M. (1995). Managing for learning: Rules, roles, and meanings in a writing class. *Journal of Classroom Interaction, 30* (2), 17–25.

Raschke, D. (1981). Designing reinforcement surveys: Let the student choose the reward. *Teaching Exceptional Children, 14,* 92–96.

Redfering, D. L., & Bowman, M. J. (1981). Effects of meditative relaxation exercise on non-attending behaviors of behavioral disturbed children. *Journal of Clinical Child Psychology, 10,* 126–127.

Redl, F. (1966). *When we deal with children.* New York: Free Press.

Redl, F., & Wattenberg, W. (1959). *Mental hygiene in teaching* (2nd ed.). New York: Harcourt, Brace and World.

Richmond, V., & McCroskey, J. (1984). Power in the classroom II: Power and learning. *Communication Education, 33,* 125–136.

Rogers, C. (1969). *Freedom to learn.* Columbus, OH: Merrill.

Rogers, C., & Freiberg, H. J. (1994). *Freedom to learn* (3rd ed.). New York: Merrill.

Rosenshine, B. (1979). Content, time, and direct instruction. In P. Peterson & H. Walberg (Eds.), *Research on teaching: Concepts, findings, and implications.* Berkeley, CA: McCutcheon.

Rosenshine, B., & Berliner, D. C. (1978). Academic engaged time. *British Journal of Teacher Education, 4,* 3–15.

Rosenshine, B., & Stevens, R. (1984). Classroom instruction in reading. In D. Pearson (Ed.), *Handbook of research on teaching.* New York: Longman.

Rosenshine, B., & Stevens, R. (1986). Teaching functions. In M. C. Wittrock (Ed.), *Third handbook on research on teaching* (pp. 376–391). New York: Macmillan.

Rosenthal, R., & Jacobson, L. (1968). *Pygmalion in the classroom: Teachers expectations and pupils' intellectual development.* New York: Holt, Rinehart & Winston.

Ross, M. (1976). The self-perception of intrinsic motivation. In J. H. Harvey, W. J. Ickes, & R. F. Kidd (Eds.), *New directions in attributional research* (vol. 1). Hillsdale, NJ: Erlbaum.

Rost, J. C. (1991). *Leadership for the twenty-first century.* New York: Praeger.

Roush, D. (1984). Rational-emotive therapy and youth: Some new techniques for counselors. *Personnel and Guidance Journal, 62,* 414–417.

Rowan, B. (1990). Commitment and control: Alternative strategies for the organizational design of schools. *Review of Research in Education, 16,* 353–385.

Ryan, B. (1979). A case against behavior modification in the "ordinary classroom." *Journal of School Psychology, 17* (2), 131–136.

Sautter, R. C. (1995). Standing up to violence. *Phi Delta Kappan, 76,* K1–K12.

Schumaker, J. B., Hazel, J. S., & Pederson, C. S. (1988). *Social skills for daily living.* Circle Pines, MN: American Guidance Service.

Schwab, R. L., Jackson, S. E., & Schuler, R. S. (1986). Educator burnout: Sources and consequences. *Educational Research Quarterly, 10,* 14–30.

Schwartz, B. (1990). The creation and destruction of value. *American Psychologist, 45,* 7–15.

Senge, P. M. 1990. *The fifth discipline.* New York: Currency Doubleday.

Sergiovanni, T. (1992). *Moral leadership.* San Francisco, CA: Jossey-Bass.

Sergiovanni, T. (1994). *Building community in schools.* San Francisco, CA: Jossey-Bass.

Shapiro, S. B., & Reiff, J. (1993). A framework for reflective inquiry on practice: Beyond intuition and experience. *Psychological Reports, 73,* 1379–1394.

Shipman, W. M. (1984). Emotional and behavioral effects of long-distance running on children. In M. L. Sachs & G. W. Buffone (Eds.), *Running as therapy: An integrated approach.* Lincoln: University of Nebraska Press.

Silberman, M. L., & Wheelan, S. A. (1980). *How to discipline without feeling guilty: Assertive relationships with children.* Champaign, IL: Research Press.

Sizer, T. (1984). *Horace's compromise.* Boston, MA: Houghton Mifflin.

Slavin, R. E., Karweit, N. L., & Madden, N. A. (1989). *Effective programs for students at risk.* Boston, MA: Allyn & Bacon.

Smead, R. (1981). *A comparison of counselor administered and tape-recorded relaxation training on decreasing target and non-target anxiety in elementary school children.* Unpublished doctoral dissertation, Auburn University.

Soar, R., & Soar, R. (1975). Classroom behavior, pupil characteristics, and pupil growth for the school year and summer. *JSAS Catalog of Selected Documents in Psychology, 5,* 873.

Sparks-Langer, G., & Colton, A. (1991). Synthesis of research on teachers reflective thinking. *Educational Leadership, 48* (6), 37–44.

Spiel, O. (1962). *Discipline without punishment.* London: Faber and Faber.

Stahelski, A., & Frost, D. (1987). *Modern managers move away from the carrot-and-stick approach.* Paper presented at the annual meeting of the Western Psychological Association, Long Beach, CA.

Stallings, J. (1975). Implementation and child effects of teaching practices in Follow Through classrooms. *Monographs of the Society for Research in Child Development, 40,* 7–8.

Sutherland, S. (1993). Impoverished minds. *Nature, 364,* 767.

Thompson, C., & Poppen, W. (1972). *For those who care: Ways of relating to youth.* Columbus, OH: Merrill.

Usher, R. S., & Bryant, I. (1989). *Adult education as theory, practice and research: The captive triangle.* New York: Routledge, Chapman and Hall.

Vygotsky, L. (1962). *Thought and language.* New York: Wiley.

Walen, S. R., DiGiuseppe, R., & Wessler, R. L. (1980). *A practitioner's guide to rational-emotive therapy.* New York: Oxford University Press.

Walker, H. (1979). *The acting out child: Coping with classroom discipline.* Boston, MA: Allyn & Bacon.

Walker, H. M., & Walker, J. E. (1991). *Coping with noncompliance in the classroom.* Austin, TX: Pro-Ed.

Weiner, B. (1979). A theory of motivation in some classroom experiences. *Journal of Educational Psychology, 71,* 3–25.

Weinstein. C. S., & Mignano, A. J. (1997). *Elementary classroom management: Lessons from research and practice.* New York: McGraw-Hill.

Werner, E. E. (1990). Protective factors and individual resilience. In S. J. Meisels & J. P. Shonkoff (Eds.), *Handbook of early childhood intervention* (p. 109). Cambridge, UK: Cambridge University Press.

Werner, E. E., & Smith, R. S. (1992). *Overcoming the odds: High risk children from birth to adulthood.* Ithaca, NY: Cornell University Press.

Wheatley, M. J. 1992. *Leadership and the new science.* San Francisco, CA: Berrett-Koehler.

Wood, M. (1986). *Developmental theory in the classroom.* Austin, TX: Pro-Ed.

Zehm, S. J., & Kottler, J. A. (1993). *On being a teacher: The human dimension.* Newbury Park, CA: Corwin Press.

Zimrin, H. (1986). A profile of survival. *Child Abuse and Neglect, 10,* 339–349.

Index